D0622974

Eternally Vigilant

ETERNALLY VIGILANT

Free Speech in the Modern Era

edited by LEE C. BOLLINGER & GEOFFREY R. STONE

The University of Chicago Press
Chicago and London

LEE C. BOLLINGER is professor of law and the
president of the University of Michigan. He is the
author of *The Tolerant Society: Freedom of Speech and
Extremist Speech in America* (1986) and *Images of a
Free Press* (1991), the latter published by the
University of Chicago Press.
GEOFFREY R. STONE is the Harry Kalven Jr.
Distinguished Service Professor of Law and provost of
the University of Chicago. He is the coauthor of *The
First Amendment* (1999) and coeditor of the annual
Supreme Court Review.

The University of Chicago Press, Chicago 60637
The University of Chicago Press, Ltd., London
© 2002 by The University of Chicago
All rights reserved. Published 2002
Printed in the United States of America
11 10 09 08 07 06 05 04 03 02   1 2 3 4 5
ISBN: 0-226-06353-4 (cloth)

**Library of Congress
Cataloging-in-Publication Data**

Eternally vigilant : free speech in the modern era /
edited by Lee C. Bollinger and Geoffrey R. Stone.
p.   cm.
Includes index.
ISBN 0-226-06353-4 (cloth : alk. paper)
1. Freedom of speech—United States.   I. Bollinger,
Lee C., 1946– II. Stone, Geoffrey R.
KF4772 .E86 2002
342.73'0853—dc21
2001027896

♾ The paper used in this publication meets the
minimum requirements of the American National
Standard for Information Sciences—Permanence of
Paper for Printed Library Materials, ANSI Z39.48-1992.

For Nancy and Jean

CONTENTS

Preface   ix

Dialogue   Lee C. Bollinger & Geoffrey R. Stone . 1

Freedom of Speech and the Common-Law Constitution   David A. Strauss . 32

Free Speech and Good Character: From Milton to Brandeis to the Present   Vincent Blasi . 60

"Clear and Present Danger" and Criminal Speech   Kent Greenawalt . 96

The Speech Market and the Legacy of *Schenck*   Richard A. Posner . 120

Reconciling Theory and Doctrine in First Amendment Jurisprudence   Robert Post . 152

First Amendment Opportunism   Frederick Schauer . 174

The Dance of Theory   Stanley Fish . 198

The Invisible Hand of the Marketplace of Ideas   Lillian R. BeVier . 232

The Censorship of Television   Owen M. Fiss . 256

The Future of Free Speech   Cass R. Sunstein . 284

Epilogue   Lee C. Bollinger & Geoffrey R. Stone . 311

List of Contributors   317

Index   319

In 1919, in *Abrams v. United States*, Justice Oliver Wendell Holmes spoke eloquently about the constitutional guarantee of freedom of speech as "an experiment, as all life is an experiment." Each day of our lives, he observed, we must "wager our salvation upon some prophecy based upon imperfect knowledge." Thus, Holmes concluded, as consequential as free speech is for the society, and despite the unproven nature of the "experiment," we must be "eternally vigilant" in the protection and defense of this freedom.

There is a deep tension in that statement. An experiment implies a tentativeness of commitment and a need for ongoing review and adjustment, while the admonition of eternal vigilance implies a commitment to something utterly foundational and continuously vulnerable that must be defended at all costs. An experiment implies something recent and novel, while eternal vigilance implies something of and for the ages.

This tension reveals something of the essence of our First Amendment freedoms of speech and press. In an important sense, the principle is embedded deep within our inherited traditions, with glorious defenses by Socrates, John Milton, and John Stuart Mill. Yet in an equally important sense, the principle is relatively new, dating back only to the second decade of the twentieth century, when the Supreme Court of the United States first began to sketch the outlines of the jurisprudence of free speech.

This book was conceived out of the sense that the turn of a century is an appropriate occasion to reflect on these dual historical realities. We therefore invited a number of eminent First Amendment scholars who have contributed significantly to our understanding of freedom of speech over the past few decades to write essays against this self-reflective backdrop.

The essays begin with a historical overview by David Strauss and an examination of the philosophical underpinnings of the First Amendment by Vincent Blasi. These are followed by essays by Kent Greenawalt and Richard Posner that explore the lessons of the initial Supreme Court decisions on the freedom of speech. Robert Post, Frederick Schauer, and Stanley Fish then offer reflections on general First Amendment theory and doctrine. Finally, Lillian

BeVier, Owen Fiss, and Cass Sunstein address contemporary free speech issues and the future of free speech. We have framed these essays with an informal exchange between ourselves, designed largely to introduce nonexperts to the labyrinth of theory, doctrine, and social texture that mark the jurisprudence of the First Amendment and the essays in the book.

Our hope is that this volume will elucidate some of the more perplexing challenges and mysteries of our nation's most daring "experiment" and that it will inspire the kind of thought, deliberation, and debate that are essential to the promise of "eternal vigilance."

BOLLINGER: Let's begin with some general observations about the development of the First Amendment and their potential implications for the future. Two characteristics stand out as especially salient.

The first is the relative *newness* of First Amendment jurisprudence—a fact that is widely unappreciated. As each of the essays in this volume makes clear, the First Amendment—as we know it today—is an invention of the twentieth century. It begins in 1919, the first time in our history that the Supreme Court interpreted the meaning and reach of the principle of freedom of speech and press. In a trilogy of cases (*Schenck, Frowherk,* and *Debs* [case citations are provided at the end of the dialogue]), each involving individuals who dissented from the nation's involvement in World War I, the Court (in unanimous opinions written by Justice Oliver Wendell Holmes) announced the "clear and present danger" standard for the limits of free speech and gave us the memorable hypothetical of a person who falsely shouts "fire" in a crowded theater (to whom, of course, freedom of speech can be denied).

From that moment on, we have witnessed an extraordinary growth of case law, scholarship, and general commentary about the First Amendment. Hundreds of judicial decisions—minutely studied, analyzed, and criticized— now constitute a highly intricate body of principles, doctrines, exceptions, and rationales.

A sign of this explosion of jurisprudence can be seen in the law school curriculum. For the past two decades, many (certainly the leading) law schools have offered an entire course just on the First Amendment. Indeed, if you or I were to return to full-time law teaching now, we might offer *three* courses involving the First Amendment: the basic course, a mass media law course, and a seminar on some aspect of freedom of speech and press such as broadcast regulation, obscenity, or free speech in cyberspace. The first point, then, is this: *what* we are talking about in this book—and certainly *how* we talk about it—is largely a creation of the twentieth century.

STONE: Your reference to Holmes's announcement of the "clear and present danger" standard and his use of the "false cry of fire in a crowded theater" hypothetical illustrate several important points about both the First Amendment and legal analysis more generally. As you note, it was in *Schenck,* the Supreme Court's initial decision on the meaning of the First Amendment, that Holmes first uttered these two phrases, and for the next half-century they shaped the course of First Amendment thinking. But in many respects they shaped our thinking in subtly misleading directions.

Where you start thinking about a problem often determines where you end up. In this case, Holmes began his inquiry into the meaning of the First Amendment by seeking a simple example of what the guarantee of freedom of speech *doesn't* protect. In a way, this is logical. Given the seemingly absolute language of the Amendment ("Congress shall make no law . . . abridging the freedom of speech, or of the press"), it makes sense to test its potential reach by seeking a limiting hypothetical. Hence, the "false cry of fire" example. The key point Holmes was making with this example was that the Amendment can't possibly mean what it seems to say. And to prove that point, the hypothetical is both powerful and persuasive.

But Holmes then took the example a step further. "Why," he implicitly asked, "can the government punish the false cry of fire in a crowded theater?" If we can answer that question, we can derive a general principle that will give meaning to the seemingly overbroad text of the First Amendment. He deduces that the government may constitutionally punish the false cry of fire because such speech creates a "clear and present danger" of harm. Thus, that is the test for restricting speech under the First Amendment.

It is a shame that Holmes did not pursue his example yet another step further. Suppose, for example, someone yells "fire" in a crowded theater, but the shout is true—that is, suppose there really is a fire. In this case, the danger of people being trampled in the rush to the exits would be equally "clear and present," but surely we would not punish the speaker. In this case the value of the speech outweighs the harm it causes, even though the harm is "clear and present."

Thus, the real lesson of Holmes's hypothetical, which Holmes himself did not discern, is not that speech necessarily may be restricted when it creates a "clear and present danger," but (at least in this hypothetical) that it may be restricted when it creates a clear and present danger *and* it is false. That is a very different lesson that would have led us into a quite different set of questions about the constitutional importance of truth and falsity, why falsity may be relevant to the meaning of the First Amendment, and what other types of expression, like false speech, might also be subject to restriction. (It is also noteworthy that the example Holmes selected involves wholly nonpolitical speech. This, too, may distort the hypothetical. Indeed, the lesson might have been quite different had Holmes begun, for example, with speech critical of the government—the sort of speech actually involved in *Schenck*.)

BOLLINGER: This leads to my second observation about the modern history of the First Amendment: it has not involved a gradual and steady amassing of decisions and doctrines protective of expression as we know it now shortly after the turn of the century, but rather an ebbing and flowing of protection. Taken as a whole, the past eighty years reflect a series of deep internal disputes about the proper scope of constitutional protection for speech.

The three opening cases (*Schenck, Frowherk,* and *Debs*) *rejected* the free-speech claims of the defendants—and the most shocking outcome (to our contemporary free-speech sensibilities, anyway) was the conviction of Eugene Debs, the leader and presidential candidate of the Socialist Party who was sent to prison merely for delivering a public speech praising those who had illegally resisted the draft. During "times of war," Justice Holmes explained for the Court, we cannot expect the society to tolerate the same degree of opposition to national policies as we would in peacetime.

Just a year later, Holmes seemed to change his attitude about freedom of speech and joined Justice Louis Brandeis in a famous series of concurring and dissenting opinions that proposed a more extensive constitutional protection of speech and that laid the foundation for the extraordinary reach of the First Amendment today. During the 1930s and 1940s, the Holmes–Brandeis perspective gained adherence and momentum in various Court decisions. This was an era in which important doctrines according wider protection to dissident speech were first enunciated (*e.g.,* the public forum doctrine and the doctrine of prior restraint).

Then came the 1950s and the post–World War II fears of racial and religious conflict and of a Communist conspiracy to overthrow democracies, and American democracy in particular. In *Beauharnais v. Illinois,* the Court held that "group libel," or what we now would call hate or racist speech, was unprotected. And in *Dennis v. United States,* a decision now reviled by the free-speech community, the Supreme Court upheld the convictions of the leaders of the Communist Party for advocating the violent overthrow of the government.

But this midcentury recrudescence of the *Schenck* et al. perspective was not to be the final word. The decade of the 1960s (and partly the 1970s) brought forth a series of foundational and highly speech-protective Supreme Court decisions that together now define free speech at the start of the new century. Advocacy of illegal conduct is protected until the point at which the speaker incites imminent and serious illegal action and such action is "likely" to occur (*Brandenburg v. Ohio*), with the upshot that the KKK and neo-Nazis can now march and speak pretty much as they like. The Court has also accorded significant protection to defamatory speech (*New York Times v. Sullivan*), indecent language in public places (*Cohen v. California:* "Fuck the Draft" on the back of Cohen's jacket worn in a public courthouse), "fighting words," obscenity, and other forms of offensive speech. Of course, the Court has not held that speech is "absolutely" protected, but the levels of protection established by the Court beginning in the 1960s went far beyond what many (perhaps even most) Americans regard as "reasonable." And this continues to be true to this day.

One important question raised in this book is whether there is any significance in this ebb and flow of First Amendment protection. What might it indicate about the stability over time of the current First Amendment perspective?

STONE: This evolution of First Amendment doctrine over the past eighty years can be seen as a reflection of larger changes in society and in the Supreme Court itself. Indeed, this evolution can be understood as a classic illustration of the very principles the First Amendment was designed to promote. As you note, in its initial efforts to make sense of the First Amendment, the Court inclined toward a rather crabbed view of its protections. The Court seemed (rather innocently) to believe that the government could effectively excise from public debate only those views that could be said to be "dangerous," without threatening free speech more generally.

But over time the Court came increasingly to understand that although each generation's effort to suppress its idea of "dangerous speech" (antiwar speech during World War I; syndicalist expression during the 1920s; Communist advocacy during the 1950s) seemed warranted at the time, each seemed with the benefit of hindsight an exaggerated and often pretextual response to a particular political or social problem. The Court came to understand that there is a natural tendency of even well-meaning citizens, legislators, and judges to want to suppress ideas they find offensive or misguided, to inflate the potential dangers of such expression, and to undervalue the costs of its suppression.

In effect, then, the Supreme Court itself was a splendid example of Holmes's "marketplace of ideas" in which competing views about the meaning and breadth of the First Amendment contested openly with one another and in which, with experience and reflection, the Court came to a more sophisticated, more subtle, and more speech-protective understanding of the meaning of the First Amendment.

As an illustration, it is worth tracing briefly the evolution of the law in the area of subversive advocacy—that is, speech that is prohibited because it can lead listeners or readers to commit unlawful acts against the established order. In ruling on prosecutions for "obstructing the draft" during World War I, the lower federal courts generally applied what was known as the "bad tendency" test. Under this test, virtually any criticism of the war could be punished because of its "tendency" to make people less supportive of the war, thus increasing the risk that draftees would refuse induction or that soldiers would be insubordinate. Such speech, in other words, has a "bad tendency."

As a counterpoint to this approach, federal judge Learned Hand proposed in his opinion in the case concerning the journal *The Masses* that the government should be permitted to punish speech on the claim that it may cause unlawful acts *only* if the speaker "expressly" incites such unlawful acts (that is, expressly urges people to refuse induction). Otherwise, Judge Hand concluded, the speech should be absolutely protected.

Shortly thereafter, in its decisions in *Schenck, Frohwerk,* and *Debs,* the Supreme Court essentially adopted the "bad tendency" approach, even though it used the phrase "clear and present danger." In a series of separate dissenting and concurring opinions from 1919 through 1927, Justices Holmes and Brandeis rejected this approach and argued in such cases as *Abrams, Gitlow,* and *Whitney,* in which the Court upheld the convictions of a series of political dissidents, that speech can be restricted in this context *only* if it creates a "clear and present" (meaning *imminent*) danger of a grave harm that "Congress has a right to prevent."

A quarter-century later, in its 1951 decision in *Dennis v. United States,* the Supreme Court finally embraced the clear and present danger standard in this area of the law, but then proceeded immediately to water it down. That is, the Court held that the degree of "clarity" and "presence" necessary for prohibition could go down as the "gravity" of the harm went up. Because *Dennis* involved the prosecution of the leaders of the Communist Party for allegedly conspiring to advocate the violent overthrow of the government— obviously, a very "grave" danger, were it to occur—the Court was satisfied with a very attenuated showing of "clarity" and "presence," over the dissenting opinions of Justices Black and Douglas, who adhered to the Holmes–Brandeis version of "clear and present" danger. Most recently, in the *Brandenburg* decision in 1969, the Court held that speech can be restricted in this setting only if it expressly advocates unlawful conduct *and* it is intended imminently to cause such conduct *and* it is in fact likely imminently to cause such conduct. Thus, as Gerry Gunther has observed, the Court in *Brandenburg* combined the most speech-protective elements of Judge Hand's test in *Masses* with the most speech-protective elements of the Holmes–Brandeis version of clear and present danger to produce a highly speech-protective standard that has remained in effect ever since.

BOLLINGER: What you have just summarized is at the core of First Amendment debates, and certainly First Amendment classes, over the last eight decades, and no doubt will continue to be so in the future. Once you decide that not all speech, not even all speech on political issues, is absolutely protected, then you must devise in words a "test" that the society—all the way from legislators to speakers to police to prosecutors to judges—can apply in specific cases. Not surprisingly, that has turned out to be remarkably difficult. Partly it's a matter of how much societal harm you are willing to endure from speech; partly it's a matter of how much you trust our institutions (the courts, juries, and so on) to implement these tests. You refer to Learned Hand's test in *Masses,* that speech is protected until the point where the speaker "expressly" urges the audience to violate the law. From his private correspondence at the time with Holmes, we know that Hand was concerned that Holmes's "clear and present danger" standard would be easily manipulated by intolerant judges and juries to imprison unpopular speakers. And, in fact, the early Supreme Court cases we have mentioned, which arose out of the widespread intolerance of the war and the subsequent period of the so-called Red Scare, could be read as proof of the validity of that concern. Hand, accordingly, wanted a test that was more hard edged, less easily twisted by the wish to persecute dissenters. So he proposed to limit the power of the state to intervene only when the speech at issue *expressly* incites others to violate the law.

But this standard has serious limitations. It means that feckless speakers, those who though explicitly urging illegality have no chance of persuading anyone to do so, may be punished. It further means that truly dangerous speakers who are also clever enough to employ innuendo and irony for their illegal ends will be fully protected and free to accomplish those harmful ends (the so-called Marc Anthony problem). One inevitably begins to wonder whether the vagueness problems of the "clear and present danger" standard are less troublesome. I suspect that is why the Hand test in *Masses* did not survive the test of time, and I am doubtful that if, as you say, it is incorporated into the contemporary test articulated in *Brandenburg* (and I'm not so sure it is) it will survive in that form either.

Again, all of this raises the question whether our current First Amendment jurisprudence is as fixed and secure as most of us seem to think. The recency of the whole development—that is, an eighty-year continuing evolution, as opposed to an accretion of interpretations stretching over centuries, which is what most people (most nonlawyers, anyway) believe has happened—indicates less of a grounding in historical experience. For the foreseeable future, therefore, it is more vulnerable to the criticism that what has occurred up to this point is the judgment of just one, or perhaps, two generations, and not the more unchallengeable judgment of the ages.

The risk of the current jurisprudence being jettisoned in the future increases when one adds in the fact of the ebbing and flowing of judicial protection during this eighty-year period. And then, too, very few of the cases decided during this period have, in fact, ever been expressly overruled: *Schenck, Debs, Beauharnais,* and *Dennis* all remain on the books as potentially viable precedents, even though most First Amendment scholars today assume that they have been implicitly overruled.

Moreover, because each of those decisions arose during what were thought at the time to be exceptional circumstances (a world war or an international communist conspiracy), there is further reason to be concerned about their being revived at another point in the future when "exceptional circumstances" are perceived to exist again. It is sometimes said that freedom of speech is counterintuitive and, therefore, perpetually vulnerable to being abandoned. But our current jurisprudence may have some built-in vulnerabilities beyond that.

STONE: Earlier, I offered a very rosy view of the evolution of First Amendment jurisprudence as an illustration of the benefits of a system of freedom of expression. There is, however, a more cynical view of this process. It is noteworthy that in each of the major confrontations with the meaning of free speech—during World War I, during the 1920s, and during the Communist era—the Court adopted an interpretation of the First Amendment that was sufficiently flexible to enable it to uphold the restrictions at issue.

Thus, during World War I the Court enunciated the seemingly speech-protective "clear and present danger" test, but then construed the test in such a way as to uphold the convictions of those who protested against the war and the draft. In the 1920s, the Court looked back on the World War I cases with some dismay, and embraced a more speech-protective interpretation of the First Amendment, an interpretation that presumably would have reversed the convictions of the earlier era, but that enabled the Court to uphold the convictions of the syndicalists. In the 1950s, the Court strengthened its protection of free speech in such a way as to call into question both the World War I cases and the syndicalist decisions of the 1920s, while enabling it to uphold the convictions of the leaders of the Communist Party.

So, on this more cynical view, one might say that the Court learns just enough to correct the mistakes of the past, but never quite enough to avoid the mistakes of the present. On the other hand, as you note, since the 1960s the Court has adopted a highly speech-protective set of doctrines that has thus far withstood all of the pressures to weaken its protections of the First Amendment, most notably the efforts to suppress the Pentagon Papers and to allow the regulation of "racist" and "sexist" expressions.

I agree, however, that the current consensus is far from secure. Freedom of speech is, indeed, "counterintuitive," and as Justice Holmes once observed, "persecution for the expression of opinion" is "perfectly logical." If we deeply believe that communist or racist or unpatriotic expression is wrongheaded, offensive, or dangerous, it is perfectly "logical" to express our "wishes in law and sweep away all opposition." It requires a deep faith in the underlying premises of the First Amendment, and a deep skepticism about the capacity of the government to decide what ideas are "wrongheaded," "offensive," or "dangerous," to resist the temptation to censor. Since the 1960s, the Supreme Court has erected strong doctrines to protect against those temptations. But they are far from impenetrable.

BOLLINGER: Let's now look more broadly at First Amendment doctrine. Up to this point, our focus has been primarily on case law dealing with so-called subversive speech, or speech advocating illegal behavior (*e.g.,* overthrow of the government, riot, even murder). The reason for that is quite straightforward: subversive speech has been the classic, seminal context in which the Supreme Court has confronted and defined the scope and meaning of free speech. It is interesting to speculate about whether the First Amendment would look much different today if this had been otherwise.

A central idea in First Amendment doctrine is that the government is prohibited from restricting speech because of its *content*—that is, except in extraordinary circumstances, the government may not restrict speech because it may persuade people to embrace "bad" ideas or do bad things (attempting to overthrow the government, say, or acting immorally) or because it may offend people. Today, this constitutes the basic methodological axis for resolving issues of First Amendment protection of expression.

STONE: This is the principle the Court gleaned from the experience of decisions like *Schenck, Debs,* and *Dennis.* It embodies the Court's very strong presumption against any form of "censorship." In effect, the Court is no longer willing to listen to arguments that certain messages are so "dangerous" that they can for that reason alone be suppressed.

But, of course, there is a qualification to this principle—namely, the Court's distinction between "high" and "low" value speech. This distinction finds its roots, like so much in contemporary First Amendment jurisprudence, in Justice Holmes's opinion in *Schenck* and his familiar example of the "false cry of fire in a crowded theater." As I noted earlier, Holmes used this hypothetical to explain both why and when speech may be punished. But he missed the point of his own vivid illustration, which was that the speech could legitimately be punished, not because it created a "clear and present danger," but because it was *both* dangerous *and* false.

It is this insight that provides the foundation for the Court's willingness to permit restrictions of incitement, obscenity, fighting words, commercial advertising, false statements of fact (such as libel), and threats. In each of these categories of expression, the Court has found that the speech is not deserving of *full* First Amendment protection and may therefore be regulated in circumstances in which other speech could not be regulated. As the Court noted in *Chaplinsky* in 1942, "there are certain well-defined and narrowly limited classes of speech, the prevention and punishment of which have never been thought to raise any Constitutional problem," for "such utterances are no essential part of any exposition of ideas, and are of such slight social value as a step to truth that any benefit that may be derived from them is clearly outweighed by the social interest in order and morality."

The Court begins with the presumption that all speech has "high" value and that only *narrowly* defined categories of speech can appropriately be characterized as less than fully protected by the First Amendment. The precise calculus that makes up the "low" value judgment is not always transparent, but the Court seems to consider such factors as whether the expression is political in nature, whether it can be said to contribute affirmatively to public debate, whether it appeals to the cognitive processes of the audience, and whether it is the sort of speech that government is likely to restrict for constitutionally impermissible reasons (that is, because of partisan or political hostility to the ideas communicated).

In general, this doctrine has played a salutary role in free-speech jurisprudence. For without this doctrine—if the Court could not allow some room for government to regulate libel, commercial advertising, threats, incitement, and obscenity—there would be irresistible pressure to dilute the overall standards of free-speech protection, even for more fundamentally important expression such as criticism of the government. But the continuing challenge of the "low" value doctrine is to decide whether other forms of speech—such as hate speech—should be added to the list of those categories that are given only partial First Amendment protection.

The question of hate speech is worthy of special note. One of the most

difficult issues in working out a system of free expression arises from the need
to reconcile a society's often competing commitments to freedom of speech
and individual dignity. This conflict is posed most poignantly in the context of
hate speech. To what extent must a society, to be true to its commitment to free
expression, tolerate speech that insults and degrades a group or individual on
the basis of race, religion, gender, or ethnic origin? On the other hand, to what
extent may a society, in furtherance of its commitment to individual dignity,
censor unpleasant racist or sexist or homophobic speech because it offends, or
even deeply offends, others? Can this possibly be a principled basis on which
to censor ideas and opinions in a society committed to open public discourse?

Over the past fifty years, the Supreme Court has wrestled with these questions. While at first the Court indicated that some regulation of hate speech
might be constitutional, it has now quite firmly, and in my view correctly,
concluded that such regulation is unconstitutional. In its 1952 decision in
Beauharnais, the Court upheld a state statute declaring it unlawful for any
person to distribute any publication that "portrays depravity, criminality, un-
chastity or lack of virtue of a class of citizens, of any race, color, creed or
religion." The Court explained that such utterances, like obscenity, are not
"within the area of constitutionally protected speech." Thus, it was irrelevant
that the leaflet in question did not create a "clear and present danger." Rather,
the Court said that it was sufficient that this was not a "purposeless restriction."

In the half-century since that decision, however, *Beauharnais* has never
been cited approvingly by the Supreme Court, and for all practical purposes
has implicitly been overruled on repeated occasions. Indeed, since *Beauharnais,* it has come to be accepted that such regulations of "hate speech" are
incompatible with the First Amendment because they suppress ideas that do
not create the kind of clear and present danger of immediate and grievous
harm that is necessary to justify the suppression of free expression.

The extent to which *Beauharnais* has been discredited was made clear in
the Court's 1992 decision in *R.A.V. v. St. Paul,* in which the Court unanimously
invalidated a city ordinance that prohibited the display of a burning cross, a
swastika, or other symbol that one has reason to know "arouses anger, alarm
or resentment in others" on the basis of race, color, creed, religion, or gender.
Although the technical issue involved in the case was quite complicated, the
Court unambiguously held that such an ordinance violates the First Amendment. The Court explained that the First Amendment "prevents government
from proscribing speech because of its disapproval of the ideas expressed."
After *R.A.V.,* it seems clear that no direct regulation of speech drawn expressly
to protect particular groups against offensive or hurtful expression will pass
constitutional muster.

Thus, just as the government cannot constitutionally restrict the advocacy of communism, or agitation against a war, or the burning of the American flag, or ideas that may offend Democrats, or Palestinians, or veterans, so too is it foreclosed from restricting speech that insults or degrades particular racial, religious, or gender groups. The Court's point is not, of course, that such expression is harmless. It is, rather, that there are better ways to address that harm than by giving government the power to decide which ideas the citizens of a free and self-governing nation may and may not express.

BOLLINGER: I think the question of protection for extremist speech (whether it is subversive advocacy or racist speech) can best be understood as just one context, albeit a very special one, in which a democratic society addresses the far broader, even generic, problem of achieving the proper balance of tolerance, given a world in which there is a general bias toward excessive intolerance. We should come back to this subject at a later point in our discussion.

Another subject we should discuss, however, is the effort within the First Amendment traditions not just to bar censorship, but actively—"affirmatively," as the first First Amendment scholar Zechariah Chafee, said—to expand opportunities for citizens to speak effectively and even to equalize those opportunities.

This "affirmative" side of the First Amendment has several manifestations within the jurisprudence. The public forum doctrine, for example, which originated in the 1930s, compels the government to make certain public property—especially public streets and parks—available for speech purposes on roughly a first-come, first-served basis. This principle has sometimes been justified as ensuring the existence of the "poor person's printing press." In a sense, the public forum doctrine has operated as a kind of constitutional "takings"—certain forms of public property have been "condemned" to equalize the opportunities for citizens to exercise the freedom of speech.

STONE: When this issue first arose, courts held that the freedom of speech prohibited "censorship," but did not guarantee individuals the right to commandeer public property for speech purposes. Thus, although courts acknowledged that the government could not constitutionally prohibit speech critical of the government, they did not even glimpse a First Amendment issue in government regulations prohibiting speeches in public parks or leafleting on public streets. These latter sorts of regulations were seen as outside the scope of the freedom of speech both because they were "content neutral"—that is, they were not directed against any particular ideas or messages—and because courts assumed that the government, "no less than a private owner of property," could control the purposes to which its property is put.

As you note, by the 1930s the Supreme Court took a major step in recognizing that even these sorts of regulations could have a serious impact on free expression. Thus, the Court announced in the *Hague* case that, "wherever the title of streets and parks may rest, they have immemorially been held in trust for the use of the public and, time out of mind, have been used for purposes of . . . communicating thoughts between citizens [and] discussing public questions." In the words of Harry Kalven, the Court recognized a kind of "First Amendment easement." Because streets and parks had historically been used for speech purposes, the government could not withdraw that permission without a very substantial justification.

This, of course, led to a further set of questions. If there is a right to make public speeches in a public park and to hand out leaflets on a public sidewalk, is there also a right to distribute leaflets on a military base or to post campaign posters on public utility poles? In general, the Court in the last thirty years has embraced a relatively narrow view of the right to a "public forum" and limited the right only to those places, like streets and parks, that have been made available "time out of mind" for "discussing public questions."

Thus, as a general matter, the Court has held that the government may prevent speakers from using other types of publicly owned property for speech purposes, so long as the government doesn't draw distinctions between speakers on the basis of the message they seek to convey. The Court seems to have concluded that there are enough opportunities for free expression that don't involve the use of government property (billboards, newspapers, radio, television, and so forth) that it isn't worth the coin for courts to get bogged down in a morass of "small" disputes about the appropriateness of an almost infinite array of administrative regulations involving the possible use of public property for speech purposes. The Court didn't want to get drawn into having to make such microdecisions. Streets and parks were enough.

BOLLINGER: A related foray into the affirmative side of the First Amendment involves cases in which the Court has held that even *private* property must be treated according to the public forum rules. Of course, the First Amendment, like the rest of the Bill of Rights, covers only "state action"—that is, the actions of the government, federal and state. But in a few cases, involving a company town and a private shopping center, the Court has held that the traditional role of government had been assumed by private ownership. According to the Court, unless these private organizations were treated for constitutional purposes as if they were the state, the goals of freedom of speech would be in jeopardy.

But certainly the largest governmental effort to redress the imbalance of opportunities for speech that arises from the unequal distribution of wealth has been in the area of regulation of radio and television broadcasting. Under an explicit rationale that the broadcast media allowed too few (and only wealthy) people to control speech on the airwaves, the Court held that the First Amendment permitted (and at one point intimated that it perhaps even required) an array of public regulations designed to compel broadcast licensees to grant access to their media to other people and viewpoints. One regulation (abandoned by the Federal Communications Commission in the 1980s), the fairness doctrine, required broadcasters to present all "reasonable" points of view on all "controversial issues of public importance." Another, the equal time provision, mandates a right to "equal time" to any candidate for public office when a broadcaster allows the station to be "used" by an opposing candidate.

These are remarkable developments in the jurisprudence of the First Amendment, but they seem to me to have faded significantly over the past decade or two. As we've already noted, the public forum doctrine, while certainly alive and well with respect to traditional forums, such as streets and parks, has not been significantly extended to other public places. It has remained relatively static. And the extension of First Amendment protections to private restrictions on speech has been flatly overruled by the Court in a subsequent shopping center case, and there appears to be not the slightest inclination to explore this area further.

With public regulation of the media, the story is more complex. The Court has emphatically and consistently refused to extend this affirmative vision of the First Amendment to the print media, in spite of a fairly powerful argument that newspapers are as monopolized as television (at least as television was at the time the Court decided the issue). My own view is that the Court has allowed two models of the First Amendment to proceed over several decades, amounting to a *dual system of freedom of press:* the model of a free and independent media represented by print and the model of public regulation represented by broadcasting. I have argued that there have been substantial First Amendment benefits from this dual system. In an era in which concentration of power is increasing through the media—a matter of grave concern to the fundamental First Amendment goal of an open marketplace of ideas—one sensible response is to permit a *limited* experiment with government regulation designed to ensure greater balance of viewpoints and public access. By restricting regulation to a newly emerging communications technology (*e.g.,* the broadcast media), while leaving the traditional media (*e.g.,* the print media) fully protected and autonomous, this constitutional compromise creates at least a partial remedy of public access for a *general* problem (*i.e.,* concentration of ownership throughout the media), while significantly alleviating the risk of improper government censorship by maintaining the autonomy of traditional media from public regulation.

At this point in time, however, it seems fairly clear to me that the appeal of the public regulation model is fading. The idea that the market knows best, and that public regulation to correct market inequities is ineffectual at best and counterproductive at worst, has deepened its hold on the legislative and judicial mind. Owen Fiss, Cass Sunstein, and I have argued in various ways that public regulation can be an important, even necessary, means of realizing First Amendment goals. But those arguments seem less persuasive at the turn of the century.

STONE: I'm not sure these arguments are any less persuasive today, but they certainly have lost ground in the Supreme Court. Indeed, in recent years the Court has generally treated cable television and the Internet according to what you call the "free and independent media" model rather than the "public regulation" model.

I suspect the Court has backed away from the public regulation model largely because it was anxious about letting the government have too much influence on the substantive structure of public debate. If government officials can determine when broadcasters and newspapers have to let others speak, they will be tempted to exercise this authority in ways designed to strengthen their own political power. Legislators are more likely to support regulations that serve their own partisan interests than those that serve the interests of their opponents. Thus, regulations of the media that may appear to be "public regarding" may in fact be designed to manipulate public debate to achieve partisan ends. I think the Court was—in my view, rightly—quite nervous about inviting elected officials to get so directly involved in the structure of public debate. The same concerns, of course, also affect the Court's view of efforts to regulate the political process and campaign finance.

BOLLINGER: Those are important points. But we should always remember that we must compare two sources of threats to an open and vital marketplace of ideas—the threat of "censorship" and distortion of public debate may come both from government and from private power.

STONE: I'd like to turn now to another point that interests me—the overall coherence of First Amendment doctrine. It is fashionable these days to criticize free-speech doctrine as inconsistent and incoherent. In my view, this criticism is largely unfounded. On the whole, free-speech doctrine makes considerable sense, leads to generally predictable and sound decisions, and serves the underlying values of the First Amendment.

The criticism generally takes the form of identifying specific decisions that are at the margin of particular doctrines to demonstrate that the fundamental doctrines that make up the corpus of free-speech jurisprudence are imperfect, or even irrational. But all rules are imperfect at the margin. That is in the nature of rules. Consider one of the simplest rules of all—the speed limit. "No one may exceed 65 miles per hour on Highway *X*." Suppose I receive a speeding ticket for going 66 miles per hour. Does that make sense? Am I really so much more dangerous than a driver who goes 65 miles per hour? Suppose I can demonstrate that I am a better driver or that my car is in better condition? Is it "coherent" or "consistent" to penalize me but not the person who drives 65 miles per hour? The answer, of course, is that this is a legitimate distinction because we need the clarity of rules despite their imperfections at the margin. The same is true of free-speech doctrine.

"Congress shall make no law . . . abridging the freedom of speech." How do we give meaning to those words? One possibility, of course, would be to ask in every case whether a challenged law "abridges" the "freedom of speech." This would be like substituting a rule that says "No person may drive unsafely" for one that says "No person may exceed 65 miles per hour." The former may allow (in theory) for the "perfect" outcome on the facts of each case because the decisionmaker could consider not only the speed at which the defendant was driving but also the road conditions, the skill of the driver, the time of day or night, the weather, the traffic situation, the condition of the car, and so on. Thus, only individuals who actually drive "unsafely" would be punished. The difficulties in such an approach are evident, however. Such a vague standard creates an extraordinary level of unpredictability; leaves broad (perhaps dangerously broad) discretion in the hands of police, prosecutors, jurors, and judges; and is extremely inefficient to administer. The same would be true of an approach to the First Amendment that asked in each case whether in the particular circumstances presented the challenged law "abridges" the "freedom of speech." We need more concrete rules to guide both citizens and governmental decisionmakers.

As we've seen, most of our contemporary free-speech jurisprudence is organized around two basic distinctions: the distinction between content-based and content-neutral restrictions, and the distinction between "high" and "low" value speech. Other doctrines help to shape First Amendment jurisprudence, but these two are the most important in helping the Court organize the problems with which it has grappled.

We've already discussed the "high" value/"low"value distinction. The content-based/content-neutral distinction is equally important in framing contemporary free-speech jurisprudence. In its very first decision on the meaning of the First Amendment, the Supreme Court recognized in *Schenck* that some rule, more clearly defined than "Congress shall make no law . . . abridging the freedom of speech," was necessary to implement the free-speech guarantee. Thus, in his opinion for the Court, Justice Holmes announced that "the question in every case" is whether the speech creates a "clear and present danger."

Now, this is a clear rule. Or is it? Terms like "clear" and "present" are not self-defining. Does "clear" mean 99 percent probable, or 75 percent probable, or 51 percent probable, or reasonably foreseeable? Does "present" mean instantaneous, or within an hour, or within a day, or within a month or a year? One can discern what such terms mean only by understanding what the Court *intends* them to mean.

The defendants in *Schenck* were convicted of obstructing "the recruiting or enlistment service of the United States" because they circulated "to men who had been called and accepted for military service" a pamphlet that stated that "a conscript is little better than a convict." Did the distribution of this pamphlet create a "clear and present danger"? What was the relevant "danger"? That the war effort would be paralyzed? That the recruiting and enlistment service would grind to a halt? That a single person might be influenced to refuse induction? The Court in *Schenck* upheld the conviction, thus apparently concluding that the distribution of this pamphlet created a "clear and present danger" of a sufficiently grave harm to warrant its punishment. This would seem to suggest that, appearances to the contrary notwithstanding, this was not a very speech-protective test, at least by contemporary expectations of what the First Amendment protects.

As we've already discussed, in subsequent decisions over the next fifty years, the Supreme Court eventually gave added bite to the "clear and present danger" test to the point where, in the *Pentagon Papers* case in 1971, the Court held that the government could not prevent the publication of stolen Defense Department documents that disclosed secret information about the conduct of the Vietnam War because the government could not demonstrate a "clear and present danger." The Court had come a long way from *Schenck*. This development is important, not only because it placed a much greater burden on the government to justify restrictions of speech, but also because it embraced an almost absolute protection against content regulation of "high" value speech, thus producing a very clear rule—somewhat akin to the 65-miles-per-hour speed limit.

BOLLINGER: In a sense, the law generally can be seen as a continuous struggle between the conflicting desires for predictability and limited discretion on the part of decisionmakers, which is manifest in clear and fixed legal rules, and the desires for doing justice in each case and preserving the discretion to accomplish justice, which is manifest in more open-ended and general legal rules. Both courses clearly carry the risk of producing seemingly "arbitrary" results, although the degree of that risk may vary in specific areas of the law. I agree with you that the First Amendment has arrived at a point where "high" value speech is virtually ensured protection against government regulation directed at its "content." You cite the *Pentagon Papers* case for that proposition. That, of course, was a case involving what the Court has defined as a "prior restraint."

Classically, a prior restraint is a licensing scheme under which every author or speaker must, in advance of publication, seek permission from the government. Early in the development of the First Amendment *(Near v. Minnesota)*, the Court characterized a judicial injunction against publication as "prior restraint," to be treated just like a licensing system. The issue in *Pentagon Papers* was whether the federal government constitutionally could enjoin the *New York Times* and the *Washington Post* from publishing the official classified documents describing the history of U.S. involvement in Vietnam. Prior restraints have been especially disfavored from a free-speech standpoint because they impose significant barriers to communication, are very likely to "chill" or discourage many speakers, and probably contain an inherent bias favoring improper censorship (that is, speech in the abstract is more likely to be regarded as sufficiently "dangerous" as to justify regulation). In any event, the decision in *Pentagon Papers,* though quite complicated because of multiple opinions from the justices, can reasonably be interpreted as imposing a virtually ironclad prohibition on prior restraints. Whether, as you suggest, the case stands for the proposition that a similar barrier applies to all comparable subsequent punishment schemes, I am not so sure. But we both agree that *Brandenburg* applies to those cases, and your general point stands: prior restraints and subsequent punishments directed at the content of "high" value speech are treated in the fashion of clear and fixed legal rules (in the neighborhood, at least, of the 65-miles-per-hour rule).

Parenthetically, we might take note here of another branch of First Amendment law growing out of *Pentagon Papers,* which incidentally also follows the path of relatively clear and simple rules for resolving immensely complex problems. *Pentagon Papers,* as we've seen, largely forecloses the option for the government of protecting state documents, even classified documents, through injunctions or penalties for publication. But what about the possible right of the press, and the public too, to gain access to government documents (or events) in order to have the information to inform the public and to participate meaningfully in the marketplace of ideas? A constitutional "right of access" is hardly a frivolous claim, especially since the government is notorious for overprotecting and overclassifying information that, if known, would benefit public debate and decisionmaking. Yet, to avoid the ceaseless and burdensome task of judicially evaluating every claim for access against the government's interests in secrecy, the Court has refused to create a right of access to information. (The only exception to this is *Richmond Newspapers v. Virginia,* where the Court established a First Amendment right of the public to be present at criminal trials.)

Yet First Amendment doctrine also contains many rules that reflect the wish to retain discretion and decide cases on an individual basis. The standard for determining the constitutionality of content-neutral regulations of speech— essentially a "balancing test"—is, of course, of that kind. The same is true even of some forms of content regulation. In the important category of "low" value expression, obscenity stands out as a prime illustration. The Court's definitions of what constitutes "obscene" speech are so notoriously vague ("appeals to the prurient interest," violates "contemporary community standards," and so on) that Justice Stewart's straight-faced line "I know it when I see it" has become the defining expression of our bemusement and frustration at contentless definitions. Indeed, the case-by-case approach to determining obscenity reached such a peak in the 1960s, initiated with a case called *Redrup,* that the Court's practice of examining the allegedly obscene materials and then declaring them (without explanation) obscene or not obscene became known as "*Redrupping.*"

I have just a few additional comments on your observation about the number of criticisms of First Amendment jurisprudence as "incoherent" or "arbitrary." Many of the essays in this book either make that claim directly or try to answer it. But virtually all of them can fairly be said to be motivated by a deeply felt need, acknowledged or tacitly assumed, that bringing order and coherence to First Amendment law is of very high importance. That in itself raises a question—one we should return to at the very end of our discussion— whether the degree of that felt need says something important about the role the First Amendment has come to play in our national life.

Finally, we should unpack a bit more the claim of lack of coherence, especially in anticipation of some of the discussions in the following essays. Sometimes the argument is that conflicting results and indeterminate theories reveal that the whole corpus is nothing more than a politically motivated enterprise. Sometimes the argument is that the results of cases cannot be squared with a single theory but rather are reflective of multiple and competing theories of free speech (which, of course, need not be a bad thing). And sometimes the argument expresses an unhappiness with the incapacity of a theory to guide results in specific cases. On this last point, it is important always to bear in mind that general theories about what we're up to in any area of law often are inconclusive when it comes to resolving particular problems. Occasionally they even point in opposite directions. As we know, those who have argued for casting certain racist and pornographic speech as "low" value expression, and therefore properly subject to greater regulation, often start from the same premise as those who resist creating further exceptions to the 65-miles-per-hour approach of *Pentagon Papers* and *Brandenburg*. The premise that the First Amendment disfavors any distortion of the marketplace of ideas, of public discussion of public issues, cuts both ways: thus, there should be no censorship of even horrible ideas of racism and pornography because they're all contributions to public debate and there should be censorship of these ideas because their natural effect is to *silence* minorities and women and hence to distort the public discussion of public issues.

STONE: We should say a bit more about the distinction between content-based and content-neutral regulations of speech. In developing its jurisprudence of the First Amendment, the Supreme Court has paid attention not only to the type of *speech* being regulated (*e.g.,* criticism of the government, obscenity, express incitement), but also to the type of *regulation* of speech being challenged (*e.g.,* content-neutral or content-based). A content-based regulation restricts speech because of its message (*e.g.,* "no person may oppose the war" or "no person may advocate communism"), whereas a content-neutral regulation restricts speech without regard to its message (*e.g.,* "no person may distribute leaflets on a public street" or "no person may erect a billboard near a highway"). What is the rationale for this distinction?

Recall that in *Schenck* Justice Holmes said that "*the question in every case*" is whether the speech creates a "clear and present danger." The implication is that the "clear and present danger" standard is the test for *all* free-speech problems. Needless to say, it would be convenient to have a single standard to apply in all disputes concerning the constitutionality of government restrictions of speech. But as the Court discovered, life—and law—are never so simple.

By the late 1930s, the Court had moved toward the notion that the strong version of the "clear and present danger" standard should govern all free-speech issues. But it soon became apparent that this would not work. Consider, for example, a law prohibiting any person to use a loudspeaker in a residential neighborhood after 8:00 in the evening. Should the constitutionality of such a law be tested by the same standard used to test the government's attempt to suppress the Pentagon Papers or general criticism of government policy? By the 1930s, the Court began implicitly to recognize that different types of free-speech issues call for different tests to assess constitutionality. In *Schneider v. State*, for example, the Court considered an ordinance prohibiting any person to distribute leaflets in any public place. The purpose of the ordinance was to prevent littering. Instead of applying the "clear and present danger" standard, the Court declared that in cases like *Schneider* the Court must "weigh the circumstances and appraise the substantiality of the reasons advanced in support of the regulation." This test, which sounds in "balancing," is quite different from "clear and present danger."

But what are the cases "like *Schneider*" to which this very different test applies? At first, it was not clear even to the Court how to draw the distinction between cases like *Schenck* and cases like *Schneider*. It gradually became evident, however, that the difference was that the restriction in *Schenck* was directed at the *content* of speech, whereas the restriction in *Schneider* was *content neutral*.

Why should this matter? Why should the Court apply a strict "clear and present danger" standard in cases like *Schenck*, but a more open-ended "balancing" standard in cases like *Schneider*? To make the point clearly, consider two laws. The first prohibits any criticism of the government's decision to prosecute a war. The second prohibits leafleting in any public place. In what ways do these two laws threaten the values underlying the First Amendment?

The first of these laws cuts to the very heart of the First Amendment. By prohibiting the advocacy of a particular point of view, it arrogates to the government the power to decide what policies may and may not be questioned. In the words of Alexander Meiklejohn, it "mutilates the thinking process of the community." The law is inconsistent with the most commonly invoked values of free expression—it precludes the free and open search for truth; it denies citizens the opportunity for meaningful self-governance; and it prevents individual self-expression. It is no wonder that the Court regards such laws as presumptively, perhaps as conclusively, unconstitutional.

The second of these laws, on the other hand, is more modest in its affront to the purposes of the First Amendment. Although it may restrict the ability of individuals to select the *means* of expression they prefer, it does not involve the government in suppressing particular points of view, it does not directly skew the "thinking process of the community," and it is less likely to be the product of constitutionally impermissible motivations (*e.g.*, the desire of legislators to preserve their power or to repress their political opponents). Thus, whereas the Court has tended to take a highly speech-protective approach to content-based restrictions of "high" value speech, it has tended to test content-neutral restrictions with a more open-ended form of balancing that weighs the relative restrictiveness of the law against the government's justifications for the regulation. This distinction, although imperfect at the margins, seems to me a sound axis on which to organize First Amendment doctrine.

I do not mean to suggest, by the way, that these doctrines—the "high" value/"low" value distinction and the content-based/content-neutral distinction—are perfect or even perfectly clear, either in theory or practice. They certainly aren't as straightforward, for example, as the 65-miles-per-hour speed limit. Moreover, there are serious questions at the margin about how we define the difference between "high" and "low" value speech, how we treat different forms of "low" value speech (*e.g.,* how we define the circumstances in which government may regulate commercial advertising, obscenity, incitement, and libel), whether some types of regulations should properly be characterized as content based or content neutral (*e.g.,* laws regulating the permissible "subject matter" of speech, such as "no one may hand out leaflets in a welfare office concerning any subject other than welfare"), and how we apply these doctrines in nontraditional situations (*e.g.,* may the government fund through the National Endowment for the Arts only "good" art or only "nonracist" art, even though it cannot constitutionally prohibit "bad" and "racist" art?). What I do mean to suggest, however, is that these are *sensible* doctrines that offer a high degree of predictability in *most* circumstances and that distinguish among different categories of problems in ways that significantly further the underlying goals of the First Amendment.

BOLLINGER: There's another facet to the architecture of the First Amendment that deserves mention. The text of the First Amendment refers to "speech" and "press." The question arises whether this should be interpreted as referring only to language communication (written and oral) or to other forms of communication as well. It is, of course, customary for people to express their political views through nonlinguistic means—by wearing armbands, marching, and so on. Given a commitment to a robust marketplace of ideas and to democratic self-government, we would naturally expect courts to understand "speech" as encompassing these methods of political expression as well.

Yet ordinary criminal behavior can also be characterized as "political expression." Trespass, assault, and assassination are sometimes committed by political actors in order to communicate revolutionary messages and to inspire followers. Clearly, courts should and do worry about giving encouragement to such behavior by characterizing these acts as potentially having First Amendment value.

The Supreme Court sensed this dilemma from the outset and for many years struggled to articulate a framework for resolving it. The Court never hesitated to interpret the First Amendment as embracing a broad set of communicative behavior. Parades, marches, public gatherings, clothing, flags (including burning flags), and other forms of so-called symbolic speech have by now received ample protection of the First Amendment. Still, the Court has always kept a watchful eye on the implications of doing so. The Court's opinions in these cases invariably contain warnings about how a more cautious First Amendment analysis is called for when "action" or "conduct" or "speech plus" is involved. Not until the mid-1970s, however, in the case of *United States v. O'Brien*, did the Court provide any guidance beyond labels.

O'Brien did double duty for First Amendment doctrine. You have noted the distinction *O'Brien* drew between regulations aimed at the content, or message, of speech and regulations concerned with other matters. This was an important clarifying step, as you point out. It also provides the basis for sorting out the "speech"/"conduct" problem. Under *O'Brien* we no longer begin by distinguishing between speakers who use words and speakers who use other forms of expression. We look only at the intention or motivation behind the regulation. If the government's purpose is to punish the message being communicated (as with a law banning all criticism of a war, whether by words or by burning draft cards), the law is presumptively unconstitutional. In all other cases, the courts will balance the free-speech interests against the societal interests compromised by the speech at issue.

STONE: The current analysis of the "symbolic speech" problem is, indeed, an excellent illustration of the content-based/content-neutral distinction. Imagine two laws, one prohibiting any person to urinate in public, the other prohibiting any person to urinate on a public building as a symbolic expression of disrespect for the government. The first is presumably constitutional because it is neutral with respect to content, it serves legitimate governmental purposes unrelated to free speech, and it doesn't have a significant restrictive impact on free expression because there are plenty of other ways to express one's disrespect for the government. The second law is presumably unconstitutional, however, because it is expressly directed at particular "content." Similarly, a law prohibiting any person to destroy a draft card, which is designed to ensure the smooth administration of the selective service system, is constitutional; whereas a law prohibiting any person to "desecrate" the American flag is unconstitutional because it prohibits *only* those symbolic uses of the flag that do not treat it with respect.

In some circumstances, however, the line is not so clear. For example, in the *Barnes* case, the Court dealt with the problem of nude dancing as a form of entertainment. Although recognizing that the element of nudity can contribute to expressive behavior in this setting, the Court nonetheless upheld a city ordinance prohibiting nudity in public, even as applied to "adults only" clubs that feature nude dancing, on the theory that the ordinance was content neutral and not directed at speech (by analogy to the hypothetical law prohibiting any person to urinate in public).

BOLLINGER: Another problematic application of this distinction concerns the question whether a judge is precluded by the First Amendment from imposing additional punishment (beyond that for trespass) on a defendant convicted of burning a cross on the front yard of a black family. There is clearly "communication" involved in such an act, yet it seems unlikely any court would hold the imposition of an enhanced penalty for the communicative injury unconstitutional. Probably the best way to describe the current doctrine is that the state cannot forbid messages pure and simple, however communicated, but can add punishment for messages when accompanied by harmful acts otherwise punishable under the First Amendment because the state is concerned about avoiding noncommunicative harms (*e.g.,* trespass or murder).

STONE: Actually, I disagree about the constitutionality of an enhanced penalty for trespass that includes cross burning, as distinct from mere trespass. Although I agree that the harm to the homeowner is both different and greater if someone burns a cross on the homeowner's lawn than if he burns a pile of leaves on that person's lawn, the difference turns entirely on the speech element of the act and is thus immune from punishment. Otherwise, this would be an impermissible way of getting at "hate speech" by the back door.

BOLLINGER: It's time we turned to the underlying theory of the First Amendment, and this is a good place to close our discussion, for as you've already noted, the various doctrines and developments we've discussed ultimately can be assessed only against an understanding of the purposes of the First Amendment itself.

It is well-accepted among the justices and legal scholars today that the fundamental purpose of free speech is to maximize the search for truth and to protect the democratic decisionmaking process. Sometimes these are seen as separate and distinct functions, but more often as overlapping. Probably, if one had to select the dominant rationale of freedom of speech, it would be its relation to democracy and self-government. If citizens are to possess sovereignty, they must have the freedom to speak their minds and exchange opinions. It is sometimes said that free speech also serves a value of personal autonomy and self-realization, which is a good in itself and not just instrumental to some other end (such as truth or democracy). But that purpose has never achieved the widely accepted status in First Amendment jurisprudence of the other two.

There are many questions one can raise about the viability of these ratio-nales. I'll focus on the most prominent issues relating to the truth-seeking and democracy functions.

One question concerns the evidence we have to support the proposition that we are more likely to reach the truth, or good political decisions, in a constitutionally sheltered, robust speech environment than in a more carefully regulated one. Justice Holmes said, in *Abrams,* that this is an "experiment," as "all life is an experiment," but that only raises a number of other questions: Why are we conducting this experiment as opposed to others? How will the outcomes of the experiment be evaluated? How long should we expect it to last before it stops being an "experiment" and becomes a "choice"?

Another point should be made at the outset of the discussion with regard to the democracy rationale. It is commonly said that the First Amendment protects the democratic prerogatives of the citizens to decide what policies the society should adopt. The government must, therefore, be stopped from interfering in those discussions by prohibiting the advocacy of particular points of view. The problem with this understanding is that it misses the fact that the restrictions on speech in nearly all of the First Amendment cases have arisen out of the democratic process itself and reflect the judgment of the majority. Nonetheless, courts have not hesitated to strike down such laws as unconstitutional. Accordingly, more of an explanation is called for. It doesn't mean that a theory of the First Amendment cannot be extrapolated from the idea of a democracy, but rather that such a theory must take account of the fact that censorship will not be allowed either by the "state" *or* by a majority of the citizenry acting under otherwise normal democratic procedures.

Now, many people might say that they are entirely comfortable with the idea that free speech serves the search for truth and the sovereignty of citizens in a democracy but express doubts about the reach of the First Amendment, as it has been interpreted by the courts. Why, in other words, should free speech extend to those who would advocate the overthrow of the government, the establishment of an authoritarian system of government (including one without freedom of speech), or the hatred or even murder of other citizens? Once again, the purported rationale fails to explain what we have done in the name of the First Amendment.

This is where First Amendment theory begins to explore human nature and develop notions of epistemology. Many, but most notably John Stuart Mill and Justice Holmes, advanced the argument that, assuming we have a paramount interest in understanding the truth and given that experience teaches us that we are not infallible, any "rational" person must therefore accept that any contrary opinion, no matter how false we may perceive it to be, may be true. It follows, it is said, that we must permit all opinions to be held and expressed, because they may be true. Mill proposed a back-up argument: namely, that even if any opinion is appropriately and rationally deemed to be "false," we still benefit from our engaging with that false view because in doing so we attain a "livelier sense of the truth." (Others have expressed in varying ways this view of the benefits to be derived from confrontation with falsehood and error.)

The principal argument for protection of extremist speech, however, is not about the benefits to truth but rather about the need to create a fortress of constitutional protection around valued speech and debate. We take First Amendment protection so far out, this argument says, because of our felt need to deflect the ever-present wish for censorship, even of good speech. I call this the "fortress model" of free speech; often it is referred to as the "slippery slope argument" for protection. To create an exception to the First Amendment, however justified that exception may seem to be in the specific case, is to risk a breach in the walls of constitutional protection or a slide down the slope of censorship. So, in any case, goes the argument.

This perspective is based on several underlying assumptions. It assumes that both the state and democratic government will be prone to implement improper restrictions on speech. It assumes that judges will not be able or willing to reject those restrictions and protect the speech that deserves protection. The fortress model is premised on a distrust of our normal institutions of self-government when it comes to speech.

The problems with the perspective are many. First, there are the costs to this strategy. Often the speech protected will be very harmful. Advocacy of genocide or of hatred toward a particular group of citizens will intimidate, silence, and anger those vilified. Some listeners may even be persuaded by the speech, perhaps even taking the constitutional protection afforded the speech as a sign that these are ideas and thoughts worthy of consideration. Furthermore, it is not clear that the protection of the core of freedom of speech will be furthered by the strategy. Some may see the protection as so unreasonable that they may lose confidence in the very idea of freedom of speech. And it has to be remembered that we already have many exceptions to the First Amendment (*e.g.*, libel, obscenity, fighting words). It is not, therefore, at all clear that one more exception will make any difference whatsoever in encouraging improper censorship. Finally, it is also possible that the fortress/slippery slope strategy may be less needed over time, as the values of the First Amendment are more internalized by the society. Have we, after nearly a century, reached such a point in First Amendment history? How would we evaluate such a question?

This kind of debate leads to the most difficult, and the most important, of all questions about the reasons for the First Amendment: assuming there are clearly benefits to the society (truth, good policy, and so on) from a policy of open, largely unrestricted debate, why should we take this one area of human behavior ("speech") and make it off-limits to the ordinary give-and-take of democratic decisionmaking? After all, we leave all kinds of very important social issues (*e.g.*, the environment, social welfare) to the democratic process, even though that process is subject to errors of judgment. Why not let "speech" be subject to this process as well? One could answer, of course, that the reason we do it this way is simply because the First Amendment says it shall be so. That may be true, but it would be good if we also knew we had a good reason for why this is the way it is.

Various explanations can be offered. Some might think—erroneously, it seems to me—that there are no social costs involved in protecting speech. It is, therefore, an easy case, which should not be left to the vicissitudes of the democratic process. Besides being based on an untrue premise (namely, that there are never any social costs to speech), it still does not fully explain why we should remove "easy" problems from the democracy. Another theory is that deciding the scope of freedom of speech is problematic and the state is less able to resolve those issues than it is when other behavior is involved. The risks of bad democratic judgments, in other words, are significantly greater when expression is at stake. Distrust of the government, even of democratic government, is therefore appropriate. The problem with this is not the simple logic of the argument but rather the evidence that political life is this way.

A variation on the last idea is this: perhaps there is no material difference in a democracy between deciding on the limits of speech and nearly all other legislative choices, but it is important to minimizing the costs of errors of judgment with respect to all other choices to leave open the possibility that those errors can be pointed out over time. This creates a kind of rule against perpetuities for democratic decisions. This idea is very much in line with the arguments noted earlier of John Stuart Mill and others (about the logic of being a "rational" person and about the benefits of confrontation with falsehoods). It may also be said that allowing for those who lose in the democratic process (entirely fairly, we might add) to continue freely to speak their minds, creates hope and lessens the significance of the loss and also makes it possible for more robust decisionmaking.

These are important arguments. It may be asked, however, why these particular and very real benefits of a liberal principle of freedom of speech should nonetheless remain part of the balance of considerations a self-governing society should be able to consider for itself. All of life, it may be said, is choosing and acting on the basis of less-than-complete information and knowledge, and the possibility of error and what should be done about it and the justice of allowing those who disagree with us to continue to confront us with their views are more or less important depending on the facts and circumstances of the particular case or the moment.

There is another way of looking at free speech, at what functions and purposes it serves in the society. All that has been said up to this point attempts to derive a theory of free speech by looking at the value, the benefits, of "speech," especially in its best uses. Thus, expression is the way we exchange ideas, exercise self-government, and develop our sense of self. Extremes of speech are seen in relation to those ideal uses (*e.g.,* interaction with extremist speech advances the search for truth or provides a fortress around speech that does). And the justification for removal of regulation of speech from the usual democratic processes is found in the unique, distinctive qualities of that particular form of behavior.

But it is also possible to understand free speech from an entirely different perspective. We may find purpose not in (or only in) preserving something of unique value but in grappling with the underlying *mentality* in the act of censorship, in the *reaction* to speech. That mentality, or that impulse to censor, need not be peculiarly present in the act of censorship. The impulse that leads us to censor can also lead us to insist on having our way in every setting—to refuse to compromise in the give-and-take of social and political conflict, to punish our opponents through means other than censorship, and to punish excessively those who violate the norms we establish.

Justice Holmes was largely right when he said: "Persecution for the expression of opinions [is] perfectly logical. If you have no doubt of your premises or your power and want a certain result with all your heart, you naturally express your wishes in law and sweep away all opposition. To allow opposition by speech seems to indicate that you think the speech impotent, as when a man says that he has squared the circle, or that you do not care wholeheartedly for the result, or that you doubt either your power or your premises."

But the state of mind Holmes described is more than a motive for censorship, it also constitutes a mind of intolerance that will have broad and debilitating effects on the character of public decisionmaking of all kinds. And while beliefs and insistence are not by any means always bad in a society, it can reasonably be said that they have a tendency to get out of control, that there is a *bias toward* intolerance that must continually be curbed and mediated for any democratic society to work well.

Under this picture of human society, it makes sense to take a single area of human behavior—we take speech—and to declare it more or less off-limits for regulation. It serves a similar function to a wilderness area in an urban society, a place where sides of our personality are singled out, developed, tested, and highlighted because they are relevant to life in general. In this way, the extremes of free speech take on their own meaning. The whole point of the enterprise is to stretch the limits of our capacities, of our self-restraint and capacity for the appropriate level of social tolerance.

In the context of discussing the controversial *Skokie* case of the late 1970s, in which a small group of neo-Nazis sought to march in the city of Skokie, home to many survivors of German concentration camps, I put it this way: "One can understand . . . [the] choice to protect the free-speech activities of Nazis, but not because people should value their message in the slightest or believe it should be seriously entertained, not because a commitment to self-government or rationality logically demands that such ideas be present for consideration, not because of a simple hope qua conviction that anti-Nazi sentiment will win in the end, not because the anti-Nazi belief will be stimulated by open confrontation and argument with the Nazi belief, not because a line could not be drawn that would exclude this ideology without inevitably encroaching on ideas that one likes—not for any of these reasons nor others related to them that are a part of the traditional baggage of the free-speech argumentation; but rather because the danger of intolerance toward ideas is so pervasive an issue in our social lives, the process of mastering a capacity for tolerance so difficult, that it makes sense somewhere in the system to attempt to confront that problem and exercise more self-restraint than may be otherwise required. We should be, in short, more concerned with addressing through the act of tolerance the potential problems of intolerance than with valuing the act of speech itself."

Many parts of our jurisprudence reflect this idea of the meaning of freedom of speech. It is manifest in the many instances in which judges and others take pride in the extraordinary tolerance achieved in the protection afforded even some of the most reprehensible speech. And its seeds are present in some of the famous statements of our seminal cases, such as Brandeis's line in *Whitney:* "Men feared witches and burned women. It is the function of [free] speech to free men from the bondage of irrational fears."

Of course, this account of freedom of speech has its own questions to answer. Is the bias toward intolerance in society a greater risk than a bias toward passivity and excessive tolerance in the face of evil? Even if it is, is this the best way to deal with the bias? How are the "lessons" derived from the extraordinary tolerance in the free-speech context communicated and learned by the broader society?

Perhaps this is an appropriate moment to acknowledge how much there is still to address in our theorizing, how little hard data there are to draw upon in our theorizing, and what small guidance we receive from either the text or the original history of the First Amendment itself. This reinforces the initial observation that we are dealing with a mere decades-old interpretation of a centuries-old right.

STONE: This calls to mind what is, in my view, perhaps the Supreme Court's single most important and most underappreciated sentence on the freedom of speech—its declaration in the *Gertz* case in 1974 that "under the First Amendment there is no such thing as a false idea." What, exactly, does this mean? Of course, it doesn't mean that some ideas are not in fact better than others, or that all ideas are equal. Rather, it is a statement about who decides such questions and how such decisions are made. What it means is that the decision about which ideas are good and which are bad, which are true and which are false, is not to be made by the government or, for that matter, by the People.

But of course this can't really be so, for the government must and, indeed, does decide every day that some ideas are better than others. Legislators, judges, and voters decide all the time that some ideas are true and others are false. When legislators enact welfare legislation or campaign finance reform, when judges change the tort law or their interpretation of the First Amendment, and when voters endorse certain candidates or referenda, they are inescapably deciding that some ideas are better than others.

This is not, of course, what the Court meant in *Gertz*. Rather, it was saying that, under the First Amendment, the government may not decide that some ideas may not be *espoused* because they are "false." As the Court explained, "however pernicious an opinion may seem, we depend for its correction not on the conscience" of legislators or judges or voters, "but on the competition of other ideas."

So, here is an important distinction. We can enact into law the "good" idea that racial discrimination by private employers should be unlawful, but we cannot enact into law the "good" idea that no one may advocate the *repeal* of such legislation. Under the First Amendment, we may decide today which ideas are true and which are false as we go about the everyday business of making public policy, but the debate on the question of whether the idea is good or bad, true or false, must be permitted to continue.

Thus, the First Amendment places out of bounds any law that attempts to freeze public opinion at a particular moment in time. A majority of the People, acting through their government, may decide an issue of policy for themselves, but they have no power irrevocably to decide that issue by preventing the continuation of the debate. This is what the Court in *Gertz* meant when it said that "under the First Amendment there is no such thing as a false idea."

But that can't be the end of the matter. For the most interesting question is not whether the majority are permitted to act on their beliefs by enacting legislation about welfare policy or taxation, but whether they have the freedom permanently to end the debate on some questions, once and for all. If we believe that racism is evil, then shouldn't we simply ban any speech that says that racism is a good thing? Can't we act on our conviction that this is a "false" idea? Can't we ban the KKK and the Nazis? And what about communism? Given recent history, can't we now conclude once and for all that communism is a bad idea, and ban the reading of Marx? And what about misogynist literature and gay rights propaganda? Can't we ban them as well?

The answer given by the Supreme Court, of course, is an emphatic "no"; that "under the First Amendment there is no such thing as a false idea," and that "however pernicious an opinion may seem, we depend for its correction not on the conscience" of legislators or judges or voters, but on the constant and ongoing "competition of other ideas." In other words, in this context at least, we are not permitted to act on our convictions.

Why should this be so? A simple answer is that we don't need to ban "false" ideas because we are confident that the People will never adopt such ideas if they are allowed to consider them in a free and open competition. But, as you have noted, we don't really believe that. We know full well that knowledge is imperfect, that the People are imperfect, and that the competition is imperfect. We surely expect that sometimes, at least, the People will accept and act upon bad or false ideas if they are left to the competition of the market. So that, certainly, is not the answer.

Rather, the explanation is that we are, in effect, balancing two competing risks. On the one hand, there is the risk that, if permitted to consider all ideas, the People will not always act wisely and will sometimes embrace bad ideas, perhaps even some very bad ones. On the other hand, there is the risk that, if given the power to censor bad ideas, the People will not always act wisely and will sometimes prohibit the discussion of good ideas, ideas that would better be left open to further debate and consideration.

In choosing between these risks, and deciding whether the People, acting through their government, should have the power to declare certain ideas to be beyond the bounds of public debate, we must consider the nature of human nature. History teaches that people are prone to undue certitude, intolerance, and in the right—or perhaps more accurately, the wrong—circumstances, even to fanaticism. This is what you have described on another occasion as the "pathology of belief," the "allure of certitude," and "belief turned fanatical." We have a deep need to believe that we are right, to believe that we know that we know, to silence others who disagree with us, and in the words of Justice Holmes, to "sweep away all opposition."

If we empower the People to act on this instinct, there is every danger that they will do so. It is not inherent in human nature to be skeptical, self-doubting, and tolerant of others. We are not naturally inclined to abide ideas "we loathe and believe to be fraught with death." The First Amendment, on this view, cuts against human nature. It demands of us that we be better than we would be.

In my view, the Court has struck the right balance. The dangers of censorship and close-mindedness are greater than the dangers of robust and wide-open debate. The point is not that we trust the People always to make the right decisions if they can hear all sides of all issues; it is that we don't trust the People to make the right decisions if they have the power to silence those whose ideas they believe to be "false." For the Supreme Court to declare that "under the First Amendment there is no such thing as a false idea" is, in effect, to insist on doubt.

Citations

Abrams v. United States, 250 U.S. 616 (1919)

Barnes v. Glen Theatre, Inc., 501 U.S. 560 (1991)

Beauharnais v. Illinois, 343 U.S. 250 (1952)

Brandenburg v. Ohio, 395 U.S. 444 (1969)

Chaplinsky v. New Hampshire, 315 U.S. 568 (1942)

Cohen v. California, 403 U.S. 15 (1971)

Debs v. United States, 249 U.S. 211 (1919)

Dennis v. United States, 341 U.S. 494 (1951)

Frohwerk v. United States, 249 U.S. 204 (1919)

Gertz v. Robert Welch, Inc., 418 U.S. 323 (1974)

Gitlow v. New York, 268 U.S. 652 (1925)

Hague v. C.I.O., 307 U.S. 496 (1939)

Masses Publishing Co. v. Patten, 244 F. 535 (S.D.N.Y. 1917)

National Socialist Party v. Village of Skokie, 432 U.S. 43 (1977)

Near v. Minnesota, 283 U.S. 697 (1931)

New York Times v. Sullivan, 376 U.S. 254 (1964)

New York Times v. United States, 403 U.S. 713 (1971)

R.A.V. v. City of St. Paul, 505 U.S. 377 (1992)

Redrup v. New York, 386 U.S. 767 (1967)

Richmond Newspapers v. Virginia Pharmacy, 448 U.S. 555 (1980)

Schenck v. United States, 249 U.S. 47 (1919)

Schneider v. State, 308 U.S. 147 (1939)

United States v. O'Brien, 391 U.S. 367 (1968)

Whitney v. California, 274 U.S. 357 (1927)

In adjudicating the meaning of the First Amendment, what sources actually guide the justices of the Supreme Court? Do they look primarily to the text of the Amendment? To the "original" intentions and understandings of the framers? To the values the First Amendment was designed to serve? According to David Strauss, the "central features" of modern First Amendment law cannot be derived from any of these sources. Indeed, Professor Strauss argues that "neither the text nor the original understanding provides much support for the principles of free expression that we today take for granted." Rather, these principles "were hammered out . . . over the course of the twentieth century, in fits and starts, in a series of judicial decisions and extrajudicial developments" that together constitute an "almost textbook" example of common-law evolution.

As Professor Strauss describes this process, the Supreme Court has "decided each of the disputes before it, articulating principles that justified its decision; that, the Court claimed, were rooted in previous decisions; and that seemed to make practical and moral sense. Subsequent decisions used those principles as starting points. The principles often had to be modified, as the justices developed a more thorough understanding of the kinds of issues involved in establishing constitutional protections for speech and the kind of free-speech regime that would make sense."

Thus, Professor Strauss concludes that although the First Amendment "is a cultural reference point," the actual substance of First Amendment jurisprudence, "one of the great creations of the law," emerged not from the text of the Amendment or from the original understandings of the framers, but from "a process in which principles were tried and sometimes abandoned, sometimes modified, in light of experience and of an explicit assessment of whether they were good principles as a matter of policy and political morality." They are a creation of what Professor Strauss calls "the common-law Constitution."—GRS

DAVID A. STRAUSS

Freedom of Speech and the Common-Law Constitution

The First Amendment to the U.S. Constitution is the most celebrated text in all of American law. With the possible exception of the Fifth Amendment, which may be more notorious than famous, no other provision of the Constitution is so widely known to nonlawyers. Many nonlawyers even know some of the language of the First Amendment verbatim ("Congress shall make no law").

But the story of the development of the American system of freedom of expression is not a story about the text of the First Amendment. That text was part of the Constitution for a century and a half before the central principles of the American regime of free speech, as we now know it, became established in the law. Nor is it a story about the wisdom of those who drafted the First Amendment. There is a habit of attributing to the framers of the Constitution great foresight about freedom of expression as well as other subjects. But the actual views of the drafters and ratifiers of the First Amendment are in many ways unclear; and to the extent we can determine their views, they did not think they were establishing a system of freedom of expression resembling what we have today. There is, in fact, good evidence that the people responsible for adding the First Amendment to the Constitution would have been comfortable with forms of suppression that are anathema today.

The central principles of the American system of freedom of expression, in other words, were not the product of a moment of inspired constitutional genius two hundred years ago, however rhetorically powerful it is sometimes to speak that way. Those principles emerged in a way that is much less dramatic—but that is in many ways a more interesting and accurate reflection of how great constitutional issues are settled, and a more thoroughgoing testimony to how free speech resonates with American political culture. The central features of First Amendment law were hammered out mostly over the course of the twentieth century, in fits and starts, in a series of judicial decisions and extrajudicial developments. The story of the emergence of the American constitutional law of free speech is a story of evolution and precedent, trial and error. It is a twentieth-century story; and, in the way I am about to describe, it is a common-law story.

The Two Traditions

There are, broadly speaking, two competing accounts of how law gets its authority. One account sees law as the command of a sovereign.[1] In the early versions of this theory, the sovereign was understood to be an absolute monarch. But the command theory can easily take a democratic form, by substituting a popularly elected legislature for an absolute ruler. According to this theory, the law is binding because the person or entity who commanded it had authority to issue a binding command, either, say, because of the divine right of kings, or—the modern version—because of the legitimacy of democratic rule. In either event, the content of the law can be traced to a discrete act of the sovereign. It follows that, if you want to determine what the law says, you examine what the sovereign did—the words the sovereign used, evidence of the sovereign's intentions, and so on.

The great competitor of the command theory—the competition has gone on for centuries—is the common-law approach. In seventeenth-century Britain, Sir Edward Coke set up the common law in opposition to the absolutist claims of James I.[2] But the common-law approach has deeper roots—medieval roots, according to some accounts.[3] The early common lawyers saw the common law as a species of custom. The law emerged in the same way that other customs emerge in a society.[4] It would make no sense to ask who the sovereign was who commanded that a certain custom prevail, or when, precisely, a custom became established. Customs do not have identifiable origins like that. Legal systems are now too complex and esoteric to be regarded as societywide customs. But still, on the common-law view, the law has many aspects of custom. It develops over time, not at a single moment; it is the evolutionary product of many people, in many generations. There is no one entity who commands the law.

Similarly, according to the common-law view, the authority of the law comes not from the fact that some entity has the right, democratic or otherwise, to rule. It comes precisely from the law's evolutionary origins and its general acceptability to successive generations. Legal rules that have been worked out over an extended period can claim obedience for that reason alone. Similarly, according to the common-law approach, you cannot determine the content of

---

1. This view is most commonly associated with JOHN AUSTIN, THE PROVINCE OF JURISPRUDENCE DETER-MINED (5th ed. 1885). *See, e.g., id., in* JOHN AUSTIN, THE PROVINCE OF JURISPRUDENCE DETERMINED AND THE USES OF THE STUDY OF JURISPRUDENCE 1 (H. L. A. Hart ed., 1954).

2. *See* Prohibitions del Roy, 12 Coke's Rep. 65. *See also* Calvin's Case, 7 Coke's Rep. 3b.

3. *See* J. G. A. POCOCK, THE ANCIENT LAW AND THE FEUDAL CONSTITUTION 36–55 (1957).

4. *See, e.g.,* A. W. B. Simpson, *The Common Law and Legal Theory, in* OXFORD ESSAYS IN JURISPRUDENCE 77 (A. W. B. Simpson ed., 2d Series 1973).

the law by examining a single authoritative text or the intentions of a single entity. The content of the law is determined by the evolutionary process that produced it. Present-day interpreters may contribute to the evolution—but only by continuing the evolution, not by ignoring what exists and starting anew.

These are stylized descriptions of the two competing views. The command view has sophisticated variations that take it far away from the absolutism of Hobbes and James I, and the common-law view has many complexities. The notion of "evolution" in the common law, in particular, is obviously vague. Still, the contrast between the two views is apparent and important, and it echoes in contemporary controversies over the interpretation of the Constitution. Perhaps the most important divide in constitutional interpretation today is between approaches that emphasize the text of the document and the original understandings of the various provisions—that is, the way that the framers and ratifiers of those provisions understood them—and approaches that deemphasize the original understandings and insist that the proper interpretation of the Constitution can change over time. These two different approaches to interpretation, which are found not just in legal arguments but in the broader political culture, directly reflect the contrast between the command and common-law views.

The First Amendment's guarantee of freedom of speech, perhaps as much as any provision of the Constitution, is often seen in the terms suggested by the command theory. The fact that the text is so well known, and so often emphasized in discussions about free speech, itself suggests this. Justice Hugo Black made a particular point of emphasizing that the language of the First Amendment is "absolute," and his arguments have worked their way into the culture. The First Amendment says that Congress shall make "no law," and "no law," the argument goes, means no law, from which speech-protective conclusions are said to follow.[5] Even on its own terms, there are problems with this argument, as I will discuss. But the appeal of the textual argument fits most naturally with the command theory: we protect speech because that is required by the authoritative text, adopted by the sovereign We the People who ratified the Amendment.

In addition, arguments for the protection of speech routinely refer to the intentions and original understandings of the framers of the First Amendment. To some extent, of course, this is a common way of talking about constitutional law generally; people attribute to the framers their own views about how the Constitution should be interpreted, without any particular historical evidence that the framers actually held those views. But there is an especially strong

---

5. *See* Hugo L. Black, *The Bill of Rights*, 35 N.Y.U. L. Rev. 865, 874 (1960).

tendency to talk about the First Amendment this way.[6] The balance between free speech and other values, Justice Black liked to say, was struck by the men who wrote the Amendment.[7] This, too, reflects the command theory. The implicit premise of such claims about the framers is that we determine the contours of the American system of freedom of expression by looking to see what was decided when the First Amendment was added to the Constitution in 1791.

In fact, however, the command theory simply cannot account for the constitutional law of freedom of speech today. Neither the text nor the original understandings provide much support for the principles of free expression that we today take for granted. Those principles are, instead, the product of an evolutionary process that follows—with some significant qualifications—the common-law approach. In a sense it is almost misleading to speak of "the First Amendment" as a description of the law governing freedom of speech in the United States. Formally, the textual basis for that law, in the Constitution, is of course the First Amendment. But the central principles that protect free expression in the United States were not established by the addition of the First Amendment to the Constitution in 1791. Those principles were developed more gradually, over an extended and relatively recent period.

The Central Principles

What are those central principles? The constitutional law governing freedom of expression is elaborate and complex, but it is possible to identify three principles that give that body of law its essential structure.

The first principle, and the one that radiates throughout the rest of the doctrine, is the importance of protecting the right to criticize the government. This was what the Supreme Court, in *New York Times v. Sullivan*,[8] identified as "the central meaning of the First Amendment": the government may not punish people for criticizing it or its officials.[9] The three most important First

---

6. Recently, some Supreme Court justices have also relied on original intent, and some scholars have sought to revive original intent as a basis for interpreting the First Amendment. *See, e.g.*, McIntyre v. Ohio Elections Comm'n, 514 U.S. 334, 358–71 (1995) (Thomas, J., concurring in the judgment); 44 Liquormart, Inc. v. Rhode Island, 517 U.S. 484, 517–18 (1996) (Scalia, J., concurring in part and concurring in the judgment); AKHIL REED AMAR, THE BILL OF RIGHTS 231–37 (1999).

7. *See* Konigsberg v. State Bar, 366 U.S. 36, 61 (1961) (Black, J., dissenting) ("I believe that the First Amendment's unequivocal command that there shall be no abridgment of the rights of free speech and assembly shows that the men who drafted our Bill of Rights did all the 'balancing' that was to be done in this field.").

8. 376 U.S. 254 (1964).

9. *See id.* at 273; Harry Kalven, *The* New York Times *Case: A Note on "The Central Meaning of the First Amendment,"* 1964 SUP. CT. REV. 191.

Amendment cases of the last half-century all concerned this principle, and together they dramatically confirmed its priority. *New York Times v. Sullivan* itself, decided in 1964, established sharp limits on the extent to which individuals could be held liable for civil damages for defaming a public official. In *Brandenburg v. Ohio*,[10] the Supreme Court said that "advocacy of the use of force or of law violation" cannot be made illegal "except where such advocacy is directed to inciting or producing imminent lawless action and is likely to produce such action"[11]—a standard that may not be entirely clear in its particulars[12] but that is plainly highly protective of dissident speakers who urge the violation of law. Finally, in *New York Times Co. v. United States*,[13] a majority of the Supreme Court agreed that the government would have to make a showing of extraordinary necessity (that a publication "will surely result in direct, immediate, and irreparable damage to our Nation or its people")[14] before it could enjoin newspapers from publishing the so-called Pentagon Papers. Taken together, these decisions establish extensive and powerful protections for speech on political subjects.

The second principle is, in a sense, a generalization of the first. Plainly not all speech should receive the same protection as speech criticizing the government. The Supreme Court has, accordingly, recognized a distinction between high-value and low-value speech. It has done so by identifying certain low-value categories: obscenity, commercial speech, false and defamatory statements, "fighting words," and—although these cases have not come before the Supreme Court—speech such as perjury, blackmail, threats, and criminal solicitation. Speech in these categories can be regulated on the basis of a much weaker showing than is needed to protect high-value speech; in some instances, the speech is of no value at all and can be regulated freely. Perhaps the most significant aspect of this development is that the default category is high-value speech. Speakers need not establish that their speech is political, or artistic, or scientific, or otherwise high value; they need only establish that it is not in one of the low-value categories. In practice the result is that speech that may be of dubious artistic, scientific, or literary merit receives full protection as high-value speech because it does not fit into one of the low-value categories.

---

10. 395 U.S. 444 (1969).

11. *Id.* at 447.

12. *See* the editors' dialogue at the beginning of this book.

13. 403 U.S. 713 (1971).

14. *Id.* at 730 (opinion of Stewart, J.). While only two justices endorsed this specific formulation, at least three others would have required an even more demanding showing from the government. *See id.* at 714–20 (Black, J. concurring); *id.* at 720 (Douglas, J., concurring); *id.* at 726–27 (Brennan, J. concurring).

The third principle is a distinction among different kinds of regulations. Many laws affect people's ability to speak. A law that prohibits people from demonstrating in a way that blocks busy city streets during business hours obviously presents different issues, and should be judged differently, from a law that restricts criticism of the president. Beyond that, many laws might, in practice, have a very substantial effect on speech: a Federal Reserve Board decision to raise interest rates—or any number of other government decisions— might ripple through the economy and end up driving many marginal publishing houses, bookstores, and periodicals out of business. But it would be unworkable to treat such a decision as presenting a serious First Amendment issue. Accordingly, the courts have elaborated a distinction among regulations that are based on the content of speech; regulations that are directed at speech (like the ban on demonstrations) but that are not based on the content of the speech; and "incidental" regulations that are directed at a wide range of activities. Content-based regulations are ordinarily the most suspect; if they restrict high-value speech, they are presumed unconstitutional. Non-content-based regulations of speech are carefully reviewed by the courts but are not assumed to be unconstitutional. Incidental restrictions are almost always constitutional, even if they have a substantial effect on speech.

These are just the basic contours of the American law of freedom of expression. But where do even these basic principles come from? Obviously they are not explicit in the spare words of the First Amendment. In fact, they are in some ways difficult even to reconcile with the words of the First Amendment. And they are also not to be found in the records of the intentions of the framers of the First Amendment. They are principles that have been worked out by the courts, principally the Supreme Court, through a common-law process. Surprisingly, perhaps, the text and the original understandings of the First Amendment are essentially irrelevant to the American system of freedom of expression as it exists today. One could, as a thought experiment, imagine forbidding any reference to the text or the original understandings; as long as the precedents could still be invoked, the operative law of freedom of expression would remain undisturbed.

Doesn't "No Law" Mean "No Law"?

The text of the First Amendment, which plays such a large role in popular understandings, in fact presents some significant problems. The first word of the Amendment is "Congress." Taken at face value, the language of the Amendment does not prohibit the president or the courts from restricting speech. No one today would suggest that the president or the courts may infringe free speech.[15] But the principle that the First Amendment applies to the entire federal government, and not just to Congress, is very difficult to square with the text of the Bill of Rights. The Second, Fourth, and Ninth Amendments refer to the rights of "the People"; the Fifth, Sixth, and Seventh Amendments speak in terms of the rights of individuals; the Third and Eighth Amendments forbid certain actions without limiting the prohibition to a certain branch of the government. The First Amendment could have been drafted with any of these locutions. But it wasn't; the First Amendment alone singles out "Congress."[16] If we focus just on the text—as the " 'no law' means no law" approach suggests—the case for protecting free speech against government infringement generally is actually somewhat weak.

Quite apart from that, it has been settled since the earliest days of the republic that the entire Bill of Rights, of its own force, applies only to the federal government, not to the states. So far as the First Amendment is concerned, then, the states were free to suppress speech in any way they wished. Today the states are limited by the same First Amendment principles that apply to the federal government, but that is because the Fourteenth Amendment, added to the Constitution in 1868, has been interpreted to apply the First Amendment to the states.

That interpretation is also not obvious from the text. There is reason to believe that the drafters of the Fourteenth Amendment were, in fact, concerned about freedom of expression; antislavery speech was viciously suppressed in many slave states before the Civil War, and that experience was a recent and important memory for the members of the Reconstruction Congress.[17] But the drafters of the Fourteenth Amendment did not include an explicit protection of speech. The Fourteenth Amendment prohibits the states from

---

15. In general, the president and the courts act pursuant to powers granted by Congress, so it might be argued that a restriction that applies to "Congress" effectively limits them, too. There are at least two problems with this argument, however. First, both the president and the courts have some inherent powers—powers they possess even in the absence of a congressional authorization. For example, the Constitution itself makes the president commander in chief of the armed forces—Congress cannot take that power away from him—but no one believes that that gives the president carte blanche in restricting the expression of members of the armed forces. (The president could not, for example, order military officials to support his party's candidates for office.) Second, as I discuss in the text, other provisions of the Bill of Rights are written in terms that leave no doubt that they apply to all branches of government, so the text makes it difficult to sustain an argument that "Congress" in the First Amendment was just shorthand for all three branches.

16. For an account of how the First Amendment came to be drafted in this way, *see* Mark P. Denbeaux, *The First Word of the First Amendment*, 80 Nw. U. L. Rev. 1156, 1165–71 (1986).

17. *See generally* Michael Kent Curtis, Free Speech, "The People's Darling Privilege": Struggles for Freedom of Expression in American History (2000).

denying anyone "liberty" without "due process of law," and it protects the "privileges or immunities of citizens of the United States" from infringement by the states. Those are the clauses that are said to have incorporated the First Amendment. So the ringing phrases of the text of the Constitution actually do not, on their face, provide any comprehensive protection of speech from government regulation. The generation of 1791 did not pay any attention to state laws suppressing speech; the post–Civil War generation did not include a free-speech clause in the Fourteenth Amendment.

Finally, even if we were to leave aside these ways in which the language of the Amendment does not support a general right to be free from government restrictions of speech, the text alone simply does not tell us much. Surely "no law" means no law, but even leaving aside the fact that it is only "Congress" that "shall make no law," the words that come after "no law" are "abridging the freedom of speech," and those words are not self-defining. It is not obvious what constitutes an "abridgement" (has the government abridged speech if it rejects an artist's application for a grant? if it prohibits demonstrations in a government-owned park?) and it is not obvious what constitutes "the freedom of speech." The complex set of First Amendment principles we have today is certainly one interpretation of that language. But many other principles— some protecting more speech, some protecting less—would also be consistent with the requirement that the government not "abridg[e] . . . the freedom of speech."

Sedition and "Those Who Won Our Independence"

Similarly, the evidence we have of the original understandings of the First Amendment does not support the idea that the framers of the First Amendment meant to establish protections of free expression comparable to those with which we are familiar today. For much of the twentieth century, the orthodox view was that at least "the central meaning of the First Amendment"—that the government may not punish dissent—was established by the framers. In the words of Zechariah Chafee Jr., the first great First Amendment scholar of the century, "[t]he First Amendment was written by men . . . who intended to wipe out the common law of sedition, and make further prosecutions for criticism of the government, without any incitement to law-breaking, forever impossible in the United States of America."[18] Justice Holmes endorsed essentially

---

18. ZECHARIAH CHAFEE JR., FREE SPEECH IN THE UNITED STATES 21 (1967). Chafee first published this conclusion in 1919 (Freedom of Speech in War Time, 32 HARV. L. REV. 932, 947), as part of what one historian describes as "his disingenuous effort to influence the Supreme Court decisions in the Espionage Act cases after World War I." David M. Rabban, The Ahistorical Historian: Leonard Levy on Freedom of Expression in Early American History, 37 STAN. L. REV. 795, 797 n.2 (1985).

this view in his dissenting opinion in *Abrams v. United States*,[19] and Justice Brandeis said similar things about "[t]hose who won our independence" in his brilliant opinion in *Whitney v. California*.[20]

Even on this central issue, though, notwithstanding Chafee and Holmes and Brandeis, it is simply not clear what the framers thought. To some extent the problems are what we always encounter when trying to figure out the original understandings of constitutional provisions. The world of late-eighteenth-century America was very different from ours, and it is difficult, probably often impossible, for us to recreate today how they understood their world and what they hoped to accomplish by adopting various legal provisions. Moreover, even if we could do that in principle, we often do not have enough evidence in the historical record to reconstruct what the framers believed they were doing. But to the extent we can reconstruct their intentions, we certainly do not find unequivocal support for a system of freedom of expression resembling ours. A few points, in particular, stand out.

First, when the framers adopted the First Amendment, they were concerned with the balance of power between the federal government and the states as well as with protecting free expression.[21] It might be tempting to treat the word "Congress" in the First Amendment as a kind of synecdoche for "government," perhaps on the theory that while the framers thought the principal threat to free speech would come from Congress, their underlying concern was with all government suppression of speech, so it is a natural extension of their work to say that the First Amendment applies to all levels of government. That is the way the First Amendment is commonly understood today in the culture at large.

For the framers, however, there was a sharp distinction between the federal government and the state governments. Under the Constitution, the federal government has only those powers that are granted to it. Some of the framers—including, initially, James Madison—thought the Bill of Rights, including the First Amendment, was redundant because the Constitution did not give the federal government any power to restrict speech or the press in the first place.[22] Madison and others were ultimately persuaded to add the First Amendment, and we now understand that the Amendment was not at all redundant. Legitimate powers granted to Congress might be interpreted to allow Congress to restrict speech; Congress might use its power to "raise and support Armies,"

---

19. 250 U.S. 616, 630 (1919).

20. 274 U.S. 357, 375 (1927) (Brandeis, J., concurring).

21. *See, e.g.*, AKHIL REED AMAR, THE BILL OF RIGHTS 20–32 (1999).

22. *See, e.g.*, GORDON S. WOOD, THE CREATION OF THE AMERICAN REPUBLIC 1776–1787, at 536–43 (1969) (recounting the Federalists' belief in "the irrelevance of a Bill of Rights").

for example, to prohibit speech that discouraged people from volunteering for military service. But the entire focus of debate over the First Amendment was on the federal government, and on making clear that the Constitution's grants of various powers to Congress, in Article I, Section 8, did not include the power to restrict speech or the press (or to establish a religion—or to *dis*establish state religious establishments, another way in which the original understandings deviate from current law). The idea that the First Amendment established a nationwide principle that speech must be free from the control of government, period, was not part of the framers' understanding.

Second, even so far as the federal government was concerned, it is not clear that the framers intended to enshrine the core First Amendment principle that the government may not punish its critics. There was a robust tradition in England of punishing political dissent—"seditious libel" as it was called. As Chief Justice Holt explained in 1704: "If people should not be called to account for possessing the people with an ill opinion of the government, no government can subsist. For it is very necessary for all governments that the people should have a good opinion of it."[23] Even truthful statements about the government were therefore subject to criminal penalties; in fact, truthful statements were especially threatening to the stability of the government, and therefore especially worthy of punishment. William Blackstone—"whose works," according to the Supreme Court, "constituted the preeminent authority on English law for the founding generation"[24]—defined freedom of expression very narrowly. According to Blackstone, freedom of speech meant only freedom from "previous restraints upon publication," such as laws requiring that a newspaper publisher receive permission from a censor beforehand, and not "freedom from censure for criminal matter when published." In fact, Blackstone vigorously endorsed suppression of a kind we would consider unthinkable today: "[T]o punish (as the law does at present) any dangerous or offensive writings, which, when published, shall on a fair and impartial trial be adjudged of a pernicious tendency, is necessary for the preservation of peace and good order, of government and religion, the only foundations of civil liberty."[25]

There is a great deal of dispute among historians over whether the framers of the First Amendment meant to repudiate Blackstone and abolish the crime of seditious libel.[26] The text of the Amendment is, as usual, of little help. In

---

23. Rex v. Tutchin, 14 Howell's State Trials 1095, 1128 (1704).

24. Alden v. Maine, 527 U.S. 706, 715 (1999).

25. 4 WILLIAM BLACKSTONE, COMMENTARIES ON THE LAWS OF ENGLAND *151–52.

26. *See, e.g.,* LEONARD W. LEVY, LEGACY OF SUPPRESSION: FREEDOM OF SPEECH AND PRESS IN EARLY AMERICAN HISTORY (1960); LEONARD W. LEVY, EMERGENCE OF A FREE PRESS (1985); William T. Mayton, *Seditious*

fact, the reference to "the" freedom of speech can be read as saying that the First Amendment protects a preexisting package of rights, something already understood as "the freedom of speech"—an interpretation that might suggest that the First Amendment just enacts Blackstone's account of the existing law of England. That is not the inevitable reading of the text, of course, and there are good reasons in the historical record to think the framers did not intend to adopt Blackstone's view. Laws licensing the press—the principal concern of freedom of speech, according to Blackstone—had long since ceased to exist in England and never took hold in the colonies, and it seems doubtful that the framers would adopt the First Amendment to deal with a nonexistent evil.[27]

So far as the historical record is concerned, though, it is simply not clear what the framers meant to do. Part of the difficulty, again, is the differences between their world and ours. For example, the framers appear to have believed that protecting the right to a trial by jury and narrowing the definition of treason (both of which were accomplished by the original Constitution and the Bill of Rights) would provide enough protection for political dissent. That belief may have been correct in the eighteenth century, but by today's standards those measures alone would still permit too much suppression, partly because one lesson we have drawn from two hundred years of experience is not to place so much confidence in juries to protect dissent. It is simply unclear what we should make of the original intentions of the framers when circumstances have changed in such a way.

To the extent we can make out the framers' intentions, though, there is at least a plausible argument that the First Amendment was not intended to outlaw prosecutions for sedition. For example, there were some prosecutions for seditious libel in states that adopted provisions like the First Amendment— suggesting that the original understanding of the language of the First Amendment permitted prosecutions for sedition.[28] And, of course, in 1798, Congress—with the affirmative votes of many of the framers of the First Amendment—enacted the Sedition Act, a federal law that expressly punished dissent. The Sedition Act controversy was highly partisan, and the various claims made about the meaning of the First Amendment were offered for partisan purposes and cannot always be accepted at face value. Some framers,

---

Libel and the Lost Guarantee of a Freedom of Expression, 84 COLUM. L. REV. 91 (1984); David M. Rabban, *The Ahistorical Historian: Leonard Levy on Freedom of Expression in Early American History*, 37 STAN. L. REV. 795 (1985).

27. *See* CHAFEE, FREE SPEECH IN THE UNITED STATES, *supra* note 18, at 18–20; LEVY, EMERGENCE OF A FREE PRESS, *supra* note 26, at xi.

28. *See* LEVY, EMERGENCE OF A FREE PRESS, *supra* note 26, at 196–98.

including James Madison, the most important figure in the drafting of the Bill of Rights, condemned the Sedition Act as a violation of the First Amendment. But there are at least serious doubts about whether the framers understood the First Amendment to stand even for what we today would consider the core principle of a system of free expression.

Finally, away from the central issue of dissent and criticism of the government, there is little doubt that the framers were comfortable with forms of suppression that we today would consider incompatible with the First Amendment. There were prosecutions for blasphemy in the early days of the republic, including in states that had First Amendment–like constitutional provisions; there is no indication that anyone argued that those provisions barred such prosecutions. Similarly, defamation was considered outside the protection of any principle of free expression. Today, a prosecution for blasphemy would be unthinkable, and defamation law is subject to many important constitutional restrictions, even in cases that do not involve public officials.

Freedom of Expression and the Common-Law Approach

The American system of freedom of expression, as we know it, did not begin to emerge as a coherent body of legal principles until well into the twentieth century—in opinions written in a series of cases decided just after World War I.[29] Those principles emerged in a way that was, in most respects, typical of the common law. Three characteristics of the development of these principles, in particular, stand out. First, the process was distinctly evolutionary; the key principles were developed over fifty years, often through trial and error, with false starts and subsequent corrections. Of course there were some key cases that established important principles once and for all. But those decisions were not written on anything resembling a blank slate; all of them were, self-consciously, the product of what had gone before.

Second, throughout the process by which these principles developed, courts—the most visible development of the principles was in the courts, although legislators' understandings evolved too, as did popular consciousness—relied most heavily on earlier judicial decisions. There was no serious parsing of the text. In no case was the text of the Amendment decisive. The framers, or the founding generation—the most likely candidates for the sovereign whose command was to govern—also played little role in the development of the law. There were recitations of Chafee-like statements about the framers, and there is some reason to think that Chafee's historical assertions,

---

29. On the development of ideas about freedom of speech before the post–World War I cases, *see* DAVID M. RABBAN, FREE SPEECH IN ITS FORGOTTEN YEARS (1997).

which have since been strongly challenged, influenced Justice Holmes. But there was very little serious historical investigation. The relationship between the law and the framers' views was essentially backward: as the principles governing freedom of expression were hammered out, those principles were attributed to the framers, without serious attention to the historical record. There was, on the other hand, an intense concern with precedent. In some very important respects, this took an odd twist: some of the most important precedents were dissenting opinions. But the precedent-centered, common-law nature of the process was dominant.

Third, the development of these principles was marked by an unmistakable concern with matters of policy and political morality—a concern with what kinds of First Amendment principles would make sense and achieve good results. On the command theory, present-day judges' views about these matters should be irrelevant. What matters is what "We the People" decided two hundred years ago, not what judges (or anyone else) today considers a good idea. But the explicit consideration of matters of policy, fairness, workability, and political morality is a characteristic of the common-law method, especially in its modern conceptions. Those considerations can play only a limited role. They must ordinarily operate within the framework established by past decisions; only very powerful arguments of morality or policy can justify casting that framework aside. But past decisions often leave room to maneuver, and even if they do not, they can be modified in incremental ways to make the law better.

It is difficult to give a precise account of how the common-law approach operates. Historically the opponents of the common-law approach have charged it, with some justification, with being mystical and obscure, a cover for the class and guild prejudices of judges. But the central idea of the common-law approach can perhaps be rendered this way: decisions made in the past, particularly if they have been reaffirmed over time, are entitled to respect even if it is not clear to us today why they are right. An individual has only a limited capacity to figure out how to deal with a complex political and social problem, such as the proper contours of freedom of expression. Even a group of people—even an entire generation—has only a limited stock of reason on which to draw. But decisions that have stood up over time reflect the combined efforts and experiences of many people over many generations, and therefore embody a kind of collective wisdom that should not be set aside just because we today are not convinced that they were right. This is a recurrent theme sounded by the defenders of the common-law approach, perhaps most vividly by Edmund Burke, the eighteenth-century British statesman who was also an important proponent of the ideology of the common law:

> The science of constructing a commonwealth, or renovating it, or reform-
> ing it, is, like every other experimental science, not to be taught *a priori*. . . .
> The science of government being therefore so practical in itself, and intended
> for such practical purposes, a matter which requires experience, and even
> more experience than any person can gain in his whole life, however saga-
> cious and observing he may be, it is with infinite caution that any man ought
> to venture upon pulling down an edifice, which has answered in any tolerable
> degree for ages the common purposes of society.[30]

The principles that we today think of as "the First Amendment" are very much
such an "edifice" that is accepted because it "has answered in a[ ] tolerable
degree for . . . the common purposes of society"—if not "for ages," then at
least for decades.

The common-law approach is not simply a matter of following what has
been decided before, however. For one thing, it is not always clear how to
interpret previous decisions. People may have honest disagreements about
what following a particular precedent, or continuing a particular past practice, would require in a specific case. In addition, the justification for adhering to precedent is not a mystical attachment to the past (although there is
plenty of that among the common-law ideologists, including Burke); it is that
there are good, functional reasons to think that past decisions, reflecting as
they do an accumulation of experience, are sound ones. When that reason is
undermined—when there is cause to doubt that previous decisions "answer[ ]
in any tolerable degree . . . the common purposes of society"—then one should
alter the edifice. And when it is unclear what precedent requires, the interpretation of precedent should be guided by a conscious decision about which
interpretation would make the most sense, as a matter of fairness, morality,
and common sense. Precedent is the starting point, because it reflects the
collective wisdom of previous generations, and precedent is never to be taken
less than seriously and never to be overthrown without careful consideration.
But precedent can be interpreted or modified (or even, in an extreme case,
discarded) when the presumption of its soundness is overcome by a thorough
conviction that it is wrong. Benjamin Cardozo, one of the greatest American
common-law judges, put it this way, in words that also capture something
central about the development of the law of the First Amendment:

> The final cause of law is the welfare of society. The rule that misses its
> aim cannot permanently justify its existence. . . . I do not mean, of course,

---

30. EDMUND BURKE, REFLECTIONS ON THE REVOLUTION IN FRANCE 58–59 (1940). For Burke's relationship
to the common-law tradition, *see* J. G. A. Pocock, *Burke and the Ancient Constitution: A Problem in
the History of Ideas, in* POLITICS, LANGUAGE, AND TIME: ESSAYS ON POLITICAL THOUGHT AND HISTORY 206–32
(J. G. A. Pocock ed., 1973).

that judges are commissioned to set aside existing rules at pleasure in favor of any other set of rules which they may hold to be expedient or wise. I mean that when they are called upon to say how far existing rules are to be extended or restricted, they must let the welfare of society fix the path, its direction and its distance.[31]

The American law of freedom of expression developed in an almost textbook common-law fashion. The Supreme Court (few decisions by other courts played an important role in the evolution) decided each of the disputes before it, articulating principles that justified its decision; that, the Court claimed, were rooted in previous decisions; and that seemed to make practical and moral sense. Subsequent decisions used those principles as starting points. The principles often had to be modified, as the justices developed a more thorough understanding of the kinds of issues involved in establishing constitutional protections for speech and the kind of free-speech regime that would make sense.

In these ways, the development of the law of the First Amendment resembled constitutional law in many other areas, where the text has been incidental and the law developed through precedent. In one striking respect, though, the First Amendment was different. The precedents that served as fountainheads for First Amendment law were dissenting opinions, written by justices whose views had not prevailed. Specifically, they were the dissenting opinions of Justices Holmes and Brandeis in a series of cases decided during and after World War I. Those dissents became authoritative in a remarkably short time. Indeed by 1950, Justice Felix Frankfurter, in a through-the-looking-glass performance, wrote an opinion in which he was at pains to explain why, although his view seemed to be straightforwardly consistent with an earlier decision of the Supreme Court, it was actually at odds with that decision.[32] The decision was one from which Holmes and Brandeis had dissented, and Frankfurter thought it important to demonstrate that he was actually following Holmes and Brandeis, not the earlier Court.

Clear and Present Danger

The First Amendment canon in the Supreme Court, however, does not begin with a ringing Holmes and Brandeis dissent defending free speech. It begins in 1919 with *Schenck v. United States*[33]—a Holmes opinion to be sure, but a majority opinion, and one upholding the suppression of speech. Schenck had,

---

31. Benjamin N. Cardozo, The Nature of the Judicial Process 66–67 (1921).

32. *See* Dennis v. United States, 341 U.S. 494, 541–42 (1951) (Frankfurter, J., concurring).

33. 249 U.S. 47 (1919).

during World War I, circulated a leaflet condemning conscription, in "impassioned language," as immoral and unconstitutional. He distributed the leaflet to men who had been called for military service, and it urged readers to "assert [their] rights," but it did not explicitly urge unlawful conduct. Schenck was convicted of violating the Espionage Act. Holmes's opinion for a unanimous Supreme Court upheld his conviction. The opinion emphasized that the speech occurred during wartime and that a jury could have found that its "tendency" and "intent" were to obstruct the draft.

Schenck did repudiate the idea, found in Blackstone, that the First Amendment applied only to prior restraints. This was the first time that limitation was squarely rejected in American law, and it has never again been seriously entertained. But the most significant contribution of the *Schenck* opinion was Holmes's statement that "[t]he question in every case is whether the words used are used in such circumstances and are of such a nature as to create a clear and present danger that they will bring about the substantive evils that Congress has a right to prevent." The so-called clear and present danger test—here used by Holmes to uphold the suppression of speech—became integral to the development of the law (and even the common cultural understanding) of freedom of expression. The words "clear and present danger" may be as well known as, or even better known than, the words of the First Amendment itself. It is a reasonable guess that many people think those words are in the text of the Constitution. And in some sense they might as well be: these words, from a judicial opinion, have been far more important in the development of the law than the actual words of the Amendment.

After *Schenck,* the next step in that development came later in 1919, in *Abrams v. United States.*[34] In this case Holmes and Brandeis dissented from a decision upholding another World War I conviction. Holmes's opinion, although in many ways unclear, asserted (at one point at least) that the "clear and present danger" test required the government to show a high-probability risk of harm that is both immediate and serious: "[W]e should be eternally vigilant against attempts to check the expression of opinions that we loathe . . . unless they so imminently threaten immediate interference with the lawful and pressing purposes of the law that an immediate check is required to save the country."[35]

Essentially this interpretation of "clear and present danger"—with variations and refinements—has become a core principle of First Amendment law. It is not enough that speech might cause harm. It is not even enough that

---

34. 250 U.S. 616 (1919).

35. *Id.* at 630.

speech is likely to cause harm. The harm has to be imminent, and serious. Versions of this test appear in the *Pentagon Papers* case and, in a way, in *Brandenburg*. But as it happens, the principle Holmes called for in the *Abrams* dissent is essentially impossible to square with *Schenck*. *Schenck* used the words "clear and present danger," and that allowed Holmes and Brandeis to claim, subsequently, that their principle was rooted in that precedent. But the prosecution did not show, Holmes did not claim, and it is certainly not clear, that Schenck's speech presented a high-probability danger of immediate, serious harm. If there was a single, inspired moment at which the central feature of the American system of freedom of expression was decreed, it was not the adoption of the First Amendment; it was Holmes's dissent in *Abrams*.

But in fact there was no such moment. Holmes's opinion was a dissent. It made no law. The principle of Holmes's *Abrams* opinion became law only because later opinions adopted it; it had broad cultural resonance; and to some extent it seemed to work well. To the extent it did not work well, it did not survive; although *Brandenburg* is descended from Holmes's test, it also modifies that test and scrupulously avoids the phrase "clear and present danger." In all of these ways, the development of free speech in the United States followed the model of common-law evolution.

This first phase of the evolution was, as many have noted, extraordinary in the degree to which Holmes and Brandeis maintained their position.[36] Holmes and Brandeis continued to urge their version of the First Amendment—"clear and present danger" as it was understood in *Abrams,* to require a high probability of immediate serious harm—in opinion after opinion. Not one of the opinions was joined by a majority of the Supreme Court; all of them dissented from the way the Court treated the First Amendment.[37] The majority of the Supreme Court said, over and over, that the law was not what Holmes and Brandeis said it was. But Holmes and Brandeis persisted, essentially refusing to accept the approach of a majority of the Court, and it was the Holmes–Brandeis view, not the majority's holdings, that eventually became integral to the law.

In retrospect, it is possible to understand what Holmes and Brandeis were doing, even though they were not explicit about it at the time, nor even, probably, fully conscious of it. All of the decisions in this period, between 1919 and

---

36. *See* HARRY A. KALVEN, A WORTHY TRADITION: FREEDOM OF SPEECH IN AMERICA 158 (1988); David Cole, *Agon at Agora: Creative Misreadings in the First Amendment Tradition,* 95 YALE L.J. 857 (1986).

37. Justice Brandeis's opinion in *Whitney v. California,* 274 U.S. 357 (1927), which Holmes joined, concurred in the result reached by the Court on the ground that the First Amendment argument had not been properly presented in the lower courts. But the Brandeis opinion vigorously disagreed with the majority's analysis of the free-speech claim.

1927, involved political speech that was highly critical of the government—either speech critical of the war, or speech advocating some form of radical change, generally anarchist or socialist. The Court allowed the speakers to be punished essentially on the theory that it was rational for the government to conclude that this speech could cause harm. Schenck's speech, for example, might not only persuade people to question the nation's involvement in the war; it might also cause potential inductees to refuse induction.

Holmes and Brandeis understood that that approach allowed dissident speech to be suppressed too easily. Speech that is harshly critical of government policies will often have some tendency to cause harm. Almost any criticism of the government might encourage people to violate the laws that the speaker criticizes. When the speakers' views are unpopular, though, it will be too easy for the government—possibly reflecting the dominant sentiment of the population—to seize on that potentially harmful tendency as an excuse for suppressing speech that it actually dislikes because the speech is critical of government policies, or of the form of government itself. As a result, the approach taken by the Court in this period could easily have led to a climate in which it would be impossible to criticize the government without risking punishment. The *Schenck* version of clear and present danger did not prevent this. But the *Abrams* dissent, and the subsequent Holmes–Brandeis opinions, seized on the language in *Schenck* and used it to fashion a test that would, if faithfully applied, prevent this outcome. In this way, the Holmes and Brandeis opinions represent an early recognition of what *New York Times v. Sullivan* later called "the central meaning of the First Amendment," and their opinions provided the raw material from which later justices fashioned First Amendment doctrine protecting political dissent.

The Emergence of Protection

The Supreme Court did not actually uphold a free-speech claim until 1931, when it reversed the conviction of a woman who had violated a California law forbidding her to display a red flag "as a sign, symbol, or emblem of opposition to organized government."[38] The opinion in that case, *Stromberg v. California*, rested mostly on technical grounds—that the law was too vague—but it did treat as axiomatic the proposition that the government could not punish people for urging changes in the law or the government by lawful means. The California law was unconstitutional, the Court said, because its vague language would permit someone to be convicted of a crime for engaging in such advocacy.

---

38. Stromberg v. California, 283 U.S. 359 (1931).

Stromberg is representative of a series of cases involving dissident speech that the Court decided in the 1930s. The Court upheld the claims of the speakers, but it did so on relatively technical grounds that did not purport to alter the rulings from which Holmes and Brandeis had dissented, and that did not establish any broad, new First Amendment principles.[39] But at least two other developments in the decade were important for the shape they gave to the law.

One was the Court's decision in *Near v. Minnesota*,[40] which involved a state law that authorized injunctions against any "malicious, scandalous, and defamatory newspaper, magazine, or other periodical." The state statute apparently permitted such a publication to be enjoined even if the material it printed was true, unless the truth "was published with good motives and for justifiable ends." The statute was applied to forbid the publication of a particularly scurrilous periodical, although the specific statements in question, which included a vituperative criticism of the chief of police, clearly concerned public affairs. The Court held that the First Amendment did not permit such an injunction.

Near has come to be the standard citation for the proposition (derived from Blackstone) that "prior restraints" on speech are almost always unconstitutional. In fact, prior restraints present complex questions—among other things, it is not immediately clear why an injunction forbidding speech is worse than a criminal law forbidding speech—and it is not even clear that *Near* presented the kind of prior restraint that Blackstone condemned.[41] Perhaps the more important aspect of *Near* is that it represents a further development of the idea that political dissent is the central concern of the First Amendment. *Near* protected dissent that took the form of a personal attack on a public official. Although the opinion emphasizes prior restraints, *Near* was, in the common-law sense, a precursor of *New York Times v. Sullivan*.

The second especially significant decision in the 1930s was *Schneider v. State*,[42] in which the Court declared unconstitutional a municipal ordinance that forbade the distribution of leaflets on the streets. This was the first time the

---

39. *See* Herndon v. Lowry, 301 U.S. 242 (1937); De Jonge v. Orgeon, 299 U.S. 353 (1937). Fiske v. Kansas, 274 U.S. 380 (1927), a case decided just after *Whitney*, can also be placed in this category.

40. 283 U.S. 1189 (1931).

41. The prior restraint in *Near* was imposed by an injunction issued by a court; the kind of prior restraints with which Blackstone was concerned were imposed by administrative licensing bodies. One of the principal reasons for the traditional hostility is that government officials whose responsibility it is to censor speech will be unduly favorable to censorship. That concern is not as strong when the restraint is imposed by a judge. In addition, in *Near* the injunction simply required the newspaper to conform to the terms of a statute—something it had a legal obligation to do in any event (although the injunction might be enforced differently). *See* Vance v. Universal Amusement Co., 445 U.S. 308, 321–24 (1980) (White, J., dissenting).

42. 308 U.S. 147 (1939).

Court had squarely addressed a non-content-based restriction on speech, and one can find in the opinion in *Schneider* the basis of almost all the current law in this area. The Court implicitly recognized that such a restriction presented different issues from a restriction on the content of speech. At the same time, though, the Court carefully reviewed the ordinance; it did not simply defer to the municipality's judgment. With some refinements, that is how the Court treats non-content-based restrictions today.

Just fourteen years before *Schneider*, in *Gitlow v. New York*[43]—one of the decisions from which Holmes and Brandeis dissented—the Supreme Court had upheld a state law that directly forbade the advocacy of "the duty, necessity, or propriety of overthrowing . . . the government by force or violence." The opinion in *Gitlow* had emphasized the importance of deferring to legislative judgments about the dangerousness of speech. The ordinance in *Schneider* was much less threatening to the core purposes of free expression than the law in *Gitlow*. Yet the Court in *Schneider* had little difficulty in second-guessing the legislative judgment that underlay the ordinance. This was a striking change in the Court's approach. A healthy system of freedom of expression probably could survive if *Schneider* had come out the other way, and if legislative judgments about the need for non-content-based restrictions were generally accepted. *Gitlow*, by contrast, deferred to the legislature in a context in which popular opinion is likely to be inflamed against a speaker and in which suppression might badly distort public deliberation. What accounted for the change in the Court's view? *Gitlow* had not been overruled, and the Court in *Schneider* did not mention it.

The answer may lie in the fact that *Schneider*, decided in 1939, came after a series of victories—in *Stromberg*, in *Near*, and in some other cases[44]—by parties claiming rights under the First Amendment. As Harry Kalven said, the 1930s was the decade in which "[s]peech [s]tarts to [w]in."[45] By the end of the decade, the free-speech "edifice," in Burke's term, no longer consisted of just the post–World War I decisions; there were now a number of cases upholding speakers' claims, and there was a trend, however incompletely rationalized, toward protecting speech. The Court accordingly had a solid common-law basis for saying that laws restricting speech should be more closely scrutinized. Again it is the ebb and flow of precedent that accounts for the shape of the law.

In the early 1940s, the Court picked up these pieces—the Holmes–Brandeis dissents, the trend toward protecting speech, and the view, no doubt prompted

---

43. 268 U.S. 652 (1925).

44. *See, e.g.*, Hague v. C.I.O., 307 U.S. 436 (1939); Lovell v. Griffin, 303 U.S. 444 (1938).

45. *See* KALVEN, *supra* note 36, at 167 (chapter heading).

in part by events in Europe, that the protection of civil liberties was vitally important—and molded them into highly speech-protective principles that foreshadow today's. In *Thornhill v. Alabama*,[46] decided in 1940, the Court upheld the right to engage in labor picketing and stated, as if it had been law all along, a version of the "clear and present danger" test that echoed Holmes's *Abrams* dissent: "Abridgement of the liberty of . . . discussion can be justified only where the clear danger of substantive evils arises under circumstances affording no opportunity to test the merits of ideas by competition for acceptance in the market of public opinion."[47] *Cantwell v. Connecticut*,[48] decided later in 1940, suggested that the "clear and present danger" test, in its Holmes–Brandeis version, was the appropriate standard for the hostile audience situation, where a speaker was prosecuted for breach of the peace because his speech antagonized his audience. In 1941, in *Bridges v. California*,[49] the Court used the same test to overturn a conviction for contempt of court, where the speaker's criticisms of a state court (and arguable threats to cause economic disruption in retaliation for the decision) allegedly interfered with the administration of justice. By 1943, in *West Virginia State Board of Education v. Barnette*,[50] the Court could announce: "It is now a commonplace that censorship or suppression of expression of opinion is tolerated by our Constitution only when the expression presents a clear and present danger" of unlawful action.[51] These four cases were written by four different justices, and they involved markedly different situations. The First Amendment had simply become, in significant part at least, the Holmes–Brandeis version of the "clear and present danger" test. A substantial part of the present-day edifice was in place.

One other decision in the 1940s is noteworthy for the effect it had in shaping the law. In *Chaplinsky v. New Hampshire*,[52] the Court upheld the conviction of an individual for using "fighting words," which it defined as words "which by their very utterance inflict injury or tend to incite an immediate breach of the peace."[53] In the course of its opinion, the Court asserted that "[t]here are certain well-defined and narrowly limited classes of speech, the prevention and punishment of which have never been thought to raise any Constitutional

---

46. 310 U.S. 88 (1940).

47. *Id.* at 104–5.

48. 310 U.S. 296 (1941).

49. 314 U.S. 292 (1941).

50. 319 U.S. 624 (1943).

51. *Id.* at 633.

52. 315 U.S. 568 (1942).

53. *Id.* at 572.

problem. These include the lewd and obscene, the profane, the libelous, and the insulting or 'fighting' words. . . ."[54]

This was the Court's first clear statement of the distinction between low-value and high-value speech, as well as a clear statement of the important corollary that speech is assumed to have high value unless it falls into one of the low-value categories. This distinction has structured modern First Amendment doctrine. At first glance, it might seem to be a questionable distinction. The text of the First Amendment does not suggest a difference between high-value and low-value speech, and the idea that courts are to assess the value of speech seems problematic. But the distinction was an outgrowth of—to a degree, the inevitable result of—the evolution of First Amendment doctrine.

Specifically, once the Court had begun to place political speech at the center of the system of freedom of expression, and to afford extraordinary protection to political speech, it was forced to recognize that not all speech could be treated the same way. No one believes that an obscene telephone call deserves the same extraordinary protection as political dissent, and if the Court were to treat all speech alike, it would end up watering down the protection of the speech that it is most important to protect. Given the evolution of First Amendment law, the Court came to realize that it would have to make some kind of distinction between speech that was entitled to the greatest protection and speech that was not. The idea that certain categories of speech should receive less or no protection began to emerge in *Cantwell v. Connecticut*, decided two years before *Chaplinsky; Chaplinsky*, purporting to restate existing law, made the distinction explicit.

To be sure, the distinction did not have to be drawn in just the way *Chaplinsky* drew it. *Chaplinsky* differentiated between categories of speech; the Court could have said that it would proceed in each case to assess the value of the particular speech involved. And the Court could have established high-value categories and made low-value speech the default position. For a time it was unclear whether the categorical approach of *Chaplinsky* would prevail; indeed at times it seemed to be at odds with the Holmes–Brandeis "clear and present danger" test, which could be taken to suggest that speech should be evaluated case by case. These matters were worked out, in common-law fashion, beginning in the 1950s.

The McCarthy Era and the *Brandenburg* Synthesis

In the 1950s free-speech issues became as politically contentious as they had been at any time since World War I. Most of the cases that came to the Supreme

---

54. *Id.* at 571–72 (footnote omitted).

Court involved measures directed at people suspected of being, or of having been, members of the Communist Party. The most important of these cases was *Dennis v. United States*,[55] which upheld the criminal conviction of leaders of the Communist Party of the United States for conspiring to advocate the overthrow of the government by force or violence. There was no majority opinion in *Dennis*. The plurality upheld the convictions on the basis of a version of the "clear and present danger" test that said the critical question was "whether the gravity of the 'evil,' discounted by its improbability, justifies such invasion of free speech as is necessary to avoid the danger."[56]

This version of the test—essentially, a kind of cost–benefit balancing— was in fact sharply different from the Holmes–Brandeis test descended from *Abrams*. The Holmes–Brandeis test required that the harm be both imminent and highly probable; the *Dennis* test did not. Instead, the *Dennis* test effectively asked judges to assign some value to the speech that was being suppressed, and to decide whether the expected costs of the harm "justifie[d]" the restriction on speech. This approach lent itself quite readily to the kind of deference to the legislature that was endorsed in *Gitlow* and effectively repudiated in *Schneider* and other cases, and indeed Justice Frankfurter wrote a concurring opinion that called explicitly for deference to the legislature. (This was the opinion in which he was at pains to explain that, contrary to appearances, he was not following the [not formally overruled] decision in *Gitlow*.)

In the years after *Dennis*, the "clear and present danger" test, so dominant in the early 1940s, came under attack from many sides. One set of critics considered *Dennis* an abomination, and thought the "clear and present danger" test was at fault. *Dennis* had permitted dissidents to be punished simply for advocacy. Justices Black and Douglas, among others, came to the view that the "clear and present danger" test had proved itself too flexible to stand up to anticommunist hysteria. Another, sometimes overlapping, set of critics said that the problem with the test was that it simplified complex issues. They reacted against the use of "clear and present danger" in areas outside its original context of dissident political speech. The "clear and present danger" test was not well suited to determining, for example, when labor picketing should be regulated. Many of these critics thought that the only plausible way to interpret the test was as calling for a kind of cost–benefit balancing, as the *Dennis* plurality did.[57]

---

55. 341 U.S. 494 (1951).

56. *Id.* at 510 (opinion of Vinson, C.J.).

57. For a summary of the criticisms, *see* Frank R. Strong, *Fifty Years of "Clear and Present Danger,"* 1969 SUP. CT. REV. 41, 56–62.

In terms of the common-law approach, the "clear and present danger" principle, so attractive at one point, had overreached its proper scope and, in *Dennis,* had—according to some—failed Cardozo's test: it proved incapable of accomplishing its most important objectives. Following *Dennis,* the "clear and present danger" test went into eclipse, and by the time of *Brandenburg,* decided in 1969, it had few friends. The Court itself backed away from both *Dennis* and "clear and present danger" later in the 1950s. In *Yates v. United States,*[58] for example, the Court held that the Smith Act, the statute under which both the *Dennis* and the *Yates* defendants were charged, did not prohibit "advocacy of abstract doctrine" even if that advocacy were "engaged in with the intent to accomplish overthrow" of the government. Rather, the Court held, the Smith Act prohibited only "advocacy directed at promoting unlawful action."[59]

This distinction—between advocacy of ideas and advocacy of action—was, like "clear and present danger," derived from the resources that the First Amendment precedents made available to the Court: the distinction between high- and low-value speech.[60] The Court in *Yates* did not explicitly speak in those terms, but the best way to understand the distinction it drew is that advocacy of ideas is high-value speech, while simply urging people to violate the law is low value. The Court subsequently elaborated this idea in a way that makes the distinction between high- and low-value speech even more apparent: in *Noto v. United States,*[61] the Court distinguished between "the mere abstract teaching . . . of the moral propriety or even moral necessity for a resort to force and violence" and "preparing a group for violent action and steeling it to such action."[62] This characterization of the kind of speech that could be forbidden sounds more like the speech involved in criminal solicitation or a criminal conspiracy, speech that is surely low value. And, of course, once one accepts the primacy of political dissent under the First Amendment, the advocacy of political ideas has to be considered high value.

The final step in this evolution, so far, is *Brandenburg.* There the Court said that the First Amendment protects "advocacy of the use of force or of law violation except where such advocacy is directed to inciting or producing imminent lawless action and is likely to produce such action."[63] *Brandenburg*

---

58. 354 U.S. 298 (1957).

59. *Id.* at 318, 321.

60. *See* Gerald Gunther, *Learned Hand and the Origins of Modern First Amendment Doctrine: Some Fragments of History,* 27 Stan. L. Rev. 719, 752–55 (1975).

61. 367 U.S. 290 (1961).

62. *Id.* at 297–98.

63. 395 U.S. at 447.

is the product of two strands of well-developed doctrinal evolution. Although it does not use the phrase "clear and present danger," the Court's emphasis on imminence and on a high probability of harm was derived directly from the Holmes–Brandeis version of the "clear and present danger" test. *Brandenburg* appears to have added to that test a requirement that the speech be low value; if the government wants to restrict speech, it must show that the speech is not advocacy of ideas but is rather "directed to inciting or producing imminent lawless action." *Brandenburg* quoted the distinction drawn in *Noto,* suggesting that only speech that borders on a criminal conspiracy is unprotected.

The *Brandenburg* Court, following the critics of clear and present danger, had apparently concluded that although the Holmes–Brandeis test captured something important about the First Amendment, it was not sufficient by itself. The evidence for that conclusion was the use to which the test had been put in *Dennis.* In the crucible of common-law testing, it had proved too easy to collapse "clear and present danger" into a simple balancing of costs and benefits. In *Brandenburg,* the Court did not abandon the Holmes–Brandeis line of precedents, but it recognized the limitations of that approach and the need to supplement it. The Court then supplemented it from another important line of cases—from *Cantwell* through *Chaplinsky* to *Yates*—that emphasized the distinction between high- and low-value speech. The building blocks of the *Brandenburg* synthesis were entirely the product of precedents—precedents that were tested and modified by being applied in case after case, just as the common-law approach suggests.

New York Times v. Sullivan and Pentagon Papers

The other mainstays of current doctrine also represent the final (so far) stage in a doctrinal evolution on the common-law model. *New York Times v. Sullivan* held that a public official cannot recover damages for defamation without proving not just that the defamatory statement was false, but that the defendant made the statement with knowledge that it was false or with reckless disregard of the risk of falsehood. *Sullivan* was an important breakthrough in many respects, but it had a solid basis in precedent. The speech in *Sullivan*—an attack on public officials for violating the rights of civil rights demonstrators in the South—was political speech. By the time *Sullivan* was decided, the Holmes and Brandeis approach, accepted by subsequent cases, strongly supported *Sullivan*'s explicit conclusion that that kind of speech was at the center of the First Amendment.

Sullivan broke new ground because it held that the law of defamation— one of the oldest branches of tort law, which historically was entirely the province of the states—was to be strictly limited by the First Amendment.

But in achieving this breakthrough, *Sullivan* again had specific support in the precedents. *Near* protected speech that defamed a public official. *Bridges*, on which the Court in *Sullivan* relied, held—on the basis of the Holmes–Brandeis test—that the First Amendment protected severe criticism of a judge. *Sullivan* was an important further step in the direction of emphasizing the protection of political dissent, but it was far from the first step. Thus *Sullivan*, too, fits in the common-law model—certainly far better than it accords with the original intentions of the framers. And once *Sullivan* was decided, it led to a series of further decisions, in common-law fashion, that have effectively constitutionalized the law of defamation.

In the *Pentagon Papers* case, the Supreme Court ruled that the First Amendment barred the government from enjoining the publication, in the *New York Times* and the *Washington Post*, of classified government documents that recounted, in detail, internal deliberations and other information about the formulation of U.S. policy toward Southeast Asia. Most of the justices in the majority emphasized that the government was seeking to impose a prior restraint on the publication of the papers, and they asserted, echoing Black-stone, that prior restraints are anathema to a system of freedom of expression. To that extent, the *Pentagon Papers* decision can be traced to the intentions of the framers—although this aspect of First Amendment doctrine had also been endorsed several times in the precedents, most explicitly in *Near v. Minnesota*.

But the concern with prior restraints cannot, by itself, explain the *Pentagon Papers* decision. The Pentagon Papers provided material that was of central importance to citizens seeking to criticize government policy about the most controversial political issue of the time—the Vietnam War—and that fact un-questionably played a role in the Court's decision. For one thing, while the opinions in the *Pentagon Papers* case emphasized that the First Amendment forbids prior restraints, it is difficult to believe that the Court would have allowed newspaper editors to be punished, criminally, after they published the Papers.[64] In addition, the standard that the Court appears to have established—that publication may not be forbidden unless it "will surely result in direct, immediate, and irreparable damage to our Nation or its people"—not only is extremely protective of speech but echoes, indeed is a heightened version of, the Holmes–Brandeis "clear and present danger" test. Thus the *Pentagon Papers* decision, too, is a direct product of the central theme in the evolution of the law of the First Amendment in the twentieth century: the vital importance

---

64. *See* Archibald Cox, *Foreword: Freedom of Expression in the Burger Court*, 94 HARV. L. REV. 1, 17 (1980).

of protecting speech on political matters, particularly speech that vigorously questions government policies, even if that speech might also have some harmful consequences.

Conclusion

The text of the First Amendment is an important cultural reference point. The fact that there is a provision of the Constitution protecting freedom of speech surely plays a role in the way society as a whole regards free expression. Beyond that, it would, in all probability, have been more difficult to establish legal principles protecting speech without some explicit provision of the Constitution to which those principles could be referred.

But that is the fundamental connection between the First Amendment and the American law of freedom of expression. The content of the law has not emerged from the text or from the original understandings. It emerged fitfully by a process in which principles were tried and sometimes abandoned, sometimes modified, in light of experience and of an explicit assessment of whether they were good principles as a matter of policy and political morality. The law of the First Amendment is one of the great creations of the law, and it is a creation of the common-law Constitution.

Judges, scholars, and political theorists have long struggled to discern why "the freedom of speech, or of the press" should be accorded special constitutional protection. In "Free Speech and Good Character: From Milton to Brandeis to the Present," Vincent Blasi examines the rationales most often presented for the constitutional protection of free expression (individual self-fulfillment, the search for truth, and self-governance) and then explores and endorses a fourth rationale—that cultures that protect expressive liberty nurture in their "members certain character traits such as inquisitiveness, distrust of authority, willingness to take initiative, and the courage to confront evil" that are valuable "not for their intrinsic virtue but for their instrumental contribution to collective well-being, social as well as political." Professor Blasi argues that "the claim here is not that truth and justice will always prevail in a fair marketplace of ideas," but that "the most dangerous ideas can only be defeated by strong persons," not by "repressive laws," and that by "denying the moral shortcut" of repression "a free-speech regime strengthens the character of its citizens."—GRS

VINCENT BLASI

Free Speech and Good Character: From Milton to Brandeis to the Present

Introduction

When pressed to defend the extraordinary priority accorded the freedom of speech in the United States—a priority not really replicated in other liberal democracies—First Amendment devotees typically invoke one or more of three basic rationales. First, the liberty to express one's thoughts and to form them by unrestricted reading and listening is an essential attribute, it is said, of human autonomy, of what it means to be a self-directed person possessed of human dignity. Second, free speech is the foundational mechanism of the search for truth, at both the individual and the societal levels. In this view, a free "marketplace of ideas" produces a more accurate, probing, and richly textured understanding of fact and value than can any prescribed orthodoxy. Third, for a society committed to the project of self-government, in which ultimate political responsibility rests with the mass of ordinary citizens, free speech is invaluable as a means of civic education and participation.[1]

This trilogy of rationales is venerable, and there is much to be said for each of them. But there are problems. Yes, we all like to think of ourselves as autonomous, but how many of us possess even a rudimentary understanding of this profound, elusive Kantian notion? And if we did, would we necessarily embrace its strong assumptions regarding human agency and also conclude that speech is special among the liberties that sustain the self? Yes, truth is important, but truth-seeking is such a different activity for the votary, the pragmatist, and the skeptic as to confound any effort to generalize regarding the priority to be accorded truth-seeking, the role free speech plays in facilitating it, and the significance of the many "market failures" that distort the flow of ideas and information. Yes, self-government is a noble ideal and one with a textual mooring in the Constitution, but what it means for citizens to give meaningful consent or to engage in meaningful participation are the very questions that

---

1. For excellent critical summaries of the traditional rationales for the freedom of speech, *see* FRED-ERICK SCHAUER, FREE SPEECH: A PHILOSOPHICAL ENQUIRY 15–72 (1982); Kent Greenawalt, *Free Speech Justifications*, 89 COLUM. L. REV. 119 (1989).

fuel the clash of modern political philosophies. This phenomenon of radical disagreement emerging from the shared commitment to self-government appears also at the level of First Amendment doctrine. Consider the issue of campaign spending limits. Must a self-governing voter be free to hear as much speech about an election as private resources can produce? Or do the risks of corruption, plutocratic bias, citizen alienation, and the diversion of energies to fund-raising justify the imposition of spending limits as a means of preserving the self-governing capacities of voters? Moreover, the justification for free speech from self-government fails to provide a reason to protect literature or scientific inquiry, an unsettling prospect even for minimalists who can live with the exclusion of commercial advertising, workplace harassment, and hard-core pornography from the ambit of First Amendment concern. In brief, the tired trilogy of conventional free-speech justifications is at best incomplete, and at worst so abstract and protean as to be of limited intellectual or practical utility.

In light of these difficulties, it is odd that a somewhat different, and to my mind less problematic, rationale for the freedom of speech has not received more attention in recent times, particularly since it figured prominently during the first three hundred years of systematic writing in defense of toleration. This is a special kind of argument from character that builds from the claim that a culture that prizes and protects expressive liberty nurtures in its members certain character traits such as inquisitiveness, distrust of authority, willingness to take initiative, and the courage to confront evil. Such character traits are valuable, so the argument goes, not for their intrinsic virtue but for their instrumental contribution to collective well-being, social as well as political. This claim plausibly can be said to form the spine of each of the renowned defenses of free speech produced by John Milton,[2] John Stuart Mill,[3] Oliver Wendell Holmes,[4] and Louis Brandeis.[5] Yet today we pick up on other features of those classic writings, usually by finding some way to enlist their observations in the service of the familiar arguments for free speech from autonomy, truth-seeking, and self-government.[6]

---

2. JOHN MILTON, *Areopagitica, in* COMPLETE POEMS AND MAJOR PROSE 716 (Merritt Hughes ed., 1957).

3. JOHN STUART MILL, ON LIBERTY (Stefan Collini ed., 1989).

4. Abrams v. United States, 250 U.S. 616 (1919) (Holmes, J., dissenting).

5. Whitney v. California, 274 U.S. 357 (1927) (Brandeis, J., concurring), *overruled in part by* Brandenburg v. Ohio, 395 U.S. 444 (1969).

6. A good example of this (misplaced) interpretative emphasis, by one of the most astute of modern commentators, is SCHAUER, *supra* note 1, at 17, 74.

In this essay I trace how two of the master builders of the free-speech tradition, John Milton and Louis Brandeis, emphasized character in their arguments against the regulation of speech. Milton and Brandeis did not value the strengthening of character for identical reasons, nor did they seek to nurture precisely the same character traits. Nevertheless, they have in common the view that character is important in large part because it is instrumental to the pursuit of collective objectives. Moreover, despite the nearly three centuries that separate their inquiries, Milton and Brandeis overlap to a striking degree in the character traits they value most and in the connections they perceive between the freedom of speech and the flourishing of those traits. After examining in context exactly what they say about character, I elaborate the basic insights of Milton and Brandeis with attention to how their observations and ideals fit contemporary conditions. In the process I seek to identify how a robust principle of freedom of speech might even today serve a number of collective goals by means of its impact on the character of the populace.

Two introductory caveats are in order. I do not mean to suggest that the argument from character ought completely to displace the rationales for free speech that have held sway in the modern era. I aim merely to redress an imbalance in the way the principle of freedom of speech is justified and thereby appreciated. Nor do I claim that greater attention to character would directly yield better First Amendment doctrines. Doctrine building is a complex endeavor that, when done well, takes into account a host of practical and institutional considerations in addition to underlying justifications. No doctrine-generating algorithm is offered or intimated here. My ambition is not to solve specific problems so much as to shore up the flagging conviction that the freedom of speech, as a general matter and as conventionally understood, really is worth the heavy costs it sometimes imposes.

Milton

Like Machiavelli before him, Milton was preoccupied with the question of political energy.[7] He saw individual character as the key to collective energy.

---

7. A particularly good discussion of Milton's focus on political energy is DAVID LOEWENSTEIN, MILTON AND THE DRAMA OF HISTORY 46 (1990). Machiavelli's crucial but difficult notion of *virtú*, which encompasses his concern for political energy and much else as well, is explicated in QUENTIN SKINNER, MACHIAVELLI 50–67 (1981). *See also* Felix Gilbert, *On Machiavelli's Idea of Virtú*, 4 RENAISSANCE NEWS 21–23 (1951). In book I, chapter 4 of *The Discourses*, Machiavelli expresses the view, original in his day but echoed in Milton's *Areopagitica*, that tumult and discord can actually benefit a republic by energizing it. *See* NICCOLO MACHIAVELLI, THE DISCOURSES 113–15 (Bernard R. Crick ed., 1970). For an extended discussion of how this idea figures in Machiavelli's later writings (the works of Machiavelli that Milton most admired), *see* Gisela Bock, *Civil Discord in Machiavelli's* HISTORIA FLORENTINE, *in*

He valued strength of will, acuteness of perception, ingenuity, self-discipline, engagement, breadth of vision, perseverance; he detested rigidity, stasis, withdrawal, timidity, small-mindedness, indecision, laziness, deference to authority. In the *Areopagitica,* his extended polemic of 1644 against the licensing of books and pamphlets, Milton emphasizes the connection between free speech and good character. "I cannot praise," he says, "a fugitive and cloistered virtue, unexercised and unbreathed, that never sallies out and sees her adversary. . . ."[8]

Responding to his own adversaries who were asserting the need for more order, more standards, more authority, more closure in the realm of religious inquiry, Milton scornfully describes the "fruits which a dull ease and cessation of our knowledge will bring forth among the people."[9] "How goodly and how to be wished were such an obedient unanimity as this, what a fine conformity would it starch us all into! Doubtless a staunch and solid piece of framework as any January could freeze together."[10] "[F]aith and knowledge," he asserts, "thrives by exercise. . . ."[11] Truth he likens "to a streaming fountain; if her waters flow not in a perpetual progression, they sicken into a muddy pool of conformity and tradition."[12]

MACHIAVELLI AND REPUBLICANISM 181, 181–201 (Gisela Bock et al. eds., 1990). Tocqueville was to pick up this theme. *See* ALEXIS DE TOCQUEVILLE, 1 DEMOCRACY IN AMERICA 248–53 (Phillips Bradley ed., 1945). For a criticism of modern civic republican theorists for invoking Machiavelli while failing to note how much he valued conflict, *see* CHANTAL MOUFFE, THE RETURN OF THE POLITICAL 36 (1993).

8. MILTON, *supra* note 2, at 728. *See* Alan F. Price, *Incidental Imagery in* Areopagitica, 49 MODERN PHILOLOGY 217, 219 (1952): "Milton is particularly hostile toward anyone who refuses to participate in the struggle between good and evil; and nearly all his more notable images are imaginative presentations of various aspects of this fundamental conflict." There may have been a patriotic dimension to Milton's contempt for withdrawal. Many English Puritans were distressed by their nation's refusal to intervene on the Protestant side during the Thirty Years War on the Continent. CHRISTOPHER HILL, MILTON AND THE ENGLISH REVOLUTION 65, 88 (1977).

9. MILTON, *supra* note 2, at 740.

10. *Id.*

11. *Id.* at 739.

12. *Id.* For an argument that the protean imagery Milton employs in *Areopagitica* is meant to embody his rejection of static forms and static convictions, *see* LANA CABLE, CARNAL RHETORIC: MILTON'S ICONOCLASM AND THE POETICS OF DESIRE 117–43 (1995).

> The image-construction that in *The Doctrine and Discipline of Divorce* had been an activity of generating inspired analysis, of imbuing the real with the ideal, becomes in *Areopagitica* an exercise in the temporality of images per se. By their vital activity, rather than by their iconic representations, the images of *Areopagitica* illustrate a principle for the right conduct not just of poetic imagery but as well of every other concern in our lives—material, intellectual, moral, spiritual. . . . The kinetic images bear witness to something they themselves cannot contain. Similarly, human beings serve the interests of truth only when a desire for truth leads them unceasingly to search beyond whatever they think they have learned of it.

Id. at 117–18.

Milton's regard for the active life was not just a cultural preference. He saw the stakes as greater than that, involving nothing less than the control of evil. Political energy, he realized, is a sometime source of progress but also a frequent cause of strife and oppression. His crucial move was to conclude that harm, even the harm that flows from malignant political energy, can best be contained and repaired by a citizenry that is energized in a countervailing way: intellectually independent, morally engaged, politically resilient, not afraid to speak out or to stand up. His views in this matter were shaped by his lifelong study of the problem of evil. As the creator of Satan in *Paradise Lost*, probably the most brilliant and destructive demagogue in the whole of English literature, Milton can hardly be accused of failing to appreciate how words can do harm. He did not believe, however, that the discovery of evil justifies the regulation of speech. In fact, Milton thought evil so pervasive, insidious, and perdurable a force in human affairs as to demand in response something more than the blunt instruments and formal gestures of the law.[13] Evil can be combatted, he was convinced, only from within: by the vigilance of a population accustomed to challenging authority; by the ingenuity and integrity that a licensing regime is bound to discourage; by the hard work of discerning, confronting, refuting, and choosing that censors seek to disburden citizens from having to undertake.[14]

This emphasis on character is at once the most distinctive and the most pervasive feature of Milton's argument for the liberty of printing. However, proponents of the regulation of speech frequently invoke concerns relating to character on their side of the debate.[15] In Milton's day as in ours, the claim that liberty improves character was, if not patently implausible, at best

---

13. Milton worried a lot about excessive reliance on law. In *Areopagitica* he states: "[H]ere the great art lies to discern in what the law is to bid restraint and punishment, and in what things persuasion only is to work. If every action which is good or evil in man at ripe years were to be under pittance, and prescription and compulsion, what were virtue but a name . . . ?" MILTON, *supra* note 2, at 733. In *Tetrachordan*, his most systematically argued divorce tract, he says: "In every commonwealth when it decays, corruption makes two main steps; first when men cease to do according to the inward and uncompelled actions of virtue, caring only to live by the outward constraint of law, and turn the simplicity of real good into the craft of seeming so by law. . . . The next declining is when law becomes [dominated by] false and crooked interpretations. . . ." JOHN MILTON, *Tetrachordan, in* 2 COMPLETE PROSE WORKS OF JOHN MILTON 636, 639 (1959).

14. For a perceptive discussion of how Milton employs various images to make this his "principal argument," *see* John X. Evans, *Imagery as Argument in Milton's* Areopagitica, 8 TEXAS STUD. LITERATURE & LANGUAGE 189, 197–205 (1966).

15. *See, e.g.*, WALTER BERNS, THE FIRST AMENDMENT AND THE FUTURE OF AMERICAN DEMOCRACY (1976); FRANCIS CANAVAN, FREEDOM OF EXPRESSION: PURPOSE AS LIMIT (1984); HARRY CLOR, OBSCENITY AND PUBLIC MORALITY (1969); Willmoore Kendall, *The "Open Society" and Its Fallacies*, 54 AM. POL. SCI. REV. 972 (1960); Henry J. McCloskey, *Liberty of Expression: Its Grounds and Limits*, 13 INQUIRY 219 (1970).

controversial. We must, therefore, look more closely at Milton's conception of character and explore what he took to be the relationship between character and censorship.

When he turns to the "manifest hurt" that licensing will cause, Milton's choice of terms is revealing. He describes censorship as a "discouragement,"[16] an "affront,"[17] a "dishonour and derogation to the author,"[18] a "servitude,"[19] a "disparagement,"[20] a "reproach,"[21] a "thraldom,"[22] "a particular disesteem,"[23] an "undervaluing and vilifying of the whole nation."[24] He objects that every author is "mistrusted and suspected,"[25] made to "trudge to his leave-giver,"[26] and then, if all goes well, to "appear in print like a puny with his guardian," displaying "his censor's hand on the back of his title to be his bail and surety that he is no idiot or seducer. . . ."[27] No doubt Milton spoke from personal experience regarding the indignity of asking for official approval to publish.[28] An author of his skill and dedication must have felt particular umbrage at having to submit to "the fearfulness or the presumptuous rashness of a perfunctory licenser."[29] Whatever the role personal pique might have played in provoking Milton's challenge to the parliamentary licensing scheme, there can be little question that he considered censorship to be genuinely corrosive of character.

Exactly how, we might ask, is character threatened by the fact that a political regime distrusts its citizens and requires them to behave as supplicants? To Milton's mind, censorship undermines character by encouraging individuals to shirk their civic and religious responsibilities. The imagery of childhood is employed repeatedly in the *Areopagitica*. A writer forced to run the censor's

---

16. MILTON, *supra* note 2, at 735.

17. *Id.*

18. *Id.*

19. *Id.* at 737.

20. *Id.*

21. *Id.*

22. *Id.* at 738.

23. *Id.* at 736.

24. *Id.*

25. *Id.* at 735.

26. *Id.*

27. *Id.*

28. *See* Abbe Blum, *The Author's Authority:* Areopagitica *and the Labour of Licensing, in* REMEMBERING MILTON: ESSAYS ON THE TEXTS AND TRADITIONS 80–83 (Mary Nyquist & Margaret W. Ferguson eds., 1988).

29. MILTON, *supra* note 2, at 736.

gauntlet must thereby appear to his readers "a pupil teacher,"[30] an instructor "under the wardship of an overseeing fist."[31] For a community to maintain its tenets and taboos by means of "law and compulsion" rather than "exhortation" is "to captivate under a perpetual childhood of prescription. . . ."[32] "What advantage is it," Milton asks, "to be a man over it is to be a boy at school" if "serious and elaborate writings" are examined like "the theme of a grammar-lad under his pedagogue . . ."[33] Citizens who are treated like children will behave like children, he implies, and one thing we know children do surpassingly well is to let adults take on the unpleasant chores.

In an age so notable for its polemics, as well as for its exhilarating scientific and philosophical formulations, can it be that inquiry and disputation were seen as burdensome chores that many persons might seek to evade? Milton certainly thought so. Consider the case of religion. Perhaps the most extended figure in the whole tract is that of the man who "finds religion to be a traffic so entangled, and of so many piddling accounts," that he "resolves to give over toiling, and to find himself out some factor to whose care and credit he may commit the whole managing of his religious affairs."[34] To this surrogate the shirking principal "resigns the whole warehouse of his religion, with all the locks and keys, into his custody; and indeed makes the very person of that man his religion. . . ."[35] With such a delegation, "his religion is now no more within himself, but is become a dividual moveable, and goes and comes near him according as that good man frequents the house."[36] Milton is unsparing in his satire of this evasion of religious responsibility: "He entertains him, gives him gifts, feasts him, lodges him; his religion comes home at night, prays, is liberally supped and sumptuously laid to sleep; rises, is saluted. . . . [H]is religion walks abroad at eight, and leaves his kind entertainer in the shop trading all day without his religion."[37]

Preachers too are at risk of shirking their duties, living off old notes, "the gatherings and savings of a sober graduateship."[38] By means of "forming and

---

30. *Id.*

31. *Id.*

32. *Id.* at 727.

33. *Id.* at 735.

34. *Id.* at 739–40.

35. *Id.* at 740.

36. *Id.*

37. *Id.*

38. *Id.*

transforming, joining and disjoining variously, a little bookcraft and two hours meditation" the "easily inclinable" clergyman can cobble together a passable sermon, assisted as he might also be by "interlinearies, breviaries, synopses, and other loitering gear."[39] However, "if his back door be not secured by the rigid licenser," if "a bold book may now and then issue forth and give the assault to some of his old collections in their trenches," such a preacher may have to do his own work, if only to "set good guards and sentinels about his received opinions."[40] Even this would represent progress, according to Milton. "God send," he says, "that the fear of this diligence which must then be used do not make us affect the laziness of a licensing church."[41]

Milton opposed censorship in large part because he placed legal regulation in the same category as reliance on factors and cribs: an effort to free ordinary citizens and ordinary worshippers from the salutary if onerous duty of cease-less personal inquiry. Because character played so large a role in his thought, these various delegations of responsibility assumed for him a special signifi-cance. "[I]f the men be erroneous who appear to be the leading schismatics," he says, "what withholds us but our sloth, our self-will, and distrust in the right cause, that we do not give them gentle meetings and gentle dismissions, that we debate not and examine the matter thoroughly with liberal and frequent audience; if not for their sakes yet for our own?"[42]

Laziness, stubbornness, lack of trust, lack of confidence—these are some of the character flaws that, according to Milton, are nurtured by restrictions on free printing. Another is "precipitant zeal," the impulse to rush to judgment.[43] We "make no distinction," he complains, when encountering persons whom we fear "come with new and dangerous opinions."[44] We "forejudge them ere we understand them. . . ."[45] No other sentence in the *Areopagitica* has so much the quality of a personal plea: Milton's own unconventional opinions on divorce—he believed incompatibility to be a legitimate ground even in the absence of infidelity—were forejudged, badly mischaracterized, and used to hold him up to ridicule in important public forums.[46] Being treated most unfairly as

---

39. *Id.*

40. *Id.* at 741.

41. *Id.*

42. *Id.* at 748.

43. *Id.*

44. *Id.*

45. *Id.*

46. *See* Arthur Barker, Milton and the Puritan Dilemma 68–69 (1942).

a licentious and irresponsible radical was very likely a formative experience for this exceptionally serious and disciplined young man.[47] On the subject of forejudgment, he knew of what he spoke.

Licensing, indeed all legal regulation of speech, must employ forejudgment to some degree. It must proceed by categorization and incomplete characterization. Problems of proof distort judgment further. Speakers, moreover, have mixed and easily misunderstood motives. Ideas have layers and textures that resist legal classification. They have the capacity to breed but also a vulnerability to misappropriation, qualities that bedevil even well-intentioned efforts to predict their consequences. All of these features make the regulation of speech a particularly imprecise endeavor. In his pragmatist mode, Milton argues that the indiscriminate nature of licensing invites partisan abuse. But he was troubled by the indiscriminate nature of licensing at least as much for its embodiment of forejudgment, a character defect he often devoted his art to exposing.[48]

Because the regulation of printing typically is imbued with imprecision and futility, the act of licensing also has the character of a formal gesture, a regulatory show. Central to Milton's thought in several domains—religion, poetry, politics, education, marriage—was his disdain for reliance on forms.[49] Those who would regulate writings judge them superficially for several reasons, but important among them is the fact that most of the time the censorship of ideas is not really meant to be a discriminating gesture. It is intended rather to be a formal discharge of regulatory responsibility or a public affirmation of conventional forms of authority and thought. This was Milton's understanding of the true nature of licensing and a major source of his contempt for the practice.

He saw formalism as a means of avoiding the challenges of a complex, changing, often deceiving and dispiriting world. If obeisance were an adequate means of coping and of seeking salvation, the avoidance implicit in formalism might not be a matter of the highest concern. Milton, however, believed that both survival and salvation require of humankind active choice. False appearances abound in life. Taken at face value, they will mislead. They are most likely to mislead a people not experienced at getting beneath formal surfaces and exercising the capacity for critical choice. Milton's poetry repeatedly forces

---

47. *Id.*

48. *See, e.g.,* Regina Schwartz, *From Shadowy Types to Shadowy Types,* 24 MILTON STUDIES 123 (1988).

49. *See* Lana Cable, *Milton's Iconoclastic Truth, in* POLITICS, POETICS AND HERMENEUTICS IN MILTON'S PROSE 135, 136–38 (David Loewenstein & James Turner eds., 1990).

the reader to make hard choices and tempts her to make wrong choices.[50] Famously signaling his break with Calvinism, he asserts in *Areopagitica:* "Many there be that complain of divine Providence for suffering Adam to transgress. Foolish tongues! When God gave him reason, he gave him freedom to choose, for reason is but choosing. . . ."[51]

That Milton built his argument for free printing around the importance of choice does not mean that he held an exalted view of the power of human reason. In 1644 the world seemed to him more complicated and inscrutable than he had previously appreciated. Apparently, he was experiencing disillusionment during this period as a result of his own poor judgment in choosing a marriage partner, the harsh response to his divorce tracts, and more generally the dashing of his hopes for a swift, decisive Reformation.[52] Abandoning the apocalyptic tone of his earlier antiprelatical pamphlets, Milton states in *Areopagitica:* "It is not the unfrocking of a priest, the unmitring of a bishop and the removing him from off the presbyterian shoulders, that will make us a happy nation."[53] Much more than such changes of form will be required, he now realizes. Only sustained effort, the determination to persevere amid the temptation to despair, the courage to choose and the strength to choose wisely and continually, will advance "the slow-moving reformation which we labour under. . . ."[54] In the penultimate book of *Paradise Lost,* the archangel Michael explains to Adam why fallen man must endure so much suffering and injustice:

> . . . good with bad
> Expect to hear, supernal grace contending
> With sinfulness of men, thereby to learn
> True patience. . . .[55]

Milton considered licensing a policy driven by impatience, and as such a threat to the character of the English people. He embraced the freedom of speech so that his fellow citizens might hear "good with bad . . . thereby to learn true patience."

---

50. *See* Susanne Woods, *Elective Poetics and Milton's Prose: A Treatise of Civil Power and Considerations Touching the Likeliest Means to Remove Hirelings out of the Church, in* LOEWENSTEIN & TURNER, *supra* note 49, at 193, 196–97.

51. MILTON, *supra* note 2, at 733.

52. *See* BARKER, *supra* note 46, at 66–69.

53. MILTON, *supra* note 2, at 742.

54. *Id.* at 748.

55. MILTON, *Paradise Lost,* bk. XI, ll. 358–61, *in* COMPLETE POEMS AND MAJOR PROSE, *supra* note 2, at 441.

The virtue of patience belongs disproportionately to those who are capable of thinking in historical terms, as Milton most assuredly was. One of the reasons for valuing the freedom of speech is that it nurtures a nation's sense of history. When permitted a hearing and a place in the historical record, dissenting currents of thought can shape the future. When exposed to independent scrutiny in the court of history, even the most powerful rulers do not have a free hand. History, of course, will exist with or without the freedom of speech. But how a nation understands and uses its history is a vital dimension of the historical process itself. Milton thought censorship threatened the historical process primarily by its impact on character. A people afraid of new ideas, trustful of censors, and hostile to bold thinkers will be left behind, he suggests, by the sweep of history. Such a people will lack both vision and the ability to learn from experience. Patriot (and historian) that he was, he did not want this to be the fate of the English nation, as he thought it had been in the fourteenth century when the nascent reformation offered by John Wycliffe was thwarted by the deadly combination of timidity, ignorance, and censorship.[56]

Perhaps the most important aspect of Milton's historical imagination is his emphasis on the process of renewal. With his command of ancient, patristic, and medieval sources, he viewed both the Reformation and the parliamentary challenge to Stuart tyranny as efforts to recover forgotten wisdom and dissipated energy. The *Areopagitica* is replete with images of decay and reinvigoration.[57] The process of renewal feeds, Milton believed, off the sense of purpose and possibility that "much arguing, much writing, many opinions" can help to engender.[58] In this view, free speech is not primarily a mechanism for deliberation and persuasion so much as a phenomenon shaping the character and aspirations of the population. Contrary to the common scholarly assumption, *Areopagitica* may not have been written with the ambition, seemingly quixotic, of persuading the Long Parliament to abolish the practice of licensing. Milton knew the reigning Presbyterian faction to be intransigent on the issue of censorship and ill disposed to his person because of his views on divorce. The tract may instead have been aimed primarily at the Cromwellian Independents in Parliament and the army, in the hope that future agents of

---

56. On the suppression of Wycliffe's heresies, *see* George M. Trevelyan, England in the Age of Wycliffe 1368–1520, at 291–332 (1963). On Milton's admiration for Wycliffe, *see* Hill, *supra* note 8, at 85–86.

57. For a discussion of Milton's images of decay and renewal, *see* Evans, *supra* note 14, at 192–96.

58. Milton, *supra* note 2, at 743.

renewal would not lose their enthusiasm for toleration once they gained the reins of power.

Although in 1644 Milton already might have seen himself as writing for a more propitious future time, it was not until 1660 that events tested to the utmost his resolve to embrace the historical perspective. In none of his writings does he better express his belief in the importance of speech than in the closing words of *The Ready and Easy Way To Establish a Free Commonwealth,* a pamphlet written in anguish to protest the headlong rush of the strife-weary English people to restore the Stuart monarchy. Blind, betrayed by his countrymen and even by his erstwhile hero Cromwell,[59] eligible for execution on account of his polemics in defense of the regicide,[60] his great epic poem nowhere near finished, Milton remained unbowed. Risking his freedom and possibly his life, he challenged the ascendant royalists by issuing an uncompromising indictment of monarchical government. As other republicans were busy trimming to protect their positions against the impending Restoration, Milton defiantly reaffirmed his commitment to the Good Old Cause, finding succor in the prospect of eventual political renewal:

> Thus much I should perhaps have said though I were sure I should have spoken only to trees and stones, and had none to cry to, but with the prophet, "O earth, earth, earth!" to tell the very soil itself what her perverse inhabitants are deaf to. Nay, though what I have spoke should happen . . . to be the last words of our expiring liberty. But I trust I shall have spoken persuasion to abundance of sensible and ingenuous men, to some perhaps, whom God may raise of these stones to become children of reviving liberty. . . .[61]

Whether speaking of responsibility, forejudgment, the worship of form, perseverance, the courage to choose, impatience, or renewal, Milton emphasizes the inner person. Censorship, he says, leads only to "the forced and outward union of cold and neutral, and inwardly divided minds."[62] More than the ideas lost or the causes squelched, such minds were for him the chief casualty of licensing.

---

59. On Milton's disillusionment with Cromwell, *see* Martin Dzelzainis, *Milton and the Protectorate in 1658, in* MILTON AND REPUBLICANISM 181 (David Armitage et al. eds., 1995).

60. As Christopher Hill notes: "Many of Milton's friends were hanged, disembowelled and quartered. He had to go into hiding whilst a like fate was discussed for him. He was arrested and imprisoned, but escaped a traitor's sentence. Because it did not happen we tend to forget how likely it seemed in all human probability." HILL, *supra* note 8, at 207.

61. MILTON, *The Ready and Easy Way to Establish a Free Commonwealth* (1660), *in* COMPLETE POEMS AND MAJOR PROSE, *supra* note 2, at 880, 898.

62. MILTON, *supra* note 2, at 742.

Brandeis

Notwithstanding the magisterial articulations of Justices Holmes,[63] Roberts,[64] Jackson,[65] Black,[66] Harlan,[67] and Brennan[68] among others, if there is a single passage in the United States Reports that best captures why the freedom of speech might be considered the linchpin of the American constitutional regime, it is the following paragraph from Justice Brandeis's concurring opinion in *Whitney v. California:*

> Those who won our independence believed that the final end of the State was to make men free to develop their faculties; and that in its government the deliberative forces should prevail over the arbitrary. They valued liberty both as an end and as a means. They believed liberty to be the secret of happiness and courage to be the secret of liberty. They believed that freedom to think as you will and to speak as you think are means indispensable to the discovery and spread of political truth; that without free speech and assembly discussion would be futile; that with them discussion affords ordinarily adequate protection against the dissemination of noxious doctrine; that the greatest menace to freedom is an inert people; that public discussion is a political duty; and that this should be a fundamental principle of the American government. They recognized the risks to which all human institutions are subject. But they knew that order cannot be secured merely through fear of punishment for its infraction; that it is hazardous to discourage thought, hope and imagination; that fear breeds repression; that repression breeds hate; that hate menaces stable government; that the path of safety lies in the opportunity to discuss freely supposed grievances and proposed remedies; and that the fitting remedy for evil counsels is good ones. Believing in the power of reason as applied through public discussion, they eschewed silence coerced by law—the argument of force in its worst form. Recognizing the occasional tyrannies of governing majorities, they amended the Constitution so that free speech and assembly should be guaranteed.[69]

This statement contains a list of propositions, succinctly stated and Delphic in tone, that do not obviously add up to a coherent philosophy. One might suspect Brandeis, the consummate lawyer, of pleading in the alternative in

---

63. *See, e.g.,* Abrams v. United States, 250 U.S. 616 (1919) (Holmes, J., dissenting).

64. *See, e.g.,* Cantwell v. Connecticut, 310 U.S. 296 (1940); Hague v. C.I.O., 307 U.S. 496 (1939).

65. *See, e.g.,* West Va. State Bd. of Educ. v. Barnette, 319 U.S. 624 (1943).

66. *See, e.g.,* New York Times v. United States, 403 U.S. 713 (1971) (Black, J. concurring); Bridges v. California, 314 U.S. 252 (1941).

67. *See, e.g.,* Cohen v. California, 403 U.S. 15 (1971).

68. *See, e.g.,* New York Times v. Sullivan, 376 U.S. 254 (1964); Texas v. Johnson, 491 U.S. 397 (1989).

69. 274 U.S. 357, 375–76 (1927).

this paragraph.[70] That view is wrong, I believe. There is one idea here, not many, and it represents Brandeis's distinctive contribution to the history of First Amendment thought. Permit me to parse this pregnant text.

> *Those who won our independence believed that the final end of the State was to make men free to develop their faculties. . . .*

Whatever may have been the beliefs of "[t]hose who won our independence," we can be certain that Brandeis considered the purpose of government to be "to make men free to develop their faculties." Some might see in this an endorsement of the view that freedom of speech is designed to promote self-development of a highly personal and subjective sort, what my colleague Henry Monaghan likes to call the "feel-good theory of the First Amendment." In light of what follows, however, it is better to read Brandeis here as affirming the principle of self-government, specifically the premise that the state exists solely by the sufferance of, through the efforts of, and for the benefit of the individuals who comprise it. The focus is on the relationship between the individual and the state.

> *[T]he deliberative forces should prevail over the arbitrary.*

This is the first of several passages that might lead one to accuse Brandeis of too rationalistic a view of the process of opinion formation. But in erecting this model of contending forces, Brandeis need not have entertained a naive faith in the wisdom and fairness of collective deliberation to prefer that process to the alternative of unilateral decree by an unaccountable sovereign. From this perspective, freedom of speech is most important for what it implies about sovereignty. Again, the foundational principle is self-government.

> *They valued liberty both as an end and as a means. They believed liberty to be the secret of happiness and courage to be the secret of liberty.*

These sentences embrace what philosophers call a strong theory of the person. A particular kind of citizen is described: one concerned with personal happiness, to be sure, but not the private, self-regarding creature celebrated by some libertarian philosophies. The happiness Brandeis considers the legitimate aspiration of humankind is gained by struggle, by drawing on the demanding virtue of courage. Liberty is valuable as an end because the often difficult experience of exercising a measure of control over one's commitments and paths of development, of choosing what to believe and how to interact with

---

70. Under one interpretation, almost every rationale for free speech that has figured prominently in modern First Amendment analysis—individual autonomy, the search for truth, political participation, the need to check government power, the futility of repression—can be found in this paragraph.

others, is personally fulfilling. Liberty is valuable as a means because persons who have made themselves what they are through the exercise of their own initiative make the best citizens; such persons achieve the most for their societies.[71]

They believed that freedom to think as you will and to speak as you think
are means indispensable to the discovery and spread of political truth. . . .
This is as close as Brandeis gets to the claim that unregulated discussion yields truth. Notice that, in contrast to Holmes, Brandeis never tells us what is "the best test of truth."[72] He never employs the metaphor of the marketplace. He speaks only of "political truth," and he uses the phrase "means indispensable" to link activities described in highly personal terms—"think as you will," "speak as you think"—with the collective goal of "political truth." His emphasis in this passage is on the attitudes and atmosphere that must prevail if the ideals of self-government and happiness-through-courage are to be realized. Brandeis is sketching a good society here, but not an all-conquering dialectic.

[D]iscussion affords ordinarily adequate protection against the
dissemination of noxious doctrine. . . .
This is a thought Brandeis twice repeats within the space of three paragraphs. He says, a few lines after the passage quoted, "the fitting remedy for evil counsels is good ones." And two pages after that: "If there be time to expose through discussion the falsehood and fallacies, to avert the evil by the processes of education, the remedy to be applied is more speech, not enforced silence." Did he really believe this? Do we believe it today?

Brandeis was no ingenue on the subject of public opinion. He knew from his sometimes bitterly fought reform battles in Massachusetts how often the triumph of even a very good idea depends on the hard work, money, savvy, and perseverance of its proponents.[73] He was a close student of Walter Lippmann,

---

71. Five years before he wrote his *Whitney* opinion, in an informal talk that he later summarized in a letter, Brandeis had described the "development of the individual" as "both a necessary means and the end sought. For our objective is the making of men and women who shall be free, self-respecting members of a democracy—and who shall be worthy of respect." ALPHEUS MASON, BRANDEIS: A FREE MAN'S LIFE 585 (1956).

72. *Compare* Abrams v. United States, 250 U.S. 616, 630 (1919) (Holmes, J., dissenting).

73. On Brandeis's systematic efforts to influence public opinion in the cause of reform, *see* LEONARD BAKER, BRANDEIS AND FRANKFURTER: A DUAL BIOGRAPHY 37–38, 57, 61 (1984); ALLON GAL, BRANDEIS OF BOSTON 101–2, 104, 111, 123, 129–30 (1980); MASON, *supra* note 71, at 108–11, 117, 158–59, 161–65, 168–70, 187, 202, 204, 281, 303, 328–31, 371–72, 408–12; PHILIPPA STRUM, LOUIS D. BRANDEIS: JUSTICE FOR THE PEOPLE, 59, 61, 64, 80–85, 89, 101, 104–7, 138–39, 153, 177–78 (1984); MELVIN UROSKY, LOUIS D. BRANDEIS AND THE PROGRESSIVE TRADITION 15, 24, 30–31, 35, 37 (1981).

who was commenting at the time on how the phenomenon of mass culture was making public opinion dangerously manipulable.[74]

It is noteworthy that Brandeis never speaks of noxious doctrine being refuted or eliminated or defeated. He talks of societal self-protection and the fitting remedy. He warns us not to underestimate the value of discussion, education, good counsels. His point is that noxious doctrine is most likely to flourish when its opponents lack the personal qualities of wisdom, creativity, and confidence. And those qualities, he suggests, are best developed by discussion and education, not by lazy and impatient reliance on the coercive authority of the state. To those who would justify censorship on the ground that purveyors of evil ideas can manipulate public opinion, Brandeis almost surely would answer that it is incumbent upon the defenders of good ideas to learn how to influence public opinion even more skillfully.

> [T]he greatest menace to freedom is an inert people; . . . public discussion
> is a political duty. . . . They recognized the risks to which all human
> institutions are subject.

The juxtaposition of these observations is revealing. Brandeis was an idealist, but he was not a perfectionist.[75] When he speaks of the benefits of political participation, his major concern is with the preservation of freedom. He does not claim that participatory democracy produces the wisest policies on a day-to-day basis. Nor does he assert, though he may well have believed, that regular and active political participation is a necessary feature of a personally fulfilling life. To Brandeis, public discussion is a "duty." It is a duty because political liberty is a fragile condition, easily lost when its institutions and traditions fall into the hands of inert people.

> [T]hey knew that order cannot be secured merely through fear of
> punishment . . . ; that it is hazardous to discourage thought, hope and
> imagination; that fear breeds repression; that repression breeds hate; that
> hate menaces stable government. . . .

Here is the counsel of a conservative, addressing the question of how best to secure order and keep government stable.[76] To some, the passage may sound like the "safety valve" rationale for freedom of speech: dissidents will do less

---

74. *See* Robert M. Cover, *The Left, the Right, and the First Amendment: 1918–1928*, 40 MD. L. REV. 349, 363–69 (1981).

75. *See* MASON, *supra* note 71, at 6, 120.

76. On Brandeis's conservatism, *see* STRUM, *supra* note 73, at 72; MELVIN UROSKY, A MIND OF ONE PIECE: BRANDEIS AND AMERICAN REFORM 53–54 (1971).

mischief if they are permitted to let off steam. The problem with this argument is that it is too tactical in inspiration, and perhaps too condescending, to serve as the basis for a constitutional principle. Moreover, it seems a crude generalization to say that most dissidents will consider the opportunity to speak a fair substitute for the redress of their substantive discontents.

Why did Brandeis want to encourage "thought, hope and imagination" in persons whose views are unlikely to win majoritarian approval? If such persons take their thoughts and hopes too seriously, are they not likely to be all the more frustrated when their ideas and their bids for power are rejected?

I do not think Brandeis wanted hopeful, vital, imaginative dissidents because he thought they could be mollified by civil liberties. Rather, he believed that in a political community personal qualities such as hope and imagination tend to be contagious and reciprocal. If the marginal, powerless members of the community retain some semblance of spirit, the mainstream is more likely to sustain its own vitality. And when dissidents become gripped by fear and hate, so too does the majority. The phrase "repression breeds hate" can be read as a double entendre: it is not just the hate experienced by the dissidents that concerns Brandeis, but also the hate that is felt by those who possess the power to punish dissent. The passage is not primarily about consequences or tactics; it is about character.

> Believing in the power of reason as applied through public discussion, they eschewed silence coerced by law—the argument of force in its worst form.

This sentence, more than any other in the *Whitney* opinion, has led many to view Brandeis's argument as dated. Perhaps an Enlightenment figure such as Jefferson could believe in the power of reason. Perhaps a Progressive like Brandeis could. But how often today do we hear experienced, observant people proclaim their faith in the power of reason?

There can be little doubt that Brandeis was sincere in asserting that power, not just wisdom or happiness, attaches to reasoning capacity. In his own life he had parlayed his extraordinary facility at reasoning into a considerable amount of personal power. He had used that power and drawn on that reasoning facility to help many people. It would be a mistake, however, to read into this passage the naive claim—naive in 1927 as well as today—that reason will almost always triumph, at least in the long run. I do not detect in Brandeis's language the echo of Milton's famous rhetorical question: "Who ever knew truth put to the worse in a free and open encounter?"[77] From personal experience, Brandeis

---

77. *See* MILTON, *supra* note 2, at 746.

knew plenty about vested interests, market distortions, and the siren songs of demagogues.

It is essential to read the sentence as a whole. His belief in the power of reason should be seen as a commitment inspired by his emphatic distaste for the alternative: "silence coerced by law—the argument of force in its worst form." How much power reason really exerts is an enduring and intriguing question. I agree with Robert Cover's conclusion that Brandeis did not resolve this question for himself by disinterested observation and reflection.[78] He resolved the question by saying, in effect, that we simply *have* to believe in the power of reason in order to preserve a system of government in which the coercive power of the state does not swamp the individual. If we abandon the faith that reason matters, we are left with a society governed exclusively by force. The First Amendment is meant to serve as a counterweight, Brandeis seems to say, to the natural tendency of all citizens, those in the majority as well as those in the minority, to lose confidence in reason and pursue their goals through force.

The importance of confidence is a theme that permeates the succeeding paragraphs of the opinion:

> *Fear of serious injury cannot alone justify the suppression of free speech and assembly. Men feared witches and burnt women. It is the function of speech to free men from the bondage of irrational fears. . . .*

> *Those who won our independence by revolution were not cowards. They did not fear political change. They did not exalt order at the cost of liberty.*

Brandeis presents his stringent standard for regulating speech as appropriate for a nation of "courageous, self-reliant men, with confidence in the power of free and fearless reasoning. . . ." These resonant sentences add up to a celebration of the virtue of courage. They are in tune with the conclusion that emerges from a close, contextual reading of the earlier paragraph: Brandeis valued a strong doctrine of free speech largely for its contribution to the character of the political community, particularly the character of those who possess the power to regulate.

Why was he so concerned with character? Why was he convinced that courage is the paramount virtue in a democracy? In her excellent biography of Brandeis, Philippa Strum suggests an answer. She describes the intensive reading program Brandeis undertook during the summer of 1914 after the

---

78. *See* Cover, *supra* note 74, at 387–88.

leaders of the Zionist movement had recruited him to their cause. She lists the several books on Judaism that he read, but notes:

> The most important book Brandeis read, and one he quoted throughout his life and made certain that all the members of his extended family read, was not about Zionism: it was Alfred Zimmern's *The Greek Commonwealth*. . . .

> Zimmern's political views paralleled those of Brandeis, and the idea of the Greek city-state matched the possibilities of Palestine. Zimmern may have been the catalyst for the ideas already circulating in Brandeis's mind, or he may have offered Brandeis a new way of looking at Zionism. Whatever the case, the book was one of the few that Brandeis considered central to his life. . . .[79]

Strum reports that Brandeis was so impressed by the book that he arranged for Professor Zimmern to accompany him a few years later on a trip to the Middle East.[80] She continues:

> In order to understand the importance of Zimmern for Brandeis, one must first appreciate the high esteem in which Brandeis held the Greeks of fifth-century Athens. The highest tribute that Brandeis could give his uncle Dembitz was that "he reminded one of the Athenians." Brandeis also compared the Founding Fathers to the Athenians in his most eloquent defense of free speech . . . , [his opinion] in Whitney v. California. He wrote, in part, "They believed liberty to be the secret of happiness and courage to be the secret of liberty." Paul Freund, who was first Brandeis's law clerk and then his lifelong friend, has identified the sentence as coming from Pericles's "Funeral Oration." Zimmern shared Brandeis's high regard for the "Funeral Oration"; the premise of his book is that the oration reflects the greatest heights ever reached by democracy.[81]

Professor Strum offers further evidence of where Brandeis acquired his regard for the virtues of courage and civic commitment:

> Other indications of Brandeis's interest in ancient Greece include the comment of the reporter who followed Brandeis around for two days in 1916 and wrote wryly, "Euripides, I now judge, after having interviewed Brandeis on many subjects, said the last word on most of them." Jacob de Haas noted,

---

79. STRUM, *supra* note 73, at 237 (footnote omitted). On the importance of Zimmern's book to Brandeis, *see also* DEAN ACHESON, MORNING AND NOON 50 (1965) ("[T]wo interacting themes seem to have dominated [Brandeis's] talk—the Greek Genius . . . and the curse of Bigness."); Paul A. Freund, *Mr. Justice Brandeis: A Centennial Memoir*, 70 HARV. L. REV. 769, 789–90 (1957) (Zimmern's *The Greek Commonwealth* "was the book most likely to be recommended by Brandeis to friends in his later years.").

80. STRUM, *supra* note 73, at 242.

81. *Id.* at 237. Professor Freund's observation regarding the sentence from Pericles in the *Whitney* opinion is in Freund, *supra* note 79, at 789.

"Greek and Roman history are as clear to him as though they were part of the morning's news." His favorite and most often quoted poem was from Euripides' The Bacchae; he clearly felt it expressed his view of citizenship and public service. In short, to discover how the model political human being would function in the model political society, Brandeis turned to the Athenians.[82]

To Brandeis, as to Jefferson whom he studied and admired,[83] the project of democratic governance depends on nothing so much as the vitality, the daring, the inventiveness, the steadfastness of individual citizens. It is revealing that among the many books on ancient Greece that Brandeis read, the one that had the most profound effect on him was that by Alfred Zimmern.[84] This is a book about government that has as its centerpiece not the discourses of Plato

---

82. STRUM, *supra* note 73, at 237–38. The poem to which Professor Strum refers apparently is the following:

> Thou hast heard men scorn thy city, call her wild
> Of Counsel, mad; thou hast seen the fire of morn
> Flash from her eyes in answer to their scorn!
> Come toil on toil, 'tis this that makes her grand.
> Peril on peril! And common states that stand
> In caution, twilight cities, dimly wise—
> Ye know them, for no light is in their eyes!
> *Go forth, my son, and help.*

See Strum's description of its importance to Brandeis in *id.* at 62. Mason confirms that Brandeis "drew enduring inspiration" from these lines. MASON, *supra* note 71, at 95. Perhaps misled by an ambiguous reference in Mason, Professor Strum mistakenly attributes the lines to *The Bacchae.* In fact, they are from Euripides' *The Suppliant Women* (11.320–30). Gilbert Murray, whose translations of Euripides Brandeis used, says of these lines: "It is Athens as the 'saviour of Hellas' that we have here. It is Athens the champion of Hellenism and true piety, but it is also the Athens of free thought and the Enlightenment." GILBERT MURRAY, EURIPIDES AND HIS AGE 46–47 (1965). On Brandeis's fondness for quoting Euripides, *see* ACHESON, *supra* note 79, at 96.

83. Some of the instances in which Brandeis's thought parallels that of Jefferson are identified in STRUM, *supra* note 73, at 59, 62, 64, 94, 103, 108–45, 185, 193, 226, 257, 273, 275, 400–2. In the *Whitney* opinion, Brandeis quotes two famous statements by Jefferson that extol free speech as a principle of fearlessness. Whitney v. United States, 274 U.S. at 375 n.3. Particularly in his later years, Brandeis repeatedly expressed his admiration for Jefferson. A few months after he wrote his opinion in *Whitney,* Brandeis made a trip to Monticello "to pay homage" and opined that Jefferson "would have had no difficulty appreciating S.B.I. [Savings Bank Insurance, Brandeis's favorite reform accomplishment]." Louis D. Brandeis, *Letter to Alice Harriet Grady (Sept. 22, 1927), reprinted in* 5 LETTERS OF LOUIS D. BRANDEIS 302 (Melvin Urofsky & David Levy eds., 1975). He returned home from the visit "with the deepest conviction of T.J.'s greatness." Brandeis, *Letter to Alfred Brandeis (Sept. 22, 1927), reprinted in id.* In various letters he referred to three different biographies of Jefferson, *id.* at 315, 411, 521, 648, and once described Jefferson as "our most civilized American and true Democrat." Brandeis, *Letter to Bernard Flexner (Nov. 16, 1940), id.* at 648. *See also* ALFRED LIEF, BRANDEIS: THE PERSONAL HISTORY OF AN AMERICAN IDEAL 478 (1936) ("Brandeis was willing to be called a Jeffersonian."). On Jefferson's emphasis on character, *see* Joyce Appleby, *What Is Still American in the Political Philosophy of Thomas Jefferson?* 39 WM. & MARY Q. 287 (1982).

84. ALFRED ZIMMERN, THE GREEK COMMONWEALTH: POLITICS AND ECONOMICS IN FIFTH-CENTURY ATHENS (1911).

and Aristotle, not the tragedies of Aeschylus and Sophocles, but the Funeral Oration of Pericles, as rendered by Thucydides.

The Funeral Oration enumerates the virtues of Athenian citizens that account for the greatness of the city. The character traits mentioned by Pericles have a noteworthy emphasis when viewed in the context of the virtues one commonly associates with the literature and political philosophy of classical Greece.[85] In the Funeral Oration there is little talk of discipline, balance, obedience, acceptance of role, respect for the gods, subordination of self, avoidance of pride, or search for the mean. There is instead talk of "free liberality," "exceptional versatility," and "adventurous spirit."[86] If Pericles can be said to have a dominant theme, it is that Athenian citizens achieve so much for their city-state because their civic commitment is not coerced but rather flows freely out of the vital and variegated quality of life the city makes possible. In pointed contrast to other city-states, says Pericles, "we do not think that there is an incompatibility between words and deeds. . . ."[87] To the contrary, Athenian civic courage depends on the cultivation of intellectual independence:

> Others are brave out of ignorance; and, when they stop to think, they begin to fear. But the man who can most truly be accounted brave is he who best knows the meaning of what is sweet in life and what is terrible, and then goes out undeterred to meet what is to come.[88]

Perhaps the passage from Thucydides that best captures what Brandeis esteemed in the Athenians comes not from the Funeral Oration but from a speech of the Corinthians warning the Spartans "what sort of people these Athenians are against whom you will have to fight."[89]

> An Athenian is always an innovator, quick to form a resolution and quick at carrying it out. You, on the other hand, are good at keeping things as they are; you never originate an idea, and your action tends to stop short of its aim. Then again, Athenian daring will outrun its own resources; they will take risks against their better judgment, and still, in the midst of danger, remain

---

85. The Funeral Oration has, of course, been interpreted in a variety of ways. For a bibliography of modern interpretations, *see* William C. West III, *A Bibliography of Scholarship on the Speeches in Thucydides 1873–1970, in* THE SPEECHES IN THUCYDIDES (Philip A. Stadter ed., 1973). For a useful reminder of the risk of reductionism when speaking of the Greek virtues, *see* ALISTAIR MCINTYRE, AFTER VIRTUE: A STUDY IN MORAL THEORY 123–53 (1981).

86. THUCYDIDES, HISTORY OF THE PELOPONNESIAN WAR 147–48 (bk. II, paras. 40–41) (Rex Warner trans., 1954).

87. *Id.* at 174.

88. *Id.*

89. *Id.* at 75 (bk. I, para. 70).

confident. But your nature is always to do less than you could have done, to mistrust your own judgment, however sound it may be, and to assume that dangers will last forever.[90]

It is this quality of initiative—the willingness to take chances, to persist against the odds, to embark on novel ventures in the face of scorn and risk, to commit oneself—that provides the essential connection between Brandeis's regard for Athenian democracy and his emphasis in the *Whitney* opinion on the virtue of civic courage.

The importance Brandeis attached to initiative can hardly be overstated. During his career as a progressive reformer he devised and fought to implement a remarkable number of creative solutions to seemingly entrenched problems.[91] One of his favorite essays was "Self-Reliance" by Ralph Waldo Emerson, which consists largely of a plea for individual initiative.[92] The political creed for which Brandeis is best known is well encapsulated by the title of one of his books, *The Curse of Bigness*.[93] All his life he railed against and resisted the modern trend toward larger units of business and governmental organization.[94] His

---

90. *Id.* at 75–76. Although he knew Thucydides's *History* well and this speech is one of its best known passages, Brandeis left no record I can find that these lines made a particular impression on him. Moreover, despite his well-documented affection for the book, one must be cautious about ascribing to Brandeis sentiments expressed in the *History* because Thucydides employed the expositional technique favored by the Sophists of presenting carefully developed opposing speeches. *See* JOHN FINLEY, THUCYDIDES 44, 254–61 (1963). Nevertheless, the Speech of the Corinthians is so consonant with the characterization of the Athenian spirit in the Funeral Oration, and also so consistent with Brandeis's general philosophy of life, that one can be confident the speech accords with his view of what character traits contributed to the success of Athenian democracy during the Age of Pericles. Another example of reference in Thucydides to the quality of initiative is the allusion in the First Speech of Pericles to the daring strategy of Themistocles at the Battle of Salamis. THUCYDIDES, *supra* note 86, at 123 (bk. I, para. 144). It has been argued that the efforts by Aeschylus, Herodotus, and Thucydides to account for the victory at Salamis by reference to the innovative character of the Athenian citizen represent the origins of Greek political theory. *See* J. Peter Euben, *The Battle of Salamis and the Origins of Political Theory*, 14 POL. THEORY 359 (1986).

91. His reform proposals covered a wide range of activities: municipal transit, employee life insurance, utility rate formulas, competition and efficiency in the railroad and shoe machinery industries, labor relations in the garment trades, scientific management of the retailing business, Alaskan land development, tariff reduction, worker participation in management. The most comprehensive account of Brandeis's efforts as a reformer remains that in MASON, *supra* note 71, at 99–464. To the regret of many of his admirers, Brandeis's reform initiatives did not cease after he donned his judicial robes. *See* BRUCE A. MURPHY, THE BRANDEIS–FRANKFURTER CONNECTION: THE SECRET POLITICAL ACTIVITIES OF TWO SUPREME COURT JUSTICES (1982).

92. *See* RALPH WALDO EMERSON, SELECTIONS FROM RALPH WALDO EMERSON 147 (Stephen E. Whicher ed., 1960). On Brandeis's regard for the essay, *see* MASON, *supra* note 71, at 39.

93. LOUIS D. BRANDEIS, THE CURSE OF BIGNESS: MISCELLANEOUS PAPERS OF LOUIS D. BRANDEIS (Osmond K. Fraenkel ed., 1934).

94. *See id.* at 351–62; STRUM, *supra* note 73, at 339–53.

major concern was that bureaucracy breeds caution and stifles initiative.[95] It is no wonder he found special meaning in those writings that emphasize the innovative quality of Athenian civic life.

Read against this background, two sentences of the *Whitney* opinion emerge as particularly important: "Those who won our independence by revolution were not cowards. They did not fear political change."[96] To Brandeis, the measure of courage in the civic realm is the capacity to experience change—even rapid and fundamental change—without losing perspective or confidence. Assessments of the benefits and risks of unregulated discussion are certain to be affected by what general disposition the decisionmaker has toward the phenomenon of change. The courageous attitude, Brandeis asserts, is that of receptivity to new arrangements and new ways of thinking. Progress, the value literally at the root of the Progressive philosophy, depends on receptivity to change. And while speech no doubt contributes directly to change by ventilating grievances and reform proposals, the freedom of speech may be most valuable for its indirect effect, profound even if subtle, on societal attitudes toward change. Those attitudes largely determine how the political community responds to the grievances and reforms that are brought to public attention. Not just judges but all of us need to be emancipated from "the bondage of irrational fears"[97] as we encounter unsettling proposals for change. The essence of Brandeis's ideal of civic courage is a healthy mentality regarding change. The character conducive to the maintenance of that mentality is what he considered the principal benefit of a robust freedom of speech.

What about Now?

It may seem that the eloquence and brilliance of Milton and Brandeis can only be dishonored by a mundane attempt to elaborate their ideas in systematic form and contemporary argot. That, however, is the task I undertake. I hope

---

95. His feelings on this point are well summarized in a closing argument he gave during an investigation he led into corruption in the Department of Interior:

> With this great government building up, ever creating new functions, getting an ever-increasing number of employees who are attending to the people's business, the one thing we need is men in subordinate places who will think for themselves and who will think and act in full recognition of their obligations as a part of the governing body. . . . They cannot be worthy of the respect and admiration of the people unless they add to the virtue of obedience some other virtues—the virtues of manliness, of truth, of courage, of willingness to risk positions, of the willingness to risk criticisms, of the willingness to risk the misunderstandings that so often come when people do the heroic thing.

MASON, *supra* note 71, at 281.

96. *Whitney*, 274 U.S. at 377 (Brandeis, J., concurring).

97. *Id.* at 376.

to demonstrate that their insights about character constitute a resource to be exploited in resolving the First Amendment disputes of today.

What then are the character traits that, in light of contemporary conditions, we might believe are especially valuable and likely to be promoted by according free speech an extremely high priority? From our study of Milton and Brandeis, several traits come to mind: inquisitiveness, independence of judgment, distrust of authority, willingness to take initiative, perseverance, courage to confront evil, aversion to simplistic accounts and solutions, capacity to act on one's convictions even in the face of doubt and criticism, self-awareness, imagination, intellectual and cultural empathy, resilience, temperamental receptivity to change, tendency to view problems and events in a broad perspective, and respect for evidence. This is a long list, yet still incomplete. Nevertheless, the character profile it generates is anything but vacuous, and certainly not to be taken for granted.

But how is character affected by a constitutional commitment? Is the key what such a commitment says, or what it does? The passions evoked by constitutional controversies often have a lot to do with what the disputants take to be the symbolic stakes. To understand the impact of a vital First Amendment culture, however, we do better to focus on material considerations. A legal system influences character not so much by preaching or teaching tolerance as by exerting coercive authority to protect dissenters.[98] The resulting environment, in which dissent is both an option and an inescapable reality, is the principal source of the effect upon character, or so I maintain. It would be wrong to discount entirely the prospect of hortatory influence, but the environmental impact of free speech deserves the greater emphasis.

The most important environmental consequence of protecting free speech is the intellectual and moral pluralism, and thus disorder in a sense, thereby engendered. In matters of belief, conventional structures of authority are

---

98. In this respect, among others, the argument advanced here differs from the most important recent effort to integrate a concern about character into First Amendment analysis, that developed by Lee Bollinger. *See* LEE C. BOLLINGER, THE TOLERANT SOCIETY (1986). Bollinger's argument is limited to one crucial character trait, the capacity to control the intolerance one necessarily must feel toward persons whose speech or conduct manifests beliefs that threaten individual or community identity. Bollinger views the protection of free speech as a commitment that can teach us how to understand and manage this pervasive, natural, morally worthy (in proportion) but often overflowing and self-destructive impulse. The character traits that I believe are nurtured by a free-speech culture are numerous and various, extending far beyond the capacity to control the impulse to intolerance. Those traits are nurtured, moreover, primarily by the experience of living in a vibrant, dynamic, contentious society rather than by the pedagogic contribution of a legal norm of toleration. Despite these differences, the debt my treatment of the subject owes to Bollinger's pathbreaking resurrection of the concern about character is considerable.

weakened, rebellion is facilitated, closure is impaired. Persons who live in a free-speech regime are forced to cope with persistent, and frequently intractable, differences of understanding. For most of us that is a painful challenge, at least in the realms that matter to us most. Being made to take account of such differences shapes our character.

For example, a person who cannot ignore the existence of understandings antithetical to her own must find some way to come to terms with her views. Such a coming to terms can take a variety of forms: blindly digging in, angry denigration of persons with different notions, self-doubt, a deepening of conviction and enhanced awareness of the grounds for one's beliefs, curiosity about the sources of disagreement, confusion, a redoubling of proselytizing zeal, or a grudging and gradual weakening of certitude that may lead eventually to a change of mind. Faced with perdurable difference, many persons will run a gamut of responses over time. What is less likely to ensue the more difference is salient is complacency about one's beliefs and the stasis that complacency engenders. Simply by energizing the experience of belief formation, a free-speech regime's legitimation of difference can nurture many of the positive character traits outlined above.

In addition to forcing persons to confront their differences of understanding, free speech influences character by altering the complex process by which authority is constituted. Few if any of us can do without authority. By requiring us to do without *inherited* authority, *unquestioned* authority, *unaccountable* authority, *unitary* authority, a free-speech regime creates a salutary void. We fill that void by creating other authoritative structures in our lives, ranging from institutions founded on collective (and revocable) consent, to social norms enforced by social sanctions, to precommitments and other sources of self-discipline. Perhaps one could label this process the exercise of autonomy, but it matters, in terms of the instrumental function of character, that the emphasis is on the role of choice in the creation of authority rather than the experience of choice as an essential attribute of personhood. Collectively and individually, we are different people, more capable of certain initiatives and sacrifices, for having helped to determine the authorities that constrain and guide us.

A third way that a free-speech regime helps to mold character is by emboldening persons for whom orthodox understandings do not ring true. In most societies, even those that celebrate free speech, despair is the common lot of the dissenter. No doubt it can be intoxicating to act out differences: rebellion has intelligible psychological roots and a whiff of romance as well. That should not obscure the point that for most of us, most of the time, it is a discomforting and often threatening experience to be out on a limb. Despite the real satisfactions of forbidden inquiry and unvarnished self-expression, the path of pleasure more frequently lies in the direction of going along. Despite the widespread perception that in modern society too many people flaunt and exaggerate their differences, the more common response still is to bury them. In many circumstances that is surely the socially desirable outcome; it is hard to imagine a functional society that was not replete with reticence and trimming. Precisely because the burying of differences is such a pervasive and necessary practice, however, the capacity to pursue differences when occasion demands serves a most important social function.

A culture that protects and celebrates free speech can help to nurture that capacity in several ways. The legitimation of dissent can reduce the degree to which persons with unorthodox ideas are viewed as deserving of ostracism or retaliation. Also, rallies, meetings, and publications can inform dissenters that they are not so isolated, not so far on the margin, as they might have assumed. Facilitating various experiences of solidarity is one of the most consequential, because most energizing, functions of a free-speech regime. In addition, the spectacle of some persons standing up to authority or convention or corruption or evil or mediocrity can enhance in others the sense of duty to take enough responsibility for their convictions to act on them.

Finally, a regime of free speech can help to develop character by requiring those who would beat back bad ideas and contain evil demagogues to pursue those worthy objectives in the most arduous, and thereby most enduring, way: engagement rather than prohibition. The claim here is not that truth and justice will always prevail in a fair marketplace of ideas. We will never have such a marketplace, and truth and justice would not always prevail even if we did. Rather, the notion is that the *experience* of confronting falsehood and evil profoundly shapes the character of a person or a society, and that such an experience is short-circuited by censorship. In this view, the most dangerous ideas can only be defeated by strong persons, not by repressive laws. The two are not, of course, mutually exclusive, but the disturbing tendency, illustrated by our recent efforts to control racism on college campuses, is to think the day's work is done when the self-congratulatory code is enacted. The passage of laws too often has the quality of a moral shortcut, and too often diverts what could be honest, if stressful, exchanges that might actually affect beliefs into shallow forensic contests over legal coverage. In denying the moral shortcut, a free-speech regime strengthens the character of its citizens.

These are some of the ways that the protection of free speech can promote certain character traits under contemporary conditions. We must next inquire why the flourishing of those character traits might be thought to serve collective well-being.

One benefit of free speech is its contribution to a system of checks and balances. Broadly conceived, such a system includes not only the efforts of different branches of the same government to keep each other in line, but also intergovernmental checks on the abuse of authority in a federal system (states checking the federal government and vice versa) and checking by private citizens via elections and less formal manifestations of public sentiment. To do their work, all the various checking agents depend on information concerning what the potential abusers of authority are doing. Often such checking agents rely heavily on the power of communication to mobilize resistance to any discovered abuses. In this regard, the freedom of speech is a mechanism that facilitates the system of checks and balances.

That is not my concern here. Particularly for a process that entails opposition to abuses by powerful actors, mechanisms and procedures cannot be efficacious if the persons who must employ them lack certain demanding personal qualities. Independence of mind is one of those qualities because abuses usually can be rationalized, excused, or ignored by observers who are temperamentally inclined not to question their inertia-driven perceptions of regularity and good faith. For the same reason, general distrust of authority is a functional attitude in this sphere. Another character trait of particular significance for the checking process is perseverance. Miscreant officials seldom go quietly once their transgressions are brought to light. Checking is work for persons who can endure counterattacks and speak truth to power not once or twice but like a broken record. By the same token, a populace accustomed to judging on grounds of evidence and argument rather than preconception or loyalty is more likely to heed the whistleblower, as is a populace not easily discouraged by complexity or delay. To the extent that the experience of living in a contentious, unruly free-speech culture nurtures these traits, the First Amendment has instrumental value for the checking process quite apart from the mechanisms of communication it provides.

Character serves collective well-being in many ways other than by helping to control abuses of power. One is by facilitating compromise. Institutions ranging from marriages to democratic governments flourish or fail depending on how skillful participants are at the difficult art of compromise. To a large degree, the capacity to compromise depends on character. A free-speech culture can help to foster some of the attitudes, skills, and even norms that successful compromise requires. This is important because when persons negotiate their differences poorly, becoming in the event manipulative or resentful or disengaged, collective well-being is not advanced. In addition to the costly side effects of such attitudes, compromises struck in their shadow are likely to be unstable.

Persons who live in a society suffused with conflicting opinions ought on that account to be more skillful at compromise. No doubt overheated rhetoric can fuel resentments and foster political greed, but not so much, I would argue, as censorship can with the fantasies of purification and domination it encourages. Frustration with the blind, stubborn resistance of those who refuse to see matters our way will always be a major source of human unhappiness. The more that frustration is chronic, endemic to the very texture of social life, the better chance we have of learning to function in the face of it.

Free speech engenders fears but also hopes, and compromise is built on hopes. It is easier to stay engaged, to find value in that half a loaf, if tomorrow may bring change for the better. Similarly, the capacity to compromise frequently depends on the self-confidence and sense of perspective of those who are asked to settle for less. Persons whose identities have been forged by experiences of doubt, challenge, and choice are more likely to possess the self-awareness and perspective that compromise demands.

Probably the single most important way that free speech serves collective well-being is by helping persons and institutions adapt to a changing world. As with checking, adaptation depends on mechanisms of communication but even more on the character of the populace. And as various forces such as technological advances and demographic developments cause the pace of change to accelerate, this process of adaptation looms larger and larger as an ingredient of well-being.

Adaptation begins with awareness. When prevailing ideas and arrangements cease to work well in an altered environment, the common tendency is to ignore or minimize the phenomenon. A society that encourages questioning, auditing, experimenting, and revising is more likely to notice problems generated by changing conditions.

At least as crucial to the process of adaptation is a temperamental receptivity to change. A free-speech culture weakens attachments to existing patterns by ventilating alternatives and increasing public awareness of changes that are already afoot. The sheer proliferation of perspectives in play all but forces individuals caught in the maelstrom to adopt a dynamic frame of reference.

Awareness of change, even receptivity to it, does not necessarily engender productive adaptation, however. Good judgment is required for a person or institution to determine how to thrive in uncharted terrain. Heavy reliance on tradition or authority is maladaptive in a rapidly changing environment. What is needed is perceptiveness, boldness, independence of mind, the willingness to experiment, flexibility—in short the capacity to make choices. Passivity and avoidance are the vices to be feared.

Whatever else the freedom of speech does or does not do, it asks its practitioners, speakers and listeners alike, continuously to choose: what to say, how to say it, whom to address, which speakers and messages to hear, what to believe. The more experienced persons are at making choices of this sort, the better their choices ought to be.

Unless, of course, too much choosing leads to decisional anomie. Successful adaptation requires not just the willingness to choose but the discipline to care about the wisdom of one's choices. Critics of what they take to be the ascendant consumerist culture of ideas worry that the celebration of free speech ends up being a celebration of destructively casual attitudes toward knowledge and belief. Surely there is something to this critique. Persons who feel overwhelmed by the choices with which they are confronted cannot be expected to stay engaged and retain perspective. Under such conditions, impulses will reign and adaptation will suffer.

The crucial question is whether a strong constitutional commitment to free speech fosters or forestalls this dangerous phenomenon of disorientation in the face of choice. Were it possible effectively to shield persons from the riot of choices produced by the conditions of modern life, were it possible to legislate simplicity and stability, we might well conclude that censorship is the cure for disorientation. But such shielding is *not* possible, at least not in a political community as large, demographically diverse and mobile, and economically dynamic as the present-day United States. The complexity of the choices we face transcends any particular policy regarding free speech. And if we cannot help but choose, far better that we be shielded from susceptibility to simplistic perceptions and expectations. Although demagogues enabled by toleration can and do peddle simpleminded nostrums, the net effect of a robust free-speech tradition, I submit, is to make audiences more familiar and comfortable with complexity and thereby more skeptical of such nostrums. To the extent that is true, the supremely important objective of productive adaptation is served.

In addition to receptivity to change and good judgment regarding how to cope with it, an adaptive society needs creative ideas. Admittedly, the well-springs of creativity are elusive; geniuses certainly have emerged in repressive regimes. Nevertheless, by tolerating unorthodox opinions and inquiries a community encourages creativity, both by valuing it and by enabling creative persons to achieve visibility and interact. A free-speech tradition appears to matter especially at what might be termed the second level of original thought, not that of rare geniuses with gifts and wills so profound as to overwhelm their environments, but among the foot soldiers of creative adaptation, the persons who diagnose and tinker and test and guess and implement. Such persons shape a culture and are in turn shaped by it. A vibrant culture of ideas can nurture the talents of such persons.

Checking, compromise, and adaptation are collective endeavors that contribute to well-being across a wide spectrum of political arrangements. When sovereignty resides in the people, however, as in a representative democracy, additional capacities that can be developed and sustained by free speech assume special importance. Among the most significant are the willingness of ordinary citizens to participate in collective projects, to assume some measure of responsibility for social outcomes, and more generally to maintain collective energy, resilience, and aspiration.

One way that a free-speech tradition fosters such capacities is by instituting an ethic of distrust and critique of all institutions, not least of government. Critique presupposes responsibility and concern. An effective critic participates in civic life and provokes others to do so. A high level of accountability can energize both the sources and the targets of critical scrutiny.

As with adaptation, however, the social psychology of civic participation is complicated, contestable, and resistant to meaningful empirical verification. Promiscuous distrust and critique could lead to cynical disengagement from collective endeavors, the postmodern equivalent of medieval quietism. Why should we believe that pervasive and telling criticism of established institutions engenders more engagement than withdrawal? It is those very institutions, after all, that serve for most persons as the predominant forums for civic participation. Loyalty to and trust in civic institutions may provide a necessary foundation for personal commitment.

Given our current point in the cycles of the public mood, we naturally tend to associate free speech with rampant negativism, if not nihilism. And surely in any age disenchantment is one of the consequences of the unremitting scrutiny of institutions. But systematic critique carries also an implicit message of hope: hope that standards of performance continue to obtain, hope that reform is possible. Otherwise, why bother? Institutions, like persons, are respected more when much is demanded of them than when they are indulged or ignored, and that holds true even when the demands are in some sense unreasonable. Moreover, the very act of participating in the practice of institutional critique, if only as a listener, connects the ordinary citizen with the collective endeavors that constitute public life. That connection is both contingent and crucial to individual and collective well-being. Loyalty and trust, the preconditions for civic engagement, flow more from connectedness than innocence.

Connectedness, responsibility, hope—these are vital ingredients of civic participation that a commitment to free speech can help sustain. At least as important to the maintenance of political energy are two virtues that typically do not receive the emphasis they deserve: perseverance and resilience. To bring about reforms, almost always it is necessary to keep knocking on the door, over and over again, refusing to take no for an answer. To preserve hard-won gains, almost always it is necessary to ride out storms of defeated expectations and consequent disillusionment. Staying power is the linchpin of efficacious civic participation. This is all the more true in a culture buffeted by multifarious forces that serve to shorten the individual and institutional attention span.

The relationship between free speech and the civic virtues of perseverance and resilience is as difficult to pin down as it is significant. On the one hand, we might fear that too much free thinking and toleration contributes to the erosion of shared standards of judgment. If so, the capacity to stay committed may be adversely affected. Citizens fighting only for their "preferences" may not be as fiercely determined and thereby as capable of enduring the slings and arrows of outrageous resistance as persons whose civic participation is motivated by notions of honor, fundamental justice, or divinely ordained (or natural) entitlement. In this view, free speech complicates perceptions, complexity sows the seeds of doubt, and doubt weakens the will, all to the detriment of staying power.

On the other hand, one might believe, as I do, that naivete is the most important characteristic of quitters. Persons who have scant experience negotiating ideological and cultural differences, who manage to insulate themselves from all but kindred spirits, are the civic actors most likely to harbor unrealistic expectations and to wilt when those expectations are defeated. In this view, perseverance flows from experience and perspective. Whatever its relationship to autonomy, truth-seeking, or fair representation, a free-speech tradition cannot help but broaden horizons and reduce naivete. If perseverance and resilience are as integral to civic well-being as I think they are, that effect should count heavily in any assessment of the benefits of free expression.

So far I have concentrated on the affirmative side of the equation. I have examined the various ways that the protection of free speech can serve collective well-being via characterological effects. A skeptic could grant the claims I have put forward in this regard and still conclude that, on balance, a robust free-speech principle disserves collective well-being precisely because of its impact on character. For a culture of free speech may be thought to foster self-indulgence and excess. The capacity to define and enforce limits is a major element of well-being, at the societal level no less than the personal. Even when free speech promotes checking, compromise, adaptation, and engagement in the ways specified above, the individual traits that help to generate those social benefits may simultaneously undercut the project of setting limits. In nurturing such traits as exuberance, independence, and savvy, free speech sharpens a double-edged sword.

Must freedom cause its practitioners to devalue and defy bounds? The assertedly natural progression from liberty to license has always figured prominently in the rhetoric of opposition to free speech. Thoughtful proponents of toleration concede the point. "Some degree of abuse is inseparable from the proper use of everything," said Madison in what is the foundational essay on the meaning of the First Amendment, "and in no instance is this more true than in that of the press."[99] Madison thought such abuses were a price worth paying, but his observations regarding the wisdom of enduring inevitable excesses were not directed specifically to effects on character. Licentiousness might be considered especially subversive when character is the concern.

Consider, for example, the Supreme Court's much heralded decision in *New York Times v. Sullivan.*[100] To encourage vigorous criticism of government and thwart efforts by the targets of such criticism to use libel law to achieve political objectives, the Court construed the First Amendment to permit recovery by a public official only upon proof that his critic published the offending statement with knowledge of its falsity or reckless disregard for the truth. Perhaps, although there is much dispute about this, the balance struck by the Court can be justified by a utilitarian calculation regarding which stories critical of officials ought to reach the public and which injuries caused thereby warrant legal redress. But the *Sullivan* doctrine does more than strike a balance in these terms: it nurtures a journalistic ethic. Factual inaccuracy is excused and thereby destigmatized; holding a story for further sourcing is discouraged. What is glorified by the Court is "uninhibited, robust, and wide-open" reporting. Over time, we might fear, the immunity from liability established by *Sullivan* will adversely affect the character of journalists, weakening their resolve to get the details of a story right. In this environment, even the consumers of critical stories about public officials might come to care less whether an exposé is strictly accurate in its particulars.

The dilemma is apparent. We do need energetic, irreverent, adroit reporters who are not seduced by the trappings of office or cowed by the threat of

---

99. James Madison, *Report on the Virginia Resolutions Concerning the Alien and Sedition Laws, in* The Mind of the Founder 299, 332 (Marvin Meyers ed., 1958).

100. 376 U.S. 254 (1964).

a lawsuit. But we also need reporters who cherish the truth and appreciate their own fallibility in finding it—reporters, that is, who understand limits. In fostering journalistic aggressiveness and independence, does *Sullivan* exact too high a price in the currency of limits? The same question could be asked about a host of other icons in the First Amendment pantheon, for example Justice Harlan's magnanimous opinion for the Court in *Cohen v. California*,[101] establishing the right to employ profane words in public settings.

As occurs at other junctures in the case for toleration, judgment on this point depends heavily on one's faith (or lack of it) in corrective dynamics. In my experience, among engaged people excesses beget reactions. The spectacle of a person or cause or profession losing all sense of balance and decency tends to bring home to others the need to reinvigorate the moral and social order, not least by attending to the character demands of that order. There are ways to deal with overzealous reporting and breaches of public decorum other than by invoking the heavy, slow-moving, clumsy artillery of the law. Informal, nonofficial sanctions and judgments, Milton recognized, will always provide the most important "bonds and ligaments" that hold a society together.[102] Reporters who take liberties with the truth will be corrected far more by demanding editors and readers than by libel judgments. Protesters who assault the sensibilities of the public will be reigned in when their tactics cause audiences to recoil and their opponents to succeed in discrediting them. Such informal limits are a function of social vitality. They depend on dimensions of character that are blunted in repressive regimes.

It might be argued that the forces of nonofficial correction gain vitality from regulatory backup. Newspaper editors, for example, could be inspired to develop rigorous internal standards for fact-checking if losing a libel suit were a more common experience. In theory, there is no reason why the legal and informal limits on speech cannot be synergetic. In operation, however, that phenomenon is more likely to be the exception than the rule. The content of laws regulating speech cannot help but be affected, in the direction of weakening the scope and strength of the limits imposed, by some severe institutional constraints: the risk of ideological bias by judges, juries, and law enforcement officials; the peculiar difficulty of describing instances of communication in the categories of legal language; the contingencies that thwart the effort to predict or measure the consequences of particular acts of expression. Because of those constraints, legal sanctions can do only a small

---

101. 403 U.S. 15 (1971).

102. Milton, *supra* note 2, at 733.

fraction of the work of setting limits. The informal sanctions on speech need to be much more substantial, pervasive, finely calibrated, and subtle than their formal counterparts could ever be. In this regard, the watered-down limits imposed by the institutionally constrained legal regime can actually impair the development of informal limits by establishing either a low benchmark or a false perception that meaningful limits are already in place. As a rule, the most effective limits on speech originate and derive their sustenance from sources other than formal laws.

In part this is so because the limits must themselves be dynamic and adaptive. The forces of excess do not follow set patterns. The transgressions of investigative reporters assume new forms as technological capacities expand, competitive pressures intensify, and audiences change. The advent of cyber-space necessitates the construction of a wholly new type of public decorum. The accelerating commercialization of American life, not excluding the life of the mind, raises issues of limits we have barely begun to address. Limits are not fixed essences to be found and enforced. They are ongoing judgments, made in response to the novel mix of threats, needs and aspirations of a particular time and place. If a free-speech tradition does indeed help citizens to confront problems, retain perspective, and exercise judgment in a changing environment, in no project are those skills more valuable than that of enforcing the tacit, uncodified standards of behavior that make for a resilient social order.

In the last analysis, behind this concern about limits lies the primordial fear of anarchy. It would be foolish to underestimate the role this fear has played—and continues to play—in disputes over free speech. No one with even a passing acquaintance with Hobbes can dismiss the threat of anarchy out of hand, or cabin it in the seventeenth century.[103] The veneer of civilization may be just that.

Anarchy can flow from self-indulgence or zeal but so too can it flow from the failure to check, or compromise, or adapt, or take responsibility for social outcomes, or confront evil. What provoked countless persons over the centuries to fight and sometimes die for the principle of freedom of speech was, more often than not, a particular form of disorder, something we might with Locke call anarchy: the unrestrained use of the coercive apparatus of the state to stamp out difference and hold on to power.[104] The limits that keep in check the anarchic impulse to wreak vengeance on persons who challenge the reigning orthodoxy are among the essential "bonds and ligaments" of a

---

103. *See* THOMAS HOBBES, LEVIATHAN (Edwin Curley ed., 1994).

104. *See* JOHN LOCKE, SECOND TREATISE OF GOVERNMENT, ch. XIX (Crawford B. Macpherson ed., 1980).

civilized society. Those limits depend on constitutional structures but even more on strength of character.

"[T]he greatest menace to freedom," said Brandeis, "is an inert people."[105] He added, echoing Milton,[106] that such a people is also the greatest menace to order.[107] That is why, for all its costs and excesses, free speech, the archenemy of inertia, is so important.

---

105. *See* Whitney v. California, 274 U.S. 357, 375 (1927) (Brandeis, J., concurring).

106. *See* MILTON, *supra* note 2, at 742:

There be who perpetually complain of schisms and sects, and make it such a calamity that any man dissents from their maxims. It is their own pride and ignorance which causes the disturbing, who neither will hear with meekness nor can convince, yet all must be suppressed which is not found in their syntagma. They are the troublers, they are the dividers of unity, who neglect and permit not others to unite those disservered pieces which are yet wanting to the body of Truth.

107. 274 U.S. at 375: "[I]t is hazardous to discourage thought, hope and imagination. . . . [F]ear breeds repression . . . repression breeds hate . . . hate menaces stable government. . . ."

The question whether the government may restrict speech because it might persuade readers or listeners to engage in unlawful conduct has long absorbed the Supreme Court's attention. This was the first issue of First Amendment interpretation to capture the Court's sustained interest, and as David Strauss explained, the debate within the Court over this issue has resulted in the articulation of a collection of doctrines and principles that have dominated the evolution of First Amendment jurisprudence.

The Supreme Court first confronted this issue in a series of cases concerning agitation against the war and the draft during World War I. The prevailing view in the lower federal courts was that individuals who spoke in opposition to the war or the draft could be criminally punished for "attempting" to obstruct the war effort on the theory that speech is not protected by the First Amendment if a "natural consequence" of the expression might be to lead others to engage in unlawful conduct. Following this approach, some two thousand individuals were prosecuted and convicted under the Espionage and Sedition Acts for their opposition to the war and the draft during World War I.

In "'Clear and Present Danger' and Criminal Speech," Kent Greenawalt examines *Schenck v. United States,* the Supreme Court's initial effort in interpreting the First Amendment, and uses this decision as a jumping-off point for a broader exploration of the problems of subversive advocacy and "criminal speech" more generally. Reflecting the profound changes in our understanding of the First Amendment since World War I, Professor Greenawalt concludes that even explicit counseling of criminal conduct in the context of public advocacy "should be constitutionally punishable if and only if (1) the speaker seriously and expressly urges the commission of a specific crime in the very near future, and (2) it is reasonably likely that the speech will contribute to the commission of the crime in the very near future."—GRS

KENT GREENAWALT

"Clear and Present Danger" and Criminal Speech

Introduction

If you ask an American when the government is allowed to step in and punish speech, he or she is likely to say, "You can't shout fire in a crowded theater," and "The government can act when there is a clear and present danger." The language of "clear and present danger" comes from the Supreme Court's opinion in *Schenck v. United States*,[1] written by Oliver Wendell Holmes Jr. This essay is partly about the dimensions of a "clear and present danger" test in *Schenck* and subsequent cases under the Free Speech and Free Press Clauses. It also analyzes what constitutional protection, if any, certain kinds of criminal speech deserve. By "criminal speech," I mean speech that contributes to criminal acts by, for example, urging that someone commit a crime, assist in commiting a crime, or agree to commit a crime.

My focus is on doctrine. Because most provisions of the Constitution are cast at a high level of generality, courts develop middle-level doctrines or tests that they apply to particular cases. Courts sometimes make up doctrines to fit results or even use doctrines to conceal other bases for decision. But doctrines matter, and established doctrinal tests frequently lead to results judges might not reach were those tests not in place. It would be naive to suppose that constitutional decision is only about doctrines, but the analysis of doctrines has continuing importance.

"Clear and present danger" has been one of the central doctrines of the First Amendment in the twentieth century. By midcentury, "clear and present danger" seemed to be an all purpose test for free-speech problems. The test has faded in significance, but a reformulated, strict version still controls the punishment of dangerous speech. Advocacy of subversive acts can be punished because of its danger, only if it "is directed to inciting or producing imminent lawless action and is likely to incite or produce such action."[2]

---

1. 249 U.S. 47, 52 (1919).

2. Brandenburg v. Ohio, 395 U.S. 444, 447 (1969).

One might think that the boundaries of a constitutional standard that has been around for eighty years would be settled, but the Supreme Court has never answered some basic questions about "clear and present danger," and states punish many communications concerned with criminal activities without anyone worrying about free speech. What is going on?

When we examine how some varieties of criminal speech relate to the "clear and present danger" test, we learn a good deal about the nature of human communication and about the underlying purposes and coverage of the Free Speech and Free Press Clauses. My overall thesis is that "free speech" concerns only some categories of communication, that much criminal speech can be punished without the government's having to satisfy any free-speech test, and that the degree of protection for speech that the First Amendment covers should depend on the kind of speech that is involved.[3] We can begin to unpeel this onion by starting with the facts and language of *Schenck.*

Schenck and "Clear and Present Danger"

Schenck had been convicted for violating the 1917 Espionage Act, adopted after the entry of the United States into World War I. Schenck had agreed to help print an antiwar tract and to circulate copies to men called for military service. The leaflet claimed that conscription violated the Thirteenth Amendment's ban on involuntary servitude. It spoke of "your right to assert your opposition to the draft." It continued, "If you do not assert and support your rights, you are helping to deny or disparage rights which it is the solemn duty of all citizens . . . to retain," and, "You must do your share to maintain, support, and uphold the rights of the people of this country."[4] Schenck was convicted of conspiring to cause insubordination among the armed forces and to obstruct recruiting.

In his opinion for the Supreme Court affirming the conviction, Justice Holmes assumed that the statute required that a defendant have an illegal purpose. He deemed the content of the leaflet sufficient to establish that purpose. Two cases decided a week after *Schenck,*[5] as well as many convictions

---

3. I develop these themes at greater length in SPEECH, CRIME, AND THE USES OF LANGUAGE (1989), and in *Speech and Crime,* 1980 AM. B. FOUND. RES. J. 645.

4. *Schenck,* 249 U.S. at 51.

5. Frohwerk v. United States, 249 U.S. 204 (1919); Debs v. United States, 249 U.S. 211 (1919). Frohwerk had printed articles favorable to Germany, claiming that those resisting the draft were "technically . . . wrong," though "more sinned against than sinning." *Frohwerk,* 249 U.S. at 208. Debs made a speech that blamed the war on the ruling classes and praised particular draft resisters. He exhorted the audience, "Don't worry about the charge of treason to your masters; but be concerned about the treason that involves yourselves." *Debs,* 249 U.S. at 214.

that never reached the Supreme Court, showed that courts had little difficulty discerning an illegal purpose in antiwar advocacy.

In *Schenck,* after discussing the statutory requirements, Holmes turned to the First Amendment:

> We admit that in many places and in ordinary times the defendants in saying all that was said in the circular would have been within their constitutional rights. But the character of every act depends on the circumstances in which it is done. . . . The question in every case is whether the words used are used in such circumstances and are of such a nature as to create a clear and present danger that they will bring about the substantive evils that Congress has a right to prevent. It is a question of proximity and degree. When a nation is at war many things that might be said in time of peace are such a hindrance to its effort that their utterance will not be endured so long as men fight and that no Court could regard them as protected by any constitutional right.[6]

This language raises four important questions. To what sorts of communications does the "clear and present danger" test apply? How great must the evil be for the test to be satisfied? Is presentness an independent criterion or is it relevant only as an indication of the likelihood that an evil will occur? What is the relation between an actual danger and an intended danger?[7] Before working through the language of *Schenck* and considering how justices have dealt with these issues in subsequent decisions, I first provide an example that raises these questions clearly. Later I consider the central question of what kinds of criminal communications warrant constitutional protection.

Amy is vacationing with her two adult children, Bruce and Cathy, in a remote part of the Adirondack mountains in northern New York. One day, Amy happens to read a *New York Times* story about the Powerball Lottery, the jackpot for which has risen to almost 300 million dollars. The story recounts the problems of Greenwich, Connecticut, one of the many states that allows sales of Powerball tickets (New York does not). The residents of Greenwich are deeply disturbed that "low-lifes" from New York have overwhelmed their peaceful, affluent community for the purpose of buying tickets. Sensing that fortune is knocking, Amy has an ingenious idea for bringing stability to the life of her beloved son Bruce, who has "drifted" without finding meaningful work.

That evening Amy takes Bruce aside. She explains that an entrepreneur who manages to set up surreptitious Powerball outlets in New York City could

---

6. *Schenck,* 249 U.S. at 52.

7. Another question, which I do not discuss in this essay, is whether the test is one for jury application or is exclusively for judicial assessment.

make a lot of money selling tickets to harassed city dwellers who have better uses of their time than trips to Connecticut. She tells Bruce that he has just the talents to manage this endeavor, and reminds him that his uncle Don, a major figure in organized crime, would be happy to help him get started. She concludes by saying, "Bruce, I don't expect you to do anything until the end of our vacation four weeks from now, but I strongly urge you then to contact Don and begin to set up Powerball outlets in the city. I am going to be very disappointed if you flub this opportunity."

Bruce, a young man blessed with more self-knowledge than drive, thinks his mother has hit upon a fabulous idea, but he lacks confidence that he can pull it off on his own. His sister Cathy has just graduated from business school, and Bruce is sure her organizational and financial skills would prove very helpful. He excitedly tells her about the idea, and Cathy is impressed. After an hour's conversation, Bruce and Cathy agree that in a month's time, they will undertake to set up Powerball outlets in New York City.

By coincidence, the state police, suspecting Amy of involvement with Don in a heroin ring, had earlier planted listening devices in the cabin where the family is staying. They acquire an exact record of the conversations, on the basis of which Bruce and Cathy are charged with conspiring to set up illegal Powerball outlets and Amy is charged with "soliciting" Bruce to commit that crime. New York closely regulates gambling within the state; setting up sites for unauthorized gambling is criminal. Does the First Amendment provide any protection for Amy, Bruce, and Cathy?

This example sharpens the four questions that the language of *Schenck* raises. The first question concerns the kinds of communications the "clear and present danger" test protects. Does it have anything to do with an agreement to commit a crime such as Bruce and Cathy's? Does it protect explicit, unambiguous urgings that people commit particular crimes that lack political overtones, such as Amy's encouragement of Bruce? *Schenck* deals with political advocacy that falls short of explicit solicitation of a crime. We need to understand the opinion's language in context. In context, it tells us very little about how the Free Speech and Free Press Clauses might apply to the very different circumstances of our story, to its agreement and explicit criminal solicitation. If we assume for the moment that Amy's comments to Bruce do not lose all First Amendment protection, how would Amy fare under the standard of *Schenck?*

Can Amy argue that the crime of establishing Powerball outlets is just not serious enough to satisfy the "clear and present danger" test? New York, after all, has its own state lottery, well advertised and replete with appealing ways for poor people to lose money; the state also runs off-track betting outlets. No doubt, New York is constitutionally permitted to protect its own enterprises and discourage uncontrolled private gambling. It can criminalize the setting up of Powerball outlets. But can one say that preventing Powerball outlets really reflects any powerful interest of a state that makes decided efforts to encourage its citizens to gamble in a similar lottery? That seems doubtful.

Notice that the language of the *Schenck* opinion seems to look in two directions on the issue of whether the evil must be serious. Holmes writes that in ordinary times, Schenck would be within his constitutional rights in saying what he said, but that when a nation is at war, things that might be said in times of peace but that hinder the war effort "will not be endured." That sounds very much as if the magnitude of the evil matters—that speech likely to cause a great evil may be punished, that otherwise similar speech likely to cause only a slight evil is constitutionally protected. But if one parses the language of what is the most explicit formulation of the constitutional test, one reaches a different conclusion. In that formulation, Holmes puts the inquiry as whether the words in context "create a clear and present danger that they will bring about the substantive evils that Congress has a right to prevent." Congress, like state legislatures, has a right to prevent slight evils as well as great ones. Insubordination in the armed forces is a crime in peace as well as war. Insubordination of even one soldier in peacetime is an evil that Congress may prevent. If words create a clear and present danger of causing insubordination, whether during peace or war, that would seem to satisfy the precise language of the constitutional test. On this understanding, Amy's words to Bruce are punishable if they create a clear and present danger that Bruce will open at least one Powerball outlet, whether that evil is big, small, or middle-sized. Thus, different passages in *Schenck* provide grist for competing contentions that "the substantial evil" must be serious and that the size of the evil does not matter.

Our next question is whether "present" in "clear and present danger" contains an independent temporal dimension or is satisfied by a substantial probability that the evil will occur. *Schenck* certainly suggests that words creating only a slight possibility of harm should not be punished, that speech is constitutionally protected unless the likelihood of harm is significant. Usually when a bad result is close in time, we can tell more easily if the harm is likely to occur. If someone aims a gun in anger we can be more certain he will shoot than if he boards a bus in New York intending to assault his victim in Los Angeles. However, the certainty of harms does not always depend on proximity in time. Those who are sure that global warming is a present phenomenon may be equally confident that serious future harms will occur, though not for decades. Similarly, medical evidence establishes that serious physical harms will occur some decades hence to a significant proportion of teenagers who now begin smoking.[8]

The passage from *Schenck* does not illuminate the significance of "present." On the one hand, the notion of a "clear" danger already imports a substantial probability that a harm will occur. Why include "present" in the test unless the evil has to follow the speech closely in time? If "present" should be given meaning, the most straightforward significance is to require a close temporal connection of speech to harm. On the other hand, one could say that a danger may be present (global warming) although the harm will not occur for many years. In *Schenck* and its companion cases, no evidence connected the speech to a likelihood that even a few men would soon be insubordinate or resist recruiting, much less to the prospect that the number of violators would soon impair the war effort.

Amy might rely on "present" to claim that her encouragement of Bruce would not produce a harm "very soon"; Bruce was not to begin to act for a month and would take longer to establish his first lottery outlet. Whether or not "present" demands that the evil be close in time, Amy might contend that Bruce was not especially likely to act at all, that any danger from her speech was neither clear nor present.

The final question I have raised about *Schenck* is the relationship between actual danger and intended danger. Suppose a well-informed outside observer were to say, "Bruce never listens to his mother's harebrained schemes. The chance that he would do what she has proposed is extremely slight." If other requirements for punishment are met, is it enough that Amy intended to cause a harm, or must the harm have been objectively likely to happen? *Schenck* seems to focus on actual danger, and when most people conceive the "clear and present danger" test, they are thinking about the actual danger speech presents, not about the speaker's aims.

We have surveyed four important questions that could matter for our example and for which *Schenck* provides no precise answer. Why is the opinion not more definite? The most generally important reason is that legal opinions

---

8. One might quibble with this way of putting it, arguing that serious physical harm occurs (or begins) now, although it does not take its toll until later. By analogy, one would say that the growth of even a few malignant cells is a serious harm, although the victim's functioning and feeling of well-being are not yet affected.

when you
can express
yourself even
if no one can
hear you,

that's mlife

AT&T Wireless

PRESORTED
STANDARD
U.S. POSTAGE
PAID
AT&T WIRELESS

AT&T Wireless
P.O. Box 944038
Maitland, FL 32794-4038

1YA2
Albie D. Burke
6231 E. 5th St.
Long Beach, CA 90803-2111

Get TEXTIN 2DAY and GAL 2NITE

(Get texting today and get a life tonight.)

Sometimes it's the noise. Sometimes it's because you're busy. And sometimes you just don't want to be overheard. That's when it's time for text messaging. Texting is the fast, fun and discreet way to hook up with friends, share news or just let someone know you're thinking about them.

You're already set up to use text, and it costs just 10¢ to send one. Or sign up to send 100 messages a month for $4.99. What's more, text messaging doesn't use up valuable calling minutes. And, unlike other carriers, AT&T Wireless doesn't charge you for receiving messages from friends or family – no matter which wireless service they have. So the next time you want to express yourself, send a text. Words rule!

GR8 DEAL: SIGN UP FOR 100 MESSAGES A MONTH FOR $4.99.

CALL 1 800 888-7600 OR VISIT ATTWIRELESS.COM/OCS

HOW 2 SPK TXT	
HCIT	How Cool Is That?
2NITE	Tonight
:-0	Wow
TTYL	Talk To You Later

You can only send messages in select geographic areas. 100 text messages for $4.99 only available for use in select geographic areas. Ability to receive messages in any geographic area is not an indication that you can send messages. In certain circumstances the network will store and re-send any messages for up to 72 hours. Messages not delivered after 72 hours will be deleted. Maximum message length is up to 160 characters, which includes the recipient's address. Any characters over the maximum will be deleted. © 2002 AT&T Wireless. All rights reserved.   YA2

(Cool. Send me the information.)

SEND
- Select **Menu.**
- Select **Messages.**
- Select **Text Messages.**
- Select **Write Message** or similar option from Messaging Menu.*
- Write your message.
- Select **Options**, then **Send.**
- Enter the 10-digit wireless phone number or select a number from Address Book.
- Select **Send** again.

RECEIVE
- When you receive a new text message, an alert tone sounds and an envelope icon appears.
- Select **Read**, then **Select** to see the full message.

REPLY
- Press **Options**. Scroll to, then select **Reply.**
- Select **As A Message.**
- Write message.
- Select **Options**, then **Send.**
- Select **OK** to confirm the number.

* Some phone models prompt for the 10-digit wireless number first.

To get more info or a demo, visit attwireless.com/text

Printed on recycled paper.

focus on the facts of a case and do not attempt to answer many questions about other related situations. The language of opinions has to be understood in context. Two other reasons help explain *Schenck*. One involves the relation between the "clear and present danger" test and other approaches to freedom of press and speech in the minds of the justices who decided *Schenck*. The "clear and present danger" test has come to signify considerable protection for speech and writing, but, prior to *Schenck*, the Supreme Court had not definitely established that the First Amendment forbids anything other than prior restraints—for example, licensing of who may write a book or make a speech. State courts typically had said that speech with merely a "bad tendency" to cause harm could be punished, thus affording state legislatures wide latitude to punish what they chose.[9] In Supreme Court cases following *Schenck*, most justices granted legislatures similarly broad scope to punish speech.[10] Since these justices joined the *Schenck* opinion, they obviously did not assume that it gave much more protection to speech and writing than did the bad tendency test.

A second and related explanation of the opinion involves Holmes's own position, about which there are two distinct views. One is that Holmes himself, right from the start, conceived "clear and present danger" as a standard that would protect speech, but that he cleverly wrote an opinion other justices could join. The second view is that Holmes's own position developed over time, that when *Schenck* was decided he had not yet come to the conviction that speech and press should receive stringent protection. Two pieces of evidence support the second view. One is the way Holmes voted in *Schenck* and its two companion cases.[11] Someone who believed in strong protection of speech probably would not have voted to uphold all three convictions. Although Holmes may possibly have voted against his own convictions in order to write majority opinions that would preserve *some* protection of speech, justices usually vote according to how they think a case should come out. The second piece of evidence is Holmes's correspondence during this time, which does not reveal a great concern for the values of speech and press.[12]

9. *See* David M. Rabban, *The First Amendment in Its Forgotten Years*, 90 YALE L.J. 514, 522–55 (1981).

10. *See, e.g.,* Gitlow v. New York, 268 U.S. 652, 667 (1925); Whitney v. California, 274 U.S. 357, 371 (1927), *overruled in part by* Brandenburg v. Ohio, 395 U.S. 444 (1969).

11. *See supra* note 5.

12. *See* Gerald Gunther, *Learned Hand and the Origins of Modern Free Speech Doctrine: Some Fragments of History*, 27 STAN. L. REV. 719, 734–35 (1975).

Subsequent Decisions

Three of the four questions I have raised about the "clear and present danger" test are substantially answered by opinions in subsequent cases, though on two of them the Court has shifted in crucial ways. In the decade after *Schenck,* while the majority of the Court permissively allowed legislatures to prohibit subversive speech if they had a rational basis for doing so,[13] Justices Holmes and Brandeis refined the "clear and present danger" test in a series of stirring dissents[14] asserting the fundamental value of free speech.

Holmes's dissent in *Abrams v. United States,*[15] during the Court's term after *Schenck,* sheds considerable light on two of our questions—the relation between intended and actual danger and the significance of "present." Abrams had been convicted under the 1918 Espionage Act for conspiring to incite resistance to the war effort against Germany and to curtail production of war materials, with an intent to hinder prosecution of that war. The circular that the defendants distributed protested U.S. involvement against the new revolutionary government in Russia and urged a general strike. The majority of the Supreme Court said that the inevitable effect of a general strike would be to harm the war effort against Germany; that was sufficient to establish intent. Holmes disagreed; he said intent in this context must be judged by the *actual* aim of Abrams and his colleagues, and that aim was to aid the revolutionary government in Russia, not to impair the war against Germany.[16] On the question of the importance of intent versus actual danger, he wrote, "by the same reasoning that would justify punishing persuasion to murder, the United States may punish speech that produces *or* is intended to produce a clear and imminent danger."[17] Eight years later in *Whitney v. California,* Justice Brandeis, joined by Holmes, wrote that the "clear and present danger" test could be satisfied if immediate serious violence "was to be expected *or* was advocated."[18] In both these formulations, speech may be punished if it actually causes a danger that is sufficient or the speaker advocates such a danger.

---

13. *See supra* note 10.

14. The opinion by Justice Brandeis in *Whitney v. California*, 274 U.S. 357, 372–80 (1927), was technically a concurrence though it strongly disagreed with the constitutional approach of the majority.

15. 250 U.S. 616, 624–31 (1919).

16. For ordinary criminal liability, Holmes's view of intent was highly "objective": a person could "intend" consequences he did not actually foresee so long as a reasonable person would have foreseen that an act of that kind would have those consequences. Holmes believed that the espionage statute required a much stricter form of intent, a conscious desire to bring about forbidden consequences.

17. 250 U.S. at 627 (emphasis added).

18. 274 U.S. at 376 (emphasis added).

Holmes's dissent in *Abrams* and the Brandeis opinion in *Whitney* tightened the notion of presentness. Holmes wrote that no one could suppose that the circulation of five thousand copies of Abrams's leaflet posed "any immediate danger that its opinions would hinder the success of the government arms,"[19] and he referred to the need for a "clear and imminent danger" of substantive evils.[20] He talked of emergencies that make it "immediately dangerous to leave the correction of evil counsels to time."[21] Brandeis picked up this theme, developing the connection between a theory of free speech and the requirement that a danger be imminent: "If there be time to expose through discussion the falsehood and fallacies, to avert the evil by a process of education, the remedy to be applied is more speech, not enforced silence. Only an emergency can justify repression."[22] On the gravity of the evil—another of our four questions about *Schenck*—Justice Brandeis's opinion in *Whitney* provides a clear approach. He wrote, "In order to support a finding of clear and present danger it must be shown either that immediate serious violence was to be expected or advocated."[23] He went on to discuss the crime of trespass. The harm of trespass would not warrant interfering with advocacy of a moral right to trespass "even if there was imminent danger that advocacy would lead to trespass."[24] Thus, in *Abrams* and *Whitney,* Holmes and Brandeis, though certainly recognizing both intended danger and actual danger as independent bases for punishment, reinforced the importance of immediacy and of the need for a grave harm.

In a prosecution of Communist Party leaders under the Smith Act, the Supreme Court in 1951 took a large step in the opposite direction. Sustaining convictions of the leaders for conspiring to advocate overthrow of the government, a plurality of justices used a version of the "clear and present danger" test that dispensed with requirement of imminence. It said that a judge should "ask whether the gravity of the 'evil,' discounted by its improbability, justifies such invasion of free speech as is necessary to avoid the danger."[25] Under this approach, an evil, such as communist overthrow of the government, might be quite distant in time and still justify the suppression of speech because the harm is so grave.

---

19. 250 U.S. at 628.

20. *Id.* at 627.

21. *Id.* at 630.

22. 274 U.S. at 377.

23. *Id.* at 376.

24. *Id.* at 378.

25. Dennis v. United States, 341 U.S. 494, 510 (1951).

The now authoritative version of "clear and present danger" is found in a per curiam opinion from 1969, in which the Court established a test for subversive advocacy more protective of speech than any previous formulation. The opinion in *Brandenburg v. Ohio*[26] was surprising because it was unnecessary; the case involved a conviction of a Ku Klux Klan speaker under a state statute that was invalid because it reached far too broadly into the domain of protected speech. Instead, the Court reviewed "clear and present danger" problems. Paying little attention to what the Court had said in 1951, it announced that previous decisions had established that a state may not forbid "advocacy of the use of force or of law violation except where such advocacy is directed to inciting or producing imminent lawless action and is likely to incite or produce such action."[27] The word "imminent" clearly signals that the harm must closely follow the speech. And, instead of requiring that the danger be clear and present *or* intended to be so, the opinion indicates that the harm must be both likely and imminent *and* intended to be so. The opinion does not exactly say that the speaker must intend imminent harm, but it does say that advocacy must be "directed" to producing imminent lawless action. In ordinary understanding, a person directs his behavior toward an object only if he intends the object.[28]

Shortly after *Brandenburg*, the Court decided *Hess v. Indiana*.[29] A demonstrator who had said "We'll taking the fucking street later," had been convicted of disorderly conduct. Although in context, Hess, if serious, must have meant the demonstrators would "take the street" later in the same day, the Court said there was no showing that Hess intended to produce imminent disorder.[30]

---

26. 395 U.S. 444 (1969).

27. *Id.* at 447.

28. Prior to the decision in *Schenck*, Learned Hand, then a federal district court judge, had reviewed the decision of the Postmaster of New York City to treat the revolutionary journal *The Masses* as non-mailable material under the Espionage Act of 1917. Masses Pub. Co. v. Patten, 244 F. 535 (S.D.N.Y. 1917), *rev'd*, 246 F. 24 (2d Cir. 1917). Hand suggested that publications violated the Act only if they "have no purport but to counsel the violation of law." *Id.* at 540. Hand's correspondence indicated that he thought his approach was apt for interpreting the First Amendment. *See* Gunther, *supra* note 12. In demanding unambiguous encouragement of criminal acts, Hand's test seemed more protective of speech than "clear and present danger"; in allowing punishment of explicit encouragement that did not pose a serious danger (either because the evil was not likely to occur or was not serious), his test was less speech protective than any objective requirement of a clear and present danger of serious evil. The *Brandenburg* test did not draw directly from Hand, and it does not use the exact approach of the *Masses* case; but in combining a requirement that speech be directed to producing illegal action with a requirement that that be likely to occur, the *Brandenburg* opinion seemed to join elements of the Holmes and Hand approaches.

29. 414 U.S. 105 (1973).

30. *Id.* at 108. The implausibility of interpreting Hess's words as a serious urging to criminal action may have affected the result.

What period of time is imminent may vary to a degree with the crime; but *Hess* shows that the Court is serious about imminence. *Brandenburg* does not directly talk about the seriousness of the crime, but the prevailing assumption is that its test requires dangers of some degree of gravity—that what Justice Brandeis said in *Whitney* on this point continues to be valid. Although the Court since *Brandenburg* and *Hess* has considered many free-speech issues and has developed a number of doctrinal protections of speech, it has not reviewed the *Brandenburg* approach.

We can see that the *Brandenburg* test looks very favorable for Amy, and for Bruce and Cathy, *if* the test applies to their communications. But does the "clear and present danger" test, in either its *Schenck* formulation or in its modern version, apply to agreements to commit crimes and to criminal solicitations made in private that have nothing to do with ideological advocacy? These questions about "clear and present danger" have never been decisively answered by the Court. I later indicate what the Court *has said* that is relevant to them. But first I want briefly to consider some aspects of human communication and the reasons for free speech.

Reasons for Free Speech and Varieties of Communication

Human communication serves many purposes. If I talk to you, I may tell you what I think is true, I may express my feelings, I may advise you what I think is the best thing for you to do in the circumstances you face. All these functions of communication have to do with the expression of ideas and emotions; they are at the core of what freedom of speech and the First Amendment protect. The right for people to express their thoughts and feelings to each other is important both for speakers and for listeners. Speaking one's mind is a crucial aspect of self-expression; listening to uncensored expression is vital for understanding others. We have no assurance that hearing the ideas of others will lead listeners to the truth, but open discourse is much more promising in this respect than expression that is tailored to fit some government program. Talk about "the truth" may make many readers uncomfortable, but there are many varieties of truth and only the most extreme skeptic doubts that one can ever speak of truth and falsity. It is true that the Nazi government killed millions of Jews, although some persons now deny that the Holocaust ever happened. It is also true that the earth is shaped like a sphere, although a few people still believe it is flat. One part of a theory of freedom of speech is that open discourse is a better guarantee of people coming to know truths of these sorts than is a regime of government supervision. Unrestricted speech has special significance as a check on government abuse and as a necessary element of political life in a liberal democracy. Voting cannot be genuinely free unless people have some realistic idea what the government is doing, and can hear candidates and others present competing points of view.

People who disagree about which aspects of free speech are most important may also disagree about what speech should be protected. Those who emphasize the informational benefits of speech may think most advertising should receive constitutional protection, but that pornography and hate speech should not. Those who emphasize a speaker's self-expression may want greater protection for hate speech and none for commercial advertising.

Whichever of these reasons for free speech are the most central, they have little to do with certain other kinds of communication. This is most obvious for orders. A superior orders a subordinate to do something—clean the table, deliver a package, kill an innocent civilian. What is the significance of this communication? It neither mainly informs others about what the speaker believes nor expresses the speaker's attitudes and emotions. Rather it directs action. As long as the speaker is in a position of authority, the order also alters the listener's normative environment. Before the speaker gave the order, the subordinate had no duty to do that particular act; once the speaker gave the order, the listener had a new duty. (Of course, if an order is blatantly illegal, a listener has no legal obligation to perform it; but within the context of the social environment, the listener may still have some kind of nonlegal duty.) I call orders "situation-altering." They alter the circumstances the listener inhabits, rather than informing him of circumstances that already exist or revealing the speaker's feelings about those circumstances. When a speaker issues an order, his overwhelming objective is to have something *done;* instead of doing it himself, he orders a subordinate to do it. He is not aiming to inform or express; his order is a direct means of achieving a practical result. Do such orders deserve protection as speech?

The answer is no, but it requires some explanation and defense against objections. Some might argue that because speech often causes harmful results, we have little basis to distinguish orders from other communications. It is true that the spread of hatred and of pernicious ideas, protected by freedom of speech, causes harmful results. The theory of freedom of speech is that these harms are worth risking because of the special value of speech. Free-speech theory is not based on the childhood taunt, "Sticks and stones can break my bones but words can never hurt me." Words can and do hurt individuals and society. The theory is that the value of speech justifies the suffering of those occasional harms. What I am claiming about orders is that they lack the value of speech. They are much more action than speech.

A second objection to putting orders outside the boundaries of free speech might be that orders do express ideas and emotions implicitly. The factual premise lying behind this objection is sound. If a boss orders an employee to clean the table, one gathers both that the boss thinks the table is dirty and the employee is capable of cleaning it and that the boss wants the table cleaned.[31] So one can glean from a typical order something of a speaker's beliefs about circumstances and his attitudes toward them. But the same may be said about every action people perform. If I climb into my car and turn the ignition key, an observer could infer that I expect and want the engine to start and that I want to travel somewhere. In this loose sense, all actions are expressive. (In a stricter sense, an action is expressive only if the actor is *trying* to express something to someone else, which is not typically the case when I start my car.)

Although orders are implicitly expressive, they are typically no more expressive of beliefs and feelings than are other actions. The idea of freedom of speech is that speech deserves special protection in comparison with other actions. If all actions are expressive, and therefore deserve protection as speech, the idea of free speech collapses. The idea is based on the importance of protecting efforts by speakers to communicate information, ideas, attitudes, and feelings. That special importance does not attach to orders.

A final attempt to bring orders within the domain of free speech is to say that, after all, orders are a form of speech and therefore deserve protection. This claim rests on a rough categorization. Most verbal and written communication of words deserves protection as speech. (Some other acts, such as painting, writing of music, and communication by symbols, also deserve protection.) Orders are communications by words, and, as we have seen, they do implicitly convey beliefs and attributes. Therefore, they, along with all other communications by words, deserve protection as speech.

One major problem with this proposal is that the domain of protected speech should be more sensitive to the reasons for freedom of speech than it acknowledges. If much communication other than words is protected speech, it is also possible that some communication in words may not be protected. A related problem with the proposal to include all communication by words as free speech is that if one tried to give it practical effect, the difficulties might easily lead to reduced overall protection for speech, perhaps drastically reduced protection.

Let us imagine that Lee owns two delivery trucks. Lee fervently believes that government regulation is too pervasive and, in particular, that antipollution

---

31. Sometimes people give orders hoping they will be disobeyed. The boss may want the employee to get into trouble for disobeying the order or he may give the order (to kill a civilian) because a superior has ordered him to do so, without wanting the order to be carried out. However, in ordinary circumstances, an order is backed by a wish that it be performed.

devices on motor vehicles infringe the liberty of owners. Interviewed on local television one night, Lee says, "The government has no business making us use antipollution devices. They are expensive, cut down fuel efficiency, and interfere with our freedom. Any car owner who disables his antipollution device is morally justified in doing so." A week later, Lee collects his tools and commences the disabling of the device on one of his two trucks. He instructs the driver of the other truck to disable its device. Before either device is disabled, an inspector appears and tells Lee and his driver to stop. Can Lee be punished?

Lee's television talk was definitely protected speech. He did not expressly urge anyone to commit a crime (though he said criminal actions would be morally justified); nor did he create a clear and present, or imminent, danger under the Holmes–Brandeis test or under the *Brandenburg* formulation. As for his own actions of disabling a device, the First Amendment provides no protection. Lee has begun to commit a crime that has nothing to do with free speech.[32] That he happens to be committing the crime backed by a political conviction does not provide him with a defense. His behavior is secretive, not expressive. What about Lee's ordering his employee to disable the other device? The order, in itself, has no more to do with expression than Lee's beginning to dismantle a device himself. If Lee had only one truck, and the employee was disabling the device under Lee's instruction, should the employee be punishable but not Lee? Almost everyone agrees that people are properly punished for giving orders to other people to commit crimes,[33] even crimes that are not extremely serious.

Those who think orders should receive *some* protection are pushed to a position of saying they should get only a little protection, less than full-value speech. Thus, Lee's order would get less protection than his television talk, even though the talk might result in more devices being disabled than his order. If judges started with the premise that all communications, including orders, deserve some protection, but that many communications deserve little protection, the result would be a complex set of doctrines about levels of protection. And some levels of protection might be very slight—so slight

---

32. The criminal law does place limits, often fairly strict ones, on which acts of preparation count as attempts to commit crimes; but these limits are thought to be warranted by uncertainty whether people who start toward a criminal act will finish it and by the wish to encourage people to stop. The limits are not conceived as concerning free speech.

33. One might contend that Lee's order is protected speech *until* it is acted upon, but ordinarily the constitutional status of speech does not depend on whether someone picks up on the idea one has expressed.

they would never make a difference. If Lee's order is said to receive *some* protection but not enough to overcome any plausible reason for the state to make the order criminal, then the protection makes no practical difference. The introduction of such minimal levels of protection may eventually dilute protection when it really should matter. It is far preferable to say that orders deserve no protection whatever.[34]

If orders do not deserve protection, neither do agreements to act. Such agreements are commitments: they alter people's situations by creating duties to act where none existed before. Like orders, agreements to act, whether in a benign or criminal fashion, are dominantly situation-altering.[35] As with orders, one can infer beliefs, attitudes, and feelings held by people who agree; but that is not what agreements are about. Agreements set people on a course to act in the way they have agreed. The law has typically punished agreements to commit crimes. It may require an overt act in furtherance of an agreement, but the act may be quite innocent in itself. What is punished is the agreement,[36] not the act. Courts rarely say this,[37] but no one supposes that the criminal law of conspiracy raises serious First Amendment problems, as it would if agreements warranted protection as free speech. Thus, in our earlier illustration, Bruce and Cathy cannot claim the benefit of any "clear and present danger" test. Their agreement to commit the crime carries them outside any domain of constitutional protection.[38]

This brings us to Amy's encouragement of Bruce, a more difficult topic. Is Amy's urging of Bruce outside freedom of speech because she (1) actually counseled him to commit a crime, (2) spoke in private, or (3) had no ideological message? Some general observations about criminal solicitation will help put the First Amendment questions in perspective.

Criminal solicitation involves explicit counseling by one person that another person commit a crime. In the language of the Model Penal Code (a

---

34. For a contrary view, *see* Franklyn S. Haiman, "Speech Acts" and the First Amendment 10–20 (1993).

35. So, also, are offers to act in a certain way if the other person agrees. The offer of a bribe is situation-altering for both the listener and speaker. It allows the listener to close out an agreement to receive the bribe; it exposes the speaker to be bound if the listener responds in that way.

36. The agreement, indeed, is regarded as so significant that agreements to commit crimes are punishable at a stage much earlier than the preparations of an individual to commit the same crime would be punishable.

37. *See* Brown v. Hartlage, 456 U.S. 45, 55 (1982); State v. Blyth, 226 N.W.2d 250, 263 (Iowa 1975).

38. Most "threats" are also situation-altering and do not deserve protection as speech; but this is a complex topic in its own right that I do not address in this essay. *See* chapters 5 and 14 in Greenawalt, Speech, Crime, and the Uses of Language, *supra* note 3.

draft criminal code whose formulations have been influential in the law of many states), a person is guilty of criminal solicitation if, with the purpose of promoting the commission of a crime, "he commands, encourages or requests another person to engage in specific criminal conduct that would constitute such crime."[39] Amy's urging of Bruce is an encouragement (or request) that he engage in the specific criminal conduct of opening Powerball outlets.

An encouragement or request is a kind of imperative. It urges the listener to act in a certain way. In my distinction between situation-altering utterances and expressions of beliefs and feeling, where do such imperatives fall? If the speaker has no authority over the listener, an encouragement or request does not alter the listener's normative circumstances as does an order.

The critical distinction between a request and an order need not be in the words a speaker uses. Social convention often leads to orders being phrased as requests. If a coach says to a player, "Please stop taking so many wild shots," the coach is telling, not asking. When I talk about encouragements or requests, I mean those made in situations in which the listener is free to refuse. That is the key. If the listener need not comply, the encouraging remarks do not change his social duties to a significant extent.

My qualification concerning a "significant extent" is important here. When requests are made by people we know, we feel under some pressure to comply. A simple request does more than reveal an existing state of desires. I may know that a friend might prefer to have a window shut, but my reasons to shut the window are strengthened when she says, "Please shut the window." It is not polite to decline requests unless one has a good reason. On other occasions, a listener may have no such sense that he should comply because of some responsibility to the speaker. If a marathon runner hears a bystander shout, "Don't slow down now," the encouragement may have an effect, but not because the runner feels he owes anything to the bystander. I call requests and encouragements "weak imperatives," weak in the sense that they do not alter circumstances to nearly the same degree as orders, threats, agreements, and offers of agreement. To return to the example of Amy and Bruce, Amy's encouragement may have influenced Bruce; but the simple fact of Amy's proposing the plan would alone have had little effect. Bruce would not enter on a criminal course of conduct just because his mother encouraged him to do so.

Encouragements and requests can be as independent of expressions of beliefs and feelings as orders. In this respect, "Please shut the window" (a request) is the same as "Shut the window" (an order). An outsider can often

---

39. Model Penal Code § 5.02 (1985).

infer a speaker's beliefs and feelings from his making of a request, but beliefs and feelings are not the heart of a request any more than they are the heart of an order. However, encouragements (especially) and requests are often not made unembellished. The speaker often explains why the listener's performing an act would be desirable or why it matters to the speaker, or both. In this aspect, Amy's encouragement of Bruce is typical. The encouragement is tangled together with expressions of why Bruce's doing what she suggests would be good for him.

We can see, in summary, that weak imperatives occupy a kind of intermediate status between what are dominantly situation-altering utterances (orders and agreements to act) and what are dominantly expressions of belief and feeling. They cannot be relegated to the territory over which free speech has no application nearly as easily as can orders and agreements.

Criminal Solicitation and the First Amendment

I now face directly the question what the "clear and present danger" test and its *Brandenburg* revision have to do with explicit criminal counseling. We need initially to see the various possibilities and their implications. One possibility is that criminal counseling is a form of "advocacy," that criminal counseling is subject to the First Amendment test for protected speech, whatever that test is. Were this the approach, an explicit counseling of a criminal act might be protected because the crime urged was not serious enough, because the crime was not likely to happen (and perhaps was not proposed to happen) in the immediate future, and (under *Brandenburg*) was not sufficiently likely to happen at all, though the counseling shows that the speaker definitely wanted it to happen.

Another possibility is that the First Amendment gives no protection to criminal counseling. On this understanding, the advocacy that the First Amendment protects falls short of explicit counseling. It protects the advocacy of positions about various subjects, not the explicit urging that someone else commit a crime. Judge Hand once said that words "which have no purport but to counsel the violation of law cannot by any latitude of interpretation be a part of that public opinion which is the final source of government in a democratic state."[40] Of course, it would be foolish to deny that advocacy may accompany explicit counseling, but one might think that the counseling goes over the edge—that one can punish the counseling without any concern about free speech more generally. I indeed have argued a similar position about orders

---

40. Masses Pub. Co. v. Patten, 244 F. 535 (S.D.N.Y. 1917), *rev'd*, 246 F. 24 (2d Cir. 1917).

and agreements to act. These may be intertwined with advocacy, but they may be punished. The same position might be taken about explicit criminal counseling.

The third, intermediate, possibility is that advocacy is too close to counseling for the latter to be unprotected altogether, but that the degree of protection is not necessarily the same as that given to speech that falls short of counseling. The precise degree of protection might depend on the circumstances in which the counseling takes place and the reasons offered to the listener who is encouraged to commit the crime.

The Supreme Court has never indicated which of these three possibilities it intends, but it has offered occasional hints. In one of the cases decided a week after *Schenck*, Justice Holmes wrote, "We venture to believe that neither Hamilton, nor Madison, nor any other competent person then or later, ever supposed that to make criminal the counseling of a murder within the jurisdiction of Congress would be an unconstitutional interference with free speech."[41] This passage could be taken to mean that Holmes considered all explicit counseling of criminal acts to be outside the protection of the First Amendment, but the comment fits as comfortably with a view that any explicit counseling to murder would satisfy the "clear and present danger" test. (Remember, Holmes thought it was sufficient that the speaker *intend* to create a clear and present danger.)[42] In his *Abrams* dissent, Holmes commented, "I do not doubt for a moment that by the same reasoning that would justify punishing persuasion to murder, the United States constitutionally may punish speech that produces or is intended to produce a clear and imminent danger of substantive evils."[43] This passage, with its reference to "the same reasoning," suggests more strongly that explicit counseling should be treated like other advocacy that creates or is intended to create a clear and present danger.

Justice Brandeis's discussion of trespass in *Whitney v. California* gives a decidedly different impression. Recall that Justice Brandeis said that trespass was not a grave enough evil to satisfy the "clear and present danger" test—that speech that creates a clear and present danger of (only) trespass is constitutionally protected. A person might advocate a moral right to trespass despite imminent danger, Brandeis wrote; but he also remarked that a state might

---

41. *Frohwerk*, 249 U.S. at 206.

42. This assumption, however, does not itself establish that every counseling of murder would satisfy the test. Presumably, any murder would be a grave enough evil to satisfy the test, but there could be explicit counseling to commit a murder at some distant time. Not every instance of explicit counseling would satisfy the proximity aspect of clear and present danger.

43. *Abrams*, 250 U.S. at 627 (Holmes, J., dissenting).

"punish an attempt, a conspiracy, or an incitement to commit the trespass."[44] Thus, Justice Brandeis assumed that explicit counseling that did not meet the gravity requirement of the "clear and present danger" test could be punished; probably he would have had the same view about counseling that does not meet the proximity requirement. The theory would be that the First Amendment protects advocacy of moral and political rights, even when the rights claimed include the right to engage in criminal behavior, but that explicit counseling to criminal acts is not part of free speech.[45]

The reformulation of the applicable test in *Brandenburg v. Ohio* made the status of explicit counseling much more important than it had previously been. The reason is its treatment of intent and actual likelihood. Under *Brandenburg,* advocacy of law violation cannot be punished unless the speaker intends imminent law violation *and* it is likely to happen.[46] So long as the government needed to prove only actual likelihood *or* intent (Holmes's assumption), any counseling to commit a serious crime in the imminent future could be punished. The only counseling that would possibly be protected would be counseling of nonserious crimes like trespass (counseling of which would not be likely to be prosecuted in any event) and urging that a specific crime be committed in the more distant future. After *Brandenburg,* even counseling of imminent crimes may be protected if the likelihood that the listener will act is slight. If a speaker explicitly urges a listener to kill a particular person, his words may be protected if an objective observer would say that the likelihood of the crime being committed was not great.[47]

Brandenburg's speech before members of the Ku Klux Klan fell short of explicit counseling of specific crimes, so it is unclear whether the Court meant "advocacy" to include counseling. In all probability, the justices did not focus on the status of explicit counseling. Hess's comment that "We'll take the fucking street later"[48] might have been construed as urging others to commit specific crimes connected with blocking the street; but the comment, in context, amounted to a counsel of moderation not to try to take the street at that moment, and may well have been too vague to qualify as explicit counseling.

---

44. *Whitney,* 274 U.S. at 378 (Brandeis, J., concurring).

45. *See* Learned Hand's earlier opinion in *Masses, supra* note 40.

46. *Brandenburg,* 395 U.S. at 447.

47. I shall pass over the perspective from which one judges actual likelihood. Suppose the listener is in fact a government agent who is extremely unlikely to commit the crime but who appears to the speaker and to an objective observer likely to commit the crime?

48. *Hess,* 414 U.S. at 107.

For both reasons, the Court's application of the *Brandenburg* test in *Hess* does not represent a clear judgment that the test must be met if someone explicitly counsels another to commit a crime. Given the Court's silence on this subject since *Brandenburg* and *Hess,* the issue is not resolved.

How should it be resolved? The *Brandenburg* test is not appropriate for every instance of criminal solicitation. If one cousin writes another cousin a serious letter in June urging that the second cousin kill an aunt, from whom both cousins stand to inherit a large amount of money, when the aunt visits the second cousin in August, the solicitation should be punishable. Such a solicitation differs importantly from public speech in which the speaker urges a specific crime for political reasons.

The three potentially significant variables for constitutional protection concern the seriousness of the crime, the reasons the speaker offers the listener for committing the crime, and the publicness of the solicitation. I can pass quickly over the crime's seriousness. As we have seen, the gravity of the crime figured in some formulations of the "clear and present danger" test and that factor probably is carried over in the *Brandenburg* test, although that version makes no explicit reference to it. The seriousness of the crime can matter in three ways. A speaker may be shielded from punishment if a crime he urges is too trivial. Further, among crimes that are grave enough to support punishment, seriousness should matter for both likelihood and imminence. That is, the test's language—"producing imminent lawless action and . . . is likely to . . . produce such action"—should be construed somewhat flexibly in terms of the crime involved. If the speaker advocates a terrorist bombing that would kill hundreds of people, a likelihood of occurrence of 20 percent might be sufficient, although for an ordinary assault a likelihood of over 50 percent might be required. Similarly, if the bombing is to happen in ten days, that might be sufficiently imminent; even though for an ordinary assault "imminent" might mean within the next few minutes or hours. Although the seriousness of the crime someone solicits bears on the balance of speech values against other values, it does not affect whether speech values are involved. An address that urges people to assassinate government officials is as much speech as an address that urges people to trespass on government property.

Whether solicitation has an ideological character has more to do with free speech than does the seriousness of the crime. Is free speech really about encouraging a listener to commit a crime so that he, and perhaps the speaker, can get rich? Free speech seems to have much more to do with moral and political advocacy, claims that tie the speaker's encouragement to the listener's moral or political responsibility. If one person urges another to bomb an abortion clinic because they believe abortion is murder, or to burn military files because they believe the country is fighting an unjust war, these messages, if we put aside the criminal counseling, are obviously the stuff that free speech is about. One cousin urging another to commit murder to inherit money is not.

The distinction between moral and political advocacy and appeals to self-interest has intuitive plausibility as a measure of free-speech value, but it is a doubtful basis for a practical legal standard. The required line is not easy to draw, as Amy's conversation with Bruce illustrates. Amy may say that she believes in self-fulfillment and that Bruce, in her view, has not been fulfilling his potential. She urges him to set up Powerball outlets so he can have the satisfaction of being responsible for a difficult enterprise. Her appeal is not exactly political or moral; but free speech concerns not just political matters, but also how people lead a "good" life.[49] Certainly it would cover claims that an aesthetic life is more valuable than one in which artistic values have no place. Amy's ideas of the good life may be more mundane, but her counseling issues from her opinion about how Bruce may achieve greater fulfillment. If the ideological persuasion that counts for free speech cannot be limited to political advocacy and direct assertions about moral rights and duties, Amy's remarks are not so easy to disqualify. A line between ideological persuasion and other grounds for urging people to commit crimes cannot bear too much practical weight for decisions about constitutional protection of explicit counseling.

A private–nonprivate distinction may have significance and work better practically. The relevance of this distinction should *not* be grounded on the view that free speech is about speech in public, not at all about private communication. The flaw in this view is that most people discuss political, social, and moral issues with family and a few close friends and associates at work, not in public settings. And these myriad conversations are likely to have more influence on what many people believe than most public addresses. It would be paradoxical, even perverse, to say that the government may freely regulate what is said in these private settings, even though it is sharply restricted in its ability to control public speech. Of course, the practical difficulty of regulating private communications is some protection against government intrusion,[50] but that is no reason to withhold constitutional protection. In general, private speech deserves protection similar to that given public speech.

---

49. I should mention that there is a minority view that free speech in the First Amendment is exclusively related to political subjects.

50. If a government is oppressive enough, turning children into informers against their parents or making broad use of electronic surveillance, it may be able to restrict private conversations.

But does this conclusion apply to criminal counseling?[51] I think not. The reason has to do with a crucial assumption that lies behind the standards of imminence and likelihood. As Justice Brandeis emphasized, a crucial assumption about free speech concerns countervailing speech. If one person or group urges people to do one thing, others are free to urge the opposite, and listeners will make their decision in the context of a variety of messages. Another aspect of public speech is that officials can know what has been said; they may be able to take precautions to lessen the chances of a crime being successfully committed.[52] However, when one person with some influence privately urges another to commit a crime, there is opportunity neither for directly countervailing speech nor for official precautions. No one else knows that an individual or a small group has been urged to commit a particular crime, so no one is in a position to caution against that course of action. And the police are not aware that the particular threat is posed. Amy's conversation with Bruce is an example. Unless Bruce happens to ask, no acquaintance is likely to tell him it is imprudent and immoral to break the state's gambling laws. Amy's remarks (apart from the fortuitous presence of an electronic bug) would not alert the police that they should be on the lookout for operatives trying to set up Powerball outlets. In these circumstances, the requirements of imminence and likelihood provide too much protection for dangerous speech.

People can reasonably disagree about whether explicit criminal counseling should *ever* receive constitutional protection and, if so, how much protection it should receive in various settings. Here are my own suggestions. Because public advocacy can be very closely tied to counseling of certain criminal actions, counseling in a public context[53] should receive protection closely similar to that provided by the *Brandenburg* test. Public speech should be constitutionally punishable if and only if (1) the speaker seriously and expressly urges the commission of a specific crime in the very near future, and (2) it is reasonably likely that the speech will contribute to the commission of the crime in the very near future.

Private nonideological solicitation should be punishable if the speaker expresses himself in a manner that conveys a fixed and potentially influential determination that the crime should be committed. This test is much less

---

51. I am not suggesting that the reasons that follow have unique application to criminal counseling, but they have special force for it because the speaker's object is to cause a crime to be committed.

52. This does depend on the nature of the crime. If a racist speaker urged members of his audience to kill a member of another race, at random, the police could do little to protect everyone at risk.

53. I am not including here public advertising designed to earn money or other benefits for the advertiser. *See* GREENAWALT, SPEECH, CRIME, AND THE USES OF LANGUAGE, *supra* note 3, at 270–71.

protective. This sort of solicitation should receive First Amendment protection only if the speaker expresses a tentative or nonserious wish that the listener should not take as a final or reflective judgment, or if the speaker reasonably believes that the remark will not have a serious effect on the listener. Otherwise, private nonideological counseling should be punishable.

Private ideological solicitation should receive somewhat greater protection. A serious private ideological solicitation should be punishable unless it fails to present a significant danger of criminal harm. Under these standards, Amy's remarks could be punished, whether one considers them ideological or not.[54]

Conclusion

We have seen that in its origins in *Schenk*, the "clear and present danger" test leaves unresolved important issues about content and coverage. Over the years, the justices have spoken to (1) whether imminence is an independent requirement, (2) whether the evil that is threatened must be serious, and (3) the relation between actual and intended danger. We now have a test for subversive advocacy whose dimensions are tolerably clear. For punishment to be permissible, the evil must be "imminent" (a term that should be understood as somewhat flexible), the speaker must intend its occurrence, and its actual occurrence must be likely. In addition, the evil must probably have a certain degree of gravity.

The hardest questions concern the coverage of the test, and most particularly whether it protects explicit criminal counseling. I have urged that the test is not relevant for orders or for agreements to commit crimes. This conclusion is widely assumed, if not often stated. Criminal counseling is more troublesome and admits of a variety of positions, all of which can reasonably be defended. Although straightforward counseling, which does not include an offer to enter a conspiracy, is not frequently prosecuted, its status is important for understanding how free speech relates to the commission of crimes. I have strongly argued that garden-variety private solicitation of crimes for private gain does not warrant *much* constitutional protection. With less assurance, I have suggested that public solicitation does warrant protection similar to that given by *Brandenburg*.

---

54. I have indicated how difficult this categorization is. I am inclined to say that proposing a crime on the ground that it will promote the listener's ordinary welfare should not count as ideological. But the crucial point is that a constitutional test should avoid making too much turn on the decision whether solicitation is ideological.

Like Kent Greenawalt, Richard Posner begins "The Speech Market and the Legacy of *Schenck*" with the Supreme Court's 1919 decision in *Schenck v. United States*. And like Vincent Blasi, Judge Posner distinguishes between "moral" and "instrumental" rationales for the constitutional protection of free expression and endorses an instrumental approach. Similar starting points, however, do not guarantee similar conclusions.

In this essay, Judge Posner argues that because "the legal conception of freedom of speech is plastic, mutable, and contestable" it may appropriately "take its shape from the practical considerations that the instrumental approach brings into view." Tracing this approach back to Justice Holmes's opinion for the Court in *Schenck*, Judge Posner offers an economic analysis of freedom of speech that attempts to identify and then to weigh in an operational manner the relevant costs and benefits of both expression and government regulation. Judge Posner notes that "the challenge to the instrumentalist . . . is to identify situations in which the variables can actually be measured . . . and the costs and benefits of free speech thus estimated." He then reformulates the First Amendment as follows: $A_x - B_x = -(pH/(1 + d)^n + 0)_x$.

Judge Posner argues that such a "cost–benefit approach, however alien to the characteristically high-flown rhetoric in which lawyers and judges tend to talk about free speech, is consistent with the Amendment's language and history." In an effort to meet his own challenge, Judge Posner then considers at length the application of this economic analysis across such diverse areas as subversive advocacy, commercial advertising, hate speech, obscenity, and campaign finance regulation.—GRS

RICHARD A. POSNER

The Speech Market and the Legacy of *Schenck*

Two Models

There are two ways in which to approach the question of the proper scope of freedom of speech. The first is the instrumental approach: freedom of speech is to be valued to the extent that it promotes specified goals, such as political stability, economic prosperity, and personal happiness.[1] The second is the moral approach: freedom of speech is to be valued to the extent that it is a corollary or implication of a proper moral conception of persons, for example that they are to be regarded as self-directing beings and therefore should be entitled both to express their ideas and opinions and to receive any ideas or opinions that might facilitate their realizing their potential as free, rational choosers.[2] In a word, what I am calling the moral approach assigns an *intrinsic* value to speech, though not necessarily a value that cannot be overridden by other values. The moral approach to freedom of speech, like other moral theories, seems to me, and not only to me, spongy and arbitrary.[3]

A revised version of this essay appears in RICHARD A. POSNER, FRONTIERS OF LEGAL THEORY 62–94 (2001), copyright © 2001 by the President and Fellows of Harvard College; reprinted by permission of Harvard University Press. I thank Stanley Fish, Lawrence Lessig, Eric Posner, Geoffrey Stone, David Strauss, and Cass Sunstein for exceedingly helpful comments on a previous draft, and Elizabeth Beetz for her very helpful research assistance.

1. For elaborations of this approach, *see* RICHARD A. POSNER, ECONOMIC ANALYSIS OF LAW, ch. 27 (5th ed. 1998); Posner, *Free Speech in an Economic Perspective,* 20 SUFFOLK U. L. REV. 1 (1986); Daniel A. Farber, *Free Speech without Romance: Public Choice and the First Amendment,* 105 HARV. L. REV. 554 (1991). For criticism, *see* Peter J. Hammer, Note, *Free Speech and the "Acid Bath": An Evaluation and Critique of Judge Richard Posner's Economic Interpretation of the First Amendment,* 87 MICH. L. REV. 499 (1988). And for a recent application, *see* Eric Rasmusen, *The Ethics of Desecration: Flag Burning and Related Activities,* 27 J. LEGAL STUD. 245 (1998).

2. *See, e.g.,* Thomas Scanlon, *A Theory of Freedom of Expression,* 1 PHIL. & PUB. AFF. 204 (1972). Does this mean that if, as in much nazi and communist speechifying, the speaker is urging the audience to despoil other people for the audience's benefit, suppressing the speech would impair the autonomy of the audience in some censurable way? Why should an audience be thought to have a moral entitlement to receive such information and encouragement?

3. For a forceful criticism of the moral approach from within philosophy, *see* Joshua Cohen, *Freedom of Expression,* 22 PHIL. & PUB. AFF. 207 (1993). Although Cohen claims to accept a mixture of intrinsic

The instrumental approach has its own shortcomings, but it has the virtue that very few Americans believe that the instrumental values and costs of freedom of speech are *irrelevant* to deciding how extensive that freedom should be. This is not to say that Americans consider freedom of speech morally neutral; but they might be persuaded that moral theory is not going to resolve free-speech issues any more than theology is going to resolve disputes under the First Amendment's religion clauses. The instrumental approach skirts contentious moral and ideological issues and allows freedom of speech to be analyzed productively by reference to whatever goals one wishes to specify—productively because it is much easier to reason about means to given ends than to reason about the ends themselves. The biggest challenge to the instrumentalist, and one that I shall particularly emphasize, is to give the approach structure, so that it is not just an invitation to judges to exercise an uncanalized discretion.

That freedom of speech is a constitutional right may seem to make speculation about its optimal scope idle. But the First Amendment uses the term "freedom of speech or of the press" without defining it; the preconstitutional history of the term is murky; and the judicial decisions construing it do not compose a harmonious pattern either across time or across the different subfields of free-speech law. In short, the *legal* conception of freedom of speech is plastic, mutable, and contestable, and so it may take its shape from the practical considerations that the instrumental approach brings into view and may change as those considerations change.

Origins of the Instrumental Approach

In fact, the instrumental approach to free speech, although certainly not commanded by the First Amendment, has a respectable constitutional pedigree. The case that first put the constitutional protection of free speech on the map and that is the occasion for this book—*Schenck v. United States*[4]—took an instrumental approach. Charles Schenck, the general secretary of the Socialist Party, had, after the United States entered World War I, arranged for the distribution of fifteen thousand leaflets to draftees. The leaflets denounced the war and urged the draftees to oppose the draft. The leaflets did not advocate illegal measures, such as refusing to serve, but Schenck (and his codefendants, other officials of the Socialist Party) did not deny that a reasonable jury could have

---

and instrumental justifications for free speech, *id.* at 230, his intrinsic justification—basically, that people like to express their opinions, *see id.* at 224–25—I would call extrinsic: it is free speech as an argument in the individual's utility function.

4. 249 U.S. 47 (1919).

found that the intent of the mailing had been to "influence [persons subject to the draft] to obstruct the carrying of it out."[5] The Court upheld the convictions, rejecting the defendants' claim that the mailing was protected by the First Amendment. Holmes's opinion for the Court concedes that "in ordinary times" the defendants might have had a First Amendment privilege to distribute these leaflets. "But the character of every act depends upon the circumstances in which it is done. The most stringent protection of free speech would not protect a man in falsely shouting fire in a theater, and causing a panic."[6] Holmes set forth the following test: speech can be suppressed when "the words used are used in such circumstances and are of such a nature as to create a clear and present danger that they will bring about the substantive evils that Congress has a right to prevent."[7] Since the country was at war, Congress had a legitimate and indeed urgent interest in preventing the recruitment of soldiers from being obstructed, and the defendants' conduct had both the intent and a tendency to obstruct that recruitment.

In the case of falsely shouting fire in a crowded theater, the harm caused by speech is immediate, palpable, grave, and nearly certain to occur. In the case of mailing antiwar propaganda to draftees, the harm (obstruction of recruitment) may be great if it occurs, but it is less certain to occur than in the case of shouting fire in the crowded theater; the *probabilistic* character of most speech harm is salient in the draft case. Holmes's "clear and present danger" test requires that the probability be high (though not necessarily as high as in the shouting-fire case) and the harm imminent; stated differently, the *danger* of harm must be great. An economist would say that to quantify an uncertain harm you must discount (multiply) the harm if it occurs by the probability of its occurrence. The greater that probability is, the greater is the expected harm and therefore the greater the justification for preventing or punishing the act, here the speech, that creates the danger.[8] And, in turn, the clearer (that is, more certain) and more immediate the danger is, the likelier is the harm actually to occur. The economist would add that the *magnitude* of the harm if it occurs is also relevant, for it is the magnitude that is discounted to determine the expected harm. I shall come back to this vital point, which Holmes's formula overlooks though it may be implicit in the contrast he draws between wartime and ordinary times.

---

5. *Id.* at 51.

6. *Id.* at 52.

7. *Id.*

8. This formulation is explicit in Learned Hand's restatement of the "clear and present danger" test in *United States v. Dennis*, 183 F.2d 201, 212 (2d Cir. 1950), *aff'd*, 341 U.S. 494 (1951).

Immediacy has an additional significance well brought out by the example of falsely shouting fire in a theater: the more immediate the harm brought about by the speech, the less feasible it is to rely on competition among speakers and on other sources of information to avert the harm without need for public intervention. In economic terms, "market failure"[9] is more likely when dangerous speech occurs in circumstances in which counterspeech, a form of self-protection, is infeasible. But to suppose that speech can be regulated *only* when the harm is immediate—as in "without a showing of likely, immediate, and grave harm, government cannot regulate political speech"[10]— is questionable from an instrumental standpoint, as it denies the trade-off between immediacy and gravity. A similar denial is implicit in requiring that the harm be both likely and grave. If it is grave enough, it should be regulable even though unlikely, and if likely enough, it should be regulable even though not particularly grave, though both judgments depend on circumstances (how likely? how harmful? how beneficial? how costly to suppress?).

The possibility of recasting the instrumental approach in specifically economic terms is suggested by Holmes's use, in his *Abrams* dissent several months after *Schenck,* of the market metaphor for freedom of speech. He said that an idea is true (more precisely, as close to true as it is possible for us to come) only if it prevails in competition with other ideas in the marketplace of ideas.[11] So government disserves truth by suppressing competition in ideas. In thus identifying a benefit of freedom of speech, Holmes, who in *Schenck* had discussed just the cost, in *Abrams* can be seen sketching in the other side of the cost–benefit algorithm.[12] The different emphases are natural because in *Schenck* Holmes was rejecting the First Amendment claim and in *Abrams* urging its acceptance. The cases were so similar that Holmes has been charged with inconsistency. In both cases extreme leftists were agitating against U.S. participation in World War I, though the specific goal in *Abrams* was to discourage sending troops to Russia to oppose the Bolsheviks, who had just

---

9. The sources of market failure in speech markets are emphasized in Albert Breton & Ronald Wintrobe, *Freedom of Speech vs. Efficient Regulation in Markets for Ideas,* 17 J. ECON. BEHAV. & ORG. 217 (1992).

10. CASS R. SUNSTEIN, DEMOCRACY AND THE PROBLEM OF FREE SPEECH 122 (1993).

11. Abrams v. United States, 250 U.S. 616, 630 (1919). Holmes owed this point to Charles Sanders Peirce and, before him, to John Stuart Mill. *See* David S. Bogen, *The Free Speech Metamorphosis of Mr. Justice Holmes,* 11 HOFSTRA L. REV. 97, 120, 188 (1982).

12. In treating Holmes's *Schenck* and *Abrams* opinions as complementary, I depart from the more common view, well argued in DAVID M. RABBAN, FREE SPEECH IN ITS FORGOTTEN YEARS 280–82, 324–25, 346–55 (1997), that they are inconsistent. Rabban bases his view in part on passages in the *Schenck* opinion that seem to undercut the speech-protective thrust of "clear and present danger." The consistency of the two opinions is argued in Bogen, *supra* note 11.

made peace with Germany. But there is an important distinction between the cases. The defendants in *Schenck* were actually trying to obstruct the draft, by mailing leaflets to draftees. The *Abrams* defendants were distributing the leaflets at large; although some draftees and munitions workers may have been recipients, no evidence was presented that the defendants had tried to get the leaflets into the hands of either group.[13] Thus the danger of an actual obstruction of the war effort was less in *Abrams*.

These two opinions of Holmes contain the germ of an instrumental conception of freedom of speech. But it is only a germ. The analysis of the costs of speech is incomplete in *Schenck* because Holmes focuses only on the probability of harm if the speech is allowed and not on the magnitude of the harm if it occurs; thus he is looking only at one determinant of the (expected) cost of free speech. And the *Abrams* dissent does not examine the possibility, an implicit premise of *Schenck*, that competition between ideas will not always yield truth—in *Schenck*, the truth that the draftees ought to fight, and in the theater hypothetical the truth that there is no fire. Indeed, it may be doubted whether "truth" was even involved in *Schenck*. The concern was not that the defendants in that case were lying, but that they were imperiling an important national project; the analogy is to disseminating a truthful formula for making poison gas. These are cases in which competition in ideas is undesired even or perhaps especially if it produces truth.

The Instrumental Approach Formalized and Defended

Can the approach introduced by Holmes be generalized and made operational? It can be formalized, though that is not the same thing. If the benefits of challenged speech are given by B; the cost (a fire, desertion, riot, rebellion, and so on) if the speech is allowed by H (for harm) or O (for offensiveness); the probability that the cost will actually materialize if the speech is allowed by p; the rate at which future costs or benefits are discounted to the present by d (like p a number between 0 and 1); the number of years (or other unit of time) between when the speech occurs and the harm from the speech materializes or is likely to occur if the speech is allowed by n; and the cost of administering a regulation banning the speech by A, then the speech should be allowed if but only if

(1) $\quad B \geq pH/(1 + d)^n + O - A,$

which, in words, is if but only if the benefits of the speech equal or exceed its

---

13. *See* Richard Polenberg, Fighting Faiths: The Abrams Case, the Supreme Court, and Free Speech 104 (1987).

costs discounted by their probability and by their futurity, and reduced by the costs of administering a ban.

The reason the administrative costs (A) must be subtracted from the costs of the speech is that if the speech is permitted, the costs of administering a prohibition of it are saved. That is why the larger A is (as well as the smaller p, H, and O are and the larger d and n are), the more likely it is that the benefits of the speech exceed its costs. Another way to see this is to rewrite inequality (1) as: ban the speech if but only if

(2) $pH/(1 + d)^n + O \geq B + A,$

which is to say, if but only if the expected costs of the speech exceed the sum of the benefits of the speech and the costs of administering a prohibition of it. The implicit assumption—that administering a *protection* of free speech is costless—is unrealistic. But the only thing that is important for the analysis is that the administrative cost of prohibition exceed the administrative cost of protection. If so, then A can be viewed as the first cost minus the second.

Here is an alternative way of formulating the essential trade-offs. Let x be the degree of strictness with which potentially harmful or dangerous speech is regulated; the bigger x is, the less freedom of speech there is. If π (for "profit") represents the net social benefits of speech, then

(3) $\pi(x) = B(x) - (pH/(1 + d)^n + O)(x) - A(x)$

That is, the net benefits of speech are the gross benefits minus the costs, including both the harm and offensiveness caused by the speech and the costs of regulating speech. Stricter regulation (a higher x) reduces both the gross benefits and the speech costs, while raising the regulatory costs (A). The optimal strictness of regulation is given by differentiating π with respect to x and setting the result equal to zero, which yields

(4) $A_x - B_x = -(pH/(1 + d)^n + O)_x$

where the subscripts denote derivatives. In words, optimal strictness is attained when one more turn of the strictness screw would add more to the cost of regulation and the impairment of speech values[14] than it would reduce the harm and offensiveness of speech.

I offer these formulas as a heuristic, a way of framing and thinking about the regulation of speech, rather than as an algorithm for use by judges. The

---

14. Because B_x is negative (an increase in the strictness of regulation reduces speech benefits), $-B_x$ is positive, as is (for the same reason—an increase in x reduces the social costs imposed by speech) the right-hand side of equation (4).

problems of operationalizing the instrumental (or any) approach to free speech are formidable, because of the indeterminacies that pervade the field. We just don't know a great deal about the social consequences of various degrees of freedom of speech.

To bring out the formulas' heuristic value requires me to say more about two of the variables—*B,* the benefits of speech, and *O,* offensiveness. The first thing to note about *B* is that it need have nothing to do with the promotion of social or scientific progress or of political freedom or stability; aesthetic or even sexual pleasure is as much a genuine benefit as democracy or truth, though it need not be as great a benefit. Second, and very important, *B* can take on a negative value. That is, some restrictions on speech actually promote speech. Consider the following variant of the Supreme Court's decision in *Arkansas Educational Television Commission v. Forbes.*[15] A publicly owned television station wishes to sponsor a debate among presidential candidates. The problem is that there are (let us say) ten such candidates, all but two from fringe parties such as the vegetarians and the socialists. If to avoid restricting speech the station invites all the candidates to participate in the debate, the time available to the frontrunners will be drastically curtailed. Yet if only because the fringe candidates have no chance of winning, what the frontrunners have to say is probably more valuable to the audience than what the fringe candidates have to say.[16] And so a debate that is limited to frontrunners may generate a larger and more attentive audience, as well as give the members of the audience more helpful information about the issues and candidates. Hence restricting the speech opportunity of the fringe candidates may increase the speech benefits of the debate overall.

As for *O,* offensiveness: If a person shouts "Fire!" in a crowded theater (when there is no fire—and maybe when there is!) and causes a panic in which other patrons are trampled, there is undeniable harm. And likewise if a sale of pornography results in a rape that would not have occurred had the sale not taken place. But what about the indignation that wells up out of the mere knowledge that pornography is being sold or atheism or socialism being propagated? Is this indignation any different from any other disutility? Mill thought so. He distinguished between "self-regarding" and "other-regarding" acts, the former term referring to acts that have tangible effects on the person

---

15. 523 U.S. 666 (1998).

16. Probably, not certainly. Major parties can originate as fringe parties, fringe parties can contribute ideas that are later picked up by major parties, and fringe candidates can become major candidates— all points illustrated, by the way, by the rise of Hitler and the Nazi Party. Such illustrations are pertinent as reminders that even free political speech is not an unalloyed blessing.

harmed by them and the latter to acts that harm a person only through the knowledge that they are occurring. Mill's example was the outrage English people felt at knowing that polygamy was being practiced openly (at the time he was writing) in Utah, thousands of miles away.[17] But a cost is a cost whether it is the result of actually seeing (for example, seeing a man exposing his genitals as a result of having been aroused by pornography) or just reading about (for example, reading about the arousal effects of pornography).

Later I shall suggest a pragmatic (not Mill's moral) argument for banishing considerations of offensiveness from free-speech analysis. For now, the most important point is that the fact that a harm is mediated as it were by thought or recollection, rather than being the product of an immediate sense impression, has no significance in itself. Another point to bear in mind is that the "clear and present danger" test is not designed for objections based on offensiveness; for the harm of offense is not deferred or probabilistic, but immediate and certain. That is why, unlike the costs that I denote by H (for harm), equations (1) and (2) treat O, the offensiveness cost, as present and certain rather than future and hypothetical. In Holmes's day the right of government to repress offensive speech of a sexual character was so taken for granted that Holmes felt no need to develop a free-speech test broad enough to encompass offensive as well as dangerous speech, though there is a sense, of course, in which the pamphlets in *Abrams* and *Schenck* were, whether or not actually dangerous, "offensive" to patriotic sentiment.

The formulas do not refer explicitly to the government's *motivation* in suppressing particular speech. For example, it might be to stifle criticism of government officials, impose ideological uniformity, or prevent opposition candidates from competing on equal terms. Tests based on motivation are often unsatisfactory, because motivation is easily concealed. Usually motivations have to be inferred from consequences, and a test that focuses on consequences invites us to cut out the middleman, as it were. A law forbidding criticism of legislators would be bad under my approach because its costs would exceed any reasonable estimate of its benefits; nothing would be added by observing that the motivation for the law was probably selfish.

The challenge to the instrumentalist, which I take up in the next section, is to identify situations in which the variables in the formulas can actually be measured, however roughly, and the benefits and costs of free speech thus estimated. But it is important to note here that *if* the approach can thus be made operational, it can be squared with the First Amendment. A cost–benefit approach, however alien to the characteristically high-flown rhetoric

---

17. *See* JOHN STUART MILL, ON LIBERTY, ch. 4 (1859).

in which lawyers and judges tend to talk about free speech, is consistent with the Amendment's language and history (including its judicial history), though it is not compelled by either. For it is just the formalization of the instrumental approach, an approach that I have noted has the sanction of influential decisions—the *Schenck* majority opinions and the *Abrams* dissent having long ago attained canonical status in free-speech law. It is not the only approach the courts have used;[18] it is merely a contender to be the governing approach. But such is the fluidity of free-speech doctrine that the instrumental approach could be given primacy without doing undue violence to precedent. It may lack the rhetorical elevation characteristic of the discourse of freedom of speech from Milton to Meiklejohn—though there is hardly a more eloquent opinion in the history of American law than Holmes's dissent in *Abrams*. Yet the approach would not even knock freedom of speech off the perch that it occupies by virtue of being classified as a "preferred" liberty. Ordinary legislation doesn't have to pass a cost–benefit test in order to comply with the Constitution, and much of it could not get within miles of passing such a test. But under the cost–benefit approach to freedom of speech, legislative or other governmental action that restricts speech is permitted only if the benefits of the restriction can be shown, with some degree of confidence, to exceed the costs. Making it harder for government to regulate speech than action is not only a constitutional dictate but also the implication of the instrumental approach, though (as we shall see) not to every form of speech that has been brought under constitutional protection.

What is needed to make the instrumental approach thoroughly orthodox is to show how the legal–doctrinal categories are isomorphic with the instrumental ones. I believe it is possible to show this, at least to a considerable extent. Take the elaborate jurisprudence of "fora."[19] There are traditional public forums, designated public forums, limited public forums, and nonpublic forums. The first category consists mainly of public streets, sidewalks, and parks, which have traditionally been available for public assembly and demonstrations. The second includes publicly owned sites that, while not traditionally dedicated to such purposes, the government has decided to throw open to them. The third kind (often treated in the cases as part of the second) consists of public sites configured for a specific type of expression, for example a

---

18. Notably, in Brandenburg v. Ohio, 395 U.S. 444 (1969) (per curiam), the Supreme Court's adopted an extremely narrow version of the "clear and present danger" test, cutting back on the essentially economic test announced in Judge Hand's opinion in *Dennis*.

19. Summarized in many places, for example *Perry Educ. Ass'n v. Perry Local Educators' Ass'n*, 460 U.S. 37, 45–46 (1983). The archaic use of the Latin plural lends a spurious air of erudition to this jurisprudence.

publicly owned theater. The fourth includes all other public property, some of which might be suitable for expressive activity (for example, the streets and sidewalks on a military base or the concourse of an airport) but none of which is intended for such activity. In categories one and two the government can regulate only the time, place, and manner of the speech; in category three it can confine the type of speech to the type for which the facility is designed; in four it can limit speech as it wishes, provided it maintains neutrality among competing points of view (this proviso applies to the other three categories as well, of course).

These distinctions make a rough kind of economic sense. The traditional and designated public forums can be used for expressive activities without great cost provided that restrictions to prevent crowding are imposed, and these are permitted. The limited-purpose forum is apt to be nonviable if the limitation is not respected; imagine what it would do to a theater if the management had to allow it to be used for demonstrations, political rallies, picketing, and like activities. This is another case, like *Forbes*, of speech values being in both pans of the balance—of restrictions on speech promoting speech.[20] Finally, the business of government could hardly be conducted if any piece of public property that was physically suitable for demonstrations or other expressive activities could be commandeered for such purposes.

Another value of the instrumental approach, besides its making practical sense out of some arcane legal distinctions, is that it invites attention—Holmes was helpfully explicit about this in *Schenck*—to the *context* of the speech that is sought to be suppressed: war versus peace, the crowded theater versus the empty theater. Attention to context can help dispel the provincialism and anachronism that lead many modern students of freedom of speech to denounce the restrictions on speech that have been (and in some cases still are being) imposed by societies very different from that of the United States today. This country is so rich, powerful, secure, and politically stable, and its people are so well informed by historical and international standards and have such easy access to divergent points of view, that allowing people to say whatever they please is, with very few exceptions, simply not dangerous. This has not always been, and still is not everywhere, true, and so the instrumentalist is neither surprised by nor necessarily critical of the fact that freedom of speech has not always and everywhere been understood as capaciously as it is today in this country. To put this differently, modern thinking about free speech is colored by the hindsight fallacy. Knowing with the wisdom of hindsight that

---

20. Still another example is copyright law, which by limiting copying increases the financial incentives to create intellectual property.

socialist agitation never posed a real threat to the country (though this was not known at the time), free-speech scholars tend to dismiss the concerns expressed by Holmes in the *Schenck* opinion. Yet many of the same people who criticize *Schenck* and *Dennis* are fearful about free speech on the Internet. The breadth of protection that the law accords to speech seems therefore to be a function not of moral insight but of the perceived harmlessness of the protected speech. And if we were consistent in our use of hindsight, we would not be in favor of a generous construal of freedom of speech across the board. If in retrospect it is apparent that socialist agitation in this country was harmless, it is equally apparent that efforts by the Weimar republic to suppress Nazi speech would have been salutary.

Speech may be harmless yet deeply offensive. But if, as seems to be the case, norms are losing their grip on the behavior of Americans—if we are increasingly a law-governed society of individualists rather than a norm-governed society of sodalities—then the level of indignation at people who flout norms is unlikely to reach a pitch of intensity great enough to mobilize the forces of government. Orthodoxy and offensiveness are the two sides of the same coin; if very little is orthodox, very little is likely to be highly offensive to a large enough national majority to precipitate serious efforts at suppression. Most Americans are somewhat religious, somewhat egalitarian, and even somewhat straitlaced; but many are not and those that are tend to be only weakly so. They are pretty hard to shock. At the local and even the state level, however, there is considerably more homogeneity, and as a result the pressures for suppression tend to be stronger at these levels. With suppression likelier but the consequences less grave, the expected cost of suppression may be no less at the local than at the national level and if so this would provide a functional reason for the Supreme Court's decision to apply the full force of the Free Speech Clause of the First Amendment to state and local action through a by no means inevitable interpretation of the Fourteenth Amendment.

Can the Instrumental Approach Be Operationalized?

An approach that makes costs and benefits its centerpiece is vulnerable to criticism if the costs or benefits are highly uncertain. This is a problem for the instrumental approach to free speech because, to begin with, determining the benefits of speech by the methods available to the law is generally infeasible, or, in economic terms, insuperably costly. What the much-ridiculed history of censorship shows is not that censorship is always and everywhere a mistaken policy but that censors are rarely able to determine the truth or other value of dangerous or offensive speech. The inherent difficulty of making such determinations is compounded by the fact that false claims and mistaken theories can have considerable social value, not only (as Mill famously stressed in chapter 2 of *On Liberty*) by stimulating the defenders of truth to think harder about their views, articulate them more persuasively, and support them with more evidence, but also by bringing to light sources of disaffection or misunderstanding that may require corrective action. Both points are illustrated by "hate speech" and verbal harassment generally (for example, verbal sexual harassment, not involving either threats or solicitations, in the workplace). To the extent that hate speech is knitted out of misconceptions about the objects of hatred, such as blacks and homosexuals, allowing it to be vented forces the advocates of these groups to go beyond pious exhortations to equality and unconvincing denials of social pathologies associated with the groups (such as criminal violence in the case of blacks and sexually transmitted disease in the case of male homosexuals). And it enables the government to identify the sources of ignorance and resentment that motivate the hate speakers and to take steps to remove the sources. It is a separate and difficult question whether and to what extent the costs of hate speech to the missions of universities and employers justify repression of such speech. I shall come back to that question later; my only point here is that such speech should not be assumed to be barren of social benefits even if it has little or even no truth value, just as it cannot be assumed to be socially beneficial just because it is true.

A related pragmatic benefit of tolerating hateful speech lies in preventing the speaker from signaling his conviction by being willing to be imprisoned or otherwise punished for his beliefs. Lenity is the antidote to martyrdom. The martyr "puts his money where his mouth is" and this enhances the credibility of his message. Paradoxically, tolerating inflammatory speech may lower rather than raise the temperature of public debate by making it more difficult for speakers to prove that they are in deadly earnest about what they are saying. The cheaper such talk is, the less credible it is; toleration keeps it cheap. Of course, it might be a good thing or a bad thing to eliminate martyrdom; this is an example of the indeterminacies that plague the analysis of free-speech issues.

It might seem that while estimating the benefits of speech on a case-by-case method might be infeasible, a categorial approach would be feasible. The approach, very popular among commentators on free speech, involves the creation of a hierarchy in which, for example, political and scientific speech receives the most protection on the ground that it is the most valuable from a social standpoint or that (in the case of political speech) it is more central to the concerns that animated the framers and ratifiers of the First Amendment. Commercial advertising receives less, along with art and entertainment, including pornography. Criminal threats and solicitations receive no protection. The categorial approach works only with the last category. If the *only* purpose and likely effect of a speech is to engender uncontroversially criminal activity, then the speech is demonstrably worthless—the left-hand side of inequality (1) is zero. And then the only issue is whether the costs of the speech exceed the costs of prohibiting it, that is, whether the right-hand side of the inequality is positive. What made the communist cases, such as *Dennis,* difficult was that the Communist Party U.S.A. was both the conspiratorial agent of a hostile foreign government and a source of potentially valuable ideas about the economy, social classes, racism, foreign policy, and other important social phenomena.

Within the broad range of types of speech that confer some lawful benefits, the hierarchizing approach confuses total with marginal benefits. It might be worse from an overall social standpoint to ban all political speech than to ban all art;[21] but that is not the choice that confronts a tribunal asked to ban a particular speech, whether it is a commercial ad, a violent television program, a graphic lesbian novel, or a topless nightclub show. Even if political speech is socially more valuable than the novel, a tract advocating genocide might have less social value than a resolutely nonpolitical novel by Henry Miller even if some of the pleasure that readers take in a Miller novel derives from its pornographic elements. I am not impressed by the argument that political speech should be entitled to greater protection because the government cannot be trusted to permit criticism of itself. The government cannot be trusted, period. It is likely to suppress any speech that is radically unpopular, whether political, religious, commercial, or aesthetic, with consequences unrelated to any hierarchy of speech values. Spain, Portugal, and Italy probably did more harm to the long-term welfare of their people by suppressing (or condoning the church's suppression of) scientific freedom in the early modern period than by suppressing political freedom. The people who want to privilege political speech are often people who simply think that politics is the most important activity that people engage in.

A better argument for giving a special dollop of protection to political speech is related to the "voter's paradox," that is, the puzzle of why anyone votes in political elections, since the probability that the election will be decided by one vote is vanishingly small. Many people do vote, but because the private value of voting is slight, the incentive to invest in becoming well informed about the issues in the election is slight. Since the private demand for political ideas is thus weak, it makes sense to try to minimize the legal costs of producing such ideas.

---

21. That is, from the standpoint of *our* society. It is by no means clear that every society would or should prioritize the political in this way. Consider Renaissance Italy, for a plausible counterexample. In our society, it might be worse to ban scientific than political speech.

If I am right that estimating the benefits of speech by the methods of law is infeasible, the focus of the cost–benefit approach should be on the costs of speech. Sometimes it may be possible to show that the costs are zero or even negative. Consider *Posadas de Puerto Rico Associates v. Tourism Co. of Puerto Rico*.[22] The Supreme Court held in that case that Puerto Rico, since it could constitutionally have banned all gambling, had not violated the First Amendment by forbidding the advertising in Puerto Rico (but not outside of it) of casino gambling, which the government of Puerto Rico had legalized. The Court's decision makes little sense to an economist even if advertising is considered to be generally less worthy of legal protection than political speech.[23] The ostensible purpose of the advertising ban was to reduce the lure of gambling to residents of Puerto Rico[24] (a purpose not inconsistent with legalizing casino gambling, for that might have been done simply in recognition of the futility of trying to suppress it). The ban may have had some effect along that line. But at the same time, it reduced the advertising costs of the casinos, and this reduction would lead them, assuming they were competitive, to reduce their prices—which in turn would make gambling more attractive than before the ban. Thus, as far as anyone knows, the ban deprived consumers of valuable information without reducing any of the unwanted side effects of gambling addiction (such as bankruptcy, penury, embezzlement, or suicide); it may even have increased them.

There are also cases in which the social costs of speech can be reduced or eliminated without eliminating, or even greatly curtailing, the possible benefits; and sometimes the benefits are enhanced. Limiting the number of participants in a televised debate, preventing demonstrators from blocking traffic, allowing the prohibition of false advertising, and providing legal remedies against copying and defamation are examples. (All but the demonstrations case are plausible examples of restrictions that increase speech on balance.) A zoning law that requires all pornographic bookstores to relocate to a "red light" distict reduces the costs associated with pornography yet at the same time preserves the essential benefits that pornography might be thought to confer. A law banning pornography would reduce the costs even more, but, to the extent enforced, might eliminate most of the benefits. And such a law would be much more costly to enforce. These points are related to my earlier

---

22. 478 U.S. 328 (1986).

23. *See* Fred S. McChesney, *De-Bates and Re-Bates: The Supreme Court's Latest Commercial Speech Cases*, 5 SUP. CT. ECON. REV. 81, 102–5 (1997).

24. By allowing the casinos to advertise out of state, Puerto Rico showed that it cared nothing about corrupting nonresidents!

point about the importance of evaluating the costs and benefits of particular forms of speech at the margin.

Costs of enforcement are an underemphasized objection to the radical feminist program for curbing pornography. The antipornography ordinance drafted by Andrea Dworkin and Catharine MacKinnon[25] would require proof that the manufacture or sale of pornography by the defendant had harmed the plaintiff. The costs of such an evidentiary inquiry, especially the error costs, would be very high, because it is extremely difficult to determine the causal relation between exposure to pornography and particular acts. A more comprehensive prohibition of pornography, one that dispensed with proof of harm, would be even more costly to administer, as experience with efforts to stamp out other moral offenses have shown. The costs of the vast and intrusive enforcement efforts necessary to make such a prohibition effective would swamp the cost savings from dispensing with proof of harm in each case.

Given these costs and the infeasibility of actually measuring the benefits of pornography as of other forms of speech, estimating the overall social costs of pornography becomes critical. Some of these costs, such as those resulting from the exploitation and abuse of models and actresses employed to make pictorial pornography, seem largely the artifacts of the formal illegality of "hard core" pornography, which deprives the models and actresses of the usual contractual and legal protections that employees enjoy.[26] The principal cost of which feminists complain, namely the tendency of pornography to perpetuate inaccurate and offensive stereotypes about female sexuality or even to incite men to rape or otherwise abuse, degrade, or disvalue women, has yet to be convincingly documented.[27] Conservative opponents of pornography tend to emphasize not the harms but the offensiveness of pornography. But like most "other-regarding" harms in Mill's sense, this offensiveness is very difficult to measure in even the roughest terms.

---

25. The ordinance entitled anyone harmed by the sale of materials that graphically depicted the subordination of women to men to bring a civil suit against the seller. The ordinance, adopted by Indianapolis, was held unconstitutional in *American Booksellers Ass'n v. Hudnut,* 771 F.2d 323 (7th Cir. 1985), *aff'd without opinion,* 475 U.S. 1001 (1986).

26. The use of children is not an effect of illegality, but it could be forbidden without a general ban on pornography. Presumably child pornography that does not involve the use of children, for example purely verbal child pornography (the novel *Lolita,* or the movie when either bowdlerized or played by an adult actress), should be treated the same as other forms of pornography, in the absence of evidence that child pornography incites child molestation, as distinct from providing masturbation aids to pedophiles. But this is abstracting from offensiveness, an alternative ground for prohibiting pornography.

27. *See, e.g.,* PAUL R. ABRAMSON & STEVEN D. PINKERTON, WITH PLEASURE: THOUGHTS ON THE NATURE OF HUMAN SEXUALITY 188–90 (1995); RICHARD A. POSNER, OVERCOMING LAW 361–62 (1995).

The combination of the high costs of enforcing a law against pornography with the uncertain social costs of the pornography itself suggests that such a law may be undesirable even if the social benefits of pornography are estimated to be zero, which seems an extreme position. But offensiveness is a wild card here; if it is very great, punishing pornography may make economic sense after all. There is, however, a pragmatic argument against putting much weight on offensiveness as a ground for restricting freedom of speech. Offensiveness is often a by-product of challenging the values and beliefs that are important to people, and these challenges are an important part of the market in ideas and opinions. People get upset when their way of life is challenged, yet that upset may be the beginning of doubt and lead eventually to change. Think of all the currently conventional ideas and opinions that were deeply offensive when first voiced. Perhaps, therefore, a condition of being allowed to hear and utter ideas that may challenge *other* people's values and beliefs should be the willingness to extend the same right to others and thus agree that offensiveness will not be a permissible ground for punishing expression. In other words, privileging offensive speech may maximize social welfare *ex ante* even though *ex post* it will result in significant disutility to many people. Pornography is a case in point. It has historically been associated with challenges to political authority,[28] and indeed with feminism;[29] today it is (in its ideological aspect) a rearguard action against feminism.

The law has not gone so far as to banish offensiveness completely as a ground for limiting freedom of speech. While the private consumption of pornography is largely protected, the government is allowed to limit its public display and, under the rubric of preventing sexual harassment, to ban it from the workplace. These exceptions, whether or not sound, need not be viewed as ad hoc or unprincipled. In the case of public or workplace display, part of the audience of the pornography is involuntary, consisting of women offended by it. In a discreet private sale of pornography, the aim is to please the consumer, not to insult, intimidate, or embarrass anybody. Such a sale can harm a woman only if the buyer of the pornography is incited by it to mistreat her. The effect is indirect, and has not been shown to be substantial.

In the case of both pornography and hate speech, and the "political correctness" movement more broadly, one has the sense that the desire to crack down on these forms of speech has little to do with demonstrable harms from it or even with its offensiveness. It has rather to do with an ideological project— in fact with the same ideological project, that of denying or occluding the

---

28. *See, e.g.*, Robert Darnton, The Forbidden Best-Sellers of Pre-Revolutionary France, ch. 3 (1995).

29. *Id.* at 114.

existence of deep-seated differences between groups (in particular men and women, and blacks and whites). Hate speakers are vociferous deniers of equality, and pornography caters primarily to a specifically male interest in women as sexual playthings for men rather than as persons in their own right who are inherently no different from men except in reproductive anatomy. (Primarily, not exclusively; there is pornography directed to women and to homosexuals of both sexes, and much pornography "advocates" sexual pleasure for women as well as for men, and even sexual equality.) Insofar as campaigns for the regulation of hate speech and pornography have the purpose and effect of correcting ideological or political "error," giving them the backing of the law interferes arbitrarily with the market in ideas and opinions.

Subsidy versus Suppression

Suppose that politically or ideologically motivated intervention in the speech market takes the form not of suppression of reprobated speech but of subsidization of counterspeech. An example would be a government-financed campaign of antipornography advertisements, similar to antismoking advertisements. This would be governmental interference with the market in ideas and opinions, all right, and it would involve the coercion of those taxpayers who disagreed with the government's position and did not want their money used to propagate it. But subsidization and prohibition are not symmetrical in their effects, at least in speech markets oriented to consumption. For any given dollar expenditure, a government campaign against some form of speech will have a larger negative impact on it if it is used to enforce a prohibition of the speech than if it is used to finance counterspeech. This is because advertising is very expensive (the ingenuity of the Dworkin–MacKinnon proposal, an example of a prohibitory approach, was that it would have involved virtually no public expenditures because the only enforcement mechanism was the bringing of private tort suits by victims of pornography) and likely to be completely ineffectual when urging contrary to the self-interest of the audience. People who enjoy pornography are not going to be impressed by advertisements that tell them not to enjoy it. Anticigarette advertising that emphasizes the health effects of smoking is more likely to be effective, because it appeals to the self-interest of the audience, than advertising designed to engender a sense of guilt in consumers of pornography.

An intermediate case is that of antiabortion advertising. The audience for the advertising are people who have choices—whether they are women who are already pregnant, the parents of teenage girls, or girls or women deciding whether to have sex and if so whether and what type of contraception to employ. These choices involve a complex interweaving of considerations of self-interest with altruistic concerns. If the choices are finely balanced, government speech may tip the balance in some cases, though probably few (as I shall argue shortly in discussing the related issue of limiting campaign financing). But unless the private abortion-speech market, in which pro-choice and pro-life advocates vociferously clash, is insufficiently competitive, which is highly implausible, it is unclear what justification there is for government's intervening on one side of it.

The difference between subsidy and suppression as policy variables is highlighted by considering the likely productivity of spending a given amount of public money on one variable versus on the other. Suppose the government spent $100 million prosecuting people who advocate abortion. Probably that advocacy would stop altogether, or at least be driven to a very low level; and as a result the number of abortions would probably fall, perhaps substantially. (A partial offset, however, would be that abortions would be cheaper because abortion clinics would perforce be economizing on advertising, as in the case of Puerto Rico's regulation of casino advertising.) Now suppose that instead the government spent $100 million on ads denouncing abortion. The effect on the number of abortions would probably be small, though greater, as I have suggested, than if the government ran ads denouncing pornography. The antiabortion ads would be an addition to privately financed such ads; the latter might well decline, because advertisers might consider the incremental contribution of their ads to the formation of public opinion slight with the government in the picture, in which event the net increment in antiabortion advertising might be slight. Moreover, the government ads would give their audience information that it already to a large extent had, with or without advertising; information that was balanced, moreover, and to that extent offset by pro-choice advertising. In short, dollar for dollar the subsidy approach would have less impact on the market in ideas and opinions than the regulatory approach, making it less problematic from the standpoint of preserving the freedom of that market. Not unproblematic, though, since it would force taxpayers to pay for propaganda in support of causes that they might abhor, which would be a source of disutility to these taxpayers.

The efforts of government to correct "unsound" beliefs should be distinguished from government speech that is ancillary to core governmental functions, such as national defense. The government can hardly be faulted for trying to recruit soldiers by appeals to their patriotism, even if pacifists are offended. When the government is a participant in labor or other markets, it should have the same rights as other participants to advertise. And when it exercises a traditional regulatory responsibility, such as combating epidemics, it should be permitted to use advocacy as one of its tools, and thus for example to advocate monogamy and safe sex in order to try to reduce the incidence of AIDS.

The Problem of Measuring the Benefits of Speech

Although it is possible to say something and sometimes a lot about the different costs associated with different forms of speech regulation, it is generally not possible to make firm recommendations for or against a given regulation if the benefits side of speech remains as opaque as I have left it. Two forms of regulation—for example, the banning of pornography and the confinement of pornographic bookstores to specified districts within a city—might differ widely in their costs, yet both might flunk a cost–benefit test because the benefits were greater than either set of costs, or pass such a test because the benefits were smaller than either set of costs. So I must try to say more about the benefits of free speech despite the doubts that I have expressed about the feasibility of measuring them.

Obviously the benefits have to be assumed to be positive. Otherwise the only speech protected from regulation or even suppression would be speech for which the cost of regulation exceeded the harm inflicted by it. This may in fact be the case with pornography. That is why I qualified with "generally" my statement that it is impossible to make firm recommendations for legal policy toward free speech without knowing something about the benefits of the speech.

If we must assume, to get anywhere, that the benefits of free speech are positive, the question becomes how great they should be assumed to be if we cannot actually measure them. One possibility—a possibility that seems in fact to have shaped the modern law of free speech—is that those benefits are great yet tend to be underestimated because of an asymmetry in the salience and probability of the costs and the benefits. If a speech touches off a riot, the costs are visible, but the benefits of the speech in contributing to truth or happiness are not—they are diffuse and indirect and almost impossible to demonstrate by the methods of litigation. As a result, there may be a tilt in favor of suppression if a jury is asked merely whether the punishment of the speaker is "reasonable" in the circumstances. The alternative is to confine regulation to cases in which the harm inflicted by the speech is *manifestly* great in relation to the amount or value of speech suppressed.

But that approach engenders decisions that strike many people as doctrinaire and foolish. Almost all the "soft core" pornographic magazines and films that pass constitutional muster, along with neonazi ravings that are even more securely within the protection of the Constitution as it is currently interpreted, seem worthless, noxious, or at best (the case of pornography, in all likelihood)

indistinguishable so far as social value is concerned from a speechless consumer product such as a sex toy. And yet if I am correct that the benefits of
speech are not demonstrable by the methods of litigation, the approach of
deeming the benefits great may make strategic sense. An analogy will help
to show this. The U.S. defense strategy during the Cold War was a forward
defense. Our front line was the Elbe, not the Potomac. The choice between a
forward and a close-in defense involves trade-offs. The forward defense is more
costly, and the forward-defense line, because it is nearer the enemy forces, is
more likely to be overrun. But the forward defense allows a defense in depth,
reducing the likelihood that the home front will be penetrated. If the home
front is very difficult to defend, the case for the forward defense becomes
compelling.

The analogy to free-speech strategy is straightforward. Rather than defending just the right to say and write things that have some plausible social value,
the courts, by following the "deeming the benefits great" approach that I have
been describing, defend the right to say and write utterly worthless and deeply
offensive things as well. The fight goes on at these outer pickets; it is costly
because the claim of free speech is weak because overextended; and sometimes
the claim is defeated. But the home front is secure, the enemy having dissipated
its strength in penetrating the outer bulwarks. And this is vital because if the
battle shifted to the home front, and the courts had to defend the value of, say,
allowing people to read *The Bell Curve* or *The Case for Same-Sex Marriage,* they
would find it difficult to establish the social value of these or any other books
against arguments that the first is poison to race relations and the second
undermines morality.[30]

The forward strategy that I have described helps to place in proper perspective the claim by Stanley Fish that " 'free speech' is just the name we give to
verbal behavior that serves the substantive agendas we wish to advance."[31] The
judges, he says, protect the "speech they want heard" and regulate "the speech
they want silenced."[32] At one level this is true. Freedom of speech is not absolute. It is relative to social conditions. It had a narrower scope for Blackstone

---

30. Vincent Blasi, in his interesting article *The Pathological Perspective and the First Amendment,* 85
COLUM. L. REV. 449 (1985), discusses a related issue: what is the best type of free-speech doctrine to
develop in periods in which free speech is not under great stress if the main concern of free-speech
law is to plug the dike in periods (such as the Red Scare after World War I or the McCarthyite period
after World War II) when free speech is under great stress?

31. STANLEY FISH, THERE'S NO SUCH THING AS FREE SPEECH, AND IT'S A GOOD THING, TOO 110 (1994). The
discussion that follows draws on chapter 4 of POSNER, THE PROBLEMATICS OF MORAL AND LEGAL THEORY
(1999).

32. FISH, *supra* note 31, at 110.

than it has for us, and it would take careful historical inquiry to substantiate a claim that he had too narrow a conception of it even for his time. People can still be punished for disseminating obscenity, for revealing military or trade secrets, for defamation, for inciting riots, for copyright and trademark infringement, for plagiarism, for threats, for perjury, for false advertising and other misrepresentations, for certain types of verbal abuse, for exchanging information in the hope of facilitating price fixing, for talking back to prison guards, for revealing confidences of various sorts, for certain forms of picketing and aggressive solicitation, for indecorous behavior in courthouses, for publicly criticizing one's employer on matters not deemed to be of public concern, for irresponsible or offensive broadcasting, even for using loudspeakers. But there is a difference between free-speech doctrine that is shaped and constrained by broadly political considerations and judicial decisionmaking that has no theoretical coherence, let alone decisionmaking shaped by preference for or aversion to the character or content of particular speech. Most of the "speech" that survives legal challenge in the United States—not just the neonazi ravings and the pornography that does not cross the line to obscenity but also blasphemous art, government documents containing diplomatic secrets (the Pentagon Papers, for example), flag-burnings, picketing, and cross-burnings—offend the mostly conservative, mostly middle-aged and elderly persons who, as judges, insist that the government allow such displays.

Fish acknowledges the latter point (that judicial decisionmaking in the free-speech area is not purely ad hoc) in discussing a parody, held constitutionally protected by the Supreme Court, published in *Hustler* magazine in which Jerry Falwell, the fundamentalist religious leader, is represented as having sexual intercourse with his mother in an outhouse.[33] The Court's inability to draw a line that would permit the suppression of so intellectually barren and gratuitously repulsive a personal attack draws a pointed remark from Fish about the judiciary's "self-imposed incapacity to make distinctions that would seem perfectly obvious to any well-informed teenager."[34] That incapacity sounds like the very opposite of ad hoc political decisionmaking. It suggests, instead, judicial commitment to what I have described as the strategy of the forward defense.

In commending that strategy and thus the desirability of keeping the government's hands off the speech market, I may seem to be assuming that this market can be counted on to operate efficiently as long as the government keeps hands off. Actually, there are reasons to doubt that the speech market will operate efficiently: It is difficult to establish property rights in information;

---

33. Hustler Magazine v. Falwell, 485 U.S. 46 (1988).

34. FISH, *supra* note 31, at 132.

there are deep uncertainties of both a practical and a philosophical nature concerning the feasibility of determining by competition or anything else the value (for example, the truth, fruitfulness, or beauty) of particular ideas, opinions, works of art, or other intellectual or expressive work; and the "market in ideas" is frequently metaphorical rather than literal because (this is related to the first point) speech often is neither bought nor sold. For all these reasons there isn't much basis for confidence that leaving the market in ideas alone will result in the production of the optimum quality and quantity of expression.[35] The possibility that markets in ideas may fail to internalize externalities is shown by such unexceptionable interventions as punishing a person who shouts "Fire!" in a crowded theater, knowing there is no fire.

Apart from imposing external costs, these markets may fail by producing "goods" that have no net value. An example is the totalitarian ideologies that wrought such extraordinary havoc in the first half of the twentieth century. Even today Americans are awash in superstitious and erroneous, even preposterous, beliefs, in part because of sensationalistic and inaccurate "news" media; many members of the intelligentsia are dupes of absurd ideas peddled by radical postmodernists; and there is a staggering amount of trash culture, both popular and highbrow. It is apparent that markets in ideas operate frequently in a setting of prohibitive information costs. This makes it difficult to retain a robust confidence in the truth- and beauty-producing properties of these markets.

Holmes was a skeptic—which in economic terms is someone who thinks information costs are *really* high—yet he was not lukewarm in his attitude toward freedom of speech. Quite the contrary; and it was on his skepticism that he based his belief in the desirability of leaving the market of ideas largely free from government regulation. A belief in the benefits of free speech need not depend on believing that markets in expression are efficient, that they produce a "reliable" product—namely, the true idea. For the very things that make these markets inefficient—extremely high costs of information—make the regulation of them inefficient. If consumers can't sort out truth from falsity, or beauty from ugliness, in the wares produced in these markets, how likely is it that censors, judges, or juries can? Not very, history teaches us. Imbued with a mission of protecting the public, and lacking any market discipline, censors are likely to go overboard in suppressing speech that they think dangerous or find offensive.

The difficulty of establishing property rights in expression makes these markets particularly vulnerable to heavy-handed regulation. The difficulty the

---

35. *See* Breton & Wintrobe, *supra* note 9.

producer has in capturing the benefits of his output will make him exaggeratedly sensitive to expected-punishment costs. The unpopular speaker bears the full costs of punishment, while the benefits of the speech may be long deferred and thus captured largely by other persons. Whenever benefits are externalized, there is a danger of underproduction. The danger is acute in the domain of speech, and the law recognizes this in a variety of ways. One is by denying a privilege to republish defamatory material without being liable for defamation. With such a privilege—that is, if only the original publisher were liable—newspapers and other news sources would be even more reluctant than they are now to risk publishing defamatory material, because they would know that their competitors could republish it without bearing any of the expected liability costs of defamation.

The fragility of speech, owing to the externalization of its benefits, is a reason independent of judgments of social value for giving commercial speech less than average constitutional protection but giving hate speech the full protection. Commercial speech is robust not because business is politically powerful, which it sometimes is and sometimes isn't, but because the commercial speaker normally expects to recoup the full economic value of his speech in the form of higher product prices or a greater output. Because of this, indeed, it is far from obvious that commercial speech should get any greater constitutional protection than commercial activity generally. In contrast, hate speech is fragile because the costs are concentrated but the benefits diffused. The student who is expelled from school for expressing racial antagonism in proscribed terms bears all the costs of his speaking out but captures little of the social benefits of giving vent to his opinion.

The skeptical position has the further significance for the defense of free speech of depriving the censor of his best argument, which is that truth and beauty are objectively determinable but only by experts, not by *hoi polloi.* (That was the view of Plato, who believed in censorship.) Where we trust expert opinion to generate reliable, "objective" knowledge, we permit censorship. Some examples are the regulation by the Food and Drug Administration of claims concerning the safety and efficacy of drugs; the regulation of the truthfulness of advertising and labeling by the Federal Trade Commission; and the determination of truth in defamation cases. Censorship in these areas has been defended as a desirable form of paternalism—"epistemic paternalism."[36] The defense is all right, but the term is not apt. All that is involved is delegation to expert, neutral, and basically trustworthy bodies of responsibility for making

---

36. Alvin I. Goldman, *Epistemic Paternalism: Communication Control in Law and Society,* 88 J. Phil. 113 (1991).

definitive factual or other determinations that a private citizen does not have the time or the training to make. The truth of political and even many scientific ideas, however, and even more plainly the beauty or delight of works of art or literature, cannot be determined reliably by forensic processes or government experts, but must be left for the competitive struggle and the test of time to "determine" (but only tentatively and always subject to revision). Once this is granted, the censor is disarmed, since competition and the test of time are not methods that he can use to carry out his duties.

The test of time is an important link between Holmes's skepticism and his strong defense of freedom of speech. An extreme skeptic would find it difficult to work up much enthusiasm for freedom of speech. He would doubt that censorship was an impediment to the discovery of truth, because he would doubt that there was truth to discover; the only objection to censorship would be the costs, which are often (though not always, as I emphasized in discussing pornography) modest, of administering the censorship program. Holmes wasn't that kind of skeptic, at least in *Abrams*. What he said there was not that truth is undeterminable but rather that it is determinable only through competition and so requires freedom of speech and is killed by censorship. A corollary is that where truth does not require a competitive process to determine, as in many advertising and defamation cases, the case for censorship is much stronger.

In sum, while markets in ideas do not come very close to the economist's ideal of perfect competition, it is difficult to see how regulation can bring them any closer except in a few areas where objectivity in a strong sense can be achieved by agencies or courts or where unregulated speech creates calamitous dangers. And looking back over the whole course of history we realize that the marketplace of ideas has been responsible for much of what we think of as civilization. The value of competition in ideas, coupled with the costs (including error costs) of effective regulation, provides some grounding for a legal approach that *deems* the benefits of free speech to be great, and thus requires proof of *great* cost (always, though, in relation to the amount of speech curtailed, which may be very little or even negative, as in some examples given earlier) to justify restricting speech.

Regulating Hate Speech, Campaign Financing, and the Internet

So far I have been discussing mainly old issues of freedom of speech. I want now to consider, though briefly, what the instrumental approach may be able to contribute to the resolution of three of the newer issues: hate speech codes, the regulation of campaign financing, and the regulation of the Internet.

HATE SPEECH

I noted one objection to hate speech codes already, that they deprive the government of valuable information about the disaffection of the persons who are harmed or offended by affirmative action, multiculturalism, and political correctness. A second objection is that it puts the government's thumb on one pan of the balance of opinion about equality. This is true even when the hate speech code is racially neutral, so that a black student can be punished for calling a white student a honkey. There is a current of opinion in the black community—it is associated with the movement known as Afrocentrism—that whites are inferior to blacks. This seems to me equally as silly as the opposite view, but I do not think it is the government's business to punish people for denying racial equality. It is after all only a dogma, and a recent dogma, that the races, sexes, and so forth are equal; and to punish people for challenging it seems as objectionable as punishing people for advocating communism or laissez-faire.

Against this it can be observed that the most carefully drafted of the hate speech codes are limited to "fighting words," a category of speech that the Supreme Court has long held to be excepted from the protections of the First Amendment.[37] Fighting words are defined as words likely to incite a breach of the peace. This is a perverse definition. It enlarges the legal rights of those who are thin-skinned and prone to violence and so encourages people to cultivate a reputation for hypersensitivity. By focusing on audience reaction it condones a kind of "heckler's veto," which the Supreme Court has properly rejected as a basis for restricting freedom of speech.[38] It discriminates against the inarticulate, putting the hate speech codes into conflict with the desire of the same liberals who support these codes to increase the access of marginal groups to the market of ideas.[39] And in adopting a norm of decorum it reveals a misunderstanding of the character of expressive activity. An abstract painting is not less expressive than an essay on the historical roots of the First Amendment. Neither, for that matter, is a political assassination. Discursive prose represents a tiny fraction of the expressive activity that has shaped history. Political assassinations are suppressed not because they do not contribute to the market in ideas and opinions—often they do contribute, sometimes crucially—but because of their costs. It is only on the score of cost that it

---

37. *See* Cantwell v. Connecticut, 310 U.S. 296 (1940).

38. Forsyth County v. Nationalist Movement, 505 U.S. 123, 133–35 (1992). Not only can the government not ban the unpopular speaker, it cannot charge him for the added cost of providing him with police protection. If it could, this would encourage the hecklers, who would hope to make the cost of protection as high as possible in order to bring financial pressure to bear on the speaker.

39. *See, e.g.,* Cohen, *supra* note 3, at 245–48 (fair access), 254–57 (hate speech).

is rational to distinguish among the various genres of expressive activity, and not on the score of verbal articulateness.

The issue of what to do about hate speech codes is, however, easily finessed, just by a reminder that the First Amendment is limited to state action. If a private university wants to have a hate speech code, there is nothing in the Constitution to prevent it. It is, to be sure, a considerable mystery why government is in the business of owning and operating colleges and universities in the first place. The mystery is not public support of education, but public operation. Many students at private universities receive public money in one way or another; but the universities are still private. If government got out of the business of operating universities, the issue of hate speech codes (like that of affirmative action) would be removed from the constitutional agenda altogether.

This discussion illustrates the general point that strict enforcement of the Free Speech Clause creates an incentive for privatization of governmental activities. By "going private," an enterprise can escape the costs of compliance with legal directives that bind only government.

CAMPAIGN FINANCING AND THE ISSUE OF "FAIR ACCESS"

There is a good deal of dissatisfaction with the existing system of campaign financing. Despite some public subsidies and some restrictions on the size of individual contributions to campaigns, the system is essentially wide open and is generally believed to constitute a thinly disguised system of quasi bribes of elected officials, or, at the very least, to tilt the playing field too far toward the wealthy and the well organized. And these effects are believed to flow in part from (or to be entrenched by) an interpretation of the First Amendment by the Supreme Court that forbids, as an infringement of free speech, the placing of limits on overall campaign spending, on an individual's right to buy political advertising with his own or family money, and on the right of an individual who, or organization that, is "independent" of the candidate to advertise with respect to campaign issues (that is, there is an unlimited right to make "soft money" donations).[40] Allowing the making of essentially unlimited private contributions to political campaigns magnifies the effect of interest groups and, of course, the wealthy on public policy—interest groups because by definition they can overcome the usual obstacles to cooperation and so raise sums of money that are disproportionately greater than what can be raised from the members of diffuse, unorganized groups that may be much larger and so democratically entitled to greater weight in the formulation of public policy. While undeniably facilitating speech by the wealthy and by interest groups, the

---

40. Buckley v. Valeo, 424 U.S. 1 (1976) (per curiam).

present system is thus said to distort the market in ideas by drowning out the speech of the unorganized and the impecunious. To put this differently, freedom of political speech has little practical meaning without access to the mass media, which requires resources that only a fraction, constituting a nonrandom sample, of the population commands. This point is related to my earlier observation, in discussing government speech, about the high cost of advertising.

With these points conceded, it would still be extremely odd to say to an admirer of the Clintons that "you should not buy 1,000 copies of *It Takes a Village* to distribute free of charge, as this would enable you to 'speak' with a louder voice than a person who could not afford such a purchase." This example makes it easy to see that restricting "soft money" donations really would be an infringement of freedom of speech and so would require a convincing demonstration of the harms caused by such speech. The harms are elusive. Individuals or groups that have more than the average amount of money have always had more than the average ability to spend it on trying to influence public opinion. We do not consider such inequality a compelling reason for limiting free speech. Somehow the market in ideas seems robust to inequalities of expenditures by the producers and consumers in this market. Consistent with my earlier discussion of government subsidies of the speech market, the elasticity of public opinion to expenditures on shaping that opinion seems very low. Is the public policy of the nation worse because interest groups use campaign expenditures to try to influence policy and wealthy people use their wealth to try to get elected to office? This has not been shown, although I suspect that most of the people who advocate limits on campaign spending believe that if money played a smaller role in the electoral process the public policies they favor would be more likely to be adopted.

The contributions are very small in relation to the resources of the contributors, and so do not burden business greatly.[41] So far as one can judge on the basis of existing data, these contributions buy access and modest influence, at best, and often just offset the contributions to competing candidates rather than cause substantial distortions in the markets in which the contributors operate.[42] It has been suggested that the problem of quasi bribery be solved by requiring that campaign donations be anonymous.[43] But there would be an

---

41. They are also extremely small in relation to the scale of modern government. *See* John R. Lott Jr., *A Simple Explanation for Why Campaign Expenditures Are Increasing: The Government Is Getting Bigger,* 43 J.L. & ECON. 359 (2000).

42. *See* Steven D. Levitt, *Policy Watch: Congressional Campaign Finance Reform,* J. ECON. PERSP., winter 1995, at 190–92.

43. *See* Ian Ayres & Jeremy Bulow, *The Donation Booth: Mandating Donor Anonymity to Disrupt the Market for Political Influence,* 50 STAN. L. REV. 837 (1998).

information cost: the identity of a donor is a clue to the likely policies of the donee should he be elected—a valuable clue if the donor has better information about the candidate than the average voter has. Moreover, the evidence is that campaign contributions do not alter votes.[44]

Limiting campaign expenditures might create its own distortion of the market in ideas by making it harder to challenge incumbents. To get a foothold in a market, a new product has to be advertised more heavily than the existing products, which are already familiar to consumers. A limit on the amount that could be spent to advertise a product would thus reduce competition in product markets, and the same possibility looms if campaign expenditures are capped. Yet spending limits might actually hurt incumbents more than challengers because incumbents generally are able to raise more money—a natural advantage that spending limits would blunt. Empirical evidence is mixed, but seems on balance not to support the claim that spending limits would help rather than (as seems more intuitive) hurt incumbents.[45] Another possibility, however, is that a reduction in campaign contributions, by reducing publicity about the political process, would actually strengthen interest-group politics by reducing both the amount of scrutiny that interest groups receive and the need of politicians to pay close attention to the policy views of ordinary voters.

To those who think it immoral that the wealthy and the organized should have advantages in the political arena, the argument just sketched will carry no conviction. But to the instrumentalist, the morality of our oligarchic system of political financing is neither here nor there; the issue is the consequences of changing it. Of course, any noninstrumental issue can be "instrumentalized" by a suitable positing of ends. If the end were equality of influence, strict limits on campaign financing could be defended as instruments to that end. Some critics of campaign financing would posit such an end, but it would be basically a *façon de parler*. Equality, especially in so specific a domain as campaign finance, is too abstract to count as an end for an instrumentalist thinker, who will insist that the proponent of equality in campaign finance explain what tangible good is supposed to come out of such equality. Will Americans be happier if campaign spending is limited? Will the poor be better off? Will there be less crime, less discrimination, or even less pollution? Will government be bigger, smaller, better, worse? Who knows?

The movement to limit campaign spending is part of a larger movement to promote "fair access" to the marketplace of ideas. I mentioned the Supreme

---

44. Stephen G. Bronars & John R. Lott Jr., *Do Campaign Donations Alter How a Politician Votes: Or, Do Donors Support Candidates Who Value the Same Things That They Do?* 40 J.L. & Econ. 317(1997).

45. *See* Levitt, *supra* note 42, at 188–90.

Court's complex jurisprudence of public and private forums, which allows the government to prevent the use of much of its property for advocacy. One way to promote fair access, it is argued, would be to require the government to throw open more of its property to advocacy.[46] The main objection is related to a point about hate speech codes. The First Amendment constrains only government action. If the courts make it difficult for government to prevent uses of its property for advocacy purposes that interfere with maximizing the value of that property, this will accelerate the national trend toward privatization. It will make public property more costly and so create, as I have already suggested, an incentive to sell it to private firms in order to get out from under the irksome constraints of an ambitious construal of the right of free speech. Suppose that the courts decide that airports and schools should be deemed public forums available for all types of advocacy—marches and other demonstrations, soapbox oratory, aggressive solicitation. Nothing in principle requires that airports or schools be public property; there is a growing private-school movement in this country; and airport privatization is a likely eventual step in air transportation anyway. The more costs that the courts pile on public entities in the name of free speech, the less governmentally protected free speech there will be if the costs tip the balance in favor of privatization.

FREE SPEECH ON THE INTERNET

Four interrelated grounds underlie the concern that this new medium of communication fosters and magnifies irresponsible and seriously dangerous speech. First it is argued that the Internet facilitates the anonymous dissemination and receipt of indecent material, including child pornography. Second that it lacks all quality control and therefore promotes the dissemination of inaccurate and misleading information, which by a kind of Gresham's Law will obliterate truthful information; it is argued, for example, that unscrupulous, unsupervised Internet journalists "force" the respectable media to report unsubstantiated rumors. Third, the Internet gives people unmediated access to huge potential audiences for their speech, which can increase the harm caused by the speech.[47] Fourth (and related to the second and third points), the Internet is said to foment antisocial behavior by enabling perverts and extremists to find their soulmates more easily. People who have weird ideas tend to keep these ideas to themselves, fearing ostracism if they express them and perhaps doubting the validity of their ideas for want of any reinforcement of them by other people; isolation destroys self-confidence in most people. Once eccentrics

---

46. *See, e.g.,* Cohen, *supra* note 3, at 247. Privatization of public colleges and universities would cut the other way.

47. This point is stressed in Cass Sunstein's contribution to this volume.

discover in Internet chat rooms and websites that hundreds or thousands of other people think the same way they do, they become emboldened not only to express their ideas but also to act upon them, their self-confidence bolstered by membership in a community of believers.

The first and second arguments seem aimed at transitory features of the new medium. There are a variety of technological and regulatory techniques for preventing the dissemination of illegal materials (such as child pornography) and also for shielding nonconsenting consumers from them; and private demand for screening for accuracy will eventually result in equipping the Internet with quality controls as effective as those of the traditional media. The fourth argument (I'll come back to the third in a moment) is more consequential but impossible as yet to give any definite weight to. All that one can say with any confidence at this point is that governmental efforts to close chat rooms and websites that attract dangerous or unstable people will have the side effect of censoring potentially socially valuable but unconventional communication. What is more, since chat rooms are open to all, including government agents, society can protect itself by governmental monitoring of these rooms, though this depends on the cost of that monitoring and in turn on technologies of surveillance of which I am poorly informed. A weak government can be undermined by free speech, but a strong government can be strengthened by it because it enables government to keep itself better informed of potential threats, assuming the cost of surveillance is not prohibitive.

The third concern, the potentially greater magnitude of harmful speech carried by the Internet because of the potentially much greater size of the audience for individuals whose speech is too harmful or offensive to get through the gateways of the conventional media, is the most worrisome. A nut who couldn't get a newspaper to publish any of his letters to it can reach thousands or even millions of people over the Internet at virtually zero cost. But it is a problem that the instrumental approach copes with automatically. The social cost of a speech is a function not only of its harmful or offensive character but also of the size of its audience; it is worse to shout "Fire!" (at least when there is no fire, and sometimes when there is one) in a large, crowded theater than in a small one.

It should be added that there is an upside to the third point, as well as to the second, which it resembles. First, anything that reduces the cost of communication increases the amount of speech. This is not an unmitigated good but it is a good and must be counted as such. Second, the Internet is a method of circumventing private censorship. Private censorship, which sometimes reaches oppressive dimensions in the "respectable" mass media, with their unwillingness to challenge the pieties of political correctness, is both a part of and an impediment to the market in ideas and opinions. Without any private censorship, the volume of speech would increase to the level of unintelligible cacophony; but with it, important ideas, information, and insights are often suppressed. The market depends on selectivity and gatekeepers, but can also be undermined by such things. The Internet is, among other things, a safety valve.

In a symposium on cyberspace, one reads: "At this formative stage in the development of these new modes of [interactive] communication, it is appropriate to ask: What impact will these changes have on freedom of expression?"[48] With all due respect, it does not seem to me appropriate to ask that. It is too soon to gauge that impact (it was even more clearly too soon six years ago, when the article from which I have just quoted was published). There is nothing like a "clear and present danger" demonstrable from the growth of the Internet. Until such a danger is demonstrated, First Amendment instrumentalists will continue to resist subjecting the Internet to greater restrictions than television, the mails, and telephony—the conventional media of which the Internet is a kind of fusion.

Implications for Scholarship

A particular value of the instrumental approach is that it highlights the deficiencies in our knowledge about expressive activity. These deficiencies are obscured by the moral approach, which by emphasizing the intrinsic values of free speech deflects attention from the operation of free speech in the real world. If the right to buy pornography is grounded in the principle that it is an infringement of human autonomy to prevent an adult from reading or seeing anything he wants to read or see, one is not likely to ask such questions as why there is a demand for pornography and what effects the widespread consumption of it has. Moral assertions are show stoppers rather than invitations to factual inquiry. Constitutional scholarship, including the scholarship of free speech, is preoccupied on the one hand with Supreme Court decisions that are notably lacking in an empirical dimension and on the other hand with normative theories of free speech that have no empirical dimension either. Vast as the literature is, very little of it is concerned with the kind of empirical questions raised by this paper. This should be a source of concern to anyone who believes that the instrumental approach to free speech should have a role to play in the formation of public policy.

---

48. Jerry Berman & Daniel J. Weitzner, *Abundance and User Control: Renewing the Democratic Heart of the First Amendment in the Age of Interactive Media*, 104 YALE L.J. 1619 (1995).

Robert Post is also interested in the relationship between the theory, doctrine, and specific results of the First Amendment. He begins with the observation that there seems to be a significant gap between the "outcomes of particular cases," which he notes are reasonably predictable by "those fluent in the law of free speech," and our efforts over the past century "to formulate clear explanations and coherent rules capable of elucidating and charting the contours" of these holdings. Like others, Professor Post explores how two primary theories of freedom of speech and press—the truth-seeking function represented in the "marketplace of ideas" metaphor and the democracy rationale—both emerged from the early decisions of the Supreme Court.

Within these powerful explanations for a principle of free speech, Professor Post says, there lurks an important ambiguity. Both theories might well support an approach to the First Amendment that would allow regulation of expression that interferes with the ultimate goal of arriving at truth or good public policy. Some speech, after all, may impede rather than advance our progress toward those ends. Sometimes (as with the commercial speech doctrine and with the regulation of broadcast media) the Court has actually followed this logic. But in a wide array of cases involving political discourse the Court has not; instead it has insisted repeatedly that offensive, insulting, and extremist speech must be endured by the society.

Professor Post argues that this is explicable under an alternative meaning of the democracy rationale of the First Amendment. He calls this the "participatory" theory, which emphasizes the need of citizens to experience "authentic self-determination" and the imperative for courts to protect the "autonomy of individual citizens." This is what constitutes our "uniquely American jurisprudence." It also provides us with a fundamental insight into the way in which the Court has developed a "lexical ordering" of the multiple purposes naturally and appropriately served by the First Amendment.—LCB

ROBERT POST

Reconciling Theory and Doctrine in First Amendment Jurisprudence

Introduction

The simple and absolute words of the First Amendment float atop a tumultuous doctrinal sea. The free-speech jurisprudence of the First Amendment is notorious for its flagrantly proliferating and contradictory rules, its profoundly chaotic collection of methods and theories.[1] Yet, strange to say, those fluent in the law of free speech can predict with reasonable accuracy the outcomes of most constitutional cases. It seems that what is amiss with First Amendment doctrine is not so much the absence of common ground about how communication within our society ought constitutionally to be ordered, as our inability to formulate clear explanations and coherent rules capable of elucidating and charting the contours of this ground.

First Amendment doctrine veers between theory and the exigencies of specific cases. The function of doctrine is both to implement the objectives attributed by theory to the Constitution and to offer principled grounds of justification for particular decisions. Doctrine becomes confused when the requirements of theory make little sense in the actual circumstances of concrete cases, or when doctrine is required to articulate the implications of inconsistent theories. First Amendment doctrine has unfortunately suffered from both these difficulties.

In a remarkable series of opinions in 1919, Justice Oliver Wendell Holmes virtually invented both First Amendment theory and First Amendment doctrine. He advanced the theory of the marketplace of ideas, and he demonstrated how doctrine would have to evolve to implement this new theory. But soon thereafter the Court articulated a competing and in some respects inconsistent theory, which focused on the practice of democratic self-government. In this

---

1. *See generally* Glen O. Robinson, *The Electronic First Amendment: An Essay for the New Age,* 899 Duke L.J. 966 (1998); Frederick Schauer, *Codifying the First Amendment:* New York v. Ferber, 1982 Sup. Ct. Rev. 285.

essay I examine each of these two theories of the First Amendment to illustrate the complex ways in which theory, doctrine, and common sense interact in First Amendment jurisprudence. My objective is to explore the sources of the current disarray of First Amendment doctrine and to assess the kinds of clarification that we may reasonably anticipate from an analytically rigorous First Amendment jurisprudence.

Laying the Groundwork: Justice Holmes's Landmark Opinions

Although First Amendment law did not spring into existence *ex nihilo* in the year 1919,[2] First Amendment jurisprudence as we now know it springs from a series of profoundly influential opinions by Justice Holmes in the spring and fall of that year. The first of these opinions, *Schenck v. United States*,[3] is the origin of the famous "clear and present danger" test. The defendants in *Schenck* were charged with violating the Espionage Act of 1917[4] by, among other things, "causing and attempting to cause insubordination . . . in the military . . . and to obstruct the recruiting and enlistment service of the United States, when the United States was at war with the German Empire."[5] They were prosecuted for circulating to draftees a leaflet opposing conscription; their defense was that the leaflet was "protected by the First Amendment to the Constitution."[6]

Holmes's opinion for the Court firmly rejected this defense, but it did so without any discussion of the distinctive purposes or policies of the First Amendment. Instead Holmes reasoned: "It seems to be admitted that if an actual obstruction of the recruiting service were proved, liability for words that produced that effect might be enforced. . . . If the act, (speaking, or circulating a paper,) its tendency and the intent with which it is done are the same, we perceive no ground for saying that success alone warrants making the act a crime."[7]

Holmes argued that because obstruction of the draft constitutionally could be punished, so could the crime of attempted obstruction. He explained that when performed with the appropriate intent, the act of speaking or writing could constitute the crime of attempt if, as a matter of "proximity and degree," the "tendency" of the communication was to cause the punishable act of

---

2. *See* David M. Rabban, Free Speech in Its Forgotten Years 23 (1997) (tracing the origins of contemporary First Amendment doctrine).

3. 249 U.S. 47 (1919).

4. Espionage Act of June 15, 1917, ch. 30, § 3, 40 Stat. 217, 219 (repealed 1948).

5. *Schenck*, 249 U.S. at 48–49.

6. *Id.* at 51.

7. *Id.* at 52.

obstructing the draft.[8] Holmes also added that "[t]he question in every case is whether the words used are used in such circumstances and are of such a nature as to create a clear and present danger that they will bring about the substantive evils that Congress has a right to prevent."[9] But the meaning of the novel phrase "clear and present danger" was obscure. It was clarified one week later by Holmes's opinion for the Court in *Debs v. United States*,[10] which held that speech merely had to have the "natural tendency and reasonably probable effect"[11] of obstructing the recruiting service in order to constitute a punishable attempt to violate the Espionage Act of 1917.[12]

Holmes's logic in both *Schenck* and *Debs* remained entirely within the domain of substantive criminal law. Speech that was connected in a sufficiently close way to a crime was equivalent to an attempt to commit the crime. The closeness of the connection was to be assessed by doctrinal tests of "proximity and degree," tests rooted in the substantive law of attempt.[13] Although in some circumstances the First Amendment might safeguard speech—circumstances that Holmes did not explore—the Constitution did not protect speech so intimately bound up in action as to constitute the crime of attempt as defined by principles of the criminal law.

Eight months after *Schenck,* the Court was confronted with *Abrams v. United States*,[14] a case that involved a prosecution under the Espionage Act of 1918.[15] This Act was quite different from its 1917 predecessor. Tracking the words of the 1918 Act, the indictment at issue in *Abrams* charged the defendants with publishing

---

8. *Id.*

9. *Id.*

10. 249 U.S. 211 (1919). *Schenck* was decided on March 3, 1919; *Debs* on March 10, 1919.

11. *Id.* at 216.

12. In *Debs,* the Court unanimously sustained the conviction of prominent socialist politician Eugene Debs for violating the Espionage Act of 1917 by attempting "to obstruct the recruiting and enlistment service of the United States." *Id.* at 212. The evidence of the crime consisted entirely of a noninflammatory speech opposing World War I at a Socialist Party convention. Holmes wrote: "[T]he jury were most carefully instructed that they could not find the defendant guilty for advocacy of any of his opinions unless the words used had as their natural tendency and reasonably probable effect to obstruct the recruiting service, &c., and unless the defendant had the specific intent to do so in his mind." *Id.* at 216.

13. For good discussions of the relationship between the "clear and present danger" test and the substantive law of attempt, *see* G. Edward White, *Justice Holmes and the Modernization of Free Speech Jurisprudence: The Human Dimension,* 80 CAL. L. REV. 391 (1992); Edward J. Bloustein, *Criminal Attempts and the "Clear and Present Danger" Theory of the First Amendment,* 74 CORNELL L. REV. 1118 (1989).

14. 250 U.S. 616 (1919). The Court decided *Abrams* on November 10, 1919.

15. Espionage Act of May 16, 1918, ch. 75, 40 Stat. 553 (repealed 1921).

[i]n the first count, "disloyal, scurrilous and abusive language about the form of Government of the United States;" in the second count, language "intended to bring the form of Government of the United States into contempt, scorn, contumely and disrepute;" and in the third count, language "intended to incite, provoke and encourage resistance to the United States in said war." The charge in the fourth count was that the defendants conspired "when the United States was at war with the Imperial German Government, . . . unlawfully and willfully, by utterance, writing, printing and publication, to urge, incite and advocate curtailment of production of things and products . . . necessary and essential to the prosecution of the war."[16]

The defendants in *Abrams* raised strenuous constitutional objections to these charges. In his opinion for the Court, Justice Clarke disposed of these objections by simple reference to *Schenck*.[17] In fact, however, the prosecutions in *Abrams* posed entirely distinct First Amendment questions from those presented in *Schenck*, questions that would push Holmes fundamentally to revise the logic of his earlier opinions.

The Espionage Act of 1917 had prohibited action—obstructing the recruitment service of the United States during wartime. S*chenck* was thus written to address the question of when speech could be characterized as a form of proscribed action. The Espionage Act of 1918, in contrast, prohibited language itself. In particular, counts one and two of the *Abrams* indictment, which essentially charged the common-law crime of seditious libel, sought to punish speech for reasons that bore no relationship to action at all. The logic of *Schenck* was therefore quite irrelevant to these counts. It made no sense to ask whether language "intended to bring the form of Government of the United States . . . into contempt" had the "natural tendency and reasonably probable effect" of causing some underlying evil that Congress had independently forbidden. The publication of such language was itself the evil that Congress wished to suppress.

Holmes immediately understood this difference. He realized that the Court was now forced, as it had not been forced in *Schenck*, to address the question of whether the First Amendment would permit the suppression of seditious libel. Holmes's answer was unequivocal: "I wholly disagree with the argument of the Government that the First Amendment left the common law as to seditious libel in force."[18] This is the precise point in American constitutional history

---

16. *Abrams*, 250 U.S. at 617.

17. *See id.* at 619.

18. *Id.* at 630 (Holmes, J., dissenting). This was a new position for Holmes. Twelve years before, he had written that the "main purpose" of the First Amendment was " 'to prevent all such *previous restraints* upon publications as had been practiced by other governments,' " and that the First Amendment consequently did "not prevent the subsequent punishment of such as may be deemed

when First Amendment theory enters into the construction of First Amendment doctrine, for Holmes's bold assertion required him to explain why the First Amendment prohibited the punishment of seditious libel.

Seditious libel is a quintessentially political crime; its purpose is to protect the "special veneration . . . due" to those who rule.[19] Holmes could therefore have offered a theory of the First Amendment that derived from the particular characteristics of American democracy, from the fact that, as Madison put it, in our form of government "the censorial power is in the people over the Government, and not in the Government over the people."[20] But Holmes chose not to elaborate a political conception of the First Amendment. Instead, he proposed the now-famous theory of the marketplace of ideas:

> But when men have realized that time has upset many fighting faiths, they may come to believe even more than they believe the very foundations of their own conduct that the ultimate good desired is better reached by free trade in ideas—that the best test of truth is the power of the thought to get itself accepted in the competition of the market, and that truth is the only ground upon which their wishes safely can be carried out. That at any rate is the theory of our Constitution. It is an experiment, as all life is an experiment. . . . While that experiment is part of our system I think that we should be eternally vigilant against attempts to check the expression of opinions that we loathe and believe to be fraught with death, unless they so imminently threaten immediate interference with the lawful and pressing purposes of the law that an immediate check is required to save the country.[21]

Holmes's *Abrams* dissent is sometimes interpreted as representing an economic view of freedom of speech, as though the metaphors of "free trade in ideas" and "the competition of the market" meant that the constitutional value of freedom of speech literally entailed the maximization of consumer

---

contrary to the public welfare. . . . The preliminary freedom extends as well to the false as to the true; the subsequent punishment may extend as well to the true as to the false." Patterson v. Colorado, 205 U.S. 454, 462 (1907) (citations omitted). There is some evidence that by the time of *Schenck* Holmes was beginning to rethink this position. For example, he wrote in *Schenck:* "It well may be that the prohibition of laws abridging the freedom of speech is not confined to previous restraints, although to prevent them may have been the main purpose, as intimated in *Patterson v. Colorado.* We admit that in many places and in ordinary times the defendants in saying all that was said in the circular would have been within their constitutional rights." *Schenck*, 249 U.S. at 51–52 (citation omitted). For a recent discussion of Holmes's famous change of mind, *see* Bradley C. Bobertz, *The Brandeis Gambit: The Making of America's "First Freedom," 1909–1931*, 40 Wm. & Mary. L. Rev. 557, 587–607 (1999).

19. Francis Ludlow Holt, The Law of Libel 90 (1816). For a good explication, *see* James FitzJames Stephens, 2 A History of the Criminal Law of England 299–300 (1883).

20. 4 Annals of Congress 934 (1794). This is the logic that the Court adopted almost fifty years later when it finally ruled that the First Amendment did indeed forbid the punishment of seditious libel. *See* New York Times v. Sullivan, 376 U.S. 254, 275 (1964).

21. *Abrams*, 250 U.S. at 630 (Holmes, J., dissenting).

preferences.[22] But in *Abrams* Holmes explicitly oriented his theory of the First Amendment toward the value of truth, which he linked to the concept of "experiment." This strongly suggests that the *Abrams* dissent is best understood as an expression of American pragmatic epistemology, with which Holmes was very familiar.[23] Pragmatists like William James were prone to using economic metaphors to capture the idea that truth must be experimentally determined from the properties of experience itself.[24] One could understand Holmes, then, as claiming that the property of experience relevant to the determination of the truth of political opinion is that democratic citizens come to believe in an idea and to act on it.

The difficulty with this interpretation, however, is that Holmes phrased his argument in terms of an account of truth generally, rather than of specifically political truth. In the spirit of the liberal philosophical position of John Stuart Mill,[25] Holmes proposed a theory of the First Amendment addressed to the abstract requirements of freedom of thought. As Holmes would write in a subsequent dissent: "[I]f there is any principle of the Constitution that more imperatively calls for attachment than any other it is the principle of free thought—not free thought for those who agree with us but freedom for the thought that we hate."[26]

Holmes's dissent in *Abrams* contains the first judicial expression of a theory of the First Amendment, and the theory had immediate and powerful doctrinal consequences. Counts three and four of the *Abrams* indictment alleged the publication of language directed to producing certain actions—resisting the U.S. prosecution of the war and curtailing the production of necessary war material. It was clear that these actions could be made criminal, and Holmes's earlier opinions in *Schenck* and *Debs* had explicitly held that language having the tendency to produce crimes and spoken with the specific intent to produce crimes could be punished as attempts to commit crimes. One could characterize the Espionage Act of 1918 as a legislative judgment that speech advocating or encouraging prohibitable actions would have the tendency to produce those

---

22. Cass Sunstein, One Case at a Time 171–76 (1999).

23. Thomas C. Grey, *Holmes and Legal Pragmatism*, 41 Stan. L. Rev. 787, 788 (1989).

24. Thus James wrote: "Pragmatism . . . asks its usual question. 'Grant an idea or belief to be true,' it says, 'what concrete difference will its being true make in any one's actual life? . . . What experiences will be different from those which would obtain if the belief were false? What, in short, is the truth's cash-value in experiential terms?' " William James, Pragmatism: A New Name for Some Old Ways of Thinking 200 (1907).

25. *See* John Stuart Mill, On Liberty (Elizabeth Rapaport ed., 1978 [1859]).

26. United States v. Schwimmer, 279 U.S. 644, 654–55 (1929) (Holmes, J., dissenting).

actions. Given the generous and elastic breadth of the "bad tendency" test Holmes had himself articulated and applied in *Debs,* this legislative judgment was no doubt reasonable.[27] It was thus only a small step for the Court to hold that this language could constitutionally be punished under *Schenck* and *Debs.*

Counts three and four of the *Abrams* indictment thus directly forced Holmes to evaluate the relationship between his new theory of the First Amendment and the doctrinal test he had himself previously announced. Holmes immediately realized that if speech could be suppressed merely because it tended to produce prohibited action, the marketplace of ideas could easily be savaged by state regulation.[28] In an admirable effort to reshape First Amendment doctrine to implement the purposes of First Amendment theory, therefore, Holmes fundamentally transformed the bad tendency test of *Debs* and *Schenck.* He reinterpreted the language of "clear and present danger" to require a showing of imminence. Holmes argued in *Abrams* that even if speech could be characterized by substantive criminal law as an "attempt," the First Amendment should nevertheless prohibit its punishment unless there were an "emergency," unless "the expression of opinions . . . so imminently threaten[s] immediate interference with the lawful and pressing purposes of the law that an immediate check is required to save the country."[29]

By tightening the constitutionally required connection between speech and action in this way, Holmes sought both to provide ample room for the functioning of the marketplace of ideas and to empower the state to regulate

---

27. In fact in 1925 Justice Sanford cleverly traded on this logic to uphold the criminal anarchy statute of New York. *See* Gitlow v. New York, 268 U.S. 652 (1925). Like the Espionage Act of 1918, the New York criminal anarchy statute prohibited language that was connected to certain harms. In the case of the New York statute, the harms were those of violent revolution. Sanford reasoned that the statute constituted a legislative "determination" that speech advocating violent revolution posed "a sufficient danger of substantive evil" to be regulated, and he shrewdly argued that, as Holmes and Brandeis had contended in other cases, legislative judgments in these matters ought be "given great weight." *Id.* at 668–70. Sanford observed that such a legislative judgment posed an "entirely different" question "from that involved in those cases where the statute merely prohibits certain acts involving the danger of substantive evil, without any reference to language itself, and it is sought to apply its provisions to language used by the defendant for the purpose of bringing about the prohibited results." *Id.* at 670–71. In the latter case, Sanford conceded, courts must independently determine whether a defendant's language "involved such likelihood of bringing about the substantive evil as to deprive it of the constitutional protection." *Id.* at 671. But, he concluded, the test of "natural tendency and probable effect" set forth in *Schenck* and *Debs* "has no application . . . where the legislative body itself has previously determined the danger of substantive evil arising from utterances of a specified character." *Id.*

28. As Holmes remarked: "Congress certainly cannot forbid all effort to change the mind of the country." *Abrams,* 250 U.S. at 628 (Holmes, J., dissenting).

29. *Id.* at 630.

speech when it was sufficiently close to causing prohibitable substantive evils. Demonstrating the seriousness of his new test, Holmes concluded that the *Abrams* defendants could not constitutionally be convicted because "nobody can suppose that the surreptitious publishing of a silly leaflet by an unknown man, without more, would present any immediate danger that its opinions would hinder the success of the government arms. . . ."[30]

The path of Holmes's development from *Schenck* to *Abrams* exemplifies the dialectical relationship between First Amendment doctrine and First Amendment theory. As he refined his understanding of the purposes of the First Amendment, Holmes was forced to revise and reshape the doctrinal tests he had himself announced only months before. This is because Holmes fully appreciated that the purpose of doctrine is to institutionalize constitutional objectives. A corollary of this insight, however, is that First Amendment doctrine will suffer if it is expected to serve conflicting or inconsistent objectives.

The potential for this problem materialized shortly after Holmes's *Abrams* dissent. In one of its very first decisions striking down a state regulation of speech, the Court in 1931 articulated a specifically political account of the First Amendment that was quite distinct from the marketplace of ideas. "The maintenance of the opportunity for free political discussion to the end that government may be responsive to the will of the people and that changes may be obtained by lawful means," the Court said, "is a fundamental principle of our constitutional system."[31]

The democratic theory of the First Amendment differs in important respects from the marketplace of ideas theory, most notably because the former protects speech insofar as it is required by the practice of self-government, while the latter protects speech insofar as it is required to facilitate the pursuit of truth. To the extent that the practice of self-government serves ends distinct from and potentially inconsistent with the pursuit of truth, and to the extent that the pursuit of truth entails practices inconsistent with self-government, these two theories diverge. Both theories have nevertheless remained influential in the Supreme Court's thinking. The Court can announce both that " '[i]t is the purpose of the First Amendment to preserve an uninhibited marketplace of ideas in which truth will ultimately prevail,' "[32] and that the objective of the

---

30. *Id.* at 628.

31. Stromberg v. California, 283 U.S. 359, 369 (1931).

32. Turner Broadcasting Sys. v. FCC, 507 U.S. 1301, 1304 (1993) (quoting Red Lion Broadcasting Co. v. FCC, 395 U.S. 367, 390 (1969)); *see also* McIntyre v. Ohio Elections Comm'n, 514 U.S. 334, 341 (1995); Hustler Magazine v. Falwell, 485 U.S. 46, 52, 56 (1988).

First Amendment is to function as the "guardian of our democracy."[33] Almost from its inception, First Amendment doctrine has been caught in the crossfire between these two theories of freedom of speech.

To explore this contested terrain, we need to have some concrete idea of the practical differences between these two distinct perspectives. The next section of this essay evaluates the theory of the marketplace of ideas, with particular attention to the tension between its doctrinal development and the actual shape of our First Amendment tradition. That section is followed by a discussion of the ambiguities and implications of the democratic theory, which in turn will lead to a comparison of the doctrinal implications of the two theories and an attempt to draw some general conclusions about the relationship between First Amendment theory and doctrine.

The First Amendment and the Marketplace of Ideas

The theory of the marketplace of ideas focuses on "the truth-seeking function"[34] of the First Amendment. It extends the shelter of constitutional protection to speech so that we can better understand the world in which we live. It would follow from the theory, therefore, that at a minimum the Constitution ought to be concerned with all communication conveying ideas relevant to our understanding the world, whether or not these ideas are political in nature. This does not mean, of course, that the Constitution would prohibit all regulation of such communication. But it does imply that regulation of such communication ought to be evaluated according to the constitutional standards of the theory.

This is in fact the way that contemporary First Amendment doctrine defines the range of communication that triggers First Amendment scrutiny. The so-called *Spence* test, for example, holds that the First Amendment will come "into play" whenever " 'an intent to convey a particularized message [is] present,' " and, given the context, " 'the likelihood [is] great that the message would be understood by those who viewed it.' "[35] This broad doctrinal rule uses the potential communication of ideas to define what will count as "speech" for purposes of the First Amendment. It thus crisply expresses the principle that the regulation of any communication capable of increasing understanding must be subjected to constitutional review.

---

33. Brown v. Hartlage, 456 U.S. 45, 60 (1982).

34. *Hustler Magazine*, 485 U.S. at 52 (1988).

35. Texas v. Johnson, 491 U.S. 397, 403–4 (1989) (quoting Spence v. Washington, 418 U.S. 405, 410–11 (1974)).

While this principle follows more or less directly from the theory of the marketplace of ideas, it does not in fact correspond to the common sense of judges, as expressed in the resolution of actual cases. Much behavior that passes the *Spence* test because it successfully communicates a particularized message is not regarded as bringing the First Amendment into play. Such conduct ranges from terrorist bombings to written warnings on consumer products.[36] It is not that regulation of this conduct is affirmatively permitted by the First Amendment; it is rather that courts do not even subject such regulation to First Amendment scrutiny. When measured by the actual shape of the law, therefore, it is immediately apparent that the *Spence* test, which defines speech in a manner that follows from the theory of the marketplace of ideas, simply cannot stand.[37]

First Amendment jurisprudence is filled with analogous disparities between actual decisions and doctrinal rules that would appear to follow from the theory of the marketplace of ideas. For example, it is black-letter law that the First Amendment applies "the most exacting scrutiny to regulations that suppress, disadvantage, or impose differential burdens upon speech because of its content."[38] Such a rule would seem to express the requirement that the state remain neutral within the marketplace of ideas, for it is formulated in such a way as to apply not merely to political speech, but to the entire range of "speech" as defined by the *Spence* test. Yet content-based regulation of speech is routinely enforced without special constitutional scrutiny, as for example when lawyers or doctors are held liable in professional malpractice for the communication of irresponsible opinions.[39] Or consider the black-letter rule that "[t]he First Amendment recognizes no such thing as a 'false' idea."[40] This rule also seems to express a central value of the marketplace of ideas, and it is accordingly also said to apply generally to "speech," and not merely to political speech. Yet "false" ideas can be regulated not only in the context of professional malpractice, but also in the context of commercial speech, where speakers can be sanctioned if they communicate in ways that are "misleading."[41]

---

36. For a typical consumer product warning case, *see* Hahn v. Sterling Drug, Inc., 805 F.2d 1480 (11th Cir. 1986).

37. For a full discussion of the inadequacy of the *Spence* test, *see* Robert Post, *Recuperating First Amendment Doctrine*, 47 STAN. L. REV. 1249, 1250–60 (1995).

38. Turner Broadcasting Sys. v. FCC, 512 U.S. 622, 642 (1994).

39. *See, e.g.*, Togstad v. Vesely, Otto, Miller & Keefe, 291 N.W.2d 686 (Minn. 1980); Carson v. City of Beloit, 145 N.W.2d 112 (Wis. 1966).

40. *Hustler Magazine*, at 51.

41. *See, e.g.*, Rubin v. Coors Brewing Co., 514 U.S. 476, 482 (1995).

There is thus a disturbingly large gap between the actual shape of our constitutional law and doctrinal rules that seem to express the theory of the marketplace of ideas. This gap suggests either that we do not believe in the theory of the marketplace of ideas, or that our doctrine has somehow misconstrued the actual implications of the theory. The latter alternative seems to me the more plausible. Although First Amendment doctrine presently understands "the truth-seeking function" of the marketplace of ideas to flow directly from the communicative properties of speech, in fact truth-seeking requires much more. It requires an important set of shared social practices: the capacity to listen and to engage in self-evaluation, as well as a commitment to the conventions of reason, which in turn entail aspirations toward objectivity, disinterest, civility, and mutual respect. Thus John Dewey once remarked that rational deliberation depends upon "the possibility of conducting disputes, controversies and conflicts as cooperative undertakings in which both parties learn by giving the other a chance to express itself," and that this cooperation is inconsistent with one party conquering another "by forceful suppression . . . a suppression which is none the less one of violence when it takes place by psychological means of ridicule, abuse, intimidation, instead of by overt imprisonment or in concentration camps."[42]

The social practices necessary for a marketplace of ideas to serve a truth-seeking function are perhaps most explicitly embodied in the culture of scholarship inculcated in universities and professional academic disciplines. Certainly this culture is what Charles Sanders Peirce had in mind when he advocated "the method of science" as a preferred avenue toward truth, a method that he explicitly contrasted with the "method of authority" which employs the "organized force" of the state to suppress "liberty of speech."[43] In this limited sense there is deep insight in the Court's often repeated observation that "[t]he college classroom with its surrounding environs is peculiarly the 'marketplace of ideas.' "[44] The augmentation of knowledge within professional

---

42. John Dewey, *Creative Democracy—The Task Before Us, reprinted in* CLASSIC AMERICAN PHILOSOPHERS 389, 393 (Max H. Fisch ed., 1951).

43. Charles S. Peirce, *The Fixation of Belief, in* VALUES IN A UNIVERSE OF CHANCE 91, 110–11 (Philip P. Wiener ed., 1958). It is likely that Holmes was exposed to this essay while he was a member of the Metaphysical Club at Harvard. *See* David S. Bogen, *The Free Speech Metamorphosis of Mr. Justice Holmes,* 11 HOFSTRA L. REV. 97, 120 (1982).

44. Healy v. James, 408 U.S. 169, 180 (1972); *see, e.g.,* Widmar v. Vincent, 454 U.S. 263, 267 n.5 (1981); Tinker v. Des Moines Indep. Community Sch. Dist., 393 U.S. 503, 512 (1969). In another sense, however, the Court's observation is fundamentally inaccurate, for the classroom itself represents a managerial domain dedicated to instruction, rather than to the open-ended pursuit of knowledge. *See* Robert C. Post, *Racist Speech, Democracy, and the First Amendment,* 32 WM. & MARY. L.

academic disciplines does not flow merely from the fact that ideas are formally free from official censorship, but rather from the fact that this freedom is embedded within what John Stuart Mill once called a "real morality of public discussion."[45] In the absence of such a morality, it is merely tautological to presume that truth is what most people come to believe after open discussion.[46]

It is thus inaccurate to infer that the theory of the marketplace of ideas requires that the First Amendment protect all speech that communicates ideas. Instead, the theory requires the protection only of speech that communicates ideas and that is embedded in the kinds of social practices that produce truth.[47] The Court's failure to offer doctrinal articulation of the social prerequisites of truth-seeking is a significant source of the gap between doctrinal rules attempting to embody the theory of the marketplace of ideas and the actual shape of our First Amendment law.

Society consists of myriad forms of social practices, and speech is constitutive of almost all of these practices. The number of these practices that can plausibly be rendered consistent with the truth-seeking function of a marketplace of ideas is relatively small. It makes no sense, for example, to locate a truth-seeking function in the speech between lawyers or doctors and their clients, or in the communication contained in product warning labels. Judges recognize this distinction; their common sense rebels against applying to such situations doctrinal rules based upon completely incompatible social presuppositions. That is why First Amendment doctrine differs from the actual shape of our law.

To implement accurately the theory of the marketplace of ideas, therefore, doctrinal rules would have to confine the scope of their application to those domains of social life where the prerequisite forms of social organization for a functioning marketplace of ideas either were present or could constitutionally be conjured into existence. Exactly where the theory could appropriately be applied, of course, would be highly debatable, but I suspect that under any fair construction the scope of its application would be quite narrow.

Rev. 267, 317–25 (1990). The marketplace of ideas most exactly applies to the enterprise of scholarship itself.

45. Mill, *supra* note 25, at 52.

46. *See* Frederick Schauer, Free Speech 20 (1982).

47. I have argued elsewhere that *any* function attributed to the First Amendment will require a form of social organization in order to accomplish its ends, and that the Court's tendency to formulate rules applicable to speech itself, independent of social organization, has for this reason been a major source of doctrinal confusion within First Amendment law. *See* Post, *supra* note 37.

The First Amendment and Democratic Self-Government

If the theory of the marketplace of ideas tends to efface the social practices by which it is in fact sustained, thereby inducing a free-floating image of pure communication, the democratic theory has not suffered any such liability. It has never been subject to the same mystification as has the marketplace of ideas. We instantly recognize self-government as a discrete and embodied social practice, and for this reason courts applying democratic theory have been clear that the First Amendment protects only speech pertinent to self-determination. Thus, for example, in the important early decision of *Thornhill v. Alabama*[48] the Court asserted that because freedom of speech was essential to "the maintenance of democratic institutions," it embraced "the liberty to discuss publicly and truthfully all matters of public concern" so that "members of society" could "cope with the exigencies of their period."[49]

Democratic theory, however, has been subject to its own ambiguities. The constitutional meaning of self-government has proved intensely controversial. It is of course generally agreed that democracy subsists in the people governing themselves, but historically there have been two competing accounts of the practice of self-determination, each with different implications for First Amendment doctrine.

One account, associated with the work of Alexander Meiklejohn, views democracy as a process of "the voting of wise decisions."[50] The First Amendment is understood to protect the communicative processes necessary to disseminate the information and ideas required for citizens to vote in a fully informed and intelligent way. Meiklejohn analogizes democracy to a town meeting; the state is imagined as a moderator, regulating and abridging speech "as the doing of the business under actual conditions may require."[51] For this reason "abusive" speech, or speech otherwise inconsistent with "responsible and regulated discussion," can and should be suppressed.[52] From the Meiklejohnian perspective, "the point of ultimate interest is not the words of the speakers, but the minds of the hearers,"[53] so that the First Amendment is seen

---

48. 310 U.S. 88 (1940).

49. *Id.* at 96, 101–2.

50. ALEXANDER MEIKLEJOHN, POLITICAL FREEDOM: THE CONSTITUTIONAL POWER OF THE PEOPLE 26 (1965). For a full discussion and critique, *see* Robert Post, *Meiklejohn's Mistake: Individual Autonomy and the Reform of Public Discourse*, 64 U. COLO. L. REV. 1109 (1993).

51. MEIKLEJOHN, *supra* note 50, at 24.

52. *Id.*

53. *Id.* at 26.

as safeguarding collective processes of decisionmaking rather than individual rights. Meiklejohn summarizes this theory in a much-quoted and influential aphorism: "What is essential is not that everyone shall speak, but that everything worth saying shall be said."[54]

The alternative account of democracy, which I shall call the "participatory" theory, does not locate self-governance in mechanisms of decisionmaking, but rather in the processes through which citizens come to identify a government as their own.[55] According to this theory, democracy requires that citizens experience their state as an example of authentic self-determination. How such an experience can be sustained presents something of a puzzle, because citizens can expect to disagree with many of the specific actions of their government. The solution to this puzzle must be that citizens in a democracy experience their authorship of the state in ways that are anterior to the making of particular decisions. The participatory account postulates that it is a necessary precondition for this experience that a state be structured so as to subordinate its actions to public opinion, and that a state be constitutionally prohibited from preventing its citizens from participating in the communicative processes relevant to the formation of democratic public opinion.[56]

If, following the usage of the Court, we term these communicative processes "public discourse,"[57] then the participatory approach views the function of the First Amendment to be the safeguarding of public discourse from regulations that are inconsistent with democratic legitimacy. State restrictions on public discourse can be inconsistent with democratic legitimacy in two distinct ways. To the extent that the state cuts off particular citizens from participation in public discourse, it *pro tanto* negates its claim to democratic legitimacy with respect to such citizens. To the extent that the state regulates public discourse so as to reflect the values and priorities of some vision of collective identity, it preempts the very democratic process by which collective identity is to be determined.

Although both the Meiklejohnian and participatory perspectives share the common problem of specifying which communication is necessary for self-government and hence worthy of constitutional protection, they differ in at least two fundamental respects. First, the Meiklejohnian approach interprets

---

54. *Id.*

55. For a discussion of the contrast, *see* Post, *supra* note 50; *see also* Robert Post, *Equality and Autonomy in First Amendment Jurisprudence*, 95 MICH. L. REV. 1517, 1523 (1997).

56. For a fully developed explanation of this view, *see* ROBERT C. POST, CONSTITUTIONAL DOMAINS 179–96 (1995).

57. Rosenberger v. University of Va., 515 U.S. 819, 831 (1995); *see also* Hustler Magazine v. Falwell, 485 U.S. 46, 55 (1988).

the First Amendment primarily as a shield against the "mutilation of the think-ing process of the community,"[58] whereas the participatory approach under-stands the First Amendment instead as safeguarding the ability of individual citizens to participate in the formation of public opinion. The Meiklejohnian theory thus stresses the quality of public debate, whereas the participatory perspective emphasizes the autonomy of individual citizens.

Second, the Meiklejohnian perspective imagines the state within the arena of public discourse as occupying the position of a neutral moderator, capa-ble of saving public discourse from "mutilation" by distinguishing between relevant and irrelevant speech, abusive and nonabusive speech, "high" and "low" value speech, and so forth. It specifically repudiates the notion that public discourse is "a Hyde Park," filled with "unregulated talkativeness."[59] The participatory approach, in contrast, denies that there can be any possible neutral position within public discourse,[60] because public discourse is precisely the site of political contention about the nature of collective identity, and it is only by reference to some vision of collective identity that speech can be categorized as relevant or irrelevant, abusive or not abusive, of "high" or "low" value. The participatory theory understands national identity to be endlessly controversial, so that national identity cannot without contradiction provide grounds for the censorship of public discourse itself.

In both of these respects the Meiklejohnian perspective is structurally quite analogous to the theory of the marketplace of ideas. Both theories focus pri-marily on maintaining the integrity of processes of collective thinking. The Meiklejohnian approach seeks to safeguard the dialogue necessary for voting wise decisions; the theory of the marketplace of ideas seeks to protect the dialogue necessary for advancing truth. Just as Holmes in his *Abrams* dissent stressed that in proposing the theory of the marketplace of ideas he was "speaking only of expressions of opinion and exhortations,"[61] so contempo-rary Meiklejohnians seek to distinguish "between cognitive and noncognitive aspects of speech" and to award "less constitutional protection" to the latter.[62] Both theories are keenly aware of the prerequisites for constructive thinking. Just as Dewey viewed "ridicule, abuse, [and] intimidation" as incompatible

---

58. MEIKLEJOHN, *supra* note 50, at 27 (emphasis deleted).

59. *Id.* at 25–26.

60. As Kenneth Karst once famously remarked, "The state lacks 'moderators' who can be trusted to know when 'everything worth saying' has been said." Kenneth Karst, *Equality as a Central Principle in the First Amendment*, 43 U. CHI. L. REV. 20, 40 (1975).

61. 250 U.S. at 631.

62. Cass R. Sunstein, *Pornography and the First Amendment*, 1986 DUKE L.J. 589, 603 (1986).

with rational discussion,[63] so Meiklejohn viewed "abusive" speech as incompatible with a well-ordered town meeting.

Reconciling First Amendment Theory and Doctrine

It is particularly significant that our First Amendment tradition decisively rejects these critical components of both the Meiklejohnian perspective and the theory of the marketplace of ideas. American courts have consistently opted to protect individual autonomy against regulations of public discourse designed to maintain the integrity of collective thinking processes. In the area of campaign finance reform, for example, the Supreme Court has forcefully asserted that "the concept that government may restrict the speech of some elements of our society in order to enhance the relative voice of others" should be repudiated as "wholly foreign to the First Amendment."[64] In contexts ranging from restrictions on pornography and hate speech to "right-of-reply" statutes applicable to newspapers, contemporary advocates of the Meiklejohnian position have sharply and frequently complained of the tendency of courts to extend constitutional protection to individual rights even when the exercise of such rights "distorts" public discussion by perpetuating imbalances of social and economic power.[65]

This commitment to individual rights is one of the hallmarks of our distinctively American free-speech jurisprudence. The one notable exception to this commitment has been the Court's approval of federal regulations of the broadcast media. These regulations, which were designed to promote a balanced and well-ordered national dialogue on public issues, were clearly inspired by Meiklejohnian principles. Before adjudging such regulations constitutional, however, the Supreme Court took extraordinary care to characterize broadcast licensees as trustees for the speech of others, rather than as themselves direct participants in the conduct of self-governance.[66] This characterization enabled the Court to regard the imposition of broadcast regulations as not infringing on autonomous participants in the process of self-determination, and hence as compatible with the participatory approach.

American free-speech jurisprudence is also unique in its refusal to permit governments to exclude from public discourse irrational or abusive speech,

---

63. *See supra* note 42 and accompanying text.

64. Buckley v. Valeo, 424 U.S. 1, 48–49 (1976).

65. *See, e.g.,* OWEN FISS, LIBERALISM DIVIDED: FREEDOM OF SPEECH AND THE MANY USES OF STATE POWER (1996).

66. *See* Red Lion Broadcasting Co. v. FCC, 395 U.S. 367, 389–90 (1969). Over time, this characterization of broadcast media has proved historically unstable. For a discussion, *see* Robert C. Post, *Subsidized Speech,* 106 YALE L.J. 151, 158–60 (1996).

or speech otherwise deemed incompatible with rational dialogue. Beginning with cases like *Cantwell v. Connecticut*[67] and *Terminiello v. Chicago*,[68] First Amendment decisions have stood foursquare for the proposition that constitutional protection should be extended to speech within public discourse that is "outrageous"[69] or "offensive";[70] that is filled with "exaggeration" or "vilification";[71] that is "indecent";[72] that ruptures the "dignity" of its recipient;[73] or that is perceived as an instrument of "aggression and personal assault."[74] According to both the Meiklejohnian tradition and the theory of the marketplace of ideas, there is little constitutional reason to protect such speech, because it runs so directly contrary to the prerequisites of constructive thinking.

The participatory approach, by contrast, explains both why such speech is protected and why this protection is limited. The participatory approach does not focus on the cognitive cogency of speech, but rather on its facilitation of democratic participation. Even irrational and abusive speech can, within particular circumstances, serve as a vehicle for the construction of democratic legitimacy. When irrational and abusive speech serves this function, which is to say when it is deemed within public discourse,[75] its regulation would both compromise the neutrality of the state and the autonomy of those participating within public discourse. But when such speech does not serve this function, which is to say when it is deemed not within public discourse, it can be and commonly is regulated.[76] The upshot is a uniquely American jurisprudence that displays an overriding constitutional conviction to interpret the First Amendment "to ensure that the individual

---

67. 310 U.S. 296 (1940).

68. 337 U.S. 1 (1949).

69. Hustler Magazine v. Falwell, 485 U.S. 46, 53 (1988).

70. Cohen v. California, 403 U.S. 15, 22 (1971).

71. *Cantwell*, 310 U.S. at 310.

72. Reno v. ACLU, 521 U.S. 844, 869 (1997).

73. Boos v. Barry, 485 U.S. 312, 322 (1988).

74. Time, Inc. v. Hill, 385 U.S. 374, 412 (1967) (Fortas, J., dissenting).

75. The boundaries of public discourse are fixed by reference to various factors, including the content of speech (whether it is about a "public figure" or a matter of "public concern") and the method of the speech's distribution (whether it was disseminated to the public at large through a "medium for the communication of ideas."). For a discussion of the nature of these boundaries, *see* Robert C. Post, *The Constitutional Concept of Public Discourse: Outrageous Opinion, Democratic Deliberation, and Hustler Magazine v. Falwell*, 103 HARV. L. REV. 601, 667–84 (1990). For a discussion of the concept of a "medium for the communication of ideas," *see* Post, *supra* note 37.

76. For examples of such regulation, *see, e.g.*, Ohralik v. Ohio State Bar Ass'n, 436 U.S. 447, 461 (1978); Florida Bar v. Went For It, Inc., 515 U.S. 618, 624 (1995); Bethel Sch. Dist. No. 403 v. Fraser, 478 U.S. 675 (1986); Contreras v. Crown Zellerbach Corp., 565 P.2d 1173 (Wash. 1977).

citizen can effectively participate in and contribute to our republican system of self-government."[77]

This analysis suggests that where the doctrinal implications of different prominent theories of the First Amendment collide, courts will tend to give priority to the participatory theory of democracy. But this does not mean that other theories do not continue to have weight and consequence when they are not inconsistent with the participatory theory. Just as the marketplace of ideas continues to inform constitutional understandings of academic freedom, so the Meiklejohnian perspective continues to structure the regulation of speakers like the broadcast media, who are not understood to be participants in public discourse.

The full force of the participatory theory is most strikingly revealed when its requirements are contrasted with a regime of speech governed by a competing theory, like the Meiklejohnian approach. Consider, for example, the area of "commercial speech." The Court has never intimated that commercial speech should receive constitutional protection because participation in such speech facilitates democratic legitimacy. Instead the Court has explained that commercial speech merits First Amendment concern because it serves an "informational function."[78] "The free flow of commercial information," the Court has argued, is "indispensable to the formation of intelligent opinions" necessary for enlightened "public decisionmaking in a democracy."[79]

This reasoning represents a classic explication of the Meiklejohnian tradition. It stresses the cognitive contribution of speech to democratic decisionmaking, rather than the legitimation producing effects of speech understood as a vehicle of participation. The pattern of constitutional protection which the Court has extended to commercial speech thus follows a distinctly different pattern than that afforded to public discourse. The Court has allowed regulations of commercial speech that are necessary to preserve the integrity of its informational function, and hence it has accorded to commercial speech a "lesser protection."[80] Commercial speech can be suppressed if it is "misleading"[81] or "overreaching"[82] or "intrusive" and invasive of "privacy."[83] Yet because

---

77. Globe Newspaper Co. v. Superior Court, 457 U.S. 596, 604 (1982).

78. Central Hudson Gas & Elec. v. Public Serv. Comm'n, 447 U.S. 557, 563 (1980).

79. Virginia State Bd. of Pharmacy v. Virginia Citizens Consumer Council, 425 U.S. 748, 765 (1976).

80. United States v. Edge Broadcasting Co., 509 U.S. 418, 426 (1993).

81. *Central Hudson*, 447 U.S. at 566.

82. Ohralik v. Ohio State Bar Ass'n, 436 U.S. 447, 461 (1978).

83. Florida Bar v. Went For It, Inc., 515 U.S. 618, 624 (1995).

commercial speech is not understood as a vehicle for participation in the creation of democratic legitimacy, such regulation is not inconsistent with the participatory approach.[84]

The example of commercial speech suggests that First Amendment jurisprudence contains several operational and legitimate theories of freedom of speech, so that it is quite implausible to aspire to clarify First Amendment doctrine by abandoning all but one of these theories. In this short essay I have been able to discuss only the most important theories of the First Amendment, but there are certainly others. Many prominent academics, for example, have argued that the First Amendment should be interpreted so as to protect a value known variously as "individual self-realization,"[85] "individual self-fulfillment,"[86] or "human liberty,"[87] and occasionally there have been court decisions that appear to be inexplicable except by reference to some such theory of "individual liberty."[88] But there are not many such decisions, and so the theory does not seem to be very powerful.

Sometimes diverse First Amendment theories converge on similar doctrinal rules. The "clear and present danger" test formulated by Holmes may well be an example of such an overdetermined rule. But sometimes diverse First Amendment theories will require inconsistent doctrinal regimes, and when this occurs courts must decide which theory is to be given priority. I have argued in this essay that on the whole courts tend to give priority to the participatory theory of democracy, so that courts will not implement the doctrinal implications of other theories when they are inconsistent with the participatory approach.

The example of commercial speech, however, indicates that courts will nevertheless feel free to impose the doctrinal implications of other theories of the First Amendment when they are not inconsistent with the requirements of the participatory theory. We might generalize this insight by observing that theories of the First Amendment can be arranged according to a lexical priority. When theories conflict with each other, courts must decide the order in which theories should take precedence. To say, therefore, that a

---

84. For a full discussion, *see* Robert Post, *The Constitutional Status of Commercial Speech*, 48 UCLA L. REV. 1 (2000).

85. Martin H. Redish, *The Value of Free Speech*, 130 U. PA. L. REV. 591, 593 (1982).

86. THOMAS I. EMERSON, THE SYSTEM OF FREEDOM OF EXPRESSION 6 (1970).

87. C. EDWIN BAKER, HUMAN LIBERTY AND FREEDOM OF SPEECH (1989).

88. *See, e.g.*, Stanley v. Georgia, 394 U.S. 557, 565 (1969). For a useful recent study of the state of scholarship on this theory of the First Amendment, *see* Brian C. Murchison, *Speech and the Self-Realization Value*, 33 HARV. C.R.–C.L. L. REV. 443 (1998).

theory like "individual self-fulfillment" or even the marketplace of ideas is not powerful is to say that it ranks low in this lexical order, and that it cannot explain many decisions whose outcomes are not also required by lexically prior theories.

This way of conceptualizing the relationship of doctrine to theory accepts that we shall always have inconsistent regimes of First Amendment doctrine. But it also promises that this inconsistency can itself display a certain kind of order. The rules of the participatory theory will be imposed when required by that theory; the rules of the Meiklejohnian perspective will be imposed when required by that perspective and not incompatible with the participatory theory; the rules of the theory of the marketplace of ideas will be imposed when required by that theory and not incompatible with the participatory and Meiklejohnian approaches; and so forth.

The nature of this lexical ordering has been obscured by the tendency of courts to speak of First Amendment rules as applying to speech generally, thus systematically effacing the domains of speech actually implicated by different First Amendment theories. For example, in describing the First Amendment regime imposed upon commercial speech, the Supreme Court will remark that "[o]ur jurisprudence has emphasized that 'commercial speech [enjoys] a limited measure of protection, commensurate with its subordinate position in the scale of First Amendment values,' and is subject to 'modes of regulation that might be impermissible in the realm of noncommercial expression.' "[89] By characterizing commercial speech as subordinate to "noncommercial expression," the Court propagates a patent falsehood. There are many areas of noncommercial expression that receive no First Amendment protection at all, as the example of consumer product warnings illustrates. Thus the Court should instead have said that commercial speech receives less protection than "public discourse," thereby making clear that what is really at stake is the priority between the participatory and the Meiklejohnian theories of the First Amendment.

Conclusion

By perennially speaking as though speech were itself the object of First Amendment doctrine, the Court has promulgated a confusing regime of conflicting doctrinal rules that cannot possibly mean what they say. This is the underlying cause of what is now generally acknowledged to be the sorry state of First

---

89. Board of Trustees of the State Univ. v. Fox, 492 U.S. 469, 477 (1989) (quoting *Ohralik*, 436 U.S. at 456).

Amendment doctrine.[90] If, as I have suggested, the plurality of legitimate First Amendment theories limits the kind of doctrinal simplicity and clarity that is constitutionally obtainable, we can nevertheless expect courts to specify the lexical priority among First Amendment theories, as well as to be clear about the domain of speech pertinent to each theory. If courts can follow these simple prescriptions, we will have come a long way toward calming the tumultuous sea of First Amendment doctrine.

---

90. *See, e.g.,* Denver Area Educ. Telecommunications Consortium, Inc. v. FCC, 518 U.S. 727, 785–86 (1996).

The First Amendment is a cultural phenomenon. It seems to define the American
identity. Undoubtedly this has benefits for
preserving our democratic freedoms and,
more specifically, for insulating freedom
of speech itself from the vicissitudes of
momentary passions. But fame and privilege
may also bring costs. Ironically, critical
thought about freedom of speech and press
itself may be less likely to occur and less
tolerated when expressed. Moreover, the
First Amendment may become a kind of
Procrustean bed into which ill-fitting social
problems are forced. Even when First Amendment interests are at stake in controversies,
the free-speech element may dominate
the discussions and divert attention away
from other interests. While sometimes this
can serve as a safe (or safer) harbor for
discussion about more volatile and sensitive
issues (in cases involving racist speech,
for example), it would seem more often to
impoverish public debate.

It is this theme of distortion and im-
poverishment, from the standpoint of
both public policy and First Amendment
jurisprudence, that is the focus of Professor
Frederick Schauer in his essay "First Amendment Opportunism." With the metaphor of
driving a nail with a pipe wrench, Professor
Schauer examines the interests at stake and
the interests actually represented in a series
of First Amendment cases that concern prohibitions on advertising of pharmaceutical
prices, nude dancing, "Don't Ask, Don't Tell,"
and campaign finance reform. At the end,
Professor Schauer proffers two philosophical visions of the First Amendment, each
with a different answer to the question
whether what he calls "First Amendment
Opportunism" is a problem.—LCB

FREDERICK SCHAUER

First Amendment Opportunism

Suppose you need to drive a nail into a board but have no hammer. You do, however, have a pipe wrench. What do you do? Faced with this problem, some people would simply abandon the task. Not possessing the right tool for the job, they would take the position that it would be better that the task not be performed than that it be performed poorly. But most of us would react differently. Especially if the task is genuinely important, we will whack away at the nail with the pipe wrench. This will take longer than it otherwise would take with a hammer, the nail will probably not go all the way into the board, and the wrench will likely be damaged in the process. But it would be better than nothing.

In many respects, the culture of First Amendment discourse and argument, both in the courtroom and in the larger culture, exhibits many of the same features as being faced with driving a nail with a pipe wrench. With surprising frequency, people and organizations with a wide array of political goals find that society has not given them the doctrinally or rhetorically effective argumentative tools they need to advance their goals. The absence of these legally or culturally accepted arguments, like the absence of the hammer, disturbs them, but it also leads them, faced as they are with immediate goals that cannot wait until the world is reordered, to look for plausibly effective but ill-fitting tools. And in looking for these imperfect but usable tools, they often find that the leading candidate is the First Amendment. Like the pipe wrench, the First Amendment is frequently called on to do a job for which it is poorly designed. The job frequently gets done but, as with driving a nail with a pipe wrench, the job gets done poorly and the tool is damaged in the process.

The writing of this essay was supported by the Joan Shorenstein Center on the Press, Politics and Public Policy, and developed out of a series of illuminating conversations with Richard Fallon. An earlier version, focusing on the campaign reform issues discussed in the fourth section of the essay, was presented at the Federalist Society annual conference at Harvard Law School on March 11, 2000, and a subsequent and broader version was presented to the Centre on American Studies of the National University of Singapore on August 28, 2000.

That the First Amendment is so often pressed into service for tasks on the periphery of its central purposes is a product of its success. Different societies have different argumentative showstoppers, but in the United States it is often the First Amendment that serves this function, and thus it is often the First Amendment that marks the attempts of those engaged in legal or political debate to capture the political and rhetorical high ground. In some cultures this role may be played by the principle of equality,[1] in others the authority of the founders,[2] and in still others the words of a sacred text.[3] In different cultures each of these serves as the rhetorical equivalent to pounding one's fist on the table, yet in the United States, with a frequency that non-Americans typically find astonishing, it is the First Amendment particularly—and freedom of speech generally—that are the readily available and moderately serviceable pipe wrenches of political and legal argument.

When people make do with whatever happens to be available to them we call them "opportunistic," a word that hovers precariously between the pejorative and the complimentary. It is consequently not implausible to label the phenomenon I have just described as "First Amendment opportunism," and my goal in this essay is to document the phenomenon with a series of doctrinal vignettes. These vignettes, taken together, may indicate something pervasive and important about the development of First Amendment doctrine and free-speech rhetoric, for if the doctrine and the rhetoric have been developed opportunistically in the service of goals external to the First Amendment rather than as a consequence of the purposes the First Amendment was designed to serve, we may as a nation find ourselves with a cultural understanding of the First Amendment that diverges substantially from what a less misused[4] First Amendment would have produced.

---

1. On a number of issues, most prominently pornography and racist speech, the issues are often seen to present a conflict between free speech and equality. That this conflict is so often resolved in favor of the free-speech claims in the United States, *see, e.g.,* R.A.V. v. City of St. Paul, 505 U.S. 377 (1992); National Socialist Party v. Village of Skokie, 432 U.S. 43 (1977); American Booksellers Assoc. v. Hudnut, 771 F.2d 323 (7th Cir. 1985); Doe v. University of Mich., 721 F. Supp. 852 (E.D. Mich. 1989); and in favor of the equality claims in Canada, *see, e.g.,* R. v. Butler, [1992] 1 S.C.R. 452; R. v. Keegstra, [1990] 3 S.C.R. 697, is less a function of differences of judicial function than it is evidence of the different roles that the two claims play more broadly in the two different cultures. *See generally* KENT GREENAWALT, FIGHTING WORDS: INDIVIDUALS, COMMUNITIES, AND LIBERTIES OF SPEECH (1995).

2. One of the best examples I know is the rhetorical power of the "Mr. Jefferson believed . . ." argument at the University of Virginia, an argument whose power is evidenced by the frequency of the response "No, he didn't!" compared to "So what?"

3. The Bible and the Koran are the obvious examples, but in the United States the Constitution may have a similar status. *See* SANFORD LEVINSON, CONSTITUTIONAL FAITH (1988).

4. As I suggest in the concluding section, to think of the First Amendment as having been "misused" suggests that there is a properly used First Amendment, and the view that there is a properly used

The First Amendment in the Service of Libertarianism:
The Case of Commercial Speech

Many people believe that economic liberty constitutes the bedrock of almost all that is valuable, and believe as well that governmental interference with economic activity is, with precious few exceptions, more for ill than for good. We call these people libertarians, and they find their philosophical sustenance in Adam Smith, in Herbert Spencer, in Friedrich Hayek, in James Buchanan, in Milton Friedman, and even in Ayn Rand. The invisible hand really works, libertarians tend to believe, and even if the invisible hand works imperfectly, libertarians still believe it works far less imperfectly than the very visible and very heavy hand of government intervention in the operation of the market.[5]

For about fifty years, from the middle of the 1880s until the middle of the 1930s, American libertarians had an important ally in the shape of the Supreme Court of the United States. At times relying on a narrow interpretation of the scope of national power,[6] at times on either the Due Process[7] or Equal Protection[8] Clauses of the Fourteenth Amendment, at times on the Takings Clause of the Fifth Amendment,[9] and at times (especially earlier) on the Contract Clause of Article Four,[10] the Supreme Court during this period persistently invalidated a host of federal and state regulations as unconstitutionally interfering with the economic liberty of those whom government sought to regulate. Laws prohibiting child labor,[11] or setting minimum wages or maximum hours,[12] or protecting labor unions,[13] for example, were cast aside in the service of a libertarian vision of what the Constitution was designed to

---

First Amendment in turn presupposes the debatable premise within free-speech theory and constitutional jurisprudence that the First Amendment is something more than the evolution of decisions over time.

5. *See* RICHARD A. EPSTEIN, SIMPLE RULES FOR A COMPLEX WORLD (1995).

6. *See* A.L.A. Schechter Poultry Corp. v. United States, 295 U.S. 495 (1935); Railroad Retirement Bd. v. Alton R.R. Co., 295 U.S. 330 (1935).

7. *See* Allgeyer v. Louisiana, 165 U.S. 578 (1897).

8. F.S. Royster Guano Co. v. Virginia, 253 U.S. 412 (1920).

9. Pennsylvania Coal Co. v. Mahon, 260 U.S. 393 (1922).

10. *See* Robert Hale, *The Supreme Court and the Contract Clause,* 57 HARV. L. REV. 852 (1944).

11. Hammer v. Dagenhart, 247 U.S. 251 (1918), *overruled in part by* United States v. Darby, 312 U.S. 100 (1941).

12. Adkins v. Children's Hosp., 261 U.S. 525 (1923), *overruled in part by* West Coast Hotel Co. v. Parrish, 300 U.S. 379 (1937); Muller v. Oregon, 208 U.S. 412 (1908).

13. Coppage v. Kansas, 236 U.S. 1 (1915), *overruled in part by* Phelps Dodge Corp. v. NLRB, 313 U.S. 177 (1941); Adair v. United States, 208 U.S. 161 (1908), *overruled in part by* Phelps Dodge Corp. v. NLRB, 313 U.S. 177 (1941).

accomplish. The most famous of these cases was *Lochner v. New York*,[14] in which the Supreme Court in 1905 held that restricting the number of hours that a baker could bake in a day or in a week interfered with the freedom of the baker and his employer to contract as to the conditions of the baker's employment. Subsequently, early in the New Deal the Supreme Court held that a wide range of New Deal legislation unconstitutionally interfered with the economic liberty of the various enterprises that the Roosevelt Administration, in the hope of alleviating the effects of the Depression, sought to control.[15]

Halfway through the New Deal the Supreme Court changed its mind (or at least its tune), and things have never been the same. Casting aside the view that the Constitution adopted a libertarian or laissez-faire view of economics, the Court began then and has continued to uphold most forms of social and economic regulation against libertarian objections,[16] concluding that with respect to such matters it was the place neither of the comparatively unchangeable Constitution nor of the unelected federal courts to interfere with the judgments of the seemingly more representative and seemingly more responsive executive, administrative, and legislative branches of government.[17]

The Supreme Court's post–New Deal approach to economic and social legislation that interfered with unrestrained economic liberty did not serve to extinguish economic libertarianism as a legal, as a political, or as a philosophical position.[18] But those who would have argued against governmental economic control on libertarian grounds now found that after the New Deal their views had neither constitutional nor cultural (the New Deal, after all, was at the time and is still considered by most of the population to have been a rousing success) support.

Facing the increasing constitutional (or at least doctrinal) weakness of arguments from economic libertarianism, economic libertarians turned their attention to the First Amendment. In the 1976 case of *Virginia Citizens Consumer Council v. Virginia Board of Pharmacy*,[19] those who a generation earlier

---

14. 198 U.S. 45 (1905), *overruled in part by* Day-Brite Lighting Inc. v. Missouri, 342 U.S. 421 (1952) *and* Ferguson v. Skrupa, 372 U.S. 726 (1963).

15. In addition to *Railroad Retirement Bd.* and *Schechter, supra* note 6, *see also* New State Ice Co. v. Liebmann, 285 U.S. 262 (1932).

16. *See* Nebbia v. New York, 291 U.S. 502 (1934); West Coast Hotel Co. v. Parrish, 300 U.S. 379 (1937); Home Bldg. & Loan Ass'n v. Blaisdell, 290 U.S. 398 (1934).

17. United States v. Carolene Products Co., 304 U.S. 144 (1938). *See also* Ferguson v. Skrupa, 372 U.S. 726 (1963); Olsen v. Nebraska, 313 U.S. 236 (1941). *See generally* John Hetherington, *State Economic Regulation and Substantive Due Process of Law*, 53 Nw. U. L. Rev. 13 & 226 (1958).

18. *See* John Gray, Liberalism (1986); Richard Epstein, *Toward a Revitalization of the Contract Clause*, 51 U. Chi. L. Rev. 703 (1984).

19. 425 U.S. 748 (1976).

would have couched their objections in terms of economic liberty now argued that Virginia's prohibition on the advertising of pharmaceutical prices violated the First Amendment. Advertising was "speech," they argued, with Webster's Dictionary at and on their side, and those earlier Supreme Court cases[20] that had excluded commercial advertising from the ambit of the First Amendment's coverage could not survive the growing strength and breadth of the First Amendment.[21] The Supreme Court agreed, invalidating Virginia's advertising restrictions not because they represented incursions on economic liberty, which they did, but instead because the Court now saw the restrictions on advertising as unconstitutional restrictions on the freedom of speech of those who would wish to advertise the prices of the goods they were offering for sale, and on the free-speech rights, indirectly enforced by the speakers, of the *listeners* who would benefit from the information previously denied them.

Yet as Thomas Jackson and John Jeffries have powerfully demonstrated,[22] the *Virginia Pharmacy* case had little to do with freedom of speech and much to do with straight economic liberty. The advertising restriction came about as a consequence of the fact that the independent retail pharmacists in Virginia had enlisted the state board of pharmacy in their economic battles with large chain pharmacies, out of concern that the chain pharmacies were threatening to make the local pharmacist obsolete by means of their aggressive pricing policies. Siding with the local pharmacists, the pharmacy board had prohibited price advertising, allegedly in the service of preventing consumers from being misled, but in reality patently depriving the chain pharmacies of their most effective method of competing with the traditional, independent druggist.

Were it not for the fact that the state's regulatory intervention came in the form of an advertising restriction, as opposed to a price restriction or a restriction on the methods of doing business, there was little that the Supreme Court could or likely would have done given the then-existing constitutional doctrine. After all, only two decades earlier the Court had refused to intervene in a similar case in which the optometrists and ophthalmologists of Oklahoma had persuaded the Oklahoma legislature that it would be wise to prevent opticians from performing eyeglass fittings,[23] even though it was clear that

---

20. Especially Valentine v. Chrestensen, 316 U.S. 52 (1942), *overruling recognized by* Payne v. Tennessee, 501 U.S. 808 (1991). *See also* Pittsburgh Press Co. v. Pittsburgh Comm'n on Human Relations, 413 U.S. 376 (1973).

21. For a more recent articulation of the position, *see* Alex Kozinski & Stuart Banner, *The Anti-History and Pre-History of Commercial Speech,* 71 TEX. L. REV. 747 (1993); Alex Kozinski & Stuart Banner, *Who's Afraid of Commercial Speech?* 76 VA. L. REV. 627 (1990).

22. *Commercial Speech: Economic Due Process and the First Amendment,* 65 VA. L. REV. 1 (1979).

23. Williamson v. Lee Optical, 348 U.S. 483 (1955).

this restriction was nothing more than the consequence of the optometrists' and ophthalmologists' success in capturing the Oklahoma legislature for their own economic interests. But in the area of economic regulation, the Court had said, even economic regulatory decisions as scantily justified as Oklahoma's was in this case would not be invalidated in the service of a libertarian vision of the role of government.

Because the chain pharmacists of Virginia would thus have had little constitutional recourse were Virginia to have severely restricted dispensing pharmaceuticals by corporations,[24] and even less were Virginia to have set uniform prices at which pharmaceuticals could be sold, it was clear that the almost fortuitous occurrence of an advertising restriction, as opposed to a price or business operations restriction, had little to do with the underlying basis for the challenge. The challenge was driven by an economic libertarianism, or at least by the interests of a particular segment of the market that would benefit from the lack of restrictions, and the fortuitous presence of words and information in the object of the regulatory approach enabled the challengers to clothe what was in fact a doctrinally weak constitutional argument for economic libertarianism in the more doctrinally and socially robust language of the First Amendment. The challengers had been opportunistic, seizing an imperfect First Amendment argument to give them at least a partial victory.

The First Amendment in the Service of Sexual Freedom: The Case of Nude Dancing

Economic liberty is not the only variety of liberty enjoying less constitutional protection than its enthusiasts would desire. In the area of sexual liberty, an equivalent degree of judicial reluctance to interfere with state and federal restrictions exists as well, with the only difference that here, unlike in the area of economic liberty, things have never been any different. For well over a century, American courts have taken the position that state restrictions on even wholly consensual sexual activity, whether commercial or noncommercial, are not constrained by the Constitution.[25] In the face of repeated challenges, both state and federal courts have with only a few exceptions refused to take the

---

24. See also New Orleans v. Dukes, 427 U.S. 297 (1976), another case in which the Supreme Court refused to intervene when one segment of an industry (traditional street vendors in New Orleans) had succeeded in securing passage of legislation keeping another segment of that industry (new entrants from a less traditional background) from gaining a foothold.

25. See Bowers v. Hardwick, 478 U.S. 186 (1986); Doe v. Commonwealth's Attorney, 403 F. Supp. 1199 (E.D. Va. 1975); Thomas C. Grey, *Eros, Civilization and the Burger Court*, 43 LAW & CONTEMP. PROBS. 83 (1980).

view that laws criminalizing or otherwise prohibiting sodomy, fornication, and other forms of sexual conduct historically thought immoral violate a constitutionally protected liberty.[26]

The view that consensual sexual activity among adults may not legitimately be restricted by the state is part of a larger view, often associated with chapter 1 of John Stuart Mill's *On Liberty,* maintaining that the state may not legitimately interfere with the self-regarding (and thus nonharmful) activities of knowing or consenting adults in full possession of their faculties. Under the Millian view, the state may not enforce morality for its own sake, and the state may not paternalistically presume that it knows better than people themselves what is best for them. Restrictions on allegedly immoral consensual activity, like restrictions on consensual use of narcotics or consensual gambling, so the Millian position holds, are impermissible restrictions on individual liberty.

From Mill's day to the present, this view of liberty and of the limits of state power has commanded much support.[27] Notably, however, it has never commanded the support of five members of the Supreme Court of the United States, at least as a *constitutional* principle, and thus the Court has persistently treated personal liberty *simpliciter* in much the same way as it has treated economic liberty.[28] Just as the Court has adopted the view of Justice Holmes, dissenting in *Lochner v. New York,* that the Constitution does not adopt Herbert Spencer's *Social Statics,* so too has it adopted the view that neither does the Constitution adopt John Stuart Mill's *On Liberty.*[29] Whether the issue be consensual sexual practices,[30] or arguably self-regarding personal conduct such as drug use or motorcycle helmet nonuse,[31] the prevailing view in the American courts remains that governmental choices to enforce sexual morality, or even to be

---

26. *See* Note, *Fornication, Cohabitation, and the Constitution,* 77 MICH. L. REV. 252 (1978).

27. *See, e.g.,* JOEL FEINBERG, THE MORAL LIMITS OF THE CRIMINAL LAW (1984); H. L. A. HART, LAW, LIBERTY, AND MORALITY (1963); MORALITY, HARM AND THE LAW (Gerald Dworkin ed., 1993); DAVID A. J. RICHARDS, SEX, DRUGS, DEATH, AND THE LAW: AN ESSAY ON HUMAN RIGHTS AND OVERCRIMINALIZATION (1982); Richard Arneson, *Liberalism, Freedom, and Community,* 100 ETHICS 368 (1990). The argument has also generated prominent opposition, as exemplified in JAMES FITZJAMES STEPHEN, LIBERTY, EQUALITY, FRATERNITY (London 1873), and PATRICK DEVLIN, THE ENFORCEMENT OF MORALS (1965).

28. *Cf.* RONALD DWORKIN, *What Rights Do We Have?, in* TAKING RIGHTS SERIOUSLY 266–78 (1978). Dworkin's argument that there is "no right to liberty" is structurally identical to the Supreme Court's position, but because Dworkin has a much more capacious understanding of particular liberties than does the Supreme Court, in practice Dworkin's outcomes come far closer to Mill's than to those of the Supreme Court.

29. *See* Paris Adult Theatre I v. Slaton, 413 U.S. 49 (1973).

30. Bowers v. Hardwick, 478 U.S. 186 (1986).

31. *See* State v. Lee, 465 P.2d 573 (Haw. 1970); American Motorcycle Ass'n v. Davids, 158 N.W.2d 72 (Mich. App. 1968*), abrogated by* People v. Poucher, 240 N.W.2d 298 (Mich. App. 1976); Note,

paternalistic, are within the scope of constitutionally permissible governmental choices, and are thus not to be interfered with in the name of the Constitution.

As with commercial advertising, however, the First Amendment has provided an often serviceable even if imperfect tool for those who continue to press for a more liberty-focused view of constitutional restrictions on state power. In the context of sexual liberty, the best example may be the case of nude dancing. Although the motivations of those who patronize nude dancing establishments (especially those establishments providing enclosed private viewing areas) are typically not dramatically different from the motivations of those who patronize houses of prostitution, and although the motivations of the state in prohibiting nude dancing are often not fundamentally different from its motivations in prohibiting public nudity,[32] nude dancing involves a performance by someone on a stage and observation by patrons in seats. In this respect it bears some (but arguably not many)[33] points of contact with performances of Shakespeare and Beethoven, and these points of contact have consequently led people to reframe their general or sexual-liberty-based objections to nude dancing regulation in First Amendment terms.[34]

Not only have those who press for a greater degree of constitutionalized sexual liberty couched their broader arguments in narrower First Amendment terms, but they have also met with a surprising degree of success in doing so. However passive the courts may be when the issue is consensual sexual conduct not involving pictures or performances, when it takes place in the context of images or performances the First Amendment and its associated judicial aggressiveness has exerted considerable force on the development of constitutional principles. Houses of prostitution may be banned completely, but peep shows and nude dancing, even in circumstances in which the context is virtually indistinguishable from a house of prostitution,[35] have enjoyed considerable constitutional protection, although a degree of protection still less than that enjoyed by enterprises whose sale and display of images and

---

Motorcycle Helmets and the Constitutionality of Self-Protective Legislation, 30 OHIO ST. L.J. 355 (1969); Comment, *The California Marijuana Possession Statute*, 19 HASTINGS L.J. 758 (1968).

32. On public nudity, *see New England Naturist Ass'n v. Larsen*, 692 F. Supp. 75 (D.R.I. 1988).

33. *See* Young v. American Mini Theatres, Inc., 427 U.S. 50, 70 (1976) (Stevens, J.) ("[F]ew of us would march our sons and daughters off to war to preserve the citizen's right to see 'Specified Sexual Activities' exhibited in the theaters of our choice.").

34. *See* Doran v. Salem Inn, Inc., 422 U.S. 922 (1975).

35. *See* Schad v. Mt. Ephraim, 452 U.S. 61 (1981). Even where the restrictions have been upheld, as in Barnes v. Glen Theatre, Inc., 501 U.S. 560 (1991), it is clear that there is far greater constitutional solicitude for the behavior than would have been the case but for the First Amendment dimension.

performances appeal to the more cerebral dimensions of our existence. Public nudity may also be banned completely, but not pictures of nudity, even when those pictures are visible to unwilling viewers.[36]

In the area of sexually explicit performances, the opportunistic use of the First Amendment to achieve the goals of sexual libertarianism—the use of Mill's chapter 2 to achieve chapter 1 goals—has had an interesting feed-back effect. Insofar as proponents of sexual liberty are judicially or culturally successful in advancing the claim that sexual activity with either an image-based or entertainment-based component raises serious free-speech issues, there is a possibility that the association of the First Amendment with sexual freedom will become closer, and that this association will persist in the minds of people even when the issue of sexual freedom does not arise in an image-based or entertainment-based context. So although issues of sexual freedom not having such components might not earlier have been thought of as raising First Amendment concerns, the extent to which the First Amendment has been imported into the sexual arena appears to have had the aftereffect that the First Amendment is now thought relevant even when neither entertainment nor images are part of the context. The consequence of First Amendment opportunism, therefore, may not only be the intended one of moving the First Amendment into areas involving images that are not part of the array of central First Amendment concerns, but also the unintended one of moving the First Amendment in such a way that it is taken as the appropriate repository, both in court and in broader public discourse, for the full range of arguments and beliefs about all forms of sexual liberty.

The First Amendment and Sexual Orientation:
The Case of "Don't Ask, Don't Tell"

A related case of First Amendment opportunism has arisen in the context of the American military's approach to gays and lesbians serving in the armed forces. Under pressure from gays and lesbians and their supporters to relax the policy by which non-heterosexuals were excluded from the U.S. military, and under pressure from members of the military and many others to adhere to the traditional policy, the Clinton Administration in its early years adopted a policy generally known as "Don't Ask, Don't Tell." Under this policy, it was deemed impermissible for military officials to inquire into the sexual orientation of military personnel. That was the "Don't Ask" part of the policy. Under the "Don't Tell" part, however, military personnel who either disclosed

---

36. Erznoznik v. City of Jacksonville, 422 U.S. 205 (1975).

a homosexual orientation or who admitted to same-sex sexual conduct could be discharged from the military or otherwise disciplined.

In part because the military appeared to be lax about "Don't Ask" and strict about "Don't Tell," and even more because of general objections to the policy as excessively hostile to homosexual members of the military, there arose numerous court challenges to the "Don't Ask, Don't Tell" policy.[37] But because existing constitutional doctrine, especially prior to *Romer v. Evans*,[38] was consistent with the exclusion of homosexuals because of their sexuality,[39] it did not appear likely to the challengers that a direct attack on the liberty-denying and equality-denying features of the policy would be successful. Instead, the attacks on the policy were typically recast in First Amendment terms, a move facilitated by the fact that the act of telling is of necessity an act of speech in the literal sense. If telling could constitute the basis for a discharge, so the argument went, then the government was in effect punishing people for their speech.[40] What had previously been a doctrinally dubious (even if morally powerful) liberty or equality argument had thus been transformed into a slightly less doctrinally dubious free-speech argument.

Litigating the "Don't Ask, Don't Tell" policy in First Amendment terms is an example of just the kind of opportunism I am exploring here. The fundamental objection to the policy was not that it limited speech. Rather, the fundamental objection was that one's sexual orientation was both none of the government's business and irrelevant to one's ability to serve in the military, and thus that the exclusion of gays and lesbians from the military represented the discriminatory exclusion of people because of an aspect of their identity that should not as a moral and constitutional matter be permitted to be taken into account. But because the fundamental objection looked to be a constitutional loser on the existing doctrine, the litigation strategy seized on the "Don't Tell" dimension of the policy—telling is, after all, a form of speaking according to the dictionary—to convert what in a constitutionally different world would have been a better equal protection or due process claim into a slightly plausible free-speech claim.[41]

---

37. *See, e.g.,* Steffan v. Aspin, 8 F.3d 57 (D.C. Cir. 1993), *vacated by* Steffan v. Aspin, 1994 U.S. App. LEXIS 9977 (D.C. Cir. Jan. 7, 1994); Cammermeyer v. Aspin, 850 F. Supp. 910 (W.D. Wash. 1994).

38. 517 U.S. 620 (1996).

39. This is the plan implication of Bowers v. Hardwick, 478 U.S. 186 (1986).

40. *See* Patricia A. Cain, *Litigating for Lesbian and Gay Rights: A Legal History,* 79 VA. L. REV. 1551 (1993); Kenji Yoshino, *Assimilationist Bias in Equal Protection: The Visibility Presumption and the Case of "Don't Ask, Don't Tell,"* 108 YALE L.J. 485 (1998).

41. For arguments that the free-speech claim was more than slightly plausible, *see, e.g.,* Nan D. Hunter, *Expressive Identity: Recuperating Dissent for Equality,* 35 HARV. C.R.–C.L. L. REV. 1 (2000);

Two dimensions of this strategy by the opponents of "Don't Ask, Don't Tell" are worth noting. The first is the one I have already discussed, that the strategy appears to have been a second-best fallback position given the doctrinal unavailability of what was the real concern—namely, the equality-denying dimensions of the policy. The second dimension is that the fallback strategy of choice turned out to be the Free Speech Clause of the First Amendment and not something else. If one were looking for a second-best constitutional argument to give sympathetic judges a doctrinal handle and possibly to persuade members of the public as well as the judiciary of the rightness of the claim, there were a number of possibilities available. Prosecuting people on the basis of what they publicly declared might be taken as self-incrimination in violation of the Fifth Amendment. Excluding people because of their sexual orientation might be argued to be a species of sex discrimination, and thus appropriately evaluated under the intermediate scrutiny established in the 1970s for distinctions based on sex.[42] Or the exclusion might be presented as a denial of the ability to express one's faith and thus a form of denial of the free exercise of religion. Other constitutionally tethered arguments might have been available as well, and some of these might, hypothetically, have been selected by gay and lesbian activists as the foundation for their arguments in courts of law and in the court of public opinion.

It should be apparent that none of these are good arguments, in the "good law" sense of the word "good." Each of the arguments would have had to confront formidable analytical and precedential hurdles, and each of them would have had a low chance of success except in the hands of a highly sympathetic judge not overly concerned with constraints by precedents from above. And as arguments in the public arena, each of them would have suffered from trying to rely on constitutional imagery and constitutional language to support a claim whose constitutional support the courts had rejected.[43] But in this respect these arguments were no different from the free-speech argument, which would have had to confront not only the fact that the mere presence of words does not

---

Taylor Flynn, *Of Communism, Treason, and Addiction: An Evaluation of New Challenges to the Military's Anti-Gay Policy*, 80 IOWA L. REV. 979 (1995); Tobias Barrington Wolff, *Compelled Affirmations, Free Speech, and the U.S. Military's Don't Ask, Don't Tell Policy*, 63 BROOK. L. REV. 1141 (1997).

42. *See* Craig v. Boren, 429 U.S. 190 (1976). *See also* Mississippi Univ. for Women v. Hogan, 458 U.S. 718 (1982).

43. This strategy is not always unsuccessful, as we can see from the considerable public and cultural success that the institutional press has had in casting its claims of affirmative press access to governmental facilities in First Amendment terms, the Supreme Court's hostility to such First Amendment claims (*see, e.g.*, Pell v. Procunier, 417 U.S. 817 (1974); Saxbe v. Washington Post, 417 U.S. 843 (1974); Gannett Co. v. DePasquale, 443 U.S. 368 (1979)) notwithstanding.

alone create a free-speech case,[44] but also, and more directly, the doctrinally well-supported principle—exemplified in *Wayte v. United States*[45] and *Wisconsin v. Mitchell*[46]—that prosecuting people on the basis of their evidentiary admissions does not violate the First Amendment even though the evidentiary admissions necessarily take the form of speech, and sometimes take the form of public political or ideological utterances (as did Wayte's public admission during a protest demonstration that he had failed to register as required with the Selective Service System). If "telling" is in this context nothing other than a form of confessing, then prosecuting people as a consequence of what they "tell" is simply another way of describing the act of prosecuting people on the basis of the crimes to which they have—with "speech"—confessed.

It may well be that there are nonfrivolous counterarguments to the claim that the *Wayte–Mitchell* category of cases would doom the free-speech attack on "Don't Ask, Don't Tell," but my point is not about which arguments might at the end of the day have prevailed with a non-predisposed but analytically acute judge. It is rather that, as a matter of prediction,[47] the empirical likelihood of the free-speech argument's prevailing as a doctrinal matter did not look a great deal stronger than the empirical likelihood of the self-incrimination, sex discrimination, or free exercise of religion arguments' prevailing. Yet in the face of this rough equivalence in viability among probably but not certainly losing arguments, it is telling that it was the free-speech argument that was selected as the winner among the array of implausible claims. The selection of the free-speech argument rather than any of the others appears to be a consequence of the cultural salience and cultural persuasiveness of a free-speech argument, as opposed to, for example, the cultural persuasiveness of a self-incrimination argument (often seen by the public as the vehicle by which guilty people escape their just punishment).[48] The selection of the free-speech argument by the opponents of "Don't Ask, Don't Tell" appears to have been based not only on the increased likelihood that some judge would be willing to press against the doctrinal barriers, but also on the greater likelihood that the free-speech argument would resonate with a sympathetic subset of the public.

---

44. *See* KENT GREENAWALT, SPEECH, CRIME, AND THE USES OF LANGUAGE (1989); Frederick Schauer, *Categories and the First Amendment: A Play in Three Acts,* 34 VAND. L. REV. 265 (1981).

45. 470 U.S. 598 (1985).

46. 508 U.S.476 (1993).

47. *See* Frederick Schauer, *Prediction and Particularity,* 78 B.U. L. REV. 773 (1998). To refer to the question as one of prediction is a trifle question-begging, however, since the issues of doctrinal sociology that I am exploring here are, under even soft versions of legal realism, relevant to predicting what some court might do.

48. *Cf.* Dickerson v. United States, 530 U.S. 428 (2000), in which Chief Justice Rehnquist remarked on the degree of cultural entrenchment of Miranda v. Arizona, 384 U.S. 436 (1966).

In the final analysis, the First Amendment arguments against "Don't Ask, Don't Tell" did not succeed in court. Although there were some early victories,[49] the eventual result was a series of decisions by the U.S. Courts of Appeals upholding the policy against free-speech challenges almost as easily as they upheld the policy against equal protection and due process challenges.[50] Yet although the free-speech challenges ultimately did not prevail in litigation, they may still have had some success, both in generating more academic, judicial, and public support for the attacks than would otherwise have existed[51] and, perhaps more important, in associating the persuasive power of the First Amendment with the movement to recognize the moral and constitutional rights of the homosexual community. By couching the objections in free-speech terms, the objectors to the policy made a strong, even if not in the final analysis successful, claim to the cultural high ground of the First Amendment.[52] And in doing so, they not only helped their own cause, but may also have helped to shape the public understanding of the First Amendment itself.

---

49. Steffan v. Aspin, 8 F.3d 57 (D.C. Cir. 1993), *vacated by* Steffan v. Aspin, 1994 U.S. App. LEXIS 9977 (D.C. Cir. Jan. 7, 1994); Cammermeyer v. Aspin, 850 F. Supp. 910 (W.D. Wash. 1994).

50. *See, e.g.*, Holmes v. California Army Nat'l Guard, 124 F.3d 1126 (9th Cir. 1997), *reh'g denied by* 155 F.3d 1049 (9th Cir. 1998); Able v. United States, 155 F.3d 628 (2d Cir. 1998); Richenberg v. Perry, 97 F.3d 256 (8th Cir. 1996); Thomasson v. Perry, 80 F.3d 915 (4th Cir. 1996); Thorne v. United States Dep't of Defense, 945 F. Supp. 924 (E.D. Va. 1996). *See* Recent Cases, 111 HARV. L. REV. 1371 (1998).

51. One piece of evidence of this is the extent of scholarly writing, some of it cited above, in support of the argument, writing that would probably not have come into being had the litigation strategy been different. And another piece of evidence is the existence of an intriguing and politically diverse group of dissenters, especially in *Holmes v. California Army National Guard*, cited in the previous note.

52. It is not implausible to suppose that this is one part of the strategy behind the "silencing" argument that is central to the feminist antipornography movement. *See* CATHARINE MACKINNON, ONLY WORDS (1993); CATHARINE MACKINNON, FEMINISM UNMODIFIED: DISCOURSES ON LIFE AND LAW (1987); CATHARINE MACKINNON & ANDREA DWORKIN, IN HARM'S WAY: THE PORNOGRAPHY CIVIL RIGHTS HEARINGS (1997); Rae Langton, *Whose Right? Ronald Dworkin, Women, and Pornographers*, 19 PHIL. & PUB. AFF. 311 (1990); Rae Langton, *Speech Acts and Unspeakable Acts*, 22 PHIL. & PUB. AFF. 293 (1993); Jennifer Hornsby & Rae Langton, *Free Speech and Illocution*, 4 LEGAL THEORY 21 (1998). Although the equality-denying and liberty-denying dimensions of certain forms of pornography (or all forms, if pornography is *defined* so that it only includes the equality-denying dimension) are as clear (or more so) as the silencing dimension, the silencing argument enables the objectors to pornography to meet the defenders of pornography on their own culturally powerful grounds by making an argument that sounds in speech suppression rather than in equality denial. If one source of political power of the defenders of pornography is their ability to make a free-speech argument, a particularly powerful rhetorical device in the United States, then the development and use of the silencing argument may represent an effort on the parts of the opponents of pornography to deny to the defenders the exclusive use of the free-speech banner. For a lengthier exploration of this possibility, *see* Frederick Schauer, *The Ontology of Censorship, in* CENSORSHIP AND SILENCING: PRACTICES OF CULTURAL REGULATION 247–68 (Robert Post ed., 1998).

The First Amendment and Campaign Finance Reform

Consider finally the recent and not-so-recent debates about campaign finance reform.[53] One way of understanding these debates is as a debate about the extent to which elections should be subject to majoritarian control. Under one view, the design of elections, like elections themselves, is at the center of the concept of democracy, and as a consequence the largest possible range of issues about the design of elections should be subject to popular control. Whether it be the length of terms, the days on which elections are held, the determinants of candidate eligibility, or the architecture of the ballots, these are examples of the types of questions that a self-governing populace should be entitled to determine. Without democratic control of these central mechanisms and procedures of democracy, so the argument goes, the idea of democracy is pointless.[54]

Although this argument has some surface appeal, there is a powerful counterargument: allowing the democratic process to determine the rules of democracy is inevitably to allow the majority to make seemingly procedural rules that will have the substantive effect of entrenching that majority's power. Just as baseball teams with speedy baserunners and error-prone infielders instruct their groundskeepers to let the infield grass grow long, so too would any majoritarian process for designing elections benefit the interests of the majority, which is the very antithesis of democracy. The solution, according to this side of the argument, is to remove from the first-order political process those second-order decisions that determine how the process will be organized.[55] In this way electoral decisions would not be based on the principle of whose ox is gored, but by the disinterested determination of an institutional designer operating under a virtual veil of ignorance regarding the substantive or political valence of the decisions that are made.

The latter view, which would include issues of campaign contributions and expenditures among the array of issues of electoral design that should not be decided by short-term, self-interested, and self-protective majorities,

---

53. For a sampling of the voluminous literature, *see* CAMPAIGN MONEY (Herbert Alexander ed., 1976); ELIZABETH DREW, WHATEVER IT TAKES: THE REAL STRUGGLE FOR POLITICAL POWER IN AMERICA (rev. ed. 1998); MICHAEL J. MALBIN & THOMAS L. GAIS, THE DAY AFTER REFORM: SOBERING CAMPAIGN REFORM LESSONS FROM THE AMERICAN STATES (1998); IF *BUCKLEY* FELL: A FIRST AMENDMENT BLUEPRINT FOR REGULATING MONEY IN POLITICS (Joshua Rosenkranz ed., 1999); Samuel Issacharoff & Richard H. Pildes, *Politics as Markets: Partisan Lockups of the Democratic Process*, 50 STAN. L. REV. 643 (1998); Kathleen M. Sullivan, *Political Money and Freedom of Speech*, 30 U.C. DAVIS L. REV. 663 (1997); *Developments in the Law: Elections*, 88 HARV. L. REV. 1114 (1975).

54. For an exploration of this argument, and the arguments against it, *see* Frederick Schauer, *Judicial Review of the Devices of Democracy*, 94 COLUM. L. REV. 1326 (1994).

55. *Cf.* Cass R. Sunstein & Edna Ullman-Margalit, *Second Order Decisions*, 109 ETHICS 432 (1999).

bears some resemblance to the view of constitutional law made famous by John Hart Ely.[56] Under this view, the Supreme Court is primarily empowered to manage the rules of the democratic process, which should be allowed to do almost anything it wishes except to set the rules for its own operation. These rules, Ely and others believe, are antecedent to democracy, and it would make no more sense to allow a democratic majority to set the rules of democracy than it would to allow a democratic majority to vote to end democracy itself.[57]

Consistent with the position just described, it might have been desirable for the Constitution to have created a fourth branch of government charged with managing the electoral process and itself immune from the vagaries of that process. But the Constitution does not create such a national election commission, and thus the fallback institution is for many who subscribe to this view the Supreme Court and the rest of the federal judiciary, which, even if not charged with managing the electoral process, at least comes with the advantage of being comparatively immune from it.

Even this fallback view that the Supreme Court can serve the functions of a national election commission, however, founders on the rocks of the fact that the Constitution does not give the Supreme Court such expansive election-managing responsibilities. In the face of this constitutional obstacle, however, we have seen from the proponents of this "rules committee" view of the design of electoral systems yet another example of First Amendment opportunism. As might be expected, the chief proponents of this view are those who would not expect to fare well politically if majorities could design electoral systems. At present and for the past several decades, these people have largely been Republicans. Conversely, those who would allow the democratic process to make the rules for its own operation are those who generally would expect to benefit from majoritarian control over the mechanisms of majority rule. And for at least several decades, these people have largely been Democrats.

Consequently, it is the opponents and not the proponents of campaign finance reform who are in need of a constitutional hook for their larger claim about the inappropriateness of majoritarian electoral regulation (and therefore majoritarian campaign finance reform), and it should come as no surprise

---

56. JOHN HART ELY, DEMOCRACY AND DISTRUST (1980).

57. This is Karl Popper's famous "paradox of democracy," implicitly adopting the view that the concept of democracy, and the rules for managing it, are antecedent to and a presupposition of democracy, rather than being subject to it. 1 KARL POPPER, THE OPEN SOCIETY AND ITS ENEMIES 124–25, 265 (5th ed. 1966).

that the most conveniently available constitutional hook has been the First Amendment. Starting with the tenuous but not preposterous claim that the money spent on campaigning itself has a First Amendment dimension,[58] and continuing to the view that the fact that most campaign expenditures are on advertising (and therefore on speech in the literal sense) makes campaign finance a First Amendment issue, the constitutional dimensions of campaign finance reform have been dominated by First Amendment rhetoric.[59] Yet once again it was hardly inevitable that this would have been the case. It could have been the Guaranty Clause, "guarantee[ing] to every State in the Union a Republican Form of Government."[60] It could have been the Equal Protection Clause, which in the past has been the vehicle for a large range of electoral issues.[61] It could have been, following Ely,[62] some sort of inference from the various different provisions of the Constitution that deal with elections. All of these arguments would have faced formidable obstacles,[63] but so too, *ex ante,* would the First Amendment argument. That the First Amendment argument was used, has flourished, and now dominates the discourse appears to be less a function of any natural affinity between the issues of control of the electoral process and the heart of the First Amendment than a function of the opportunistic seizing upon the First Amendment as the most likely persuasive of the various fragile arguments then available to those who would oppose campaign finance reform. That the other arguments would probably have been less successful is not so much because they are less connected to the issue than because they are less likely to carry the judicial and public resonance that in this society attaches to the First Amendment.

---

58. Buckley v. Valeo, 424 U.S. 1 (1976). *See* J. Skelly Wright, *Politics and the Constitution: Is Money Speech?* 85 YALE L.J. 1001 (1976). The argument is tenuous not only because a vast range of activities that are not themselves protected can be said to be conducive to effective speech, including education, social standing, talent, and charisma, but also because the "conducive to effective speech and therefore protected" argument has, in the context of education, been explicitly rejected by the Supreme Court. San Antonio Indep. Sch. Dist. v. Rodriguez, 411 U.S. 1 (1973). The fact of explicit rejection of an argument by the Supreme Court may not be very probative on the question of the soundness of the argument, but it is generally thought to give some indication of how likely it is that the Supreme Court will accept it.

59. *See,* most recently, Nixon v. Shrink Mo. Gov't PAC, 528 U.S. 377 (2000); Colorado Republican Fed. Campaign Comm. v. Federal Election Comm'n, 518 U.S. 604 (1996).

60. U.S. CONST. art. IV, § 4.

61. *See, e.g.,* American Party of Texas v. White, 415 U.S. 767 (1974); Lubin v. Panish, 415 U.S. 709 (1974); Dunn v. Blumstein, 405 U.S. 330 (1972); Bullock v. Carter, 405 U.S. 134 (1972); Harper v. Virginia State Bd. of Elections, 383 U.S. 663 (1966). On the migration of what are essentially the same arguments from the Equal Protection Clause to the First Amendment, *see* GERALD GUNTHER & KATHLEEN M. SULLIVAN, CONSTITUTIONAL LAW 893–95 (13th ed. 1997).

62. Ely, *supra* note 56, at 67–78.

63. For example, the nonjusticiability of the Guaranty Clause. *See* Luther v. Borden, 48 U.S. 1 (1849).

Why the First Amendment?

These four examples—five if we include the footnoted example of the feminist antipornography movement, six if we add the way in which opponents of workplace sexual harassment sanctions have succeeded in transforming a sexual harassment issue into a free-speech issue,[64] and seven if we append the emerging tendency to seize on the existence of computer language or computer code as a way of converting commercial disputes about the ownership of information technology and intellectual property into free-speech claims[65]— likely only scratch the surface. In numerous other instances,[66] political, social, cultural, ideological, economic, and moral claims that are far wider than the First Amendment, and that appear to have no special philosophical or historical affinity with the First Amendment, find themselves transmogrified into First Amendment arguments. Having identified the phenomenon, it is worthwhile pondering its cause.

As I have suggested, the fact that general arguments—from economic liberty, from sexual liberty, from management of an electoral system, and many others—migrate to the First Amendment seems hardly fortuitous. When there is a good argument to be had, whether it is the First Amendment or not, those who would benefit from its acceptance are likely to use it, both in court and in public discourse. But when there is no good argument to be had, or when any argument is likely to confront some number of doctrinal, psychological, cultural, or political hurdles, we have much to learn from the fact of which arguments are selected by those with the greatest interest in prevailing.

The arguments selected, however, are less likely under these circumstances to be selected for their intrinsic merit than for the likelihood that they will succeed. And if the First Amendment appears likely to succeed more than other arguments that on their face present the same or equivalent doctrinal or precedential obstacles, then this in turn can tell us much about the power of the First Amendment today as a political force and a rhetorical device in the United

---

64. I document the phenomenon of the transformation of a sexual harassment–equality issue into a free-speech issue in Frederick Schauer, *The Speech-ing of Sexual Harassment, in* NEW DIRECTIONS IN SEXUAL HARASSMENT LAW (Catharine MacKinnon & Reva Siegel eds., 2000).

65. *See, e.g.,* Universal City Studios, Inc., v. Reimerdes, 111 F. Supp. 2d 294 (S.D.N.Y. 2000), in which U.S. District Judge Lewis Kaplan was asked (unsuccessfully, as it has turned out so far) to rule that the First Amendment protects the distribution of a software program called DeCSS, which enables users to bypass the encryption on DVD players and watch DVD movies on their computers without payment to the owners. *See also,* and more prominently, A & M Records, Inc. v. Napster, Inc., 114 F. Supp. 2d 896 (N.D. Cal. 2000).

66. A good example might be privacy, which even after Roe v. Wade, 410 U.S. 113 (1973), is still more often conjoined with free speech than with general liberty. *See* Symposium, *The Right to Privacy,* 17 SOC. PHIL. & POL'Y 1 (2000).

States. When Antonio observes in *The Merchant of Venice* that even "the devil can cite Scripture for his purpose,"[67] he makes an important observation about the texts or sources that are selected as the authorities of choice. For not only is it the case that "Scripture" is sufficiently vague, ambiguous, and internally contradictory as to allow a panoply of mutually exclusive uses, but it is also revealing that the devil, along with many others, chooses to cite Scripture rather than any of a host of other and equally capacious texts. Similarly, the fact that the First Amendment is the authority of choice when no authority is on point, and when all available authorities are equally not on point, says a great deal about the way in which the First Amendment functions in American society, even as its non-American equivalents tend, interestingly, not to be used in the same way in other societies.

All of this is of course the armchair sociology of doctrinal evolution. One can imagine ways of examining the seemingly persistent appearance of the First Amendment with greater care. One way would be to conduct a series of in-depth interviews with those who made the original rhetorical and argumentative choices. Another way would be more systematic, trying to design a method of controlling for the empirical[68] strength (or persuasiveness for a given audience or decisionmaker) of the primary argument, controlling for the empirical strength of the available secondary arguments, and then attempting to determine where the First Amendment ranks among equally available but equally tenuous arguments. And although it might be impossible to specify all of this with complete precision, it is the product of this kind of inquiry that I have in mind when I hypothesize that the First Amendment appears to be, in the United States in the last thirty years, the argument of choice for those who find that their intrinsically preferred argument is unlikely to prevail.

If it is true that the First Amendment occupies this kind of pride of place among constitutional arguments, then it would be worth exploring why this is so. Here the issue is not only what has caused the First Amendment to assume this position in society, but also the consequences of its having done so. Does the rise of First Amendment opportunism indicate that judges, politicians, and public figures are especially unwilling to be seen as "against" the First Amendment?[69] Does the first recourse to the First Amendment provide

---

67. WILLIAM SHAKESPEARE, THE MERCHANT OF VENICE, act 1, sc. 3, l. 99.

68. I stress that the empirical strength of an argument is its likely persuasiveness to a given population of argumentative targets, and that this is not to be confused with the persuasion-independent soundness of an argument. Among many in the United States, an argument from astrological signs is quite empirically strong, even though such an argument has no scientific basis whatsoever.

69. The "especially" is important here. The hypothesis is that influential decisionmakers fear being branded as hostile to the First Amendment more than they fear being branded as hostile to the Fourth

evidence for the fact that First Amendment arguments are especially likely to attract powerful but otherwise ideologically distant allies, as when the American Civil Liberties Union (ACLU) allies itself with the Ku Klux Klan,[70] or when ABC Television, America Online, the National Association of Broadcasters, and the Society of Professional Journalists support the publisher of a manual of instructions for murder for hire?[71] Does the persistent enlistment of the First Amendment into a wide range of causes suggest that the litigant or public advocate who clothes herself in the First Amendment is like the politician who clothes himself in the American flag? Does the emergence of the First Amendment as the American argument of choice owe something to the fact that an enormous influence on public opinion—the institutional press—is itself one of the primary beneficiaries of the First Amendment? Does the cultural penetration of organizations like the ACLU explain part of the way in which the First Amendment has come to be accepted by the political and cultural elite? Did the early emergence of the First Amendment as the protector of largely nonthreatening dissenters such as the Jehovah's Witnesses help produce more cultural celebration of the First Amendment than would have existed had the First Amendment been perceived—as the Fourth Amendment is perceived—as a genuine impediment to pressing social policies? Although it is not possible in this essay to pursue fully the causes of the ascendency of the First Amendment as an American cultural icon and the American argument of choice in both judicial and nonjudicial settings, the outline I have given of these phenomena may help us begin to understand why the First Amendment appears to be both the first and the last refuge of saints and scoundrels alike.

Is First Amendment Opportunism a Problem?

So what? Even if I am correct in noticing that litigational and public rhetorical opportunism calls on the First Amendment more than it calls on other equally available (or equally unavailable) constitutional provisions, even if I am correct in concluding that this says something important about the place of the First Amendment in American culture, and even if I am correct in believing that this phenomenon itself influences the judicial development and popular

---

Amendment or even hostile to the Equal Protection Clause. If this hypothesis is true, then one cause of this might be the fact that the press, itself a very important player in the creation of public opinion, has a special interest in the First Amendment, and wise public decisionmakers rarely forget the dictum: "Never argue with a fellow who buys ink by the barrel."

70. See, e.g., Knights of the Ku Klux Klan v. Curators of the Univ. of Mo., 203 F.3d 1085 (8th Cir. 2000); Church of the Am. Knights of the Ku Klux Klan v. Safir, 1999 U.S. App. Lexis 28106 (2d Cir. 1999).

71. Rice v. Paladin Enters., 128 F.3d 233 (4th Cir. 1997).

understanding of the First Amendment, is it clear that this is the problem I have implicitly suggested?

The view that First Amendment opportunism is a problem is premised on a view that there is something to the ideas behind the First Amendment other than the particular circumstances in which First Amendment arguments may assist one side or another.[72] Put differently, and perhaps tendentiously to some, the First Amendment is not, at its core, strictly pragmatic. Just as an antipragmatic view of justice or gravity would understand these concepts to have a meaning (an "essence," to be even more tendentious) apart from the way in which they are used instrumentally in certain contexts, so too would an antipragmatic view of the First Amendment understand it as embodying a particular idea or set of ideas. For some these are typically associated with the concept of the marketplace of ideas;[73] for others they relate to the way in which the First Amendment serves a particular function in democratic deliberation;[74] for others the core idea is one of toleration;[75] for others it is autonomy of a certain kind;[76] for still others the self-expression by speech is different in kind from,[77] and more important than, the full range of nonspeech forms of self-expression. And there are of course even more justifications or ideas that could easily be added to this list. But whatever ideas may be thought to be embodied in the First Amendment—whether few or many, philosophical or empirical—a large number of people believe they can identify the functions, goals, purposes, justifications, or whatever of the First Amendment in a way that is both temporally and logically antecedent to the particular instances of its application.

Under this rule-based view of the First Amendment, in which its "essence" precedes its application, any misapplication is a problem, and a series of misapplications is a large problem. If the First Amendment is not at its core about economic liberty, but finds itself steered in that direction by the opportunism

---

72. This seems to be the position at times suggested in STANLEY FISH, THERE'S NO SUCH THING AS FREE SPEECH, AND IT'S A GOOD THING TOO (1994).

73. Although the marketplace theory has not fared well in the academic literature, *see, e.g.,* Alvin I. Goldman & James C. Cox, *Speech, Truth, and the Free Market for Ideas,* 2 LEGAL THEORY 1 (1996); Stanley Ingber, *The Marketplace of Ideas: A Legitimizing Myth,* 1984 DUKE L.J. 1, it is still a staple of popular free-speech rhetoric.

74. *See, e.g.,* CASS R. SUNSTEIN, DEMOCRACY AND THE PROBLEM OF FREE SPEECH (1993).

75. *See* LEE C. BOLLINGER, THE TOLERANT SOCIETY: FREEDOM OF SPEECH AND EXTREMIST SPEECH IN AMERICA (1986).

76. *See* David Strauss, *Persuasion, Autonomy, and Freedom of Expression,* 91 COLUM. L. REV. 334 (1991).

77. *See* C. EDWIN BAKER, HUMAN LIBERTY AND FREEDOM OF SPEECH (1989).

of commercial advertisers wishing to be freed from state restrictions,[78] then the consequence is a distorted First Amendment. If the First Amendment is about political deliberation but is molded into a different cultural artifact by its persistent use in the service of the commercial sex industry, then the First Amendment that evolves is something other than the First Amendment best understood. And so on. In this sense the phenomenon of First Amendment opportunism is a problem under any view that takes the First Amendment to be substantially, even if not entirely, something other than a particular set of social, political, and ideological moves that are available at a particular point in time. Moreover, this is not just the tautological observation that particular misapplications produce over time a general misapplication. Rather, it is that arguments that are the second-best arguments of choice in a widely disparate range of settings may be susceptible to a form of systematic misapplication different in kind rather than just in degree from the misapplications that are a routine part of any decisionmaking environment. If First Amendment opportunism is as widespread as I suspect, and as some of the documentation here may suggest, then the First Amendment, precisely because of its cultural salience and consequent empirical persuasiveness, may be especially vulnerable to the kind of misuse and consequent distortion that I am suggesting. If there is no hammer handy, and if the pipe wrench is within easy grasp on the top shelf of the tool chest, then the pipe wrench more than any of the other tools in the chest may over time lose its ability to perform the function for which it was originally designed.

The previous paragraph assumes that there *is* some situationally antecedent core of the First Amendment. Another possibility, however, is that there is not. It may turn out that in the final analysis none of the justifications for a distinct free-speech principle is sound,[79] and that the First Amendment is revealed to be merely the raw material of opportunism and nothing else. To put it differently, perhaps the history of the First Amendment will reveal that it has always served as a second-best argument for those whose arguments for a broader liberty are unlikely to succeed, and that this historical evolution of the First Amendment

---

78. *See* C. Edwin Baker, Advertising and a Democratic Press (1994).

79. I have some sympathy for this view, *see* Frederick Schauer, Free Speech: A Philosophical Enquiry (1982); Frederick Schauer, *The Phenomenology of Speech and Harm*, 103 Ethics 635 (1993), although I find increasingly congenial the view, itself an instantiation of First Amendment opportunism, that the First Amendment serves as a way of providing special privileges or immunities to certain social and cultural institutions—the institutional press, libraries, the institutions of the arts, the institutions of higher education—that have been shown to be in particular need of special protection for socially valuable, institutionally autonomous decisionmaking. *See* Frederick Schauer, *Principles, Institutions, and the First Amendment*, 112 Harv. L. Rev. 84 (1998).

tracks the lack of any defensible philosophical or empirical justification for treating speech differently from other forms of behavior producing the same or equivalent consequences.[80] And if this turns out to be the case, then First Amendment opportunism can no longer be perceived as a problem, but will have told us something revealing about just what the First Amendment is.

First Amendment Opportunism and the Nature of the Common Law

In describing the view that there might be an antecedent conception of the First Amendment as "rule based," I meant to contrast it with an even more familiar method in Anglo-American law, namely, the method of common-law decisionmaking.[81] Here the role played by an antecedent "essence" of ideas is minimal, and our understanding of the Amendment is formed by the process of case-by-case doctrinal accretion. Is there a concept of a "tort" independent of something closely related to the law of torts as it has been developed by the common law? If there is not, it is because the law of torts is itself the product of a long process not at all dissimilar to what I have been calling "opportunism." Torts opportunism is different from, and odder-sounding than, First Amendment opportunism, and that is precisely because we understand the law of torts to be a creature of the common law, and we understand the common law to be opportunistic in my sense. Common-law doctrines, concepts, and principles develop through a series of litigation opportunities in which the litigants are almost always concerned only with winning. If a concept or set of doctrines that has no independent conceptual underpinnings wears on its sleeve the marks of its opportunistic development, we are not in the least surprised.

If First Amendment opportunism is a problem, therefore, it is because First Amendment opportunism is perceived as distorting, and if First Amendment opportunism is perceived as distorting it is because there is some conception of a legally undistorted idea of the First Amendment. An undistorted idea of the First Amendment, however, sounds more palatable than a legally undistorted idea of torts only if we conceive of the First Amendment as more legally antecedent than we understand torts to be. But if instead we see the First Amendment as intrinsically, fundamentally, or even just largely as an artifact

---

80. This way of formulating the central question of free-speech theory owes its origin to T. M. Scanlon, *A Theory of Freedom of Expression*, 1 PHIL. & PUB. AFF. 204 (1972).

81. On this contrast, *see* FREDERICK SCHAUER, PLAYING BY THE RULES: A PHILOSOPHICAL EXAMINATION OF RULE-BASED DECISION-MAKING IN LAW AND IN LIFE (1991). On the common law generally, *see* MELVIN A. EISENBERG, THE NATURE OF THE COMMON LAW (1988); LEGAL THEORY AND COMMON LAW (William Twining ed., 1986).

of a constitution that is itself a common-law document,[82] then it would be hard to make sense of the idea of the First Amendment, and arguably of the idea of free speech, apart from what the courts have made of it, and apart from the necessarily and nonproblematically opportunistic way of the common law.

If, as I intimated in the previous section, there may not be a philosophically defensible and legally antecedent core to the First Amendment, and if, as I have intimated in this section, the First Amendment as we know it has developed over the course of its deployment in the process of common-law opportunism to serve goals not necessarily related to speech as such, then the consequence will be that opportunism provides the best way we have of understanding the role that the First Amendment plays in this society, and the way in which the incentives to opportunism have shaped what we now understand to be the First Amendment. But if, alternatively, the opportunism of the First Amendment culture has, through the mechanism of the common-law process, produced a misshapen First Amendment, then understanding how opportunism misshapes the First Amendment may help prevent further distortions. In either event, and I do not purport to address this primary question of free-speech theory here, understanding the opportunistic dimension of the development of the First Amendment can help us understand both the causes and the consequences of a culture in which the idea of the First Amendment seems, as an empirical matter, especially powerful.

---

82. *See* David A. Strauss, *Common Law Constitutional Interpretation*, 63 U. Chi. L. Rev. 877 (1996); Frederick Schauer, *Is the Common Law Law?* 77 Cal. L. Rev. 455, 470 (1989).

It is a familiar philosophical question whether there is anywhere outside of one's own substantive views and outlook from which to develop a knowledge of the world and of how to act within it. The enormous literature on the "theory" of freedom of speech and press has in recent years puzzled over that question when it comes to understanding the First Amendment. Contemporary perspectives from literary and cultural theory applied to First Amendment jurisprudence have confounded, without always clarifying, earlier certainties about the social meaning and functions of free speech.

In "The Dance of Theory," Stanley Fish leaves no doubt where he stands on this general issue: any "theory" of free speech must reflect a "substantive political content." Thus, "the abstractions at the center of First Amendment jurisprudence—freedom of expression, the free flow of ideas, self-realization, self-governance, quality, autonomy—do not in and of themselves point us to the appropriate distinctions or help us to order a set of facts on the way to rendering an opinion." Professor Fish closely analyzes the attempts of several commentators who argue that First Amendment law is incoherent and who then offer a substitute perspective. He tries to show that the criticisms reflect our unwillingness to come to terms with the "unavailability of neutral standards or of a general theory of free speech or of a core free-speech principle or of a formal mechanism for making decisions about regulating and not regulating" speech. "Theory" can, and should, only spring from the "knowledge" that comes from our "being situated moral beings."—LCB

STANLEY FISH

The Dance of Theory

One of the first questions I always ask students and audiences is "What is the First Amendment *for?*" I ask the question not because I want to recommend a particular answer but because I want to say that if you have *any* answer to the question, *any* answer at all, you are necessarily implicated in a regime of censorship. The reason is that when you say the First Amendment is *for* something—perhaps for giving the truth the chance to emerge, or for providing the minds of citizens with the materials necessary for growth and self-realization, or for keeping the marketplace of ideas open in a democratic society—it becomes not only possible but inevitable that at some point you will ask of some instance of speech whether it in fact serves its high purpose or whether it does the opposite, retarding the search for truth, stunting the growth of mature judgment, fouling the marketplace.

This is not an empirical but a logical inevitability; for if you have a consequentialist view of the First Amendment—a view that values free speech because of the good effects it will bring about—then you must necessarily be on the lookout for forms of action, including speech action, that threaten to subvert those effects. Otherwise you would be honoring the means above the end and cutting the heart out of your moral vision. And to continue the logic, at the point you discern such a threat and move against it, you will not be compromising the First Amendment; you will be honoring it by performing the act of censorship that was implicit in it from the beginning.

By placing censorship inside the First Amendment, I join those who have been chipping away at First Amendment theory. For most of the twentieth century the dance of First Amendment theory was a two-step. The first step was to identify the essence or center of First Amendment freedoms; the second step was to devise a policy that protected and honored the center so identified. Within this general structure of analysis and argument there was considerable

---

An earlier version of this essay appeared in Stanley Fish, The Trouble with Principle 115–50 (1999), copyright © 1999 by the President and Fellows of Harvard College; reprinted by permission of Harvard University Press.

room for disagreement. One might disagree as to whether the free-speech center should be defined in relation to some desired consequence (the emergence of truth, the free flow of ideas and information in a democratic society, the fashioning of well-informed citizens capable of independent judgment, the encouraging of dissent as a check against the tendency of state power to perpetuate itself) or whether a free-speech regime follows from a moral imperative (autonomous agents should be accorded the liberty of expressing their own views and making their own choices without interference from the state) that is indifferent to consequences and cannot be relaxed just because a particular consequence is either feared or sought.

If one is a consequentialist, one will still debate which of the consequences is primary in the sense that the hope of its realization should guide policy. And if one is a nonconsequentialist, one will still debate which of the proffered moral imperatives (liberty, autonomy, equality, tolerance) is so strong that it should trump any policy considerations (eliminating racism, suppressing error, fostering civility) a would-be regulator might invoke. Even when consequentialists or nonconsequentialists settle in the same doctrinal corner, they can still debate whether the historical record of court decisions reflects and confirms their preferred view or whether that history displays a regrettable departure from the principle they have now revealed to be the true one. Obviously, then, the field will always be full of contest, but everyone will pretty much agree about the point of the contest and the prize to be won—the right to specify the correct free-speech principle and the policy that follows from it.

In the past fifteen or twenty years, however, a number of commentators have begun to tell a different story. They say things like "There is no free-speech principle," or "There is no such thing as free speech," or "There is no such thing as speech," or "There is no such thing as a principle." They reach these provocative conclusions through a variety of routes:

- by undoing the distinction between speech and action and thus depriving First Amendment theorists of an object to clarify;

- by declaring that any so-called procedural value is always and already hostage to a substantive vision and thus making viewpoint discrimination (a fancy name for politics) the *content* of the First Amendment rather than the evil it is supposed to keep at bay;

- by arguing that First Amendment mechanisms do not, as is claimed, neutralize power by giving everyone an equal chance to speak but instead work to consolidate the power of those who benefit from the maintenance of the status quo and to disempower those already marginalized and silenced;

- by insisting that words do not simply describe the world but make it and that, therefore, one cannot expect the world to remain what it always was no matter what is or is not said;

- by pointing out the manifest incoherence and absurdity of current First Amendment doctrine which regulates in the name of nonregulation, draws bright lines no one can clearly see, and recognizes so many exceptions to its rules that it is finally as ad hoc and haphazard as the world it fails to order.

What is remarkable, however, is that after having demonstrated (at least to themselves) that the first step of identifying the free-speech center cannot be taken, these same revisionists still believe they can take the second step and derive a policy from the unavailability of what the traditionalists have sought in vain. They believe, in short, that something follows from the fact (if it is a fact) that there is no principle or doctrine or overriding value for a First Amendment policy to follow. They contrive to turn the absence of normative grounds into a ground for making normative decisions. They think to substitute for the (discredited) sequence "Because the essence of X is Y, we should do Z" the brave new sequence "Because X does not exist, we should do Z."

What the revisionists refuse to see is that if step one is a nonstarter, there is no basis for taking step two other than the prudential basis that recommends itself to a situated political agent. What they refuse to see is that the only alternative to a principled consequentialism—a consequentialism tied to an outcome (such as self-realization) that everyone desires or should desire—is a consequentialism tied to an outcome some particular one (or group) desires.

One suspects that Robert Post knows all this, although he will be my first example of a theorist who cannot let go of his theory even after he has cut away its ground. Post begins his 1995 article, "Recuperating First Amendment Doctrine," by declaring that First Amendment doctrine is "striking chiefly for its superficiality, its internal incoherence, its distressing failure to facilitate judicial engagement with significant contemporary social issues."[1] Post attributes this unhappy situation to a disconnect between the doctrinal pronouncements of the Supreme Court and its behavior in particular cases, and he attributes this disconnect to the fact that the Court often speaks as if it were defending speech "per se" (1272)—an abstract entity prior to any of the social contexts in which it might occur—and therefore couching its justifications in terms (like the intent to communicate a message) appropriate to that level of generality.

---

1. Robert Post, *Recuperating First Amendment Doctrine*, 47 STAN. L. REV. 1249, 1250 (1995).

But, says Post, there is no such thing as speech per se, only speech uttered (or written) in "the social contexts that envelop and give constitutional significance to acts of communication" (1255). Rather than being an independent value whose primacy is to be honored no matter what the circumstances, speech is of consequence only in circumstances, and the value we assign to it (not as an abstract category but as a particular instance) is a function of the value already assigned the circumstance. In so-called open forums (town meetings, Hyde Park corners, radio talk shows) speech will be largely unfettered and unregulated (except for the regulation requiring each to wait his or her turn) not because we revere speech in and of itself but because the very point of open forums is to encourage as much varied expression as possible. In other contexts (Post cites the military, the medical, and the classroom contexts), the production of speech is incidental to the institutional or social point, and it makes no sense to prefer speech interests to the interests that give such contexts their reasons for being.

Post's conclusions to this analysis are sweeping. Because speech "does not itself have a general constitutional value" but attaches itself to the values already "allocated to . . . discrete forms of social practice," "the search for any general free speech principle is bound to fail" (1272). That failure is only thinly disguised by the contortions the Court has recourse to when it attempts to "force the entire spectrum of state regulation of forms of social interaction into conformity" with a chimerical "single value." The better course, the one Post is recommending, would be to make "the unit of First Amendment analysis . . . not . . . speech, but rather particular forms of social structure," with their particular purposes and goals (1273).

This suggests a new and urgent project, "a kind of interpretive charting of the ambient social landscape. Such a charting is necessarily creative and dialectical: values already recognized as constitutional may precipitate the perception of practices deemed prerequisite for their realization, while actual but untheorized practices may spur the explicit articulation of new constitutional values" (1275). Such a charting would also, I think, be provisional and ever in need of revision and updating, because what it would be charting is the *political* process whereby specific practices move in and out of the category "worthy of constitutional regard." There is no end (as there was no beginning) to the creation of new constitutional values in the wake of the decision (a word that suggests more rationality than may be present) to find constitutional value in a practice that previously was not seen to contain it. When Post says that if someone were to deface public property by inscribing on it (or into it) "a particularized message that is likely to be understood by his audience," "no court in the country would consider the case as raising a First

Amendment question" (1252), he should have added "at this time"; for it is easily imagined that some court will extrapolate from cases dealing with flag-burning, sleeping in public parks (as a form of protest), trampling on public grounds (in the course of a march), and so on, a constitutional value for what we now dismiss as graffiti (and remember there are graffiti "artists," both self-described and recognized by others) or vandalism. Constitutional value is not something that hovers above the judicial process and guides it; constitutional value (as everything in Post's discussion implies) is what emerges from the process, sometimes in this form, sometimes in that, but never in a form so perdurable that one can be confident that its invocation will always secure the desired effect.

In the course of his exposition, Post characterizes the conclusions he has been reaching as "radical" (1273); but when he turns to consolidate the gains of his analysis, what may have seemed radical (at least as I would under-stand the term) becomes something quite familiar and traditional. The hinge sentence is this one: "I have . . . surveyed in some detail the court's opinions dealing with the regulation of speech within governmental institutions, and I have found that the pattern of the court's decisions is largely what would be predicted by the preceding discussion" (1275). When I first read this I thought that the pattern he found was one that would further dash the hopes of those in search of a "generic constitutional value for speech" (1275) because it revealed the extent to which the court's decisions varied with the "specific and discrete kinds of social practices" (1272) that displayed speech as a feature—practices that were not only discrete but ever on the move, capable of metamorphosing into something quite other than they had been and thus gaining or shedding constitutional value along the way. I thought, in short, that Post would follow his rejection of "any general free speech principle" (1272) with a critique of the claim that doctrinal analysis is normative rather than ad hoc and rhetorical (as much of what he had been saying suggested that it was).

Instead, Post shifts the level at which doctrinal analysis will be both ex-planatory and guiding. Although the universalism (and utility) of notions like self-realization or the search for truth is repudiated because the "abstract world" (1276) in which they live exists only in the mind of theorists, a new universalism, or essentialism, is embraced in the forms of the social practices that will be the new unit of First Amendment analysis. While no overarching, single value exists—the search for which has "blinded" (1275) the Court—there is a single value, Post believes, appropriate to specific social structures, structures whose "charting" (now revealed to be a taxonomic task that can be performed once and for all) will enable us to sort everything out and proceed in a coherent fashion. All we need do is match up discrete social practices with the single values (whether constitutional or not) animating them, and we will know what to do and, in contrast to the present sorry situation, there will be a fit between what we do and the vocabulary within which what we do is justified.

All at once the chaotic world of First Amendment jurisprudence and the radical implications of saying that there is no general free-speech principle are tamed by finding general free-speech principles that are local. What "the pattern of the court's decisions reveals," Post tells us, is not the absence of a doctrinal coherence but a doctrinal coherence it has not itself recognized, with the result that its performance, pretty much what one would desire, is misrecognized by its theory, which is "thoroughly disconnected from the actual levers of its judgment" (1275). Although the Court "has been completely unable to craft a clear and useful doctrinal expression" (1275) of what should, and does, guide its deliberations and opinions, that lack has now been supplied by the First Amendment theorist.

Indeed, when the theoretical dust clears and Post descends to particulars, it turns out that there is a general First Amendment principle after all, and along with it a single overriding value. It is not general in the old way: it does not envelop the field. Rather it sits at the field's center and generates the distinctions between practices that can then be the basis of determining in which of them speech activity should be of constitutional concern and in which of them speech can be regulated in accordance with the goal and point of the enterprise. (It is not that I think the drawing of such lines would be impossible or even difficult; it is just that the lines would be drawn in the context of background assumptions—about whether a particular practice, like the practice of graffiti artists, rises to the level of constitutional notice—that could themselves be challenged at any point; and if the challenge were successful, the entire map would have to be redrawn.) It is because it sits at the center that this principle/value is called a "core" (1275), a word and concept one would have thought Post had let go of when he let go of "speech as such," "self-realization," "the conveying of particular messages," and "expressive conduct" as failed candidates for the central value the First Amendment was designed to protect.

Moreover, Post's candidate for "core" is so far from being radical as to be commonplace and absolutely centrist. It is, he announces with a flourish, "democracy," that "specific kind of social order, which seeks to sustain the value of self-government by reconciling individual and collective autonomy through the medium of public discourse," with the goal of facilitating "the emergence of 'a common will, communicatively shaped and discursively clarified in the political public sphere'" (1275). Although this "kind of social order" is said to be "specific," it is not (as the word suggests) just one among equals. Rather, the aspirations and imperatives of democracy order the entire landscape. The social practices (like the military, the medical, and the scholarly) that are not held to its requirement of allowing as much unfettered speech as possible are released from the requirement not in opposition to, or sequestration from, democracy but by its leave. When a teacher is permitted to restrict both the material and the scope of discussion in the classroom, it is not because he is being given permission to be undemocratic; rather, the controlled space of the classroom is deemed to be contributory to the "material conditions of the specific social order of democracy" (1275), one of which is the fashioning of well-informed citizens.

Democracy, thus conceived, *is* the abstract universal Post has scorned in the pages preceding its emergence, and the clear sign that this is so is the citing of Jürgen Habermas as his source for the idea of a "structure of governance" always open to revision. (As far as I am concerned, any positive reference to Habermas in the course of an argument is enough to invalidate it.) Habermas, after all, is the philosopher of the "ideal speech situation" (identified by him as the desirable form of the public forum), a situation inhabited by participants who leave behind the points of view and senses of interest and desires for particular outcomes attached to their local and partisan existence and enter the room intent only on offering propositions that have a claim to universal validity and can be tested against similar claims in a communal effort to arrive at general truths. The fact that Post can declare that there are no general truths (1278) *after* he has enlisted Habermas as an authority is an indication of the tension between his "radical" repudiation of the abstractions underlying traditional First Amendment doctrine and his rehabilitation (or recuperation) of traditional First Amendment doctrine in the name of one of those same abstractions. Thoroughly conversant with those discourses—feminist, poststructuralist, postmodern, Foucaultian, Derridean, pragmatist, and so on— that have challenged every concept and notion on which the intelligibility of First Amendment jurisprudence depends, he nevertheless retreats from those discourses just as their strongest (and most disturbing) implications come into view. He says that there is no such thing as a free-speech principle and ends up delivering one that has all the properties he has taught us not to believe in.

He does it again, and in a smaller compass, in an introduction to the rich collection, *Censorship and Silencing.*[2] Post reports that the upshot of much

---

2. CENSORSHIP AND SILENCING: PRACTICES OF CULTURAL REGULATION (ISSUES & DEBATES) (Robert Post ed., 1998).

recent work in social and political theory is to cast doubt on the usefulness of censorship as a coherent category, as a category naming an act that can be circumscribed and seen by everyone to be bad and even evil (as in "but that's censorship"). What we have now learned (and Post clearly includes himself in the "we") is that censorship is the "means by which discursive practices are maintained," and that since "social life largely consists of such practices . . . censorship is the norm rather than the exception" (2). Moreover, not only is censorship unavoidable, it is good because rather than inhibiting free expression, it is "the very condition of free expression" (3). Without the lines censorship draws between the permissible and the impermissible, the central and the peripheral, the desirable and the undesirable, no one would have positions or views and there would be no point to expressing them or encouraging them or fearing them.

The consequences of this new account of censorship, Post sees, are enormous; for absent the clear understanding of censorship as bad and unlimited expression as good, and absent the possibility of easily and uncontroversially identifying censors on the one hand and victims on the other, the entire rationale of free-speech doctrine, dedicated to the protection against censorship of what censorship is now said to produce, falls to the ground. No sooner has Post given voice to this conclusion than he recoils from it: "These are exciting and important intellectual developments. For all their undeniable power, however, they seem to miss something of importance featured in more traditional accounts" (4). What they miss, he tells us, is the exemplary force of free-speech heroes, like the "Pakistani writers resisting the oppression of a tyrannical regime" (4). It would seem that the "undeniable power" of these new intellectual developments is quite easy to deny, for that is what Post is doing when he assumes an unproblematic identification of oppressor and oppressed. It is not that the opposition between the Pakistani writers and a tyrannical regime cannot be framed, but that framing it thus is an act performed *within* the perspective of the Pakistani writers; presumably the tyrannical regime would frame it differently and would not accept for itself the designation "tyrannical." The new intellectual developments Post cites do not take away anyone's ability to characterize his or her party as bravely resisting the imposition of state censorship, but they do take away the ability to support the characterization by invoking a normative standard to which all the parties in the political landscape would subscribe. Such a standard, were it available, would be universal, and it would thus provide what Post says the newer theoretical views "miss": a vantage point from which the specification of censor and censored, and therefore of hero and villain, could be made uncontroversially.

But surely "miss" is the wrong verb to describe what Foucaultian based thought does to the possibility of such a vantage point; "demonstrates the unavailability of" or "shows to be illusory" or "destroys the basis of" would be verb phrases that better capture the relationship in all its corrosiveness. The "new scholarship of censorship" (4), the insights of which Post by and large accepts, does not "miss" the moment when someone or some group unambiguously stands up for free expression against the forces of moral and intellectual darkness. It says that there is no such moment, and it says this for all the reasons Post rehearses: the impossibility of sharply distinguishing censorship and free expression, each of which is constituitive of the other; the complicating of "any simple opposition between power and person" or state and individual; the emptying of the category "power as such" and the dispersal of power (to be sure in different and differently efficacious forms) to all the positions in a social or intellectual structure; and (the sum of all of these) the diminishment, almost to nothing, of "the force of censorship as a normative concept" (1–2).

Although Post assents to the force of these reasons, he nevertheless resists their implications when he criticizes the "Foucaultian perspective" because it "seems to flatten distinctions among kinds of power, implicitly equating suppression of speech caused by state legal action with that caused by the market, or by the dominance of a particular discourse" (4). Yes and no. These (and other) actions are equated only in that they are all exercises of power. It follows that if there are to be distinctions between them, the presence or absence of power or a calculation of greater and lesser power (made in relation to power as an isolatable and measurable concept) cannot be their basis. Rather, the distinctions will be established, if they are established, by partisan agents who are working to sort forms of activity into separate categories in the hope that such a sorting will lead to legislative and judicial outcomes they desire, outcomes that will constitutionalize some forms of speech regulation and outlaw others.

Of course, the distinctions so established will be no more firmly settled than the political process that will have produced them; and when that process takes another turn (as it always will), other partisan agents will have substituted the distinctions (and the outcomes) they favor for the ones that for a time seemed so securely in place. What will never be achieved is the establishment of distinctions immune from the political process, distinctions that one can invoke with the confidence that everyone will always find them perspicuous and determinative.

The unavailability of distinctions that preside over and guide the political process does not mean that the force of the normative is lost and that, as

Post fears, there is no longer any basis for distinguishing between legitimate and illegitimate state action. Rather, it means that the normative is *inside* the political process, where it is a prize and not a given, at least not until the process registers a victory (temporary, although it may stand for hundreds of years) by one of the contending parties whose norms will for a while be the ones that can be unproblematically invoked.

Nor does this mean that the norms in which you believe and to which you adhere are ungrounded; it is just that they are not grounded in anything outside or independent of the reasons, evidence, assumptions, goals, imperatives, ranked values, preferred outcomes, and so on that are at once the content of your consciousness and determinative of what you see and what you will take to be the obviously right course of action in a particular situation. Much confusion has resulted from failing to see that saying there are no independent normative justifications—no justifications higher than those your belief system already recognizes—is not the same as saying there are no normative justifications. The first assertion says nothing more than that our convictions have no support in anything external to their structure and history. The absence of such support, however, is not a reason for doubting our convictions; rather, it is the explanation, not the reason—a reason would be too positive—of why we could not doubt them except by mechanisms built into them. A doubt introduced by an outside source or authority would not register except as a message from an alien context. One's consciousness is always fully formed and riding along quite nicely on the track of its own presuppositions.

To be sure, the content of your consciousness can change; you can be persuaded. Nothing, not even your deepest conviction, is invulnerable to the vicissitudes of that process. This does not mean that, as liberals often urge, it is your duty to expose your deepest conviction to every peril that might undo it. That would be the mistake of turning an inevitability (your opinions will change) into a positive moral program (you must work affirmatively to change your opinions). Nor is there any mechanism that will arrest the process, freeze-frame the play of politics, or protect the presently achieved normative judgments (even the judgment that the state cannot discriminate on the basis of race) from future alteration. To put it from the other direction, any mechanism designed to arrest the play of politics will be itself political— effective only as the extension of some partisan triumph—and will therefore always be available to a challenge from the very forces it has for a time managed to still.

Post suggests that this Foucaultian lesson—that politics or "agonism" is everywhere—has the effect of creating a new universalism; and unlike the old universalisms, which at least provided a basis for evaluation and choice, this new one takes away the basis of evaluation by rendering everything the same: "Agonism, is precisely universal. It is precisely omniscient" (4). But this is to make agonism or politics into a *thing* (of the kind some want free speech or the marketplace of ideas to be), whereas in fact it is a condition-universal, to be sure, but not a value to be invoked, as one might invoke academic freedom or the search for truth or the free flow of ideas. No one says, or even thinks, "Let's do this for the sake of politics, for the sake of conflict and disagreement as such, not as prerequisites for the flourishing of a good (full participation, the maximization of information) but as goods in and of themselves."

In short, politics or agonism is not something you can choose or reject: it is the medium (the soup, the air) within whose ever-expanding confines (there is nothing outside it) one makes the kind of choices—so-called principled choices—to which it is rhetorically opposed. The fact that politics is everywhere has no normative or antinormative implications; it provides you with no program, nor does it take any away from you; it points you in no direction but only tells you that, whatever direction you find yourself taking, politics will be there, not as a byway or a danger or an impurity but as the very condition of action.

In short, politics and censorship are one, and are alike inescapable. The wonder is that even those like Post who see this are forever trying to escape it, usually by resurrecting in only a slightly disguised form the very concepts, ideals, and talismanic phrases they have recently laid to rest.

Richard Abel is another case in point. In *Speaking Respect, Respecting Speech,* he shows himself less inclined to philosophical analysis than Post, but his arguments and conclusions clearly place him in the ranks of those for whom First Amendment jurisprudence is a field without a doctrinal center or clear lines of opposition or principled means of settling disputes.[3] He describes his style as more "narrative" than theoretical. "I let my stories do the talking (without denying my ventriloquism)" (ix). His stories are many, but each of them helps to illustrate a set of related points:

- First Amendment disputes are everywhere;

- parties to First Amendment disputes claim to be serving the same abstractions (freedom, neutrality, autonomy, truth);

- those abstractions (especially free speech) are never encountered in the real world because the very conditions of social life—the conditions of structure, hierarchy, and direction—require their violation;

---

3. RICHARD ABEL, SPEAKING RESPECT, RESPECTING SPEECH (1998).

- since the disputes can't really be about the abstractions everyone ritually invokes, they must be about something else, and what they are about is "status politics," the efforts of various groups "to preserve, defend, or enhance the prestige of its own style of living" (59);

- since each group " 'operates with an image of correct behavior which it prizes' " (59, quoting Joseph Gusfield) and there is no overriding standard of correctness (or truth or liberty) that might adjudicate their claims, there is no room for compromise ("Both sides see the conflict as a zero-sum game" [108]); and therefore

- "these controversies seemed insoluble" (55).

Along the way Abel considers and dismisses the usual devices or mantras for resolving them:

- *the marketplace of ideas:* "The markets for speech, and thus the worth of messages are constructed" by state actions intent on "protecting ownership interests" (149);

- *individual freedom:* "Private freedom is a mystification" because "the dichotomy between the public as a realm of constraint and the private as a realm of liberty" just doesn't hold up; "expression is always subject to constraints, private and public" (195);

- *neutrality:* "Neither possible nor desirable" (159), a "chimera" beloved by those "hoping to escape politics and evade responsibility for choice" (246);

- a *general theory of the value of speech:* "Because each constraint raises unique moral issues, there can be no general theory of free speech" (198).

All there can be are contexts, themselves not clearly configured in ways that everyone acknowledges and filled at every point and level with counterclaims, mutual recriminations, and conflicting characterizations of what is at stake. Since expression "is always subject to constraints" and since in any situation of constraint the constraint will function to advance the interests of some group and retard the interests of some others, what we are left with is "the inevitability of prudential judgments weighing the value of speech in a particular context against the multitude of countervailing considerations" (195). We are left, in short, with politics as the realm that demands choice but can offer no recipe for making it. Because "judgments vary among people"—that's why politics is necessary; if judgment could be normalized, politics would have no reason for being—they "must be concrete" (195), that is, not general, abstract, theoretical, or principled.

It follows, then, that both the extreme positions one occasionally finds at either end of the First Amendment spectrum won't work. Absolute nonregulation won't work because, as Abel says again and again, regulation is a constitutive feature of social life, not a deformation of it. Regulation *tout court* won't work because, given the capacity of human beings to recontextualize utterances, including the utterances of would-be regulators, the machinery of regulation will itself be appropriated by the play of interpretive agendas. "Legal efforts to regulate speech founder on the ineradicable ambiguity of meaning deployed by the ludic imagination" (243). Because "context is all. . . . the moral content of symbols depends on the identities of a relationship between speaker and audience it can reverse instantly, like the optical illusion in which figure and ground oscillate between a vase and other profiled faces" (243).

After all this, the last thing one would expect is a proposal designed to stabilize the effects of speech by the production of more speech (the familiar Brandeis admonition), by the saying of something in a way that will surely (or even likely) have the effect of undoing or neutralizing or canceling out what has already been said. Yet that is what Abel proposes as the "antidote" (245) to harmful and "degrading" speech: "The best antidote to degrading speech is more speech, but of a particular kind: only an apology can rectify the status inequality constructed by harmful words. To achieve this, the social settings within which respect is conferred should encourage victims to complain through an informal process that evaluates speech in context and makes offenders render an apology acceptable to both victim and community" (245–46).

The problems with this proposal can be surfaced by subjecting it to questions Abel himself has posed throughout his book. Why should an apology be a privileged speech act, one whose effects could be more or less counted on? Abel spends considerable time recounting in rich detail the story of Salman Rushdie's back-and-forth response to the furor surrounding his *Satanic Verses*—at times defiant in the face of criticism, at other times issuing apologies (even converting and unconverting) that were accepted by some, rejected by others, and accepted and then unaccepted by still others. Not only did the apologies "take" differently, but, in the eyes of some, apologizing was a wrong step because there was nothing to apologize for. And of course the fact that Rushdie alternated apology with defiance cast doubt both on the apologies he had already made and (prospectively) on any apologies he might make in the future. What this history shows is that rather than stopping or damping down dispute, an apology will more than likely be the occasion for extending and complicating a dispute. An apology is just like any other verbal action; the relationship between the intention of its speaker (and what exactly the intention is can remain a mystery even to that speaker) and its reception will always be contingent on a myriad of unpredictable factors, factors that can neither be controlled nor mapped.

Moreover, there is a prior question: what would move someone already party to a deep conflict about the correct way to conduct public life to apologize in the first place? An apology is an admission of error: I'm sorry I did that or said that; I was wrong. But it is a feature of the conflicts Abel analyzes that no one thinks himself to be wrong: "Each antagonist championed fundamental values" (48); "Adversaries sought to score points, not to listen" (56); "Both sides see the conflict as a zero-sum game" (108). Therefore, there would seem to be no reason for anyone on either side to announce publicly that a previous utterance is now regretted (and every reason for those on the other side to suspect that any such announcement was merely strategic).

Only persons who valued peace and fellowship more than they valued the convictions in whose name they were fighting—that is, only persons whose strongest conviction was that peace was to be prized above anything—could perform an apology without reservation or subterfuge. And were there such persons, it would be hard to understand why they had ever painted themselves into apparently intractable corners in the first place, since the premium they placed on the achievement of communal harmony would have diminished their partisan ardor before it ever got out of control.

Abel's proposal, in sum, requires either disputants who are ready to withdraw from their most cherished beliefs (and I ask again, why should they be ready to do that?) or antidisputants whose most cherished beliefs are that we should all get along and that it is the obligation of the more advantaged to defer to the sensitivities of the less advantaged in the case of mutual accusations of disrespect. It is not that there are not such people; it is just that they are a special breed—call them classical liberals—for whom the highest obligation is to transcend or set aside one's own sense of interest in favor of a common interest in mutual cooperation and egalitarian justice. In short, the imperative to apologize flows from an ideology, one that universalizes respect and derives from that universalization an obligation, and it is an ideology subscribed to by none of the antagonists whose behavior Abel so amply reports. Rather it is *his* ideology, imposed (at least theoretically) on protagonists for whom it has little or no force, as he acknowledges under the rubric "Hard Questions": "My proposal is consciously partisan. It represents a decision not only to value status equality but also to favor some categories over others. In the zero-sum competition for status it is impossible to respect *both* Jews and anti-Semites, gays and homophobes, minorities and racists, women and misogynists" (273).

In fact, his proposal is *both* partisan and universalizing, as we can see from his paired opposites. Those who believe that homosexuality is unnatural and abhorrent wouldn't describe themselves as homophobes but as persons trying to hew to biblical precepts; those who cite evidence showing (to their satisfaction) that intelligence or some other positive feature is to be found more in some races than in others wouldn't describe themselves as racists but as persons intent on pursuing the truth, wherever it leads; those who resist the entry of women into the political and mercantile spheres wouldn't describe themselves as misogynists but as persons eager to respect the natural talents and capacities of women. In each instance the descriptive noun on the right side of Abel's opposition is conferred from the perspective of those situated on the left side; the very framing of the sequence is thus partisan.

It is also universalizing because the epithets are applied confidently and casually, as if there could be no doubt that the characteristics they name are transparently the properties of the persons so designated. When Abel says "racist" or "homophobe," he is not adding "as I see it" but implying (by never stating) "as everyone sees it or should see it." His "partisan" judgment issues from a perspective presumed to be general, and it is a judgment on behavior that is obviously deviant only in relation to a norm he represents. When he declares that it is impossible to respect both gays and homophobes, it is clear which he respects, and it is clear too that he believes that it is a respect every right-thinking person should perform. Racists and homophobes simply don't deserve respect, which is why Abel gives away so little when he labels his proposal "partisan"; it is the proposal of those who are partisans of the good and the true.

In saying this I shouldn't be understood as criticizing Abel. He does what everyone does when he presupposes the normative status of his own convictions and then configures the social and political landscape accordingly. He does no more or less than what those whose intractability he laments do; and because he is just like them in that respect—intractable in his beliefs, and especially in the belief that there must be status equality—his proposal will operate not to equalize status but further to entrench the status hierarchy implied by and inherent in his ready stigmatization (as racists, misogynists, homophobes) of those with whom he strongly disagrees. He is not the solution but more of the problem, insofar as the problem is the unhappy spectacle of antagonists brandishing fundamental values like clubs and refusing to listen to reason.

But that is a problem only if one thinks that there are alternatives to the endless wars of truth that make up human history, and to think that is to think (with classical liberals) that there is an alternative to politics, to the conflict between the visions of the good that compete for the right to order social life.

Abel, however, has declared and massively documented the pervasiveness of politics, and one wonders, as in the case of Post, why in the end he fails to follow out the implications of his own lesson.

The puzzle is not solved but just provided with another piece when, just as in the case of Post, Habermas turns up to support the idea of a "structured conversation between victims . . . and offenders" (here assumed to be uncontroversially identifiable [265]), ending in a formal apology. Habermas's conversation is not labeled "ideal" for nothing; it requires, as I have already said, the shedding of all the baggage of belief, interest, desire, aspiration that, as Abel shows so persuasively, is inseparable from the condition of being human. It is not that the ideal conversation is a bad idea; it is an impossible idea, and it should certainly be regarded as impossible by someone, like Abel, who has repudiated the search for a First Amendment essence, who has insisted that constraints are everywhere and unavoidable, who has debunked neutrality and abandoned the hope of a general theory, and who has proclaimed, first, that context is all, and, second, that context is infinitely interpretable, if only by virtue of "the ineradicable ambiguity of meaning deployed by the ludic imagination" (243). When he brings in Habermas (if only in a footnote) Abel acts as if his own arguments have not been made and as if the hopes those arguments have exploded can find harbor in another theoretical construct.

Judith Butler knows better. She too cites Habermas, but only to explain why he would be an inappropriate resource for those who (like her) have tumbled to the fact that censorship, rather than being an exercise of power by one person intent on stifling the free expression of another, is constitutive of what both can and cannot be freely expressed (no censorship, no expression), and that therefore it is foolish to place one's hopes in a regime (or a principle, or a theory, or a bright line) that will see to it that only the right things are said and the wrong things remain unspoken.

"On the assumption that no speech is permissible without some other speech becoming impermissible, censorship is what permits speech by enforcing the very distinction between permissible and impermissible speech" (139), she writes in *Excitable Speech: A Politics of the Performative*.[4] The trouble with Habermas is that he wants to arrange things in advance so that what Abel calls the "ludic" energies and Butler the "performative" energies of language are held in check and only a certain kind of speech—one that aims to express universally valid propositions—is allowed to occur. This requires, as Butler observes, a "consensually established meaning," a linguistic safe house in which (the words are Habermas's) "the productivity of the process

---

4. JUDITH BUTLER, EXCITABLE SPEECH: A POLITICS OF THE PERFORMATIVE (1997).

of understanding remains unproblematic" because "all participants stick to the reference point of possibly achieving a mutual understanding in which the same utterances are assigned the same meaning" (86). What Habermas urges is a form of benign censorship that banishes equivocation, deception, intimidation, verbal manipulation (all the traditional enemies of truth-seeking usually stigmatized under the rubrics of rhetoric and mere politics) from the public sphere, which will then be populated only by persons who mean one thing and say it straightforwardly in a way that cannot be misunderstood.

Butler's response to this linguistic utopianism (at least from the vantage point of rationalist philosophy) is a barrage of questions: "But are we, whoever 'we' are, the kind of community in which such meanings could be established once and for all? Is there not a permanent diversity within the semantic field that constitutes an irreversible situation for political theorizing? Who stands above the interpretive fray in a position to 'assign' the same utterances the same meanings? And why is it that the threat posed by such an authority is deemed less serious than the one posed by equivocal interpretation left unconstrained?" (87).

These questions imply that the Habermasian project is at once impossible and unworthy. It is impossible because the multidirectional fecundity or "diversity" Habermas fears is a property of language, not a misuse of it. The very words in which an edict mandating an interpretive straight line was promulgated would themselves be subject to interpretive swerves; interpretation cannot be closed down. And the Habermasian project is unworthy because closing down interpretation is what it aims to do, and Butler finds this aim (which she believes to be unachievable) retrograde and antidemocratic: "Risk and vulnerability are proper to democratic process in the sense that one cannot know in advance the meaning that the other will assign to one's utterance, what conflicts of interpretation may well arise, and how best to adjudicate that difference. The effort to come to terms is not one that can be resolved in anticipation but only through a concrete struggle of translation, one whose success has no guarantees" (87–88).

There are two strains of argument here, and one of them, as we shall see, takes Butler back in the direction of the essentialism and universalism she repeatedly rejects, whether it assumes Habermasian form or any other. The first strain insists (correctly, in my view) that effects cannot be designed in advance and that there is no way (verbal or physical) of acting that eliminates or precludes consequences other than those one hopes for. Politics, whether of speech or action, is not a medium capable of being stabilized; it can always take another and unexpected turn, and no amount of careful planning will ensure either that it will stop on a particular dime or that it will respect no-entry signs even if they have traditionally been obeyed. Whatever one intends by a word or a deed (a distinction Butler, like Post and Abel, finally complicates), the career of its reception or "uptake" (a technical term in J. L. Austin's *Speech Act Theory) is* unpredictable and may well include effects that subvert the intention or mock it.

Butler's example is the speech act of threat:

> The fantasy of sovereign action that structures the threat is that a certain kind of saying is at once the performance of the act referred to in that saying. . . . The threat may well solicit a response, however, that it never anticipated, losing its own sovereign sense of expectation in the face of a resistance it advertently helped to produce. Instead of obliterating the possibility of response, paralyzing the addressee with fear, the threat may well be countered by a different kind of performative act, one that exploits the redoubled action of the threat . . . to turn one part of that speaking against the other, confounding the performative power of the threat. (12)

Technically—that is, according to speech act theory as developed by Austin and John Searle—this is not quite right. The fact that a given speech act may draw an unanticipated response does not mean that it has not succeeded, for the attempted performance of an illocutionary act like the act of threatening is successful the moment the intention to perform it is recognized by the addressee. Illocutionary acts are conventional; one performs them by following a stipulated script or recipe known in advance to both parties. When party *A* says to party *B* something both understand as portending a future action *C* assumed to be unwelcome and injurious to *B*, a threat has occurred.

To be sure, there are ways for attempted illocutionary acts to fail: *A* may have misjudged *B* who may in fact desire the "infliction" of *C*, or the condition *C* would bring about already obtains (you can't threaten someone with an unhappy consequence he is already experiencing). But these are not the failures Butler has in mind when she notes the many ways in which "speech can be 'returned' to its speaker in a different form [and] can be cited against its originary purposes" (14). Rather, she has in mind what can happen after the illocutionary formula has "taken"—you understand the speaker's intention—and the threat has thereby been performed. What can happen, as she indicates, is almost anything, because recognizing that you have been threatened entails no necessary response beyond the (wholly conventional) response that is the content of the recognition. You can know you have been threatened and feel afraid; you can know you have been threatened and feel indifferent; you can know you have been threatened and feel angry; you can know that you have been threatened and you can laugh. It is in this important sense that Butler is right when she declares that "speech is always in some ways out of our control" (15).

It is those ways that interest her and solicit her positive concern. She argues not only that they cannot be shut down—control of speech and its effects is not a possibility—but that they should not be shut down because it is in the discursive space between an utterance and its work in the world that the possibility of resignification, revaluation, counterappropriation, and, in a word, change opens up. One of her examples is the counterappropriation by gays of epithets hurled at them as terms of opprobrium: "The revaluation of terms such as 'queer' suggest that speech can be 'returned' to its speaker in a different form . . . and perform a reversal of effects" (14). This is but one instance of "the performative power of appropriating the very terms by which one has been abused in order to deplete the term of its degradation or to derive an affirmative from that degradation" (for example, "Black is beautiful" [158]). This "kind of talking back," Butler says, "would be foreclosed" if the reins on potentially harmful speech were tightened, even for benign reasons (15). Such a foreclosing would operate to forestall the performance of the "insurrectionary acts" that occur when ordinary or sedimented (and perhaps unfortunate) meanings are challenged (145). In many cases the very power of an addressee derives from the speech act directed against her, and that power would be diminished if regulation deprived her of the opportunity to turn speech meant to be injurious into an occasion for self-affirmation and political progress: "Insurrectionary speech becomes the necessary response to injurious language, a risk taken in response to being put at risk, a repetition in language that forces change" (163).

It is this last assertion or claim—"a repetition in language that forces change"—that veers in the universalizing direction I noted (but did not ex-plain) earlier. The capacity of language to change and to initiate change even when the "same words" are repeated—or, more precisely, the incapacity of lan-guage and its effects to remain the same in the temporal space of repetition—is a *general* or theoretical capacity (or incapacity). It is a truth about language independent of its employment in any particular situation, and therefore it is a truth about language that has no necessary implications for its employment in any particular situation. You may know that when you say "If you don't come tomorrow, I'll disinherit you" your attempt to threaten may backfire or misfire because language's destination is never sure; but that (theoretical) knowledge will not weigh on your decision to utter or not utter the threat. What might weigh is knowledge of the person you are attempting to threaten, whether he or she is likely to be easily intimidated or whether the attempt at intimidation is likely to be met with resistance and so on. Your calculation will be made in relation to such contextual variables (which in institutional settings will include the particular local conventions that tacitly govern the production and reception of speech; members of Congress know that in some contexts they can say things with no danger that anyone will take them seriously) and not in relation to some highly abstract truth the realization of which will always be mediated by those same variables.

Similarly, it may be true that in some ultimate sense censorship is impossible because, as Butler observes, it names and produces that which it would suppress; and it may also be true that elimination of constraints on speech is equally impossible because, as Abel and Post observe, constraints are a precondition of expression. But knowledge of those general truths will not stop the would-be regulator who may have good reason to believe that in the short run his effort to curtail a certain kind of expression will succeed; nor will it prevent the would-be liberator from trying to remove a restriction that frustrates his desire to proclaim his views. General theories of language (even for persons so odd as to be persuaded by one) do not determine or even influence verbal behavior because there is no direct line from the abstract level of their operation to the very particular level of lived life where threats are made, apologies given, commands uttered. General theories of language, in short, do not dictate or enable a politics, for politics, as everyone has now learned to say, is local.

There is one exception to this rule, and it may be an exception of which Butler's argument is an instance. General theories of language may dictate a politics that is universal, or, as I would put it, a politics that is not a politics. This would be the case if, when Butler celebrated the capacity of language (in the course of being revalued or counterappropriated) to force change, she was interested only in the capacity and not the nature of the change being forced or the state of affairs the change was unsettling. She would then be privileging change as a universal good rather than worrying about whether a particular change was desirable or achievable. That this is so is indicated by her description of the counterappropriative performative as one that can "compel a critical perspective on existing institutions" (158), and by her praise of the "insurrectionary moment . . . the moment that founds a future through a break with [the] past" (159).

If you ask which institutions will be the object of this critical perspective, the answer seems to be any and all institutions; and if you ask "Break with which past?" the answer seems to be any past. The insurrectionary moment is welcomed and courted not for what it specifically brings about but for what it brings about in general, the "overthrowing" of "established codes of legitimacy" (147), whatever they happen to be. "The possibility for the speech act to take on a nonordinary meaning, to function in contexts where it has not belonged, is precisely the political promise of the performative, one that positions the performative at the center of a politics of hegemony, one that offers an unanticipated political future for deconstructive thinking" (161).

A politics of hegemony is a politics in which one party or interest gains dominance over another or over many others, and it is to this that Butler opposes her preferred politics of deconstructive thinking. But all politics is the politics of hegemony, for politics is only necessary or possible when there are contending visions of the good and no God or self-interpreting scripture to decide between them. Given that condition—the human condition—you must struggle to establish the vision to whose truth you are persuaded; you must struggle to establish hegemony. The alternative—and, not surprisingly, it is the alternative offered in the liberal tradition that stretches from Mill to Rawls—is a politics (if that is the word) impelled by no vision except one in which all visions are suspect as "historically sedimented" (159) pretenders to universal authority; and in the context of that politics, what you do and do endlessly is "rethink" (162) whatever views you happen to hold. This, says Butler, is "to rethink one's politics" (162), but in fact it is to substitute rethinking *for* politics, to substitute for the project of implementing your agenda the project of submitting your agenda, whatever it might be, to the searching scrutiny of deconstructive interrogation.

One might argue that in fact this is a politics, and call it "the politics of rethinking"; but there is no *politics* of rethinking, just an assumption that rethinking is a general obligation that overrides the obligations that might come along with the political programs to which you have become attached. This assumption is not argued for; it is more like an article of faith, a faith that rethinking or revaluing or counterappropriating will lead to a better world populated by better persons. And it is a universalizing assumption because it is indifferent to outcomes, to how things turn out in the world, and concerned only to enjoin a single activity (rethinking) that is, like virtue, its own reward.

This indifference to outcomes is signaled when Butler describes the "political future" deconstructive thinking will make possible as "unanticipated" (161). That is, where it will take us is not known, and that is what's good about it. Not constrained or controlled by hegemonic purpose but driven only by the purpose to unsettle the ordinary and the sedimented, deconstructive thinking will bring us to a brave new world of whose outlines we are necessarily (and happily) ignorant.

It should hardly be a surprise that this is exactly the promise (if it can be called that) held out by the fabled marketplace of ideas. If we forgo our natural tendency to regulate and if we allow speech to flourish more or less unconstrained, our reward will be the emergence of general and self-evident truths rather than the imposition (through censorship or state-enforced adherence to favored views) of someone's or some group's truths. Particular outcomes are less important than the process that ensures that no one outcome will either be mandated or ruled out in advance. Like Post and Abel, Butler entertains and approves a radical critique of the components of First Amendment jurisprudence, only to come back in the end to its familiar conclusions and recipes. Where traditional First Amendment jurisprudence counsels distrust of received opinion and puts its faith in a future-oriented proceduralism, Butler counsels a "break with [the] past" (159). Where traditional First Amendment jurisprudence tells us that the answer to speech is more speech, Butler tells us that the answer to speech is counterappropriative speech. Where traditional First Amendment jurisprudence sees itself as the extension of the democratic preference for resolutions that emerge from a free-for-all competition between opposing views, Butler wishes to promote the "risk and vulnerability" that are "proper to democratic process" (87). (In saying this, she seems to imply that risk and vulnerability are the *goals* of democratic process, whereas it would be more correct to say that risk and vulnerability are inescapable features of the conditions within which democratic process unfolds.)

The politics of rethinking turns out to be pretty much indistinguishable from the politics of classical liberalism, with its insistence that nothing be foreclosed and everything be left open to revision and its disinclination to allow any commitment or value to be regarded as sacrosanct. The politics of rethinking turns out, in short, to be the antipolitics—suspicious of closure and downright hostile to the notion of anyone's winning—that has been with us at least since Mill's *On Liberty*.

Or so would be the case if Butler really meant it, if she, like the libertarians who now supply so much of First Amendment rhetoric, were really indifferent to how issues were resolved so long as the process remained radically open. In fact, however, she is not at all indifferent and has quite specific ideas about how certain First Amendment disputes should be adjudicated. She thinks that pornographic representations should not be regulated, but that racist messages, especially those that take the form of "symbolic" speech like the burning of a cross on a black family's lawn, should be. The question, of course, is how to justify the distinction (which I am neither endorsing nor challenging, only reporting), and the answer involves her not in the generalized activity of rethinking but in the very particular activity of manipulating First Amendment categories in order to bring about a desired political result. Before our very eyes, the theorist turns rhetorician (in saying this I am bestowing a compliment), at once deriding the playing of games and playing the games she derides.

The game that most concerns her is the manipulation of the speech/conduct distinction. She notes that, depending on its direction, this manipulation can serve diametrically opposed political ends. A Supreme Court disinclined to take racial injury seriously might employ a nonperformative view of speech—a view of speech as merely a medium for delivering messages—"to defend certain kinds of racist conduct" by moving that conduct into a category of protected actions; while in the other direction, the direction of a Catharine MacKinnon, a court might employ a performative view of speech—a view of speech as producing effects in the world—in order to extend "the power of state intervention over graphic sexual representation" (21–22). In one case the power of the state will be curtailed, in the other augmented. But in either case, a court will have put the prudential horse before the theoretical cart. First comes the result it desires or thinks intuitively right, and then comes the invocation of the view of speech (performative or nonperformative) that will aid in producing the result.

As an account of how the courts have dealt with pornography and racist speech issues respectively, this seems to me exactly right, as does Butler's conclusion that what we see in decisions like *R.A.V. v. St. Paul* and *Miller v. California* is the manipulation of "the distinction between speech and conduct in order to achieve certain political aims" (22). ("This same court has been willing . . . to use the very rationale proposed by some arguments in favor of hate-crime legislation to augment its case to exclude obscenity from protected speech" [62].) What I find curious is the note of complaint in the account, first because such manipulation is exactly what one would expect if, as Butler herself says, discursive categories are inherently unstable and always subject to dispute and revision (were the line between speech and conduct drawn by nature, fashioning a coherent and generally acceptable First Amendment jurisprudence would be easy), and second because manipulation of doctrinal distinctions is what she herself is doing, and necessarily so (only if such distinctions were self-interpreting would manipulation—another word for interpretation—be unnecessary and the clear occasion for moral blame).

That is to say, Butler resists blurring the distinction between speech and conduct not as a matter of principle but because she fears that a court hostile to lesbian and gay interests might seize an opportunity to regulate acts of speech whose proliferation she favors. Any "extension of state power" would, she says, "represent one of the greatest threats to the discursive operation of gay and lesbian politics," a large part of which consists of " 'speech acts' that can be, and have been, construed as offensive and, indeed, injurious conduct" (22).

This is admirably straightforward. In effect she says: I value and desire to protect certain utterances and images (regarded by some as pornographic) central to gay and lesbian culture. Their protection is more likely if the speech/conduct distinction is maintained. Therefore, it should be maintained. Except, that is, in the case of at least some racist utterances and images I do not value or wish to protect. Then I argue that what has been called a message is really conduct, and conduct of a kind the state should move to prevent. To be sure, Butler gives reasons for her uneasiness at transmuting an act like the burning of a cross into a speech act in which someone sends someone else a message. Such a classification, she says, "refuses the dimension of social power that constructs the so-called speaker and the addressee of the speech act in question" and "refuses as well the racist history of the convention of cross-burning by the Ku Klux Klan . . . which portended a further violence against a given addressee" (55). But as she no doubt knows, antipornography theorists like Catharine MacKinnon give similar reasons, also referencing power and recalling the unhappy history of a convention, in order to argue for the regulation of speech *they* consider harmful.

One can, as Butler does, *assert* a difference—"the visual text of pornography cannot 'threaten' or 'demean' or 'debase' in the same way the burning cross can" (21)—but the differences will not have been generated by the reasons marshaled to support it. Rather, the difference is assumed as a constitutive center of Butler's worldview, and it is within its assumption that the reasons will be seen as reasons and fall into their prepared place. It is not that I am unpersuaded by Butler's arguments; it is just that when I am persuaded it is not because her theoretical distinctions are independently perspicuous but because her political investments dovetail (at least in part) with mine, and together we move toward the conclusion we have both desired from the beginning.

Butler might well agree, for the best comment on her performance in *Excitable Speech* is one she provides: "It would be a mistake to think that working out the theoretical problems of the speech act will offer a set of clarifying solutions to the contemporary political operation of the speech act. The relation between theory and politics tends to work the other way. Theoretical positions are always appropriated and deployed in political contexts that expose something of the strategic value of such theories" (20). 1 would balk only at "expose," which suggests that the strategic value of a theory is something it possesses inherently and that certain political contexts serve to bring it out. In fact, theories are the products of political contexts—of the need in a particular situation for an explanation of what has already been done or for an apparently principled justification of what you are about to do—and when the abstract (and substantively empty) vocabulary of a "theoretical position" is appropriated by a political agenda other than the one in whose service it was first thought up, its strategic value will have changed.

Butler both reports on such changes—when she criticizes courts for using the same theoretical formulas to reach conclusions that are manifestly *inconsistent with* one another—and performs them—when she first attacks the universalism of Habermas and others, then produces (as do Post and Abel) a new universalism in the form of the politics of rethinking, and then reveals (and this is what puts her one-up on Post and Abel in my book) that the politics of rethinking is to be selectively employed (rethink this, but not that) and subordinated to her (plain old) politics.

Nor could it be otherwise. Those who have read this far will know before I say it that I am not faulting Butler for filling her theoretical and doctrinal vocabulary with a substantive political content. That is what everyone does and what everyone has to do because a vocabulary with no substantive political content could not be linked up (except in a wholly arbitrary way) with the real-world situations in relation to which one might wish to invoke it. That is to say, the abstractions at the center of First Amendment jurisprudence— freedom of expression, the free flow of ideas, self-realization, self-governance, equality, autonomy—do not in and of themselves point us to the appropriate distinctions or help us to order a set of facts on the way to rendering an opinion. Before we can proceed to do those things, the abstractions have to be filled in with specifications of what is included in their scope, specifications they themselves do not provide.

Although free-speech values supposedly stand alone and are said to be independent of circumstance and political pressure, they only become thick enough to provide a direction for decisionmaking when definitions and distinctions borrowed from particular circumstances (and borrowed selectively in relation to some substantive agenda) are presupposed as their content. You must determine what you mean by "expression" or what is and is not a "free flow" or what does and does not constitute "self-realization" in relation to what notion of the self before any of these so-called principles will have any bite. And since these are not determinations those principles can make for themselves, when they do have bite, when invoking them actually gets you somewhere, it will be because inside them is the outside— substantive values, preferred outcomes, politics—from which they are rhetorically distinguished.

It is the resistance to this insight that accounts for the persistence of theory even in the thought of those like Post, Abel, and Butler who spend much of their time challenging the coherence and intelligibility of the theory project. On the one hand, these commentators are persuaded that there is no road from a (nonexistent) general theory of free speech to the outcomes they desire; but on the other hand, they do desire those outcomes and cannot quite bring themselves to urge them "nakedly," that is, as deriving from their substantive visions of what is good and desirable rather than from a formal procedural vision in which the question of what is good and desirable has been bracketed. So what they do in their different ways is veer back in the direction of theory and a universalizing proceduralism in order to give their substantive agendas the kind of pedigree they have just shown to be unavailable.

To this one might say (and I myself am tempted to say it), "So what? Dressing up one's agenda in procedural garb so as to increase its chances of getting enacted might be a good, even necessary, strategy, and if the strategy works, what's the harm?" One answer to this question has been given by a series of articles in which it is suggested that those who work to frame their agendas in the language of formal theory may become confused about what their own agenda actually is and pursue lines of argument inimical to their interests. This is the conclusion reached by Peter Weston in his "The Empty Idea of Equality."[5] Weston's basic thesis is the one I have been urging throughout: formal abstractions have no content of their own, and to get content they must go to the very realm of messy partisan disputes about substantive goods of which they claim to be independent:

> Equality . . . tells us to treat like people alike; but when we ask who "like people" are, we are told "they are people who should be treated alike." Equality is an empty vessel with no substantive moral content of its own. Without moral standards, equality remains meaningless, a formula that can have nothing to say about how we should act. With such standards, equality remains superfluous, a formula that can do nothing but repeat what we already know. (547)

In a footnote to this passage, Weston declares, "Equality is not alone in its emptiness." Any abstract principle (he instances freedom) will have this twin liability of having nothing of pointed urgency to say to us (because without specific moral content it says too much and too little) and of being superfluous if we have gotten our moral content elsewhere (if your substantive convictions are already telling you what to do, why invoke an abstraction that adds nothing but the illusion of higher legitimization?). Even the idea of justice falls to this analysis. It is, says Weston, "entirely formal" (556), that is, without any guiding specification. "It requires that persons be given their 'due' but does not itself define what is their 'due' " (557). In order to remedy this deficiency,

---

5. Peter Weston, *The Empty Idea of Equality*, 95 HARV. L. REV. 537 (1982).

"one must look beyond the proposition that every person should be given his due to the substantive moral or legal standards that determine what is one's 'due' " (557).

The same reasoning holds for the familiar legal principle "Treat like persons alike," a mainstay mantra of First Amendment and affirmative action jurisprudence. Substantive notions of racial justice or the right to free exercise do not derive from the injunction but give it content and direction. Unless the relevant likeness and unlikeness has already been specified in moral/empirical terms, saying "Treat like persons alike" will be entirely unhelpful and obfuscatory. "Rights of religion and speech and religion, rights of race and sex, can be stated without reference to 'likes' or 'equals.' " Indeed, "not only can they be so stated, they must be so stated, because they provide the standards by which people are rendered 'alike' or 'unlike.' " (565).

It is a question always of what comes first, and Weston is saying that contextual judgments as to what is and is not morally relevant come first, and then and only then will formal formulas tell us anything, and even so they will be telling us what we already know. If the process is reversed and you begin with the formal formula, you will be proceeding in an entirely haphazard fashion because the relevant judgments have not yet been made: "When one is ignorant as to whether people are likely to be alike in morally significant respects, a presumption in favor of treating people alike is as unjustified as a presumption in favor of treating them unalike," for "each presumption creates an unjustified risk that it will deny people the treatment to which they are actually entitled" (573).

Weston acknowledges an apparent paradox in his argument: he is asserting that equality and other formal universals are empty and add nothing to determinations already made on other bases, and yet he is urging that invoking such universals leads to bad results, which suggests that they may not be so empty after all (how can something without content affect content?). He responds by arguing that when decisionmakers wield concepts that give them no genuine help and confer instead only a baseless confidence, they will be directed away from the real issues and produce opinions that serve only to muddy the waters: "Although equality is derivative [useful only when it is informed by substantive distinctions brought in from elsewhere], people do not realize that it is derivative, and not realizing it, they allow equality to distort the substance of their decisionmaking" (592). "As a form of analysis, equality [one could substitute freedom, justice, neutrality, autonomy] confuses far more than it clarifies" because "by masquerading as an independent norm, equality conceals the real nature of the substantive rights it incorporates [unknowingly] by reference" (579).

One year after Weston's article was published, Larry Alexander and Paul Horton made basically the same argument with respect to the formal principle of "freedom of speech." Whether your First Amendment analysis rests on deontological assumptions or consequentialist assumptions, whether you are concerned to protect individual autonomy or increase the free flow of ideas, " 'freedom of speech' will not have its own principle, but instead will be part of a more general liberty," or subordinate to the desire for a specific outcome.[6] The moment one seeks to justify the principle of freedom of speech, the principle, as something freestanding, will have been compromised: " 'Free speech is justified because. . . .' What comes after the 'because' inevitably will link free speech with something else, usually more basic, and thus will destroy free speech's independence. Put differently, any attempt to justify, rather than merely to identify, a free speech principle will require acceptance of principles that are broader than the free speech principle itself, with respect to which the free speech principle is not independent" (1356).

The reasons Alexander and Horton give for this judgment are familiar and constitute a summary of the points made by Post, Abel, Butler, and other free-speech revisionists: " 'Speech,' we contend, does not denote any particular set of phenomena. Everything, including all human activities, can 'express' or 'communicate,' and an audience can derive meaning from all sorts of human and natural events. Moreover, 'speech' is regulated and affected by regulation in a multitude of different ways and for a multitude of different reasons. Finally, with respect to any value, 'speech' both serves and disserves that value in an indefinite variety of ways and degrees. Considering these points, it would be truly amazing if 'freedom of speech' really did have a coherent and independently justifiable principle all its own" (1322). Given the impossibility of identifying an independent free-speech principle, there is no basis for any "special treatment of 'speech' " such that it would be obviously and uncontroversially "distinguished from other activities" (1349). And in the absence of either a freestanding principle or a notion of speech that marks it off clearly from the more inclusive category of action, there is nothing *general* to say about speech with respect to regulation. "Instead," Alexander and Horton conclude, "there are merely some improper regulations of speech, just as there are some improper regulations of other activities. And we may put our pretheoretical intuitions aside, to await a narrower articulation of free speech principles in the specific contexts in which specific governmental regulations of specific communicative activity are brought to our attention" (1357). That is,

---

6. Larry Alexander & Paul Horton, *The Impossibility of a Free Speech Principle*, 78 Nw. U. L. Rev. 1319, 1321 (1983).

we must await the identification of what is and is not "improper" in relation to moral and empirical determinations no principle of free speech will generate, for it is only when such determinations are arrived at by other means that the so-called principle will be armed and alive. In short, we must await, and work for, the outcomes of politics.

In a more recent article, Alexander generalizes this argument so that it extends to all procedural rights and imperatives, which, he argues in a now-familiar vein, "just *are* substantive rights."[7] Whenever we have procedural rights, they are "secondary to substantive rights because they are rights about official determinations of the facts governing the application of substantive rights" (23). Moreover, because these determinations are made not from a God's-eye perspective but from a perspective that is partial, they provide only a challengeable and corrigible ground for identifying what our rights and duties are: "We each calculate the probabilities of adjudicative facts differently because our perspectives are different; and the calculations of probabilities themselves, and not just the probabilities about adjudicative facts, will also differ due to differences in perspective" (23).

The implications of this argument for the theory project and for liberalism in general are far-reaching and dire. Liberalism begins in the recognition of the plurality of perspectives and pins its hopes on the possibility of carving out a realm within which differing perspectives can be accorded equal procedural rights. But if the specification of those rights and of their application is dependent on a prior perspective-sensitive interpretation of moral and empirical facts, there is no merely procedural realm; and rather than offering a rational alternative to substantive, agenda-driven judgments, procedural rights and rules are merely one form (and that a self-deluding form) that substantive agenda-driven judgments take. Procedural rights and rules, despite their promise to save us from agonism and politics, are politics by another name.

I have quoted extensively from the work of Weston, Alexander, and Horton because they at once provide support for what Post, Abel, and Butler say about the impossibility of a coherent and workable First Amendment theory and enlarge the argument so that it includes the theory project in general. Where, however, does this leave us? First of all, it leaves us without a ground of justification more basic or higher than the grounds given us by our moral convictions and determinations of fact. There is no theory or principle or bright line that will allow us to rise above or step to the side of the conclusions we have reached as situated political agents. This is the lesson read to us by all the theorists examined in this essay, and to it I have added the lesson that nothing

---

7. Larry Alexander, *Are Procedural Rights Derivative Substantive Rights?* 17 LAW & PHIL. 19 (1998).

of a positive or helpfully negative kind can be derived from this lesson. An awareness that a free-speech principle is unavailable will not equip you with resources to deal with the next free-speech dilemma that comes your way. At the very most it will (or should; remember the examples of Post, Butler, and Abel) tell you where not to look and will refocus your attention on questions that actually have answers because they are rooted in an understanding of what is really at stake—*never* an abstraction like equality or free speech—and of the possible alternative courses of action.

This, at any rate, is the hope harbored by Frederick Schauer in a recent essay. Schauer's subject is censorship, and he begins by making and accepting the point made by Post, Abel, and Butler. Censorship, he reminds us, is usually thought of as an external constraint on one's individual expressive preferences; but what if our preferences were themselves determined by the same kind of external constraint? This would mean that censorship, broadly conceived as a restraint on expressive action, was an inescapable ingredient of all expression, and that would mean that the notion could not be used to mark off a desirable condition (freedom of expression) from an undesirable one (coerced or regulated expression). "For if the [traditional] use of the word *censorship* presupposes that censorship is a readily identifiable subset of the set of human activity, then it makes no sense to identify as such a subset something that is part and parcel of all human activity."[8]

It would then be the case (as Schauer thinks it to be) that to characterize something as censorship is to mark a difference between speech acts you think should be regulated and speech acts you think should not be, not to explain it: "I am tempted to conclude that the word *censorship,* which is largely even if not exclusively pejorative (and that is why censors always deny that they are censoring, even when they are censoring for good purposes), does not describe a category of conduct, but rather attaches an operative conclusion (ascribes) to a category created on other grounds" (160).

Those other grounds are the grounds of politics, the grounds on which one decides that some forms of speech are valuable and others are not; it is not to censorship per se that people object but to "the particular substance of the censorious acts that are necessary for the maintenance of language as we know it" (153). In other words, censorship is the name you give to censorious acts of which you disapprove; censorious acts that have effects you like will receive another name and be attached to some principle (good order, equality, democratic process) you take them to be protecting or promoting.

---

8. Frederick Schauer, *The Ontology of Censorship, in* CENSORSHIP AND SILENCING: PRACTICES OF CULTURAL REGULATION (ISSUES & DEBATES) 149 (Robert Post ed., 1998).

In any controversy, therefore, the choice is never between censorship and noncensorship, constrained speech and free speech, but between different operations of constraint and authority. So that the "question . . . is not whether artists should be censored"; rather, the question is "whether the judgments of curators should be preferred to the judgments of the state and whether the forces of the market should be preferred to the forces of politics" (162).

Forces there will always be—no zone of freedom in this argument—and thus the traditional language of censorship, assuming as it does an autonomous agent whose autonomy can be infringed, is inappropriate. "The language I would substitute for the language of censorship is thus the language that we might use in making [any and all] social decisions about the allocation of content-determining authority and the language that a society might use in negotiating competing claims for the right to exercise that authority" (163). That language would not itself do normative work but would record the result of normative work done in the crucible of social life, with its disputes and (temporary) resolutions; it would "identify whose choices we as a society wish to privilege and whose choices we wish to suspect" (163). And, it cannot be said too often, those choices will be political, not theoretical. Thus, for example, "in the context of funding for the arts, the question is whether the judgments of artistic peers, themselves infused with the politics of art . . . should be preferred to the judgments of public officials, which are equally infused with politics of a different kind" (162–63). Not politics or the avoidance of politics, but politics proceeding from this set of interests rather than that.

Schauer, then, comes out just about where Weston, Alexander, and Horton do, with a warning against employing the misleading and empty vocabulary of abstraction and formal principle and an injunction to keep one's eye on the true question of concern (What do we think good and what part of the machinery of First Amendment jurisprudence and of law in general will help us to realize it?) and not involve ourselves in profitless questions directed at entities (free speech, equality, freedom, justice) that do not exist. As some of the writings I have examined in this essay show, the advice will be hard to follow, in part because the lure of the formal universal with its promise of a space insulated from political "distortion" is so powerful that it inflects even our framing of an issue.

Consider, for example, what has often been called the "problem" of hate speech, to which several of those I discuss obsessively return. I put "problem" in quotes so as to flag it as a noninnocent usage. The problem with "problem" is that, unqualified, it means "problem for everyone," or a problem universally, as in the problems (for everyone except perhaps fanatic Malthusians) of hunger and disease. Hate speech, however, is not such a problem; rather, it is the pejorative designation by one party of the way of thinking and talking central to the beliefs and agenda of another party. Moreover, not only is it a mistake to term hate speech a problem, and thus to imply that a cure for it may someday be found in a pill or a book whose consumption will render any reader morally healthy, it is a mistake with consequences. It gets in the way of thinking about strategies for dealing with that which you regard as dangerous and a source of evil. If the evil is given no particular location but is regarded more or less as a virus that mysteriously infects some people and leaves others uninfected, you will think in terms of remedies or, in cases where the disease is too far gone, of quarantine. But if the evil is given a location in a worldview you despise and fear—not an irrational worldview (calling speech you loathe "irrational" is another form of universalizing and trivializing) but a view equipped with reasons, evidence, and authorities you reject and find truly harmful—you will think in agonistic and political terms and begin to figure out how you can stigmatize, oppress, and in general get the better of an enemy.

Here is another example of the way in which the liberal tendency to turn substantive convictions into formal abstractions—either good as in freedom or equality or bad as in hate speech or bigotry—can trick you into mistaking the true nature of your objective (not freedom or equality but some politically realizable state of affairs) and minimizing (by universalizing) the threat to its being accomplished. So long as hate speech, bigotry, and discrimination are conceptualized as "problems" rather than as the names you have given to acts of discrimination other than those you think good and right, you will never get a handle on them and you will be reduced, as liberals have been in the past twenty years, to handwringing and pious exhortations.

I recognize the harshness of this conclusion, which is more Hobbesian than Millian or Rawlsian. It is a conclusion Sanford Levinson reaches reluctantly after he surveys the pro and con arguments for state regulation of monuments and statuary and finds himself on one side or the other depending on whether or not he approves the purposes of the state in a given instance. "I am happy with the state's playing a tutelary role . . . as long as I am happy with the state's substantive decisions as to whom to honor (or dishonor)."[9] Immediately after saying this, Levinson recoils against it: "Does it simply boil down to whose ox is gored or cultural symbol honored? One would like to say 'No,' especially if one is a liberal yearning for neutral standards that enable us to transcend our own substantive politics. . . . But I do not know what those standards are" (211).

---

9. Sanford Levinson, *The Tutelary State: "Censorship," "Silencing," and the "Practices of Cultural Regulation," in* CENSORSHIP AND SILENCING: PRACTICES OF CULTURAL REGULATION (ISSUES & DEBATES) 211 (Robert Post ed., 1998).

Not to worry; nobody else does either. And the large lesson to be taken from the "new" (anti)theorists of the First Amendment—a lesson they occasionally resist even as they teach it—is that the unavailability of neutral standards or of a general theory of free speech or of a core free-speech principle or of a formal mechanism for making decisions about regulating and not regulating does not prevent us either from knowing what is good or working to bring it about. That knowledge is ours by virtue of being situated moral beings; and if we go with it and do not disdain it in favor of empty abstractions, it will direct us to the resources, wholly and benignly political, by means of which our deepest convictions and aspirations might be realized.

But, one might ask, what exactly are (or should be) our deepest aspirations and convictions? I shall not answer that question because, were I to do so, I would be urging some particular vision of the good, whereas it is my purpose only to argue that particular visions of the good are unavoidable. That argument, in and of itself, is not and could not without contradiction be an argument for either affirming or rejecting any particular vision. *That* kind of argument, in which I am happy to engage, would take place in some historical context of substantive dispute, exactly the context neutral principles were designed to bypass or transcend. Denying that there are any such neutral principles commits me to nothing substantive, but neither does it place me in a position of detachment from substantive conflict. Rather, it tells me (and you) that such detachment is impossible and that any claim to have achieved it is either empty or part and parcel of a substantive strategy (or both).

I am aware that on the surface this might seem to be my version of the neutrality I so often deride. But it is not. The difference is that liberal neutrality is positive; it directs you to do something, to bracket or set aside your substantive convictions; my neutrality (if that is the word, and it isn't) leaves you where you always were, in the grip of whatever substantive convictions have become yours by virtue of experience and education. It is the minimalism, rather than the neutrality, of my position that should be emphasized. If that position finds you in the condition of always and already being in the embrace of your convictions, it does not claim to have *produced* the condition it finds, only to report on it. Embracing your convictions is not (by my argument) an option; therefore I could not be recommending it, only trying to explain why it is inescapable, an explanation that does no positive work, pushes you in no particular direction, but tells you that being in a particular direction is both the limitation (no transcendence available) and the glory (a field of opportunity is always opening up before you) of your situation.

In "The Invisible Hand of the Marketplace of Ideas," Lillian BeVier addresses the question whether the decline of "legal accountability of participants in public debate" that has occurred through the progressive expansion of First Amendment rights has brought unwarranted, and unaccounted for, costs to the society. For example, the removal of legal liability for false statements uttered in the course of public debate might well encourage false statements, which seemingly would result in increased harm to individuals and, more importantly, to public discourse as well. There is a paradox here, too, for while legal accountability for harmful speech has been constitutionally diminished, legal liability for other harmful behavior has risen substantially over the last century (for example, the law governing the liability of manufacturers of defective products). Professor BeVier notes that "the political information industry—the press—is now the only major profitable industry in the U.S. economy that is not routinely held legally accountable for the harms that defects in its product cause, either to the electorate as a whole or to particular victimized individuals."

In her analysis, Professor BeVier finds "hitherto underappreciated features of the market for political information" and "mechanisms other than liability rules [that] seem to encourage the press to perform its constitutionally significant role." Drawing on a wide array of concepts from economics and game theory, Professor BeVier parses the working assumptions of First Amendment jurisprudence that tend to reflect a far greater concern for the need to stimulate the quantity of political information by diminishing legal liability for errors than any concern about the adverse effects from removal of incentives to produce high-quality information. "All things considered," she concludes, "the relative lack of formal legal accountability of the press does not have consequences that are on balance perverse." Competition saves us.—LCB

LILLIAN R. BEVIER

The Invisible Hand of the Marketplace of Ideas

Introduction: "Developments in the Law"

Despite the doctrinal litter that clutters the First Amendment landscape, one trend is clear: the First Amendment's domain has expanded significantly in recent years. The Supreme Court has interpreted both the substantive reach and the methodological imperatives of the First Amendment so as substantially to diminish government's power to regulate, control, or punish speech.[1] Because of this, a genuine contraction in the *legal* accountability of participants in political debate has taken place.

Consider, for example, the liability of publishers for making false statements of fact about public officials or public figures. As every lawyer knows, before *New York Times v. Sullivan*,[2] publishers of false defamatory statements about

---

1. In terms of the substantive reach of the First Amendment, *compare, e.g.*, Dennis v. United States, 341 U.S. 494, 510 (1951) ("In each case, [courts] must ask whether the gravity of the 'evil,' discounted by its improbability, justifies such invasion of free speech as is necessary to avoid the danger"), *with* Brandenburg v. Ohio, 395 U.S. 444, 447 (1969) ("The constitutional guarantees of free speech and free press do not permit a State to forbid or proscribe advocacy of the use of force or of law violation except where such advocacy is directed to inciting or producing imminent lawless action and is likely to incite or produce such action."); Chaplinsky v. New Hampshire, 315 U.S. 568, 571–72 (1942) ("There are certain well-defined and narrowly limited classes of speech, the prevention and punishment of which have never been thought to raise any Constitutional problem. These include the lewd and obscene, the profane, the libelous, and the insulting or 'fighting' words"), *with* New York Times v. Sullivan, 376 U.S. 254, 269 (1964) ("[L]ibel can claim no talismanic immunity from constitutional limitations. It must be measured by standards that satisfy the First Amendment."); and Valentine v. Chrestensen, 316 U.S. 52, 54 (1942) (The First Amendment imposes no "restraint on government as respects purely commercial advertising."), *with* Virginia State Bd. of Pharmacy v. Virginia Citizens Consumer Council, 425 U.S. 748, 770 (1976) ("[C]ommercial speech, like other varieties, is protected" by the First Amendment.). In addition, such doctrines as prior restraint, *see, e.g.*, New York Times v. United States, 403 U.S. 713, 714 (1971) ("Any system of prior restraints of expression comes to this Court bearing a heavy presumption against its constitutional validity."); vagueness, *see, e.g.*, Smith v. Goguen, 415 U.S. 566, 572–73 (1974) (Vagueness doctrine "requires legislatures to set reasonably clear guidelines for law enforcement officials and triers of fact in order to prevent 'arbitrary and discriminatory enforcement.' "); and the rule against content discrimination, *see, e.g.*, Police Dep't v. Mosley, 408 U.S. 92, 95 (1972) ("[A]bove all else, the First Amendment means that government has no power to restrict expression because of its message, its ideas, its subject matter, or its content.") embody increasingly stringent methodological imperatives.

2. 376 U.S. 254 (1964).

public officials and their performance of their official duties were strictly liable for defamation. Truth was a defense, but the defendant had the burden of proof on the issue. Successful plaintiffs could recover presumed and punitive damages, and defendants could not escape liability even if they published with reasonable grounds to believe that what they were publishing was true. Today, though, on account of what the Court perceives to be required by the First Amendment, publishers of false statements of fact about public officials (as well as about public figures involved in matters of public interest and concern) are not liable even for actual damages unless they publish with actual malice, that is, knowledge of falsity or reckless disregard of the truth.[3] The burden of proof of falsity has also shifted. Truth is no longer an affirmative defense; instead, it is plaintiff's burden to prove falsity.[4] Finally, plaintiff must prove all the elements of her cause of action by clear and convincing evidence. And when reviewing a trial court's finding of actual malice, the appellate court is not limited by the clearly erroneous standard; rather it must exercise independent judgment to determine that the record supports the finding with convincing clarity.[5]

New York Times and its progeny signal a trend in the direction of diminished legal accountability for the press that stands in sharp contrast to developments in other legal domains. For example, a shift in the opposite direction has occurred with regard to the liability of commercial advertisers to their rivals for false statements of fact about their own products. In fact, the legal rules that today specify the liability of producers of political information and of commercial advertising when they make false statements of fact are almost exactly the converse both of one another and of what each was a half-century ago. Fifty years ago it was virtually impossible for a competitor to sue a commercial rival for making false statements of fact in advertising about the rival's own product.[6] Now, however, on account of the way the courts interpreted and Congress subsequently amended § 43(a) of the Lanham Trademark Act, such suits are commonplace. Moreover, liability—for false or misleading statements—is strict, causation is often effectively presumed, a

---

3. Curtis Publishing Co. v. Butts, 388 U.S. 130 (1967); Gertz v. Robert Welch, Inc., 418 U.S. 323 (1974); Dun & Bradstreet v. Greenmoss Builders, 472 U.S. 749 (1985).

4. Philadelphia Newspapers v. Hepps, 475 U.S. 767 (1986).

5. Bose Corp. v. Consumers Union of the United States, 466 U.S. 485 (1984).

6. *Cf., e.g.,* Ely-Norris Safe Co. v. Mosler Safe Co., 7 F.2d 603 (2d Cir. 1925), *rev'd,* 273 U.S. 132 (1927). *See generally* Gary S. Marx, *§ 43(a) of the Lanham Act: A Statutory Cause of Action for False Advertising,* 40 WASH. & LEE L. REV. 383, 389 (1983) ("The common-law rule in 1927 . . . was that competitors had no standing to enjoin nondisparaging, deceptive advertising outside the palming off context unless the plaintiff had a monopoly position in the market such that sales were necessarily decreased by the deception.").

reasonable belief in the truth of the statement is no defense, and seven-figure damage awards are becoming familiar if not yet quite routine.[7] The Supreme Court does not view the First Amendment as impeding this particular trend toward increased liability. Indeed, with the Court's implicit blessing and with no discernible resistance from First Amendment commentators, the trend has accelerated since the Court extended First Amendment coverage to commercial advertising in 1976.[8]

In addition, if we think of a false statement of fact by the producer of political information as in the nature of a defective product—which seems a reasonable enough way to think about it if we consider that "no rational person ever wants to act on the basis of a false statement of fact"[9]—we will become aware that the legal rules that govern liability of producers of defective political information now depart drastically from the regime of strict liability that has come to govern producers of other defective products. In the first half of the twentieth century, manufacturers were liable to consumers who were injured by defects in their products only if the consumer could prove that the product had been negligently manufactured. In 1965, confirming the trend of case law,[10] the American Law Institute promulgated § 402A of the Restatement (2d) of Torts, announcing that any seller of a product in a "defective condition unreasonably dangerous to the user" was strictly liable in tort for personal injury or property damage resulting from that defective condition. The "liability explosion"[11] was underway, and it has continued apace.

It is a fair generalization to note that the political information industry—the press—is now the only major industry in the U.S. economy that is not routinely held legally accountable for the harms that defects in its product cause, either to the electorate as a whole or to particular victimized individuals. Those who gather and report the news have no legal obligation to be competent, thorough, or disinterested. Those who publish and broadcast it have no legal obligation to warrant its truthfulness, to guarantee its relevance, or to ensure

---

7. *See, e.g.,* Alpo Petfoods, Inc. v. Ralston Purina Co., 997 F.2d 949 (D.C. Cir. 1993); U-Haul Int'l v. Jartran, Inc., 793 F.2d 1034 (9th Cir. 1986), *aff'g in part and rev'g in part* 601 F. Supp. 1140 (D. Ariz. 1984) (*Jartran II*).

8. Virginia State Bd. of Pharmacy v. Virginia Citizens Consumer Council, 425 U.S. 748 (1976).

9. David A. Strauss, *Persuasion, Autonomy, and Freedom of Expression,* 91 COLUM. L. REV. 334, 366 (1991).

10. In 1960, the New Jersey Supreme Court decided *Henningsen v. Bloomfield Motors, Inc.,* 161 A.2d 69 (N.J. 1960), which came to be understood as holding that a manufacturer is strictly liable in tort to an injured consumer. California explicitly followed suit in *Greenman v. Yuba Power Prods., Inc.,* 377 P.2d 897 (Cal. 1963).

11. *Cf.* WALTER K. OLSON, THE LITIGATION EXPLOSION (1991).

its completeness. And they are only liable to public officials or public figures about whom they publish defamatory falsehoods if they have acted with egregious indifference to their rights.

It is also a fair generalization that, for all their disagreements about underlying premises and empirical verities, few theorists challenge the First Amendment appropriateness of this regime. Instead, there is at least on one level a surprising consensus that the First Amendment requires these outcomes—because of the centrality of political discourse to the enterprise of representative democracy, because of the necessity that the press perform a "checking function" in order to expose and halt the abuse of government power, because of the great *benefits* of speech and the excessive *costs* of regulation. In this essay, I do not propose to challenge this consensus. Instead, I want to suggest a way of discussing what the First Amendment is about, and of thinking about the "marketplace of ideas," that may deepen our appreciation of the processes by which the freedom implemented by these doctrines serves constitutional values.[12] I focus not on the benefits of *speech* but on the benefits of *freedom of speech*.[13]

I turn first to the marketplace metaphor. I have already noted that recent decades have witnessed a constitutionally compelled contraction in the legal liability of producers of false political information, while in nearby courtrooms the legal liability of producers of defective products and of false commercial information about products has steadily expanded. In the next section of the essay I describe an interesting, seldom-noticed aspect of these developments, which is that each is often justified with reference to a particular kind

---

12. I warn readers that the First Amendment literature on the "marketplace of ideas" is voluminous, and that this essay's portrayal of the market may seem somewhat though not wholly idiosyncratic. It approaches the market in terms of the incentives that appear systematically to confront producers and consumers of information. For a similar approach, *see* BRUCE M. OWEN, ECONOMICS AND FREEDOM OF EXPRESSION: MEDIA STRUCTURE AND THE FIRST AMENDMENT (1975). In addition, this essay talks not about the market's capacity to produce "truth" with a capital *T,* but rather of its capacity to produce factually accurate information.

Much of the existing literature is critical, in the sense that it concludes that for one reason or another the marketplace of ideas fails to produce socially optimal results. Commentators approach the market in terms of what they allege to be its underlying assumptions—that truth is objective, humans are rational, and access is equally available to holders of all ideas. Finding these assumptions flawed, they question the intellectual and legal hegemony of the marketplace metaphor. *See generally* C. EDWIN BAKER, HUMAN LIBERTY AND FREEDOM OF SPEECH 1–24 (1989); Stanley Ingber, *The Marketplace of Ideas: A Legitimating Myth,* 1984 DUKE L.J. 1; Jonathan Weinberg, *Broadcasting and Speech,* 81 CAL. L. REV. 1101 (1993).

13. I agree with commentators like Professor Schauer who point out that speech can do harm to innocent victims and that the present legal regime may sometimes unfairly impose costs on undeserving individuals. *See* Frederick Schauer, *Uncoupling Free Speech,* 92 COLUM. L. REV. 1321 (1992). I put these unpleasant realities aside for the moment.

of failure in the relevant market—for political speech, for products, and for commercial information about products, respectively. Then, in the following section, I speculate about the validity of some of the empirical assumptions that support the market failure hypothesis with reference to the market for political information. I conclude that, though the free and unregulated market for political information is not an unqualified success (in that it may tend to produce information in suboptimal quantities and of inferior quality), it does serve democracy surprisingly well.

Three Liability Regimes and Their Rationales

Consider first, and most briefly, the expansion of liability of producers of defective products and of defective warnings about unavoidably dangerous products. An important rationale for this expansion is that, without the prod of legal liability, market forces generate inadequate incentives for producers either to establish and maintain appropriate standards of quality or to provide consumers with sufficient information to permit them to protect themselves from harm.[14] The supposed result is that while producers can readily internalize the social *benefits* of their productive activity, they do not always internalize the full social *costs*. Consumers are unable to detect defects before purchase or to take appropriate precautions afterward. They are incapable of rationally assessing the risks, especially of latent defects, in the design of the products they buy. Yet, unaware of their own ignorance, they cannot translate their presumed willingness to pay for nondefective products into a demand that at least some producers would exploit. The distrust of the market implicitly reflects as well the view that producers of goods and services are systematically inclined to shirk on safety, and that without the threat of legal liability they would willingly and profitably subject their customers and innocent bystanders to serious risks of harm. Absent liability imposed by law, the market thus permits producers to escape accountability for the costs of their own mistakes, and for their failure to discern what it is that consumers "really" want. The function of liability, then, is to correct for this market failure by supplying a mechanism that will have the effect of internalizing these costs to the producers and thus of requiring the producers to take account of them.

This essay is not about tort law, of course, and it will not challenge the assumptions of market failure on which the tort liability explosion has been based. Noting them, however, serves both to highlight the fact that the liability regimes that presently govern commercial and political speakers also rest on

---

14. For a useful, if skeptical, account of this rationale, *see* Alan Schwartz, *Proposals for Products Liability Reform: A Theoretical Synthesis*, 97 YALE L.J. 353 (1988).

assumptions about how the respective markets work and to introduce the thought that unpacking these assumptions might enrich doctrinal analysis.

Given the role that market failure arguments play in supporting *expanded* liability for defective products, it is perhaps ironic that a dominant line of argument supporting the regime of *relaxed* liability for producers of political information is also often cast in market failure terms, albeit different from those that support the expansion of liability for other producers. The argument begins by tracing the connection between political speech and democratic government: a viable democracy requires a politically well-informed citizenry. More than a rhetorical embellishment of First Amendment opinions,[15] this observation captures a central insight about how representative democracy works. Citizens must know what their elected representatives are doing if they are to be responsible voters. Information in the hands of citizens is indispensable to their being able to hold their government to account, which is in turn indispensable almost by definition to democracy. Asymmetries of information between citizens and government officials present the latter with opportunities to shirk their public duties and to pursue their own—or some special interest group's—ends instead.[16] The more citizens know and understand about what their government is doing, and the more reliable their access to such knowledge and understanding, the more likely they will be to detect any shirking that might take place. And the more likely they are to detect shirking, the greater will be their ability to deter it *ex ante* and to punish it when it occurs. For this reason, representative democracy needs a market that produces more and better political information instead of one that produces less and worse. Thus the press, as supplier of political information, appears to have a constitutionally significant role to play, a role that even turns out to imply criteria helpful for judging the quality of political information. In order to enable citizens better to know and understand what government is doing, political information must be factually accurate, reasonably complete, and relevant. Political information that is false, incomplete, or irrelevant, accordingly, may be fairly characterized as defective.

---

15. *See, e.g.,* Richmond Newspapers v. Virginia, 448 U.S. 555, 587 (1980) (Brennan, J., concurring in the judgment) (First Amendment has "a *structural* role to play in securing and fostering our republican system of self-government" implicit in the assumption that "valuable public debate—as well as other civic behavior—must be informed."); Pell v. Procunier, 417 U.S. 817, 862 (1974) (Powell, J., dissenting) (First Amendment performs "societal function" of "preserving free public discussion of governmental affairs.").

16. *Cf.* Gary C. Jacobson, *Campaign Finance and Democratic Control: Comments on Gottlieb and Lowenstein's Papers,* 18 HOFSTRA L. REV. 369 (1989) (viewing debate on campaign finance reform through lens of agency theory).

The market failure argument supporting press freedom from liability for the harms that defects in its product cause takes democracy's need for more political information as its implicit starting point. The argument does not ask whether holding the press accountable for the *harm* would improve the *quality* of political information but rather whether liability might have an intolerably discouraging effect on *quantity*. Claiming to discover that the market has a systematic tendency to supply "too little," the argument grounds press freedom from liability on the need to correct for this undersupply by providing a constitutional privilege to publish false statements of fact about public officials and public figures, a privilege that subsidizes information providers by reducing their exposure to liability.[17] Thus the reverse twist on the market failure arguments that support increased liability in other markets: providers of political information must be protected from liability because the market fails to permit them to internalize the full social *benefits* of their activity, whereas producers of other products must be subjected to liability because the market permits them to externalize some of their *costs*.[18]

---

17. *See generally, e.g.,* Daniel A. Farber, *Free Speech without Romance: Public Choice and the First Amendment,* 105 HARV. L. REV. 554 (1991); Richard A. Posner, *Free Speech in an Economic Perspective,* 20 SUFFOLK U. L. REV. 1 (1986). There are those, too, who argue that the market failure implicit in the market's tendency to undersupply political information requires not more freedom but less. *See, e.g.,* CASS A. SUNSTEIN, THE PARTIAL CONSTITUTION 220 (1993) ("[T]he market will produce too little information. . . . For this reason a regulatory solution, solving the public good problem, is justified.").

18. The market failure rationale is not the only significant argument linking press freedom to the role of information in sustaining democratic government. Freedom insulates the press from both the threat and the reality of government censorship, thus enabling it to perform its constitutionally mandated task of informing the citizenry. This fact supplies a coherent and indisputably useful premise—the premise of distrust—for reasoning about what the content of First Amendment rules ought to be. *See generally* JOHN HART ELY, DEMOCRACY AND DISTRUST 106 (1980) ("Courts must police inhibitions on . . . political activity because we cannot trust elected officials to do so: ins have a way of wanting to make sure the outs stay out."). Distrust of government is not the subject of this essay, except perhaps obliquely insofar the essay celebrates *freedom* of speech, a concept in which distrust of government inheres.

Beginning with *New York Times v. Sullivan,* the Court's opinions justifying the constitutional privilege to publish falsehoods about public officials and figures contain a number of striking features. None of these features renders the opinions necessarily inconsistent with the "market failure" explanation, though none articulates the explanation in so many words.

First, the opinions affirm the connection between the First Amendment, the provision of political information by the press, and democracy. Justice Brennan's opinion in *Sullivan* famously insisted on considering the "case against the background of a profound national commitment to the principle that debate on public issues should be uninhibited, robust and wide-open," 376 U.S. 254, 270 (1964), and the Court has never questioned the relevance of this principle to its defamation jurisprudence. Second, the opinions self-consciously rest on judgments about how the scope of publisher liability for defamation affects the *amount* of information that publishers are likely to produce. Third, they reflect the Court's implicit decision that the incentive effects of the various liability rules ought to be a principal determinant of the scope and content of the constitutional privilege. Fourth, the

Now consider commercial advertising. The First Amendment protection of commercial speech does *not* include a privilege to make false or misleading statements of fact. Precisely to the contrary. The Court appears to believe that constitutional protection for *true* commercial speech is in instrumental terms merely the flip side of the common law of fraud, which of course regulates *false* statements.[19] Thus, in its treatment of false or misleading speech, the contours of First Amendment protection of commercial speech differ significantly from the protection afforded political speech.[20] Though the differences stem in part from the different theoretical bases for the two sets of doctrines, they also reflect the "common sense distinctions"[21] between commercial and noncommercial speech that the Court perceives. The Court has explicitly accepted an account of how the market for commercial advertising works that differs in crucial respects from conventional wisdom about the market for political speech. It regards the information about products that commercial advertising provides as more objective and readily verifiable than the information about public officials and about matters of public interest and concern that noncommercial speakers provide. Moreover, it thinks that "commercial speech may be more durable than other kinds. Since advertising is the *sine qua non* of commercial

---

opinions give scant attention to the fact that the Court has deliberately privileged the publication of *false* information, nor do they often concern themselves with what the effect of such false information on the overall quality of political debate might be. Justice Brennan asserted in *Sullivan* that "[a]uthoritative interpretations of the First Amendment guarantees have consistently refused to recognize an exception for any test of truth," *id.* at 271, and speculated that "[e]ven a false statement may be deemed to make a valuable contribution to public debate, since it brings about 'the clearer perception and livelier perception of truth, produced by its collision with error,' " *id.* at 279 n.19. And though the Court has since disavowed the latter speculation, *see* Gertz v. Robert Welch, Inc., 418 U.S. 323, 339 (1974) ("there is no constitutional value in false statements of fact"), its defamation opinions tend to suppress the issue of truth versus falsity in favor of rhetorical endorsements of the presumably unequivocal value of "uninhibited, robust, and wide-open" discussion. The Court is clearly convinced that, under a rule imposing strict liability for false statements of fact, "would-be critics of official conduct may be deterred from voicing their criticism, even though it is believed to be true and even though it is in fact true, because of doubt whether it can be proved in court or fear of the expense of having to do so." It remains noteworthy, however, that the Court has paid almost no attention to the possibility that systematically privileging the publication of false statements of fact might have a perverse effect on the quality of political debate.

19. In 44 Liquormart, Inc. v. Rhode Island, 517 U.S. 484, 496 (1996), the Court stated: "[T]he same interest that supports regulation of potentially misleading advertising, namely the public's interest in receiving accurate commercial information, also supports an interpretation of the First Amendment that provides constitutional protection for the dissemination of accurate and nonmisleading commercial messages."

20. The Court has said, for example that it is "less necessary to tolerate inaccurate statements for fear of silencing the speaker, . . . [It is permissible] to require that a commercial message appear in such a form, or include such additional information, warnings, and disclaimers, as are necessary to prevent its being deceptive . . . and the prohibition against prior restraints" is inapplicable. Virginia State Bd. of Pharmacy, 425 U.S. at 771–72 n.24.

21. *Id.*

profits, there is little likelihood of its being chilled by proper regulation and forgone entirely."[22]

The Court also appears to assume that, left unregulated, the market for commercial information is prone to quality failures. It seems to assume that, absent regulation of false advertising on the one hand and constitutional protection of truthful advertising on the other, producers of commercial information will far too readily be able to mislead consumers.

Challenging Premises; Rethinking Implications

Thus the Constitutional doctrines that govern the permissible scope of liability for false statements of fact about public officials on the one hand and false statements of fact in commercial advertising about products on the other hand rest in significant measure on unproven empirical assumptions about how the respective information markets work and on the particular kind of market failure to which each is prone.[23] The constitutional privilege to make false statements of fact about public officials makes up for a supposed failure along the *quantity* dimension, by in effect subsidizing producers. To the extent the Court has worried about the impact of the privilege on the *quality* of reporting about public events, it has either managed to convince itself that the effects on quality are benign or that routinely engaging in efforts judicially to determine quality *ex post* poses unacceptable risks of error and creates perverse effects on producers' incentives to publish information about important public events.[24] On the other hand, denying advertisers a constitutional privilege to publish false or misleading statements of fact responds to a supposed failure along the *quality* dimension of commercial speech by permitting legal penalties for falsehood to substitute for inadequate market incentives for truth-telling. And, by the simple expedient of assuming away any effect of regulation on the activity levels of commercial information producers, the Court has been able to ignore regulations' potential impact on the *quantity* of commercial information.

Some of the empirical assumptions on which these First Amendment doctrines rest seem incomplete. The assumptions that support the constitutional

---

22. *Id.* The Court's assumptions have not gone unchallenged. *See, e.g.,* Jeffrey P. Singdahlsen, Note, *The Risk of Chill: A Cost of the Standards Governing the Regulation of False Advertising under § 43(a) of the Lanham Act,* 77 VA. L. REV. 339 (1991) (arguing that the uncertainty of the standards that courts apply in § 43(a) cases chills the production of truthful advertising).

23. Although this essay does not purport to be based on extensive empirical research, it does represent an effort to observe the world and to understand it as it actually seems to be. I have tried to pay "careful attention to facts as well as theory," because my goal here has been to avoid the pitfalls of "theorizing without concern for factual predicates." Lucas A. Powe Jr., *The Supreme Court, Social Change, and Legal Scholarship,* 44 STAN. L. REV. 1615, 1616 (1992).

24. *Cf. supra* note 18.

privileging of false statements of fact in the political realm seem most worthy of note, since the privilege runs counter to other legal trends and since it is political speech that is the central concern of the First Amendment. The assumptions upon which the nonprivileging of false statements in the market for commercial information rest are worth comparing, though a rigorously empirical look at either market is not the point of this speculative essay and its account of both markets accordingly will be cursory. The analysis will generate no firm conclusions. It may, however, suggest some hitherto underappreciated features of the market for political information and highlight the fact that mechanisms other than liability rules actually do seem to be in play to encourage the press to perform its constitutionally significant role.

Certain conceptually separate but mutually reinforcing characteristics of political information have led commentators and legal policymakers to conclude that the private market fails to produce it in optimal amounts. First, on the supply side, information is a public good. Because public goods are nonrival and nonexclusive, they tend to be underproduced in ordinary markets. Property rights are the principal vehicle that in our economy permit producers of tangible goods and services to appropriate the full social benefits of their efforts and thus encourage them to produce the full amount that society wants. On account of the difficulty in excluding nonpayers from enjoying their benefits, however, property rights in public goods are inherently difficult—and sometimes as a practical matter impossible—to maintain and enforce.

Consider information. It is intangible and thus has no physical boundaries that would permit the ready identification of a "thing" to which property's exclusive rights of use, possession, and transfer might be said to attach. Because property rights in their output are so difficult to establish and maintain, those who gather information—in particular for purposes of this essay, those who gather political information—encounter systematic difficulty in appropriating the full social benefits of their efforts. Since they must contend with the pervasive possibility that the "investment they make in producing information will benefit others as well as themselves,"[25] they will tend, *ceteris paribus,* to underproduce it relative to its full social value. This general tendency of markets to underproduce information is conventionally regarded as an important source of "failure" in the specific market for political information.

Collective action problems, which are now understood to present a pervasive challenge to representative democracy, exacerbate this political information market failure. Information about government initiatives whose burdens or benefits will be widely diffused among large unorganized groups of citizens

---

25. Posner, *supra* note 17, at 19.

tends to be underproduced because no individual member of the group has the incentive to produce it. Special interest groups might overcome collective action problems, but many commentators seem convinced that in practice interest groups tend to make the problem worse.[26] Groups that stand to receive concentrated benefits from government programs have incentives to produce information about the programs' benefits but not to publicize their costs. Accordingly, the "potential victims . . . may each be so slightly affected that the expected private gain from contributing to a joint effort [to produce information about them] would be zero. Then the problem will be worse than a mere underproduction of information"[27]—though underproduction there will no doubt be.

In addition, though the value to a democratic society of a politically well-informed citizenry is great, the private demand for political information does not reflect its full social value. In the first place, the good government that a well-informed citizenry will produce is itself a "public good" whose benefits (or costs) will accrue to all citizens regardless of whether they are politically well-informed. Many citizens seem likely therefore to free ride on the information-acquiring efforts of their fellows rather than to incur the costs of becoming informed themselves. In addition, when individual incentives to acquire political information are assumed to derive from the appropriable expected value of information as an input to voting, they appear very weak indeed. Considered as an act whose aim is to affect the outcome of an election, voting itself has negative expected value. It is costly to vote, but the chance that any one's vote will affect the outcome is minuscule. Thus few citizens can be expected to vote, fewer still to incur the costs of becoming politically well-informed.[28]

Many commentators who have identified these tendencies of the market to underproduce political information turn their attention at once to the task of deriving appropriate policy implications,[29] one of which is endorsement of

---

26. *See, e.g.,* Lillian R. BeVier, *Campaign Finance Reform: Specious Arguments, Intractable Dilemmas,* 94 COLUM. L. REV. 1258, 1274–76 (1994) (noting that special interest groups have the capacity at once to overcome and to exacerbate collective action problems).

27. Posner, *supra* note 17, at 22.

28. The phenomenon identified in text is commonly referred to as "rational ignorance," and it was first identified by Anthony Downs. ANTHONY DOWNS, AN ECONOMIC THEORY OF DEMOCRACY (1957).

29. A typical suggestion is that of Professor Farber, who recommends that "if the government intervenes in the market at all, it should *subsidize* speech rather than limit it. Legal restrictions on information only further reduce a *naturally inadequate supply of information.*" Farber, *supra* note 17, at 559. Judge Posner similarly notes that "if it is true that the main benefits of information are external, anything that raises the costs of producing information is questionable on its face," Posner, *supra* note 17, at 20, and that "a frequent common law response to the problem of external benefits is to

the subsidy embodied in less-than-strict liability for false statements of fact. A closer look suggests that, while relaxed liability may in fact be defensible on other grounds, conventional market failure analysis may overdefend it on account of exaggerating the extent of both the undersupply of and the weak demand for political information. A few examples help make the point.

On the supply side, producers of political information appear spontaneously to have devised a variety of strategies for appropriating ever more completely to themselves the benefits of their efforts.[30] The most pervasive example of a spontaneously generated market solution is advertising. The important real-world fact is that the sale of advertising at a price that varies according to the number of recipients of the sponsored information permits information providers to appropriate the benefits of producing a product that many people value but for which it is infeasible to charge them directly. Advertising, in other words, has the effect of transforming information from a public into a private good. It obviously does not do so perfectly, because it does not overcome producers' inability to charge consumers directly in proportion to how much and what kind of information they would be willing to pay for[31] and because large audiences do not always want the kind and amount of political information that the public needs to be optimally informed[32]—but perfect solutions are will-o-the-wisps in any event.[33]

---

allow the enterprise to externalize some of its costs," *id.* And Professor Sunstein endorses the notion that, especially in the context of the broadcast media, "a regulatory solution, solving the public good problem, is justified." SUNSTEIN, *supra* note 17, at 220.

30. *Cf.* Harold Demsetz, *Toward A Theory of Property Rights,* 57 AM. ECON. REV. 347–57 (1967) ("Property rights develop to internalize externalities when the gains of internalization become larger than the cost of internalization.").

31. *Cf.* THOMAS KRATTENMAKER & LUCAS A. POWE JR., REGULATING BROADCAST PROGRAMMING (1995) (in broadcast market, consumers cannot express the intensity of their preferences by offering to pay more for what they value more highly because advertisers care about how many people watch and not about how much they value watching).

32. *Cf.* OWEN, *supra* note 12, at 31 ("The basic problem is that the advertiser buys audience while the consumer buys content."). *See also* CASS A. SUNSTEIN, DEMOCRACY AND THE PROBLEM OF FREE SPEECH 70–71 (1993) (Advertisers do aggregate individual preferences and thus help to overcome the public good problem, but they do not overcome the problem of inadequate information about public affairs because programs with large audiences may not provide information at all because documentary movies "hardly ever appear on the list of the most popular shows," and because the economic interests of advertisers often "argue against sponsorship of public service or controversial programming.").

33. *Cf.* Harold Demsetz, *Information and Efficiency: Another Viewpoint,* 12 J.L. & ECON. 1 (1969) (criticizing the arguments of Kenneth J. Arrow, *Economic Welfare and the Allocation of Resources for Invention, in* THE RATE AND DIRECTION OF INVENTIVE ACTIVITY 609–25 (1962), on grounds that Arrow's analytical framework seduces him into committing the "Nirvana fallacy," in which the practitioner "implicitly presents the relevant choice as between an ideal norm and an existing 'imperfect' institutional arrangement.").

On account of their desire for advertising revenue, many information providers have adopted the strategy of packaging the "information" they supply in entertaining formats, so as to increase the size of their audiences. Such strategies are deplorable to some commentators, because they require catering to the lowest common denominator of public taste[34] or because they entail a wealth-based bias.[35] They do, however, have the significant virtue on the supply side of permitting information producers to capture more of the benefits of their efforts (thus partially alleviating chronic undersupply) and on the demand side to strengthen the appeal of an otherwise undervalued product (by providing the spoonful of sugar that helps the medicine of political information go down).[36]

I turn next to the demand side, where the crucial step is simply to take note of the obvious fact that the private demand for political information is not solely a function of its negligible expected value as an input to voting. Not all citizens place an identical value on information about politics, nor do they appear to demand such information solely because it contributes to their ability to cast a well-informed vote. In fact, it seems to be the case that citizens vary widely in the intensity of their demand for political information. Some simply enjoy knowing about politics; some travel in circles where prestige and reputational value inhere in being politically in the know; some need political information in order to advance professionally; and some are so ideologically committed that political information is to them as a sword to a knight—it enables them to fight the good fight, whatever the cost to themselves. Finally there are the lobbyists across the spectrum of industries, trades, professions, and interests whose influence depends on knowing and reporting about political developments of interest to their constituencies. In other words, the demand for political information is far more robust than one would predict from simply aggregating the preferences of hypothetical "average rational citizens."

On account, however, of the perception of egregious market failure on the

---

34. *See, e.g.,* Rodney A. Smolla, *Report of the Coalition for a New America: Platform Section on Communications Policy,* 1993 U. CHI. LEGAL F. 149.

35. Weinberg, *supra* note 12, at 1153.

36. *Cf.* Farber, *supra* note 17, at 582 ("The entertainment component of certain items containing information may be closer to being a standard consumer good than a public good."); Posner, *supra* note 17, at 23 (The fact that most people probably attach little value to political information and will readily substitute other forms of news and entertainment for it "may be why most television news is packaged and formatted as entertainment rather than information."). This latter virtue is in turn a vice in the eyes of some commentators, who decry "infotainment" and celebrate the achievement of "public television stations [that] have 46 percent more public affairs programming than do their commercial counterparts." SUNSTEIN, *supra* note 32, at 5–6.

quantity side, the Court has substantially relaxed the legal tools available to control the *quality* of political information. Thus the next task is to look at the factors other than the threat of legal liability that affect the quality of political information.

Several factors appear to bear on the quality of the supply of political information, though their influence is often difficult to assess. First, the news industry regularly generates sizeable revenues and appears to be highly profitable. Of relevance to the quality of the supply of political information is the fact that a substantial portion of the news media's revenues comes from advertisers. But whether advertisers exert a negative, a positive, or a neutral influence on the quality of political information is unclear, and the task of assessing its influence is complicated by the difficulty of specifying what a world of political information *not* supported by advertising would be like. Analysts often fail to acknowledge that dependence on advertisers is at once an artifact of and an ingenious solution to certain ineluctable realities such as technological constraints, weak citizen demand, and the public-good character of information. No doubt it is well to remember that the alternative to depending on advertisers is depending on direct government funding, a dependence that if it came to be universal would be much like inviting the fox to guard the chickens, and moreover would seem even less likely to be correlated with dependably reliable information about government than is dependence on advertisers.

A second factor that has an obvious bearing on the quality of political information is that it comes daily in the form of "the news" from television, radio, and newspapers. Certain institutional facts pervasively affect news content. For example, a number of salient economic and organizational constraints characterize the "news" or "political information" industry and exert influence on the quality of its product. Consider the fact that news organizations must produce news in accordance with rigid deadlines every day, and that they must structure their news-gathering and editing operations around this requirement.[37] Among other effects, this has led to the development of the beat system, which assigns reporters routinely to cover newsworthy places, officials, or branches of government, in order to ensure that there will be news product on any given day.[38] The beat system carries the risk of turning reporters into "insiders" whose close relationships with their news sources jeopardize their ability to remain detached, skeptical, and relatively autonomous.[39] In addition

---

37. *See, e.g.*, BEN H. BAGDIKIAN, THE MEDIA MONOPOLY 18–21 (1983).

38. BERNARD ROSCHO, NEWSMAKING 73 (1975).

39. *See* Vincent Blasi, *The Newsman's Privilege: An Empirical Study*, 70 MICH. L. REV. 229, 242 (1971); *see also* HERBERT J. GANS, DECIDING WHAT'S NEWS 177 (1979).

news organizations rely heavily on government press offices, as well as on third-party sources who provide more-or-less reliable, more-or-less complete information through both official and unofficial channels.[40]

"Objectivity" has become a pervasively touted norm of popular journalism,[41] but if it is meant normatively to characterize the content of news as governed by a set of universally shared, clearly defined, articulable standards external to the producer, objectivity remains an illusory goal. This is because "news" is unavoidably an artifact of a myriad of discretionary choices.[42] It is quite possibly the case, however, that journalists claim to be objective as a means of bonding their reliability and of shielding themselves and their profession from accusations of bias and the public distrust that such accusations would bring in their wake.[43] If consumers of political information believed journalists' claims to objectivity, and if the speciousness of the claims were to go without challenge or threat of exposure, the implications might be cause for concern. Biased reporting successfully disguised in the sheep's clothing of objectivity could have a negative impact on the ability of citizens to monitor their government agents. But so long as competing information suppliers are free, as they are, to challenge one another, to expose one another's biases and thus alert consumers, there seems little cause for concern that concealed "bias in the media" presents a *systemic* threat, as opposed to a possibly worrisome, too-frequent departure for a norm of perfect disclosure.

The Newspaper Editors' "Statement of Principles" (1975) contains a statement representative of journalism's explicit norms.[44] Asserting the lofty purposes and responsibilities of the press ("to serve the general welfare by informing the people and enabling them to make judgments on the issues of the time . . . to bring an independent scrutiny to bear on the forces of power in society"),[45] the Principles embrace reciprocal self-imposed obligations of independence, truth, accuracy, fairness, impartiality, clear distinctions between

---

40. GANS, *supra* note 39, at 281–82; *cf. also* MARTIN A. LEE & NORMAN SOLOMON, UNRELIABLE SOURCES: A GUIDE TO DETECTING MEDIA BIAS 45 (1990).

41. *See* MICHAEL SCHUDSON, ORIGINS OF THE IDEAL OF OBJECTIVITY IN THE PROFESSIONS: STUDIES IN THE HISTORY OF AMERICAN JOURNALISM AND AMERICAN LAW 1830–1940, chs. 6, 7 (1990).

42. *Cf., e.g.,* Linda Greenhouse, *Telling the Court's Story: Justice and Journalism at the Supreme Court,* 105 YALE L.J. 1537 (1996).

43. *See* GANS, *supra* note 39, at 186.

44. AMERICAN SOCIETY OF NEWSPAPER EDITORS, STATEMENT OF PRINCIPLES (1975), *reprinted in* James C. Thomas Jr., *Journalistic Ethics: Some Probings by a Media Keeper, in* QUESTIONING MEDIA ETHICS 56 (Bernard Rubin ed., 1987).

45. SIGMA DELTA CHI, CODE OF ETHICS (1973), *id.* at 58. The "Code of Ethics" is quite similar to the "Statement of Principles" in both tone and substance.

news reports and opinions, and respect for the rights of people involved in the news. It is noteworthy, however, that the press vehemently resists being held formally to any standard of quality and exhibits surprising unwillingness to subject its own behavior to the routine systematic, though informal, scrutiny that it devotes to the behavior of others.[46]

Insofar as the demand side of the quality dimension is concerned, a key point of this essay is that, because producers of political information are not legally accountable for defects in the quality of the information they produce, their incentives to produce accurate, relevant, and reasonably complete information about government are almost entirely extralegal or market driven. It becomes important to ask, therefore, whether the demand is robust enough to create systematic incentives for political information providers to produce a high quality of information.[47] The question cannot be answered simply by assuming, however reasonable it might be to do so, that citizens prefer accurate, relevant, and reasonably complete information to that which is partial, irrelevant, and false. The answer requires analysis, also, of whether consumers generally can detect inaccuracy, irrelevance, or incompleteness in the political information they receive. If they can detect these quality defects, analysis must turn to whether they would be inclined to punish—by withholding their future patronage from—suppliers who have disappointed them in the past. Even if the average individual consumer cannot detect quality defects and/or is not particularly inclined to punish occasional lapses from the highest standards, there may be *some* consumers who can more readily detect defects than can the average citizen, and some who more insistently demand a high quality of information. It then becomes important to ask how the demands of these more discerning consumers affect the overall incentives of information producers. Finally there is the question of whether, if consumers cannot readily detect defects in the quality of information they receive but still would prefer better to worse information, competition among suppliers of political information

---

46. A handful of newspapers have appointed full-time ombudsmen who investigate and publicize complaints about the news organization. David Pritchard, *The Impact of Newspaper Ombudsmen on Journalists' Attitudes,* 70 JOURNALISM Q. 77, 78 (1993). And few newspapers hire media critics to assess news gathering and presentation in the same way they routinely review other industries. *See* Jerry Knight, *Self-Criticism Not a Journalistic Pastime,* WASHINGTON POST, Aug. 13, 1984, at Wash. Business 1 (criticizing media's reluctance to self-regulate). An example of this "double standard" is that the media seldom disclose their own political contributions or activities and those of other industry participants. Sheila Kaplan, *The Powers That Be Lobbying—One Special Interest the Press Doesn't Cover: Itself,* WASHINGTON MONTHLY, Dec. 1989, at 36.

47. We ask about whether producers confront appropriate externally generated incentives because otherwise we would have to indulge in the plainly counterfactual assumption that producers of political information, alone among human beings, are systematically spontaneously inclined to conform their behavior to socially optimal norms.

tends systematically to discourage publication of inaccurate or misleadingly incomplete information.

Begin by assuming that individual citizens possess identical capacities to evaluate and identical preferences for quality political information. Assume also that citizens' preferences, and hence their demand, for quality political information are solely a function of the information's value as an input to voting, itself an act to which many citizens—perhaps rationally—appear to attach little value.[48]

Except with respect to its relevance, individual citizens are not well positioned to monitor the quality of political information they receive. For the individual citizen, the accuracy and completeness of political information is beset by an irreducible and intractable uncertainty that she can neither guard against nor resolve. In this respect, political information stands in stark contrast to information contained in commercial advertising. Indeed, if consumer ability to detect quality defects in information were a controlling factor in gauging whether information producers ought to be liable for false statements of fact, it would make far more sense to relieve commercial advertisers from liability than it does to relieve political information providers.

Contrast, for example, the citizen's ability to assess the accuracy and completeness of political information with the consumer's ability to assess the quality of information contained in advertising. The information content and systematic reliability of commercial advertising are functions, first, of consumers' ability to verify the information either by prepurchase *search* or postpurchase *experience* and, second, of consumers' tendency to discount all producer-provided information.[49] With respect to information about qualities of a product that consumers can discern before purchase—its price, for example, or its color—consumers can readily detect falsity and thus can easily protect themselves against being duped. Accordingly, producers have little to gain by conveying false information about such "search" qualities. With respect to information about qualities that consumers cannot detect prepurchase but that will manifest themselves in the course of a product's use— "experience" qualities such as a food's taste, for example—consumers know

---

48. *See, e.g.,* FRANCES FOX PIVEN & RICHARD CLOWARD, WHY AMERICANS DON'T VOTE (1988).

49. The seminal work distinguishing "search" from "experience" characteristics, identifying the kind of information likely to be contained in advertising with respect to each, and articulating the implications of the analysis with respect to the likelihood of deceiving consumers was done by Professor Nelson. *See* Philip Nelson, *Advertising as Information,* 82 J. POL. ECON. 729 (1974); Philip Nelson, *Information and Consumer Behavior,* 78 J. POL. ECON. 311 (1970). *See also* Mark F. Grady, *Regulating Information: Advertising Overview, in* THE FEDERAL TRADE COMMISSION SINCE 1970, at 222 (Kenneth W. Clarkson & Timothy Muris eds., 1981).

that they cannot detect falsity until they experience the product. Because they are aware of their own ignorance, and because in any event they discount the information to account for producer self-interest, consumers are wary of producer-provided information about such qualities. Their wariness is in turn tempered because they know they have the ability to detect falsity in the course of their use of the product and to punish the producer by failing to make repeat purchases should the advertising about it prove to have been false. Because in the usual case advertising does not pay if consumers in fact do not become repeat purchasers, and because consumers can detect falsity after purchase and then retaliate against producers who disappoint them, producers have little incentive to convey false information about experience qualities.[50] In fact, they have little incentive to convey direct information about such qualities at all, since they know consumers will be unlikely to believe it. For this reason, perhaps, producers have developed means of signaling the reliability of their advertisements. They invest in brand name reputations, for example, thereby signaling to consumers "the presence of firm-specific selling costs"[51] and thus conveying the indirect message that consumers are likely to be satisfied by the product since if they fail to make repeat purchases, the producer's specific investment will be forfeited.

With respect to accuracy and completeness, however, political information is neither a search nor an experience good. Whereas citizens can determine for themselves whether the political information they receive is relevant to their political decisionmaking, they can neither cost-effectively verify the information prepurchase nor detect falsity or incompleteness by "experiencing" the information postpurchase. Political information is what economists would call a "credence good."[52] Because in the typical case they cannot cost-effectively determine for themselves whether the political information they receive from the press is either accurate or complete, individual citizens are inherently incapable of distinguishing "good" quality political information from "bad"— unless they receive additional costly information.[53] This does not necessarily mean that citizens are going to be systematically fooled into believing false information and relying upon incomplete accounts. Its more likely consequence

---

50. *Cf.* Lillian R. BeVier, *Competitor Suits for False Advertising under § 43(a) of the Lanham Act: A Puzzle in the Law of Deception,* 78 Va. L. Rev. 1, 8–12 (1992) (arguing that, with respect to search and experience qualities, deceptive advertising does not pose a significant risk to consumers).

51. Benjamin Klein & Keith Leffler, *The Role of Market Forces in Assuring Contractual Performance,* 89 J. Pol. Econ. 615, 630 (1981).

52. *See* Michael Darby & Edi Karni, *Free Competition and the Optimal Amount of Fraud,* 16 J.L. & Econ. 67 (1973).

53. *Id.* at 69.

is that, unless they can find means to assure themselves of its reliability, they will apply a systematic discount to all political information.[54] Consumers will not discount political information's reliability on account of producers' self-interest, unless they detect that the information is hopelessly infected with the producers' biases. They will, however, discount the information on the basis of their inability to verify it. If that were all there were to the story, the possibility of bad information coupled with citizens' knowledge of their own inability to tell the difference between good and bad might well have the perverse tendency to drive good quality information from the market altogether.[55] Since no individual citizen can tell the difference between them, good and bad information will sell at the same price and competition among information providers, far from serving to improve the quality of information generally available, will tend to drive out the good.

Moreover, since the expected value of a vote to an individual citizen is so low, a citizen whose demand for quality is solely a function of the information's value as an input to voting would not be likely to push hard for excellence. This complacency would be exacerbated by the way political information is marketed in the mainstream media: it is offered as part of a total package that includes both heavy doses of entertainment and a wide variety of information on many subjects—from sports to stock prices to the weather—that is of more intense and immediate personal interest to consumers than is politics. Accordingly, consumers' willlingness to punish particular providers of bad quality political information by declining in the future to purchase their particular total package is likely to be quite attenuated.

Another way to think about the individual citizen's problem in evaluating the quality of political information that the press provides is in terms of the principal–agent heuristic, with the citizen as principal and the news provider as agent. Conceptualized in this way, the citizen's difficulty in evaluating political information emerges as yet another manifestation of the ubiquitous agency cost phenomenon. Indeed, with respect to providing information about government, the press has often portrayed itself, and the Court has often characterized it, as the public's agent: "In seeking out the news, the

---

54. *Cf.* BeVier, *supra* note 50, at 13 ("The more costly it is for the consumer to verify the claims of the producer . . . the less inclined she will be to believe them . . . .").

55. George A. Akerlof, *The Market for "Lemons": Quality Uncertainty and the Market Mechanism,* 84 Q.J. ECON. 488 (1970). Professor Farber appears to believe that the discount consumers apply to information they cannot verify will somehow enable them to "screen out more false statements than true ones and hence [make them] more likely to accept true statements." Farber, *supra* note 17, at 561 n.26. He does not explain, however, how consumers are able to tell the difference between false and true statements when they cannot independently verify the information.

press acts as an agent of the public at large. [The] underlying right is the right of the public generally. The press is the necessary representative of the public's interest in this context and the instrumentality which effects the public's right."[56]

As we know, however, agents do not always have the interests of their principals at heart, and principal–agent relationships are routinely beset by "problems of diverging interests and asymmetrical information."[57] There is no reason in principle to believe that the principal–agent relationship between the public and the press is exempt from such tensions. Principals seek cost-effective ways to monitor their agents' behavior. Agents in turn seek means of bonding the integrity of their performance. The fact that individual citizens are intrinsically incapable of distinguishing good from bad quality political information renders them as individuals poor monitors of the reliability of their information providers' performance even though they each prefer good to bad political information. The fact that the press is not legally accountable for defects in the quality of the information it provides deprives it of the ability to bond itself by adherence to an exacting legal standard.

This analysis suggests that we need to be looking elsewhere than to the individual citizen-consumer as the information market's principal quality-control mechanism. One place to look is to the press itself, and one question to ask is whether the press can bond the quality of its political information by means other than adhering to exacting legal standards. In other kinds of markets where buyers cannot tell the difference between high- and low-quality products, producers develop a variety of means of providing relatively trustworthy guarantees.[58] Given the pervasiveness of constraints other than legal ones on the behavior of all market participants, it would certainly not be surprising if at least some political information providers had found credible means of bonding the reliability of their output. In fact, suppliers of political information do appear to bond the quality of the political information that they supply in a variety of ways, some more credible than others.

Their most obvious bonding mechanism is reputation. Many producers in the mainstream media appear to have invested heavily in earning a reputation for providing trustworthy information. To the extent that an information provider puts assets at genuine risk in support of building and maintaining a reputation for the accuracy and completeness of the facts it reports, it can

---

56. Saxbe v. Washington Post, 417 U.S. 843, 863 (1974) (Powell, J., concurring).

57. Jacobson, *supra* note 16, at 369.

58. *Cf.* Akerlof, *supra* note 55 (institutions such as guarantees, brand names, chain stores, and official licensing provide relatively trustworthy information about quality).

be seen to have attempted credibly to bond its output.[59] Obvious reputational investments that represent fairly clear and unambiguous commitments of assets are not frequently to be observed, however. More frequently, information providers' attempts to bond the quality of their information are somewhat less credible, either because they are not so clearly supported by the commitment of specific assets or because they are so blatantly self-serving that they invite skepticism rather than credulity. Touting the virtues of—and their own adherence to—journalistic norms of objectivity, for example, is one way that information providers attempt to signal their commitment to quality. Even the press's stubborn unwillingness to admit its own errors, its occasional self-righteous posturing, and its frequently pursued strategy of fighting libel suits tooth-and-nail can plausibly be regarded as strategies—even if not particularly convincing ones—to bond the quality of their product.

Given that individual citizens who value information only as an input to voting are poor monitors of information quality, another question to ask about the demand for quality is whether other monitors can be identified. The most obvious monitoring mechanism is competition among journalists and publishers of political information. Competition creates an environment that is more conducive to accuracy than it is congenial to lies or half-truths. Journalistic careers can be made by exposing the errors of others, and they can be ruined when a journalist is revealed to be careless about the truth. Such a reality creates powerful incentives for journalists not to make mistakes.[60]

In markets for other kinds of goods, buyers who care more rather than less about the quality of products they buy, and are thus more willing to expend resources searching for quality—"searchers"—are often able to protect consumers who care somewhat less—"nonsearchers."[61] If such searchers exist in the market for political information, and if they are able effectively to translate their preferences into demands that even a few producers of political information have incentives to satisfy, then individual nonsearching citizens—and the

---

59. When the Dow Jones Company was approached several years ago, for example, to sell the right to identify its stock market index to the Chicago Board of Trade so that the latter could peg its futures contracts to a "reliable index," Dow Jones refused the offer, citing its desire to preserve its reputation for providing financially conservative information untainted by any association with speculation or gambling. The refusal, entailing the obvious opportunity cost of foregoing the offered price, can be viewed as an investment in preserving its reputation. The Illinois appellate court sustained the refusal. Board of Trade v. Dow Jones & Co., 439 N.E.2d 526 (Ill. App. 1982).

60. Cf. OWEN, supra note 12, at 13 (noting that the editor who competes with other editors for survival is a surrogate for the consumer).

61. Alan Schwartz & Louis Wilde, Product Quality and Imperfect Information, 1985 REV. ECON. STUD. 251. See also Alan Schwartz & Louis Wilde, Intervening in Markets on the Basis of Imperfect Information, 127 U. PA. L. REV. 630 (1979).

society at large—can free ride on the more reliable information that searchers will encourage producers to produce. Observation reveals that searchers do exist in the political marketplace: citizens do differ from one another in both the *amount* of political information that they demand and in their inclination and ability to evaluate its *quality.*

Although citizens' tastes differ from one another in a host of ways that predictably generate wide variations in the intensity of their demand for quality political information, even the most discerning among them cannot readily judge for themselves the accuracy and completeness of the political information they receive from the mainstream press. Fortunately, they need not rely on the mass media. To satisfy their demand for a higher quality of political information—more accurate, more complete—producers have supplied them with a vast array of alternatives. This is not, after all, surprising, given the rewards that the competitive market offers to those who identify consumer demands and satisfy them. The point here, though, is that these alternative sources, which cater to a wide variety of particularized preferences and intensities of demand for quality, can be viewed both as players in the information market in their own right and as monitors of the quality of others' play. Their very existence—and the fact that more of them might enter the market at any time—constrains the extent to which even the mainstream press can shirk its quality obligations.

The existence of highly differentiated information products attests both to the diversity of preferences of the citizenry for political information and to the ingenuity of information suppliers in satisfying their demands. Prodded by their various audiences, and reflecting their constituents' particular concerns, these alternative information suppliers will often delve more deeply into apparent realities, interpret events with greater sophistication, and analyze data more thoroughly than the mainstream media is inclined to do. In doing so, of course, their principal motivation is to satisfy their own customers. While pursuing this goal, they serendipitously constrain, even if they do not completely eliminate, the mainstream media's ability to portray falsehood as truth or to omit key facts from otherwise apparently complete accounts.

Conclusion

These speculative observations lead me to a confident conclusion, though not an unequivocal one. All things considered, the relative lack of formal legal accountability of the press does not have consequences that are on balance perverse. This is because of the dynamic, highly decentralized, occasionally chaotic market for political information—because, that is, of the variety of buyers and sellers, the heterogeneity of the interests, the multiplicity of the preference intensities, the diversity of incentives in play. The First Amendment does not, I think, "anoint" the press and of its own force place it "above the law." What the First Amendment promises is freedom of political participation for everyone, thereby creating if not a level playing field at least a crowded and extremely lively one on which no single institution can anticipate achieving permanent dominance nor realistically hope that any single statement of fact—whether true or false—will go unchallenged. Perhaps it is appropriate to celebrate the role that freedom of speech and of the press play in preserving the ability and incentives of private actors—the press, special interest groups, individual citizens—to hold one another *and their government* to account.

One of the most interesting facets of First Amendment jurisprudence over the past century has been the development of rules and principles for dealing with new technologies of communication, most notably radio, broadcast television, and cable television. From the outset, Congress devised a regulatory system over these media for the explicit purpose of ensuring that they serve the "public interest, convenience, and necessity." The administration of this system has been vested in the Federal Communications Commission. Cable has also been subject to oversight by local communities. These regulations have included rights of public access, requirements of fairness and balance in coverage of public issues, and special restrictions on indecent language and programming. None of these regulations has been constitutionally permitted in the more traditional print media. This is the basis, therefore, of the extraordinary "dual system" of freedom of the press in this country, which has generated considerable debate among courts and commentators as to its rationality and wisdom.

In "The Censorship of Television," Owen Fiss focuses on several of the most current debates in this area of regulation of new media. Specifically, he takes up Supreme Court cases involving the regulation of indecent programming on cable (*Denver Area*), the so-called must-carry requirements for cable (which mandate that cable operators must carry the programs of local over-the-air broadcasters) (*Turner*), and a decision by a public television station to exclude from a televised debate a candidate for public office who, in the station's view, was not a "serious candidate" (*Forbes*). In his essay, Professor Fiss draws our attention to a distinction in First Amendment law between state censorship and what he calls "managerial censorship." These recent cases are significant, he argues, because they represent the "Court's effort to come to terms with . . . 'managerial censorship,' a form of censorship in which the censor is not the state but an actor within the television industry itself." This "engagement" has "represented a striking new development in the law and posed challenges of a wholly different order" from cases involving the more traditional problems of state censorship. Professor Fiss finds especially significant the opinion of Justice Breyer in the *Turner* case, which constitutes, he concludes, "an important first step toward the recovery of a jurisprudence that sees the First Amendment more as a protection of the democratic system than as a protection of the expressive interests of the individual speaker."—LCB

OWEN M. FISS

The Censorship of Television

Democracy is a system that vests the ultimate power of governance in individual citizens. As evidenced by the rule requiring universal distribution of the franchise and our commitment to the one person, one vote principle, much of democracy's appeal flows from a postulate of the moral equality of citizens: the views of one person are assumed to be as worthy of respect as those of others.

This postulate causes many to cringe because we know that certain people are in fact more qualified than others to exercise the power of governance. They are smarter, better informed, more aware of the world around them, and much more capable of exercising wise judgment. This fact has caused some to turn their backs on democracy altogether. Others have responded by seeking to allocate the franchise according to criteria that presumably test for knowledge and understanding. Although Americans have tried this alternative at various points in our history, we have since come to reject it, largely because it had been used unfairly to disenfranchise blacks and other minority groups. Our present strategy is more inclusive: we try to enlarge the knowledge and understanding of all citizens, not in an effort to eliminate distinctions among them, but rather to ensure that they are all capable of exercising the power of governance in a wise and intelligent way.

This, I believe, is one of the central functions of the formal education system and an important reason why we make elementary and secondary education mandatory. The purpose of such a system is not simply to endow individuals with the skills necessary to make them fully productive and sociable members of society. The system is also, and perhaps more importantly, designed to enable all of us to discharge the duties of citizenship. In this way, mandatory education gives substance to the egalitarian premises that underlie democracy.

A portion of this chapter appeared in the summer 1999 issue of the Northwestern University Law Review, vol. 93, p. 1215, published by the Northwestern University School of Law. My research assistants, Dana Wagner and Renato Mariotti, made many important contributions to this chapter for which I am especially grateful.

The American formal education system, with both its public and private components, is vast and abundant. Indeed, it is one of the greatest treasures of our nation. But it is not without limits. Although some citizens pursue formal education well into their adult years, for most it comes to an end by their early twenties. By that time, it is fair to assume that the proper foundations have been laid. Yet democracy requires that the educational process continue— citizens must be able to update and reevaluate their knowledge as the world around them changes and they find themselves in new situations. A well-functioning democracy not only depends upon a formal education system, but also upon an ongoing informal education system.

In the United States, this informal education system has many components—films, newspapers, books, journals of opinion, magazines, radio, political campaigns, billboards, marches, workplace conversations—but none is as important as television. Television was first developed in the 1920s and 1930s and was commercially exploited on a large scale in the years after World War II. Its use has become more and more common, and today television stands as the most important public medium in our informal education system. Television was able to achieve this dominance over, say, the print media because it combines audio and visual messages; provides easy and rapid access to the citizenry; is capable of instantly transmitting information from around the globe; and pervades every domain, including the most intimate— the home.

These days television is often taken for granted, and attention is lavished on the communicative technologies recently introduced by the personal computer and the informational network—the Internet—created by linking computers together. One such communicative technology is electronic mail, or "e-mail." Much like the telephone, though now in written form, e-mail effectively renders geographic distance meaningless and thereby greatly enhances the ability of individuals to interact with and learn from one another. Another computer-based communicative technology, the World Wide Web, has also had an enormous impact on the informal education system, giving citizens direct and immediate access to vast sources of knowledge. Over the course of just a few years, a great deal of the information stored within the major research libraries of the world has suddenly become available on the Web to every citizen who has access to a personal computer and learns to use it.

These computer-based means of communication, and the others that may emerge, will undoubtedly make citizens less dependent on television as a source of information. We must, however, be careful not to overstate their value to democracy. Almost every household has a television, but only about

50 percent have computers, and a wide variety of factors—for example, income, race, ethnicity, and age—has caused what has been called a "digital divide," that is, a difference among various groups in terms of their access to computer-based means of communication. Although approximately 40 percent of all American households have Internet access, to take one statistic, the number for the households of blacks and Hispanics is significantly less—about 20 percent.[1]

The natural passivity of most citizens also limits the role of the computer in the informal educational system. The Internet and the Web can provide vastly more information than television, but will reach citizens only if they actively seek it out. Television informs even the passive observer.

Another source of television's importance, as opposed to that of the computer, in our informal education system stems from its unique capacity to create a shared understanding. It defines the public. Computerized communication is private in the sense that citizens use computers to pursue individually what interests them and also to communicate individually with those they already know or want to know. With television, on the other hand, millions of families watch the same show or the same news broadcast, often at the same time. For instance, every week more than 10 million households watch the news program *60 Minutes*,[2] and more than 40 million households tuned in for the final episode of *Seinfeld*.[3] Television is unique in its capacity to produce this type of shared experience and for that very reason can be regarded, at least today, as the paramount public medium.

Although most attention today is focused on the computer industry, the television industry has also recently experienced substantial technological changes, particularly in the methods by which programs are transmitted. In the past two decades, cable television has proliferated—almost 70 percent of all homes with television now have it,[4] and that number is likely to grow.[5] Cable television, as its name suggests, is transmitted into the home through a cable rather than via over-the-air broadcast signals. This method of transmission

---

1. *See* National Telecomms. and Info. Admin., Falling Through the Net: Toward Digital Inclusion (October 2000).

2. *See* Nielsen Media Research, 1998 Report on Television (1999).

3. *See id.; Seinfeld Goes Out on Top*, CFRA News/Talk Radio (visited May 19, 1998) < http://interactive.cfra.com/1996/05/19/35308.html >.

4. *See Television Bureau of Advertising Online* (visited March 14, 2001) < http://www.tvb.org/tvfacts/ tvbasics/tv_basics3.html > (citing Nielsen Media Research, *supra* note 2), putting the number today at 68.0 percent.

5. *See* Research & Policy Analysis Dep't, National Cable Television Ass'n, Cable Television Developments: Industry Overview §§ 1-A, 2-A (Fall 1994) (finding that the percentage of television households with cable television has grown every year in the past two decades).

improves reception quality and increases the possible number of channels—today we have roughly eighty standard cable channels and five hundred digital ones. Those individuals who subscribe to premium satellite transmission services may have access to even more channels.

Although the proliferation of channels is of great significance to the television industry, to the individual television viewer, and of course to the governing regulatory regime, it will not lessen the importance of television as a public medium. The number of channels may proliferate almost indefinitely as a result of technological advances, but economic factors, including the costs of gathering news and producing television programs, make it highly probable that a relatively small number of channels will continue to dominate the spectrum. These channels will remain the principal institutions that construct the public agenda and shape public understanding.

Given television's crucial role in our informal education system, it is essential that we protect it from threats that might impair its ability to perform this role properly. Traditionally, one of the greatest of such threats has been "state censorship"—attempts by governmental actors to limit, directly or indirectly, the information and variety of opinions available to the public. The threat of state censorship is always present, and it has received a fair amount of attention from the Supreme Court, past and present. But of even greater significance in recent years has been the Court's effort to come to terms with what I call "managerial censorship," a form of censorship in which the censor is not the state but an actor within the television industry itself. Whereas the Court's decisions concerning state censorship have extended a well-established tradition, its engagement with managerial censorship has represented a striking new development in the law and poses challenges of a wholly different order.

State Censorship

"Congress shall make no law . . . abridging the freedom of speech, or of the press." This is the text of the First Amendment, and though it is not clear exactly where television fits into this provision as a purely exegetical matter—Is it speech? Is it the press? Would it be either as understood by the original framers?—it is now well settled that the Constitution protects television from threats to the discharge of its democratic mission. As previously indicated, one such threat comes from what can be termed state censorship: action by state agencies or actors that seek to control television programming.

One particularly egregious example of state censorship came in the early 1970s, when President Nixon attempted to get the Federal Communications Commission (FCC) to impose sanctions against broadcasters who criticized his administration.[6] The sanctions he proposed included withdrawing the licenses of stations carrying such broadcasts. In that instance, the state interference stemmed from the president's anger over what the broadcasters had to say about him and his policies. Rarely can this type of motive be identified, and such motivation is not a necessary condition for a First Amendment violation. For example, President Nixon's subsequent attempt to suppress the publication of the Pentagon Papers was justified on the grounds of national security, not on the basis of his dislike of the account those documents gave of our military involvement in Vietnam.[7] Of course, the national security rationale may have been pretextual, a mere cover for a disagreement that no doubt existed. Nonetheless, the Court's review—which would have been identical if the Papers were to have been published on CBS rather than in the *New York Times*—was not grounded on that assumption. The Court took the Administration's actions at face value and assumed that the request for an injunction was predicated completely on national security grounds. The question was whether this justification was sufficient given the necessary adverse effect of the injunction sought: a limitation of the public's access to information.

In recent years, the threat of state censorship has been posed more by Congress than by the president. Congress has proceeded through the en-actment of general rules—as opposed to actions aimed at specific speech, as in the *Pentagon Papers* case—and has done so in the name of decency rather than national security. A case in point is the Cable Act of 1992,[8] which was aimed at patently offensive depictions of sexual activity. The statute in question did not so much prohibit certain television programs, as would a criminal statute or an injunction, but rather interfered with the public's access to them. Specifically, the 1992 law and its implementing regulations required cable operators—companies that assemble the programs and transmit them to individual viewers—to place indecent programs on a separate channel, to block this channel, to unblock it within thirty days of a subscriber's written request for access, and to reblock it within thirty days of a subscriber's re-quest for reblocking. These restrictions only applied to programs on "leased access channels," which are channels that federal law requires cable operators to reserve for commercial lease by unaffiliated third parties. In addition to imposing the above restrictions, the regulations required the programmers of

---

6. *See* WILLIAM E. PORTER, ASSAULT ON THE MEDIA: THE NIXON YEARS (1976).

7. *See* New York Times v. United States, 403 U.S. 713 (1971) (the *Pentagon Papers* case).

8. Pub. L. No. 102-385, 106 Stat. 1460 (1992).

leased channels to alert cable operators of their intent to broadcast indecent material at least thirty days before the scheduled broadcast date. In the *Denver Area* case,[9] the Supreme Court held this scheme unconstitutional. The Court's opinion, written by Justice Breyer, strikes me as an important deepening of the First Amendment tradition against state censorship. I say this for two reasons. One arises from the Court's sensitivity to the speech-restrictive dimensions of the regulatory scheme. The instrument of censorship in the *Pentagon Papers* case was an injunction that would have flatly prohibited the publication of certain information. In contrast, the concern in *Denver Area* was with inconveniences, burdens, obstacles, and costs—all of which might impair the free flow of information to would-be viewers, but none of which has the bite of an injunction or of any other instrument of the civil or criminal law. Of concern to Justice Breyer was the burden on the viewer who might want a single show, as opposed to the entire channel; or the viewer who might want to choose a channel without any advance planning (the "surfer"); or the one who worries about the danger to his reputation that might result if he makes a written request to subscribe to the channel (as opposed to simply flipping on the remote).[10] None of these viewers faced insurmountable burdens—each of them, if determined, could get access to the desired programming by following the established procedures—but it is to the Court's credit that it nonetheless protected them against the statute's impairments.

The Court's sensitivity to the impairment of viewer freedom is all the more remarkable because the standard it employed was a comparative one. The Court did not hypothesize or advocate an absolute freedom, but rather acknowledged—by noting that the declared purpose of the regulation (the protection of minors) is a compelling one—that some regulation might well be appropriate. It struck down the segregate-and-block requirement of the 1992 Act not because it completely impaired viewer freedom, but because it was more of an impairment than many other alternatives. The Court's concern was with the incremental impairment created by the segregate-and-block requirement as opposed to that entailed in, for instance, requiring operators to scramble and block individual programs, requiring them to code programs so that they can be blocked using V-chip technology, or requiring them to provide viewers with screening devices known as "lock-boxes."[11] Because the 1992 segregate-and-block requirements compared unfavorably with these

---

9. Denver Area Educ. Telecommunications Consortium, Inc. v. FCC, 518 U.S. 727 (1996).

10. *See id.* at 754.

11. *See id.* at 755–60.

alternatives, they were struck down as being "overly restrictive" (a phrase Justice Breyer used repeatedly).[12]

The second way in which *Denver Area* represents an advance over the past concerns the nature of the material censored: sexual material. In the *Pentagon Papers* case, the content of the publication to be censored was of great and obvious political importance. The Court could therefore justify its action in terms that gave full expression to the democratic theory of the First Amendment; the suppression of the Papers would have severely compromised the citizen's right to be informed fully about matters of public concern—specifically, the conduct of the American government in the Vietnam War. In *Denver Area*, on the other hand, the state censorship was aimed at sexual depictions and sought to preserve certain standards of decency. There is no denying that the depiction of sexuality is an important part of cultural freedom and that political freedom is inextricably linked to culture (as Alexander Meiklejohn was fond of saying, you need to read *Ulysses* in order to vote).[13] Nonetheless, the case for First Amendment protection is less clear and compelling in this context than it is when the material to be censored relates directly to public policy.

For most of our history, the Court tolerated some state censorship of sexual material, either as a concession to original understanding, or as a reflection of a doubt as to the importance of such material in our political life, or as an effort to accommodate strongly held popular sentiments, or perhaps in anticipation of more recently expressed feminist concerns about equality. Starting in the late 1950s, however, the Supreme Court limited the power of the state censor by creating a constitutional definition of what could validly be proscribed: obscenity. If, and only if, the material satisfied the three criteria that the Court used to define obscenity (namely, that the material appealed to a prurient interest in sex, was patently offensive, and was without redeeming social value) could it be censored.[14]

Over the past forty years, the Court has confronted many attempts to water down this constitutional definition of obscenity or, to put it differently, to enlarge the scope of the censor's jurisdiction over sexually explicit material. Thus far, the Court has by and large resisted such efforts, and the constitutional definition of obscenity has become a fixity of the First Amendment. However, the Court has on occasion created exceptions to this definition and the protections it provides. One exception, created in a case decided after *Denver Area*, allowed

---

12. *See, e.g., id.* at 760.

13. *See* Alexander Meiklejohn, *The First Amendment Is an Absolute,* 1961 Sup. Ct. Rev. 245, 263.

14. *See* Miller v. California, 413 U.S. 15, 24 (1973).

the National Endowment for the Arts to use indecency as a negative factor in its assessment of applications for grant money.[15] This exception was justified by reference to the special rules that relate to subsidization—denying a grant is not the same as suppressing independent speech—and has only limited applicability to the regulation of television. The same cannot be said of the other exceptions. The Court has allowed the definition of obscenity to be lowered in order to protect children from sexual material,[16] and it has also allowed the FCC to use a decency standard when regulating the content of radio programs.[17] In creating this latter exception, the Court was greatly moved by the presence of radio in the home and the difficulty in shielding children from its broadcasts.

Perhaps encouraged by the creation of these exceptions, Congress has become persistent in its attempts to enlarge the scope of the censor's jurisdiction over sexually explicit material; it has repeatedly sought to move the law from an obscenity standard to an indecency standard (the crucial difference being the elimination in the latter of the third criterion—the requirement that the sexual depiction be without redeeming social value). The Court has generally resisted these efforts as well. For instance, in *Reno v. ACLU*,[18] it held unconstitutional those provisions of the 1996 Telecommunications Act that prohibited indecent transmissions on the Internet, and it took a similar position in *Denver Area* when it struck down the 1992 Cable Act's segregate-and-block provisions.

Although the *Denver Area* Court acknowledged that the segregate-and-block provisions protected children and thereby furthered a compelling interest, it was equally mindful of the provisions' adverse impact on the programming available to adults.[19] The Court affirmed and emphasized the principle of *Butler v. Michigan:* the Constitution does not permit the state to reduce the material available to adults to the level of what is appropriate for children.[20] The Court was also careful to distinguish and thus contain *FCC v. Pacifica Foundation,* which had upheld a ban on indecent language on a radio show in the interest of protecting children.[21] In *Pacifica,* the Court had noted that radio shows come into the home without any warning or advance notice, thereby increasing the risk of exposing children to material they should not hear and

---

15. *See* National Endowment for the Arts v. Finley, 524 U.S. 569 (1998). *Compare* OWEN M. FISS, THE IRONY OF FREE SPEECH 27 (1996) [hereinafter IRONY] *with* Robert Post, *Subsidized Speech,* 106 YALE L.J. 151 (1996).

16. *See, e.g.,* Ginsberg v. New York, 390 U.S. 629 (1968).

17. *See* FCC v. Pacifica Found., 438 U.S. 726 (1978).

18. 521 U.S. 844 (1997).

19. *See Denver Area,* 518 U.S. at 755–59.

20. 352 U.S. 380 (1957).

21. *See Pacifica,* 438 U.S. at 726.

undermining parental control.[22] In *Denver Area,* the Court acknowledged the similarly invasive nature of television—like radio, it becomes available in the home with a mere flick of a switch—but refused to let this feature of the medium become the predicate for a broad extension of the censor's power over sexually explicit material.[23] The *Pacifica* ban was aimed at afternoon shows, so the interests and needs of adults could easily be accommodated by shows at night.[24] No analogous limitation confined the ban at issue in *Denver Area.*

Through both its sensitivity to the speech-abridging aspects of regulation and its protection of sexual material, the *Denver Area* Court deepened and strengthened the First Amendment's protections against state censorship. Indeed, using the *Pentagon Papers* case of 1971 as a benchmark, I think it is fair to say that many of the Court's recent decisions, above all *Denver Area,* have extended these protections as they apply to television.

Managerial Censorship

Protection against state censorship is a traditional domain of First Amendment jurisprudence, and therefore the Court's recent strengthening of such protection, while highly laudable, has in some respects been fairly unsurprising and straightforward. The Court's contribution in dealing with another form of censorship—what I have called managerial censorship—is more difficult to assess, though here too I detect a subtle, but favorable, shift in the law, once again spearheaded by Justice Breyer.

Under the model of state censorship, we assume two autonomous agencies—some government officials and, say, a television station—and we further assume an antagonistic relationship between the two. The action of the government officials impinges upon the freedom of the television station in a way that limits the information available to the public. From the standpoint of the media industry, the threat of such censorship is external. With managerial censorship, the threat is internal: it arises from operating decisions made within the industry itself, which may serve to interfere with or preclude public access to certain information.

The managerial censorship model is predicated on a more nuanced understanding of the relationship between the media and the state than that hypothesized by the state censorship model and, more generally, by classical liberal theory. Rather than assuming that there is always and everywhere an antagonism between the state and the media, the notion of managerial

---

22. *See id.* at 748–49.

23. *See Denver Area,* 518 U.S. at 744–47, 755–59.

24. *See id.* at 744.

censorship recognizes that in fact every media organization receives significant benefits from the state. Some such benefits can be found in the laws of contract, property, and corporations, and in the provision of services such as police and fire protection that are generally available to all citizens. In addition, the government has played a leading role in the development of television technology, and it continues to provide distinct benefits and privileges to the various entities within the television industry. Each over-the-air broadcaster receives a license from the federal government that gives it exclusive permission to use a portion of the electromagnetic spectrum; cable operators receive easements from local governments that permit them to run their wire cables through town streets; and public television stations receive direct subsidies from all levels of government, though these vary in amount from station to station and from year to year.

Such entanglements between the state and the television industry create a special risk of state censorship. As the Nixon example mentioned earlier illustrates, the state might manipulate the award or renewal of broadcast licenses to favor the administration's friends or punish its enemies. Alternatively, the grant of easements or the award of subsidies might be controlled with similar purposes in mind. For the most part, however, these dangers have not materialized. The television industry, including both its private and public components, has not become the puppet of the political branches of government, but rather has emerged as a collection of autonomous decision centers.

Although regulators have looked at the content of programs when awarding broadcast licenses, they have only done so to make certain that there is sufficient coverage of public issues and to enforce well-defined boundaries regarding depictions of sexuality. Localities have placed a price on the grant of easements, but only to provide public access to cable as a means of communication. Furthermore, public television has been permitted a strong measure of autonomy from funding agencies, and for many constitutional purposes it is treated in much the same way as the private sector of the industry. This was the overarching message of FCC v. League of Women Voters, in which the Supreme Court invalidated a ban on editorializing in the Public Broadcasting System.[25] This ban would have been unthinkable in the private context, and it was struck down largely for that reason.

Unlike the more traditional conception of censorship, the theory of managerial censorship does not differentiate between state-financed and privately financed stations, nor does it make much out of the grant of easements and licenses. It treats all television stations as autonomous decision centers. The

---

25. 468 U.S. 364 (1984).

focus is instead on the way in which these stations exercise their autonomy. This may seem like a perverse source of concern, since the tradition that guards against state censorship seeks to increase and protect the autonomy of media organizations. Under the managerial censorship theory, however, this autonomy is conceived as serving only instrumental purposes: it exists so that citizens may learn what they need to know to exercise their democratic prerogative properly. The theory recognizes that the exercise of managerial control can sometimes interfere with the achievement of this end. Thus, the desirability of media autonomy becomes entirely contingent on how the media serves the informational needs of the public.

CABLE OPERATORS AS DECENCY POLICE

The danger that managerial censorship poses to First Amendment interests was another issue raised by the 1992 Cable Act and addressed by the Court in *Denver Area*. As previously discussed, one provision of the 1992 Act required cable operators to segregate and block indecent material appearing on leased channels, and the Court struck down this provision as an impermissible form of state censorship. Another contested feature of the 1992 Act did not impose a requirement on cable operators, but rather authorized them to prohibit indecent programs on two types of channels—leased channels and public access channels—over which they would ordinarily possess no editorial control.[26] In both instances, the authority given to the cable operator acted as a double check—Breyer refers to it as a "veto"[27]—on the programming decisions of another media organization. This double check was upheld for the leased channels but not for the public access ones.[28]

Public access channels are channels that cable operators dedicate to municipalities in exchange for the easements that allow them to run their wires through city property. Within each city, the control of the programming on these channels is vested in a supervisory board or manager, typically a nonprofit organization financed by municipal funds. These boards and managers are capable of screening out indecent shows and thus protecting interests, such as the well-being of children, that might otherwise be threatened. This itself is a form of managerial censorship, but the Court was willing to leave it in place. What it objected to, as evidenced by its invalidation of the further veto power of the cable operator, was a second tier of managerial censorship.

In defense of this second tier, the proponents of the 1992 Act pointed to

---

26. *See Denver Area,* 518 U.S. at 734–36.

27. *Id.* at 763.

28. *See id.* at 737.

the risk of a mistake in the first tier (the public access channel's manager or supervisory board). The Court acknowledged the risk of such a mistake: the supervisors might not screen out indecent shows that should be excluded.[29] The problem for the Court, however, was the risk of error on the other side: as Breyer put it, "the risk that the veto itself may be mistaken; and its use, or threatened use, could prevent the presentation of programming, that, though borderline, is not 'patently offensive' to its targeted audience."[30] By itself, this response is not wholly adequate, for it merely leaves us to choose between two risks—the risk that the supervisory manager will screen too little and the risk that the cable operator will screen too much. In invalidating the veto power of the cable operator, the Court might have been making some pragmatic or offhand judgment as to which kind of error is more probable. Or, more plausibly, it might have been implicitly making a normative judgment about the quality of the errors. From the First Amendment perspective, the error of the cable operator is worse than that of the public access channel's supervising manager—more speech is better.

The Court was, however, less sensitive to the dangers of managerial censorship—or perhaps more tolerant of them—when it came to the cable operator's control over the leased channels. The 1992 Act gave cable operators the same authority to prohibit sexually explicit programming on leased access channels that it gave them over public access channels, but the Court chose to uphold this authority in the former context while invalidating it in the latter. In making this distinction, the Court was expressing greater confidence in public managers than in the operators of leased channels to strike the right balance between speech and the welfare of children. Justice Breyer repeatedly described the managers of public access channels as "locally accountable" and "publicly accountable."[31] In contrast, the program managers of leased channels are driven by considerations of profit; their programming will be as sexually explicit as the market will allow. Although these managers must consider the size and profile of their audiences and the willingness of advertisers to become associated with their programs, the resulting constraints are likely to be weaker than those that discipline the managers of public access channels. Of course, the cable operators themselves are also driven by considerations of profit, but these operators are selling a different product—the cable service itself—and though they tend to have monopoly positions in each community, they are accountable to the public agencies that grant these monopolies. Their

---

29. *See id.* at 763.

30. *Id.*

31. *See Denver Area,* 518 U.S. at 763.

ability to veto programming on leased channels will undoubtedly be somewhat restrictive of speech, but Breyer, never an absolutist, must have assumed that their censorial power would be less pernicious in this context than in the public access context.

In dissent, Justice Thomas denied that the public has any independent First Amendment interest in receiving information or that cable programmers have a First Amendment right to have their shows transmitted.[32] In his view, cable operators manage a purely private communication system, and have complete discretion over what to transmit. He compared the rights of cable operators to the right of newspapers to choose which pieces to publish or the right of bookstores to choose which books to put on their shelves.[33] As he put it, "Like a free-lance writer seeking a paper in which to publish newspaper editorials, a programmer is protected in searching for an outlet for cable programming, but has no free-standing First Amendment right to have that programming transmitted."[34]

Breyer disputed Thomas's analysis of the property law regime. He argued that programmers were not intruding into private property, as Thomas would have us believe, but rather were using what might be seen as a public easement that government created over private property.[35] Breyer's response seems entirely correct, but the dispute between them seems contrived. It is hard to believe that the system of allocating property rights was what truly divides them, given the unsettled character of the property regime in the electronic domain—it is hard to know who owns what. My sense is that the real dispute between Thomas and Breyer was over whether the public has any independent First Amendment rights. Thomas denied that they do, but Breyer was of an entirely different view. Breyer saw the First Amendment as an instrument for democracy, and in a way that he would more fully articulate in *Turner Broadcasting*, construed the First Amendment to grant the public a right to receive information.[36]

THE MUST-CARRY OBLIGATIONS OF CABLE OPERATORS
In *Denver Area*, the Supreme Court confronted two distinct regulatory techniques that Congress had employed to curb the prevalence of so-called indecent

---

32. *See id.* at 817.

33. *See id.* at 817, 824.

34. *Id.* at 817.

35. *See id.* at 760.

36. *See* Turner Broadcasting Sys. v. FCC, 520 U.S. 180, 226–27 (1997) (Breyer, J., concurring) (discussed *infra* in the text accompanying notes 47–50). *See generally* Dana R. Wagner, *The First Amendment and the Right to Hear*, 108 YALE L.J. 669 (1998).

programs on cable. With leased channels, cable operators were empowered to prohibit indecent material and, at the same time, obliged to segregate such material onto a separate channel, where it would be blocked until a subscriber requested access. With public access channels, they were simply given the veto power. The grant of the veto power and the segregate-and-block requirement could both be viewed as enhancements of cable operators' managerial powers over other components of the television industry, notably the programmers who utilize leased channels and public access channels. On the other hand, the 1992 Cable Act also restricted the managerial decisions of cable operators by requiring them to carry the programs of over-the-air broadcasters, thereby guaranteeing that cable subscribers will receive those programs.

This portion of the 1992 Act, known as the "must-carry" provisions, came before the Court on two separate occasions. On the first (*Turner I*), a sharply divided Court remanded the case for further evidentiary hearings.[37] Four of the justices thought the must-carry provisions were invalid. Justice Kennedy wrote the opinion supporting the remand, which he argued was necessary to determine whether sufficient facts existed to support the law; but he had only four votes. The ninth justice—Stevens—was prepared to sustain the law without any further inquiry, but acquiesced in the remand in order to form a majority. On the second occasion (*Turner II*), the Court upheld the must-carry provisions as a valid exercise of congressional authority.[38] The original four dissenters adhered to their view, and once again Kennedy wrote for four justices. In *Turner II*, however, Stevens was one of those four and wrote a separate concurrence to praise Kennedy's opinion and to underscore its central theme. But the pivotal difference in *Turner II* was that one of Kennedy's original bloc—Justice Blackmun—had retired and was replaced by Breyer. As the must-carry provisions returned to the Court, all eyes turned to him. Breyer supplied the crucial fifth vote to sustain those provisions, but, as articulated in a separate concurrence, on a different theory than Kennedy's.

Crucial to Kennedy's analysis in both *Turner I* and *Turner II* was his view that must-carry requirements are not a form of content regulation. The segregate-and-block and the double-check provisions of the 1992 Act had specifically targeted programs on the basis of their content, and for that reason, Kennedy had insisted in *Denver Area* that a strict standard of review was necessary: not only did the statute's end need to be compelling, which he was willing to concede, but the fit between its means and this end had to be

---

37. *See* Turner Broadcasting Sys. v. FCC, 512 U.S. 622 (1994) [hereinafter *Turner I*].

38. *See* Turner Broadcasting Sys. v. FCC, 520 U.S. 180 (1997) [hereinafter *Turner II*].

tight.[39] Because he did not believe that the fit was sufficient, he was prepared in that case to strike down all of the contested provisions of the 1992 Cable Act, including the one upheld by the majority (that is, the one that gave cable operators a veto power over sexually explicit programming on leased channels). With the must-carry provisions at issue in *Turner,* however, Justice Kennedy used a more lax standard of review—intermediate scrutiny rather than strict—and he justified this approach by denying that the provisions of the 1992 Act at issue were a form of content regulation.[40]

In fact, some of the must-carry provisions of the 1992 Act were defined in terms of content. The must-carry provision for low-power broadcast stations— which Kennedy refused to address, surely to keep to the lower standard of review—was conditioned on an assessment of the station's capacity to cover "local news and informational needs."[41] In addition, there was a separate must-carry provision for public, noncommercial broadcasters, and it is fair to read that provision as being structured in terms of program content as well. Still, these provisions, and the must-carry obligation in general, differ from the segregate-and-block and double-check provisions of the 1992 Act, which were aimed at forcing programs off the air entirely, or at least out of the home, on the basis of their content. So although the must-carry provisions were a species of content regulation insofar as they affected the mix of programs available to viewers, they were fundamentally different from the regulations at issue in *Denver Area.*

The rationale for the restrictions on managerial prerogative contained in the must-carry provisions was ambiguous. On one reading, these provisions were a form of antitrust regulation: their purpose was to preserve competition in the television industry. Many cable operators own cable programming firms, and the fear may have been that these operators would favor their own program-mers to the detriment of over-the-air broadcasters. Cable is the growing sector of the industry, and over-the-air broadcasters would not survive economically if the cable operators dropped them.

On another reading, the concern behind the must-carry provisions was not the maintenance of competition but rather the availability of information to the public. Because only 60 percent of the television market then had access to cable, the collapse of the over-the-air broadcasting industry would mean that 40 percent of the market would be left without television and thus deprived of an important source of information. At that juncture, some further number

---

39. *See Denver Area,* 518 U.S. at 780 (Kennedy, J., concurring in part and dissenting in part).

40. *See Turner I,* 512 U.S. at 623; *Turner II,* 520 U.S. at 189.

41. 47 U.S.C. § 534(h)(2)(B) (1998).

might decide to subscribe to cable, but that would still leave without television those who could not afford such a subscription (over-the-air broadcasting is free) and those who live in communities that cable providers do not yet serve. From this perspective, the must-carry rules do not seek to further antitrust policy but rather free speech. The power of cable operators is curbed in order to enlarge the communicative freedom and capability of the ordinary citizen.

There is no logical inconsistency between the antitrust and free-speech rationales—a highly competitive industry is a step toward freedom insofar as it proliferates sources of information. However, antitrust policy, as it is presently understood, does not protect competitors but competition, and in many circumstances this allows it to tolerate significant degrees of concentration. The antitrust and free-speech rationales for the must-carry provisions therefore begin to diverge once it can be shown that the cable operators' decision to favor cable programmers, either their own or those of others, is justifiable as a matter of economic efficiency. If this is the case, antitrust policy would permit the collapse of the broadcast industry, and some significant portion of the public would be left without the information television provides. Efficient markets can be a source of freedom, but they can also constrain it.

In both *Turner I* and *Turner II*, Kennedy analyzed the must-carry provisions in antitrust terms. The remand in *Turner I* was to ascertain whether there was adequate factual basis to justify Congress's concern as to the danger of anticompetitive practices by cable operators, and in *Turner II* he concluded that there was. Congress had ample reason, he said, to fear that cable operators would engage in predatory practices that would disfavor over-the-air broadcasting and work to the advantage of cable programmers, particularly those owned by the cable operators themselves.

The vertical integration in the cable industry is indeed considerable—cable operators integrated with programmers serve 70 percent of all subscribers—yet the antitrust warrant for the must-carry provisions is unclear. As Judge Williams pointed out early in the proceedings, the risk of predatory practices arising from the integration of the cable industry calls for a rule against discrimination, not a must-carry policy.[42] In response, Justice Kennedy pointed to the resource burdens that broadcasters would bear when bringing individual antitrust suits against predatory cable operators.[43] He was therefore prepared to treat the must-carry provisions largely as a kind of preemptive antitrust

---

42. *See* Turner Broadcasting Sys. v. FCC, 910 F. Supp. 734, 754 (D.D.C. 1995) (Williams, J., dissenting).

43. *See Turner II*, 520 U.S. at 189.

measure. Importantly, however, he did nothing to disclaim or disassociate himself from the free-speech rationale.

Justice Breyer was not so politic. His primary purpose in writing a separate concurrence was to disassociate himself from the antitrust rationale on which Kennedy's opinion relied. For Breyer, the value of free speech was powerful enough to sustain the statute on its own. What was of concern to him were the homes without cable and the loss to them—indeed, to all of society—that would result if over-the-air broadcasters were dropped, regardless of the economic desirability of such an occurrence. Citing with manifest approval the classic decisions that gave life to the democratic theory of the First Amendment—Justice Brandeis's concurrence in *Whitney v. California,*[44] *Associated Press v. United States,*[45] and *New York Times v. Sullivan*[46]—Breyer conceptualized the must-carry rules and their curtailment of managerial prerogatives as furthering a "national communication policy" that seeks "the widest possible dissemination of information from diverse and antagonistic sources."[47] He then went on to state, "That policy, in turn, seeks to facilitate the public discussion and informed deliberation, which, as Justice Brandeis pointed out many years ago, democratic government presupposes and the First Amendment seeks to achieve."[48]

Breyer was very clear about the costs to speech that the bar on managerial prerogative entailed. "It interferes," he wrote, "with the protected interests of the cable operators to choose their own programming; it prevents displaced cable program providers from obtaining an audience; and it will sometimes prevent some cable viewers from watching what, in its absence, would have been their preferred set of programs."[49] He rooted each of these three interests in the First Amendment and acknowledged that the must-carry policy "exacts a serious First Amendment price," which he unashamedly characterized as a "suppression of speech."[50] But he then went on to state that there are "important First Amendment interests on both sides of the equation,"[51] thereby fully recognizing that occasionally some speech has to be restricted in order to further other speech. In such a situation, Breyer maintained, the statute at issue

---

44. 274 U.S. 357, 375–76 (1927) (Brandeis, J., concurring).

45. 326 U.S. 1 (1945).

46. 376 U.S. 254 (1964).

47. *Turner II,* 520 U.S. at 226–27 (Breyer, J., concurring).

48. *Id.* at 227.

49. *Id.; see supra* notes 32–36 and accompanying text.

50. *Id.*

51. *Id.; see also* IRONY, *supra* note 15, at 19.

should be upheld if two conditions are met: (1) there are no alternative ways of achieving the furtherance of the speech objectives that are significantly less restrictive than the one chosen, and (2) the speech-enhancing consequences dominate the speech-restrictive ones.[52] In describing the last condition, Justice Breyer spoke of requiring a "reasonable balance" between the speech-restricting and speech-enhancing elements.[53]

Thirty years ago, the Supreme Court announced a similar approach in the *Red Lion* case, which upheld an FCC regulation that was specifically aimed at the problem of managerial censorship, the so-called fairness doctrine.[54] One aspect of this doctrine gave people personally attacked in broadcasts a right of reply; another gave political candidates an opportunity to respond to editorials; and a third, perhaps the most important, required radio and television broadcasters to cover issues of public importance in a fair and balanced way. For the past thirty years, the Supreme Court has turned its back on the decision to uphold these regulations and the principle that *Red Lion* announced: sometimes, when there are speech interests on both sides of an issue, one form of speech must be sacrificed for another. This precedent has remained on the books, but subsequent decisions have drained it of much of its vitality. As recently as *Turner I*, the Supreme Court construed *Red Lion* as being rooted in the technology of over-the-air broadcasting—specifically, the use of the electromagnetic spectrum and the resulting technological scarcity.[55]

In his opinion in *Turner II*, however, Justice Breyer cited *Red Lion* approvingly twice, and he applied its underlying principle to the cable industry.[56] He thereby freed this principle from its technological moorings and introduced the idea that what is crucial, at least for the democratic theory of the First Amendment, is not spectrum scarcity but economic scarcity. In limiting, and thus justifying, his approach, Breyer underscored the economic power of cable operators: because cable systems are "physically dependent upon the availability of space along city streets," they face "little competition" and constitute "a kind of bottleneck that controls the range of viewer choice."[57] It matters not, he quickly added, whether the operators use this "economic power for economic predatory purposes."[58]

---

52. *See Turner II*, 520 U.S. at 227 (Breyer, J., concurring).

53. *Id.*

54. Red Lion Broadcasting Co. v. FCC, 395 U.S. 367 (1969).

55. *See Turner I*, 512 U.S. at 622.

56. *See Turner II*, 520 U.S. at 226–28 (Breyer, J., concurring).

57. *Id.* at 227–28.

58. *Id.* at 228.

Breyer's entire approach represents a revitalization of *Red Lion,* and his discussion of the economic power of cable operators allows the principle of that case to transcend the specific technological context in which it was born. This is an important move in the law, and my sense is that Breyer was very much aware of this move and was especially anxious about it, as it enables the suppression of some speech in the name of enhancing other speech. His anxiety broke through most acutely when he reminded us of the particular form of state intervention involved in the case before him. He wrote, "In particular, I note . . . that some degree—at least a limited degree—of governmental intervention and control through regulation can prove appropriate when justified under O'Brien (at least when not 'content based')."[59] One is left to wonder why *Red Lion* is one of the cases cited immediately following this sentence and, furthermore, what he meant by "at least." The appearance of this particular phrase twice in one sentence—once within the parenthesis, once between dashes—suggests that these qualifications were inserted during the final moments of the editing process, when he began to feel the full weight of what he was doing.

PUBLIC TELEVISION AND CANDIDATE DEBATES

Breyer's unease became even more apparent in *Arkansas Educational Television Commission v. Forbes,*[60] decided in May 1998, in which the Supreme Court once again attempted to come to grips with the problem of managerial censorship. Here the Court dealt not with the prerogatives of cable operators, but rather with those of the managers of a public television station. The station in question had decided to hold a public debate among congressional candidates, and it had excluded one person running for office, Ralph Forbes, on the grounds that he was not a serious candidate. Forbes brought suit in federal court, challenging this exercise of managerial prerogative. His case made its way up through the appellate process and ultimately reached the Supreme Court, which refused to provide him with relief.

Justice Kennedy wrote the Court's opinion, in which he asked whether the debate on public television amounted to a public forum, decided that it did not, applied a lax standard of review, and then concluded that this standard was satisfied.[61] His mode of analysis could not be attractive to Breyer, who in *Denver Area* had studiously avoided such a formalistic and categorical approach and who for that very reason had been sharply criticized by

---

59. *Id.* at 227–28.

60. 523 U.S. 666 (1998).

61. *See id.*

Kennedy.[62] It is therefore somewhat surprising that Breyer joined Kennedy's opinion. True, *Denver Area* involved cable, one of the so-called new technologies (though it was hardly new anymore), and *Forbes* involved over-the-air broadcasting. But Breyer did not indicate in *Denver Area* that his refusal to apply the traditional public-forum analysis was due to technological differences in the method of transmitting cable and broadcast signals. Indeed, in that case, Justice Souter wrote a separate opinion to defend Breyer's analysis and therein made reference to technological changes and the need to have a freer hand when facing new situations,[63] but Breyer himself did not emphasize this point. My own sense is that Breyer did not use the categorical analysis in *Denver Area* simply because he did not find it useful or illuminating. He was, however, willing to acquiesce to Kennedy's use of that mode of analysis in *Forbes* as a gesture of deference; he most likely acted on the principle that the author of the Court's opinion was entitled to use whatever mode of analysis he found helpful.

Although Justice Breyer's acquiescence in Kennedy's mode of analysis is somewhat puzzling, it is not difficult to identify important substantive differences between *Turner II* and *Forbes* that might have led him to be more respectful of managerial prerogatives in one case than in the other. First of all, in *Forbes* the Court dealt not with cable operators, but with a television station and the officials who make programming decisions. In *Turner II*, Breyer was very clear that the economic power of cable operators provided a basis for compromising their speech interests to further those of listeners and other programmers;[64] he took a similar position in *Denver Area*, at least when it came to analyzing the veto powers of cable operators.[65] In contrast to cable operators, station managers lack the economic power that so worried Breyer in the earlier cases. They are powerful, but it is hard to think of them as "bottlenecks." Moreover, the prerogatives of those who make the programming decisions for a station appear more central to First Amendment concerns than those of cable operators. In choosing the array of programs, cable operators engage in a form of editing, but the creative and artistic elements of those who make programming decisions for a station are more pronounced and might be seen as giving rise to a more powerful First Amendment claim.

Second, the issue before the Court in *Forbes* was not whether it was permissible for the state to intervene, as in the *Turner* cases, but whether the state

---

62. *See Denver Area*, 518 U.S. at 780 (Kennedy, J., concurring in part and dissenting in part).

63. *See id. at* 774 (Souter, J., concurring).

64. *See Turner II*, 520 U.S. at 227–29 (Breyer, J., concurring).

65. *See Denver Area*, 518 U.S. at 738–39.

was obliged to do so. Ralph Forbes claimed that the station had violated his free-speech rights and those of the public by excluding him from the debate, and he turned to the federal court to provide him with access as a remedy for that violation.[66] In so doing, he was effectively asking that court to constrain the managerial prerogatives of the station. At that point, the station would claim that any such interference with its prerogatives would itself constitute an abridgement of its First Amendment rights. In his *Turner II* concurrence, Breyer had articulated a framework for dealing with precisely this type of situation— a situation where speech interests lie on both sides of the equation—but the answer in that case came more easily because he was able and willing to defer to another branch of government. He allowed Congress to regulate and thus to make the choice between the speech interests. The question in *Forbes,* however, was not one of permission—was it permissible for Congress to constrain the managerial prerogatives of cable operators?—but rather one of obligation—did the First Amendment require the station to provide Ralph Forbes with access to the debate? As a result, sentiments of deference could not provide any help in resolving the conflict between the two speech interests.

Justice Kennedy was aware of all of these factors, particularly the distinction between permission and obligation, and he carefully limited the reach of the *Forbes* holding accordingly: "This is not to say the First Amendment would bar the legislative imposition of neutral rules for access to public broadcasting. Instead, we say that, in most cases, the First Amendment of its own force does not compel public broadcasters to allow third parties access to their programming."[67] Earlier in the opinion, he emphasized the headaches and dangers courts would face if access were a constitutional obligation. As indicated by the phrase "in most cases," however, he in fact recognized an exception, and in dicta created a limited right of access. This right was defined by two features: (1) access may be compelled for candidate debates, but only if (2) the station has denied the candidate the opportunity to participate in the debate "on the basis of whether it agrees with [the] candidate's views."[68]

In thus creating a limited right of access, Justice Kennedy curbed the reach of managerial censorship in much the spirit of *Denver Area* and *Turner II.* Ralph Forbes lost, but over the long run the true significance of the decision, and perhaps the key to Breyer's willingness to join Kennedy's opinion, might lie in the annunciation of this access right. The emergence of this right is all the more striking because, in that case, it operated against a television station

---

66. *See Arkansas Educ. Television Comm'n,* 523 U.S. at 670–71.

67. *Id.* at 675.

68. *Id.* at 676.

(as opposed to a cable operator) and arose in the obligation (rather than the permission) context.

In confining the limited right of access announced in *Forbes* to candidate debates, Justice Kennedy emphasized the unique role these debates play in our political life. He also explained that the format of such debates makes it unlikely that viewers would attribute the views of one speaker (the candidate seeking access) to those of another (the station). Fears about such false attribution have long made the Court uneasy about creating rights of access or even tolerating them when they have been created by others. In contrast, the other limitation that Kennedy imposed on the right of access—that access must only be granted to overcome an exclusion based on a disagreement with the candidate's views—seems less sensible.[69]

In justifying this particular limitation, Justice Kennedy explained that such viewpoint discrimination would inevitably skew the electoral debate. What he overlooked is that every exclusion, regardless of its reason, will inevitably have this same effect. The only difference between a viewpoint-based exclusion and a viewpoint-neutral exclusion is the justification. Admittedly, as noted with the Nixon example in the earlier discussion of state censorship, disagreement with a particular viewpoint is clearly not a proper justification for suppression or exclusion. But there may be other grounds for exclusion that are equally unable to justify the inevitable skew it produces. Such grounds can be deemed "arbitrary" and should not be permitted. Suppose, for instance, that a station excludes a candidate not because it disagrees with the candidate's view, but because it believes the candidate is not popular or is not likely to win, or does not have the economic resources needed to mount an effective campaign. All of these rationales strike me as arbitrary and insufficient to justify the skew that the exclusion will produce.

The *Forbes* dissent, written by Justice Stevens and joined by Justices Souter and Ginsburg, focused on these problems and in so doing made an important contribution to our understanding of managerial censorship. Like Breyer, Stevens is no friend of the categorical approach,[70] and he did not get involved in the public forum issue that so preoccupied the Kennedy opinion. That is,

---

69. In other contexts, the Court has disaggregated the state among its many functions, and applied a lesser standard of review, close to the one applied to private entities. For example, the Court curbed political activity on post office sidewalks and in airport terminals, where the state might be thought to be acting as property owner as opposed to sovereign. *See* OWEN M. FISS, *Silence on the Street Corner, in* LIBERALISM DIVIDED 55–66 (1996). In those earlier cases, Justice Kennedy complained about the disaggregation, but in *Forbes* he reached the same result by rather unconvincingly characterizing the candidate debate on public television as a "non–public forum." *See infra* note 70 and accompanying text.

70. *See generally* John Paul Stevens, *The Freedom of Speech*, 102 YALE L.J. 1293 (1993).

he did not dwell on whether the televised debate constituted "a designated public forum" or "a non-public forum." (In a footnote, however, he noted almost as an aside that if, as claimed, the station admitted all "viable" or "newsworthy" candidates, then it created a designated public forum and not the non-public forum that Kennedy concluded existed.)[71] Rather, Stevens argued that regardless of how the candidate debate is categorized under public forum doctrine, the First Amendment will not tolerate arbitrary definitions of its scope, and while viewpoint discrimination would constitute arbitrary exclusion, it is clearly not the only potential source of arbitrariness.

At this juncture, Stevens could have in fact inquired into the grounds for Forbes's exclusion and determined whether it was arbitrary, but he instead chose another, more procedural tack. Drawing on a vital part of First Amendment state-censorship jurisprudence, he faulted the station for lacking "narrow, objective, and definite standards" for its exclusions.[72] With a burst of real insight, he analogized the public television station managing its debate to a local authority issuing parade permits.[73] In both cases, he said, there exists "a constitutional duty to use objective standards," and the station must announce these standards in advance.[74] Stevens traced this duty to the *Shuttlesworth* case,[75] which arose from Dr. King's 1963 Birmingham campaign, but in truth it goes all the way back to the Supreme Court's 1938 decision in *Lovell v. City of Griffin*[76] and the very beginning of the First Amendment tradition.

The appeal of the duty espoused by Stevens is manifold. For one thing, it would limit the ability of managers to use arbitrary standards, as the very construction of a list of objective criteria would produce an open discussion about the permissible grounds for exclusion. Every criterion would have to be openly defended and justified. Also, the duty to use objective, pre-announced standards would give the excluded candidate a better chance to prove that his or her exclusion was arbitrary or, under the rule of the majority, a form of viewpoint discrimination. As things currently stand, such proof can usually only be indirect; no manager is likely to create direct evidence that the candidate was excluded because of disagreement with his or her views. Once the standards for exclusion were promulgated, the manager would have to justify

---

71. *Arkansas Educ. Television Comm'n*, 523 U.S. at 694 n.18 (Stevens, J., dissenting).

72. *Id.* at 684.

73. *See id.* at 690–91.

74. *Id.* at 694.

75. Shuttlesworth v. City of Birmingham, 394 U.S. 147 (1969).

76. 303 U.S. 444 (1938).

the exclusion in terms of one of the publicly announced criteria. The excluded candidate would then have a chance to show that this criterion had not been met, which would create a powerful indication that viewpoint discrimination or some other arbitrary basis for exclusion had been used.

In creating this duty, Stevens was very much aware of the practice of commercial stations and even made reference to it; he explained that he was asking no more of public stations than what was common practice in the industry in general.[77] Yet, by drawing on precedents governing the issue of parade permits, he seemed to suggest that the duty to use objective standards was confined, as a constitutional matter, to public stations. After all, the First Amendment only applies to state actors. Similarly, Kennedy's limited right of access appears confined to public stations. There is, however, reason to question whether either Stevens's duty to use objective standards or Kennedy's limited right of access should be limited to public television.

Commercial stations dominate the television industry. They are often thought of as "private"—in contrast to the public ones—because they are not financed by government funds; they receive their revenue largely from advertisements and in some cases by viewer subscriptions. However, these stations are fully entangled with the state, which gives them many substantial benefits, including the licenses and easements I described before. Is this sufficient? It is hard to be precise about these matters but if race cases such as *Burton v. Wilmington Parking Authority*[78] are any guide, certainly there seems to be enough involvement by the state in the operations of commercial stations to satisfy the state action requirement. True, there is not likely to be a nexus between the government's involvement with a particular station—say, through the conferral of its broadcast license or the grant of an easement— and that station's exclusion of a candidate; in such a situation, the government would not have required or in any way endorsed the exclusion. But the same argument could be made in the public broadcasting context: there is no nexus between the state's subsidy of a station and the station's decision to exclude.[79] There is therefore reason to believe, or at least to hope, that the duties Justices Stevens and Kennedy crafted in the public broadcasting context may, in time, be extended to the television industry as a whole.

---

77. *See Arkansas Educ. Television Comm'n*, 523 U.S. at 685–86 (Stevens, J., dissenting).

78. 365 U.S. 715 (1961).

79. No nexus was present, for instance, in the classic state action case of *Shelley v. Kraemer*, 334 U.S. 1 (1948), although Justice Rehnquist insisted upon the existence of such a nexus in *Moose Lodge No. 107 v. Irvis*, 407 U.S. 163 (1972).

A Turn in the Law

Those of us who write or teach are privileged. We can keep up with the world and explore issues of social importance by attending public lectures, by spending hours in the library, or by performing extensive online investigations. Most citizens, however, do not enjoy these luxuries and have come to depend on the mass media—and most notably, television—for their knowledge about issues and events beyond their immediate experience. It is only through television that they get a glimpse of candidates for public office and elected officials. A candidate debate, a news story, an elected public official's broadcast, or even a talk show may be the only occasion a citizen has to consider issues of public importance and to hear conflicting viewpoints on them.

The Supreme Court's recent decisions in *Denver Area, Turner,* and *Forbes* are premised on this understanding of the medium's significance. To their great credit, these decisions appreciate the role of television in our informal education system, and they seek to construct a set of rules that enables television to perform this role more effectively. Not all of the factors that can impair television's ability to perform its educational role are within the Court's reach; some are technological, others are economic, and still others have their roots in the frenzied pace of contemporary life. Yet in a modest but deliberate manner, the Court has focused on two factors that have greatly interfered with television's ability to discharge its democratic responsibility: state censorship and what I have called managerial censorship. Of the two, the latter has proved more difficult for the Court to grasp and conceptualize.

To some extent, this difficulty is due to the fact that curbs on managerial prerogatives interfere with the very autonomy that the state-censorship tradition seeks to secure. To put the same point differently, remedying managerial censorship requires a measure of speech-abridging state action. This is most clearly the case in *Turner II,* where the imposition of the must-carry provisions was upheld, but it is also the case in *Forbes,* where the corrective action sought was a judicial decree granting a candidate a right of access to a televised debate, thereby curbing the station's autonomy. *Denver Area* is rather peculiar in this regard, insofar as it involved a challenge to an act of Congress that gave cable operators a power they otherwise would not have, but it too deals with the conflict between protecting media autonomy and maximizing the information available to the public.

The other difficulty with the concept of managerial censorship stems from the challenge of defining the prohibited conduct with specificity. We cannot define the prohibited conduct in purely quantitative terms because, under conditions of scarcity, every programming decision has a censorial aspect—

to run one program or carry one channel is necessarily to exclude another. Of course, we might try, as I have on occasion, to use some qualitative standard: the people should have the information they need to discharge their responsibility of governance properly. But giving concrete meaning to such a phrase is fraught with difficulty. Accordingly, what we find in the cases is a cautious and piecemeal effort to question particularized abuses of managerial prerogatives: a risk that cable operators might drop over-the-air broadcasters and thereby leave 40 percent of American households without television; a power to veto sexually explicit programming on public access channels; a decision to exclude a congressional candidate from a televised debate on public television.

Given these difficulties with the concept of managerial censorship, it is no wonder that it has divided the Supreme Court and that the fullest elaboration of the theory in recent times—Breyer's opinion in *Turner II*—lacked the endorsement of a majority. In fact, no one else joined that opinion. We should be careful, however, not to ignore the significance of Breyer's opinion. Admittedly, Breyer spoke only for himself, but his opinion was crucial for the formation of a majority, and though Kennedy did not explicitly endorse Breyer's position, he in no way disputed or disavowed it. Perhaps Breyer's opinion has as much right as Kennedy's to claim the authority of the judgment. I would go further, however, and say that even if Kennedy had obtained a majority there is a special force to Breyer's concurrence in *Turner II* that must be reckoned with.

The theory Breyer expounded in that opinion is not entirely new. It had been developed by a number of scholars in recent decades. Yet in Breyer's hands it achieved an authority that can only come from the fact that it served as the predicate for a judicial judgment, and for that purpose it mattered not whether the judgment it supported obtained the vote of one justice, five justices, or nine. Breyer spoke as a public official. He was informed by the adjudicatory process and disciplined by the rules that govern it, and as a result his words are part of the law itself. His *Turner II* opinion has an authority and generative power that a scholar's work can never achieve.

Turner II was handed down in March 1997. Three years later, Justice Breyer extended his analysis to another sharply contested First Amendment area—campaign finance—and there gained the support of Justice Ginsburg, who had dissented in both *Turner I* and *Turner II*. The specific issue before the Court in the more recent case was the validity of a state law imposing dollar limits on contribution to candidates running for state office.[80] The law was attacked on the ground that it interfered with the First Amendment freedom of individuals to advance the candidacy of those they favored. A majority of

---

80. Nixon v. Shrink Missouri Government PAC, 120 S. Ct. 897 (2000).

the justices brushed this challenge aside, relying upon their 1976 decision in *Buckley v. Valeo,* which had upheld ceilings on campaign contributions in federal elections on the ground that such regulations minimize the risk of quid-quo-pro corruption.[81]

Responding to high-pitched dissents calling for a reexamination of *Buckley* itself, Justice Breyer once again wrote a separate concurrence. His purpose was to avoid reliance on the Buckley anticorruption rationale. To achieve that end he deployed a strategy analogous to the one developed in *Turner II* to avoid Kennedy's antitrust rationale, arguing that the purpose of the campaign regulation was not to avoid corruption but to further the First Amendment itself. Breyer openly acknowledged the interference with First Amendment freedoms that stemmed from the ceiling on campaign contributions, but pointed to larger First Amendment interests served by such regulations. As he explained, "they seek to build public confidence in [the electoral] process and broaden the base of a candidate's meaningful financial support, encouraging the public participation and open discussion that the First Amendment itself presupposes."[82] He saw no principled reason for denying the state the power to favor these First Amendment interests over those that might be served by a rule that allowed the wealthy to make whatever campaign contributions they wished. Repeating the formulation he first used in *Turner II,* but now with a nod from Ginsburg, Breyer emphasized that "this is a case where constitutionally protected interests lie on both sides of the legal equation."[83]

Seen in this light, Breyer's concurrence in *Turner II* should be understood as a new turn in the law—a movement away from the libertarian doctrine that has so dominated the Court for the last twenty-five years. It constitutes an important first step toward the recovery of a jurisprudence that sees the First Amendment more as a protection of the democratic system than as a protection of the expressive interests of the individual speaker. Justice Brandeis originally articulated the foundation for this approach in a separate concurrence in *Whitney v. California,* which was joined only by Holmes.[84] As suggested by the subsequent history of that opinion and the authority it has garnered over the years, First Amendment doctrine, like the Amendment itself, has an uncanny tendency to pay special heed to dissident voices.

---

81. 424 U.S. 1 (1976).

82. *Shrink Missouri Government,* 120 S. Ct. at 911.

83. *Id.; see* note 51 *supra.*

84. *See Whitney,* 274 U.S. at 375–76 (1927) (Brandeis, J., concurring).

In "The Future of Free Speech," Cass Sunstein seeks "to cast some light on the relationship between democracy and new communications technologies." Focusing on the growing power of individuals to "filter" what they read and learn, Professor Sunstein argues that "in a heterogeneous society" individuals should be "exposed to materials that they would not have chosen in advance" and that "most citizens should have a range of common experiences." He expresses concern that by fostering "fragmentation" and "group polarization," the new technologies threaten to undermine "both self-government and freedom, properly conceived."

Professor Sunstein then asks whether "the free-speech principle bars government from responding to this situation" by attempting "to improve the operation of the speech market." In answering this question in the negative, Professor Sunstein argues that the First Amendment should be understood as most fundamentally about promoting "deliberative democracy" rather than consumer individual "sovereignty."

Because the "emerging technologies" enable individuals "to wall themselves off from topics and opinions that they would prefer to avoid" and thus pose "serious dangers" to a well-functioning deliberative democracy, Professor Sunstein concludes that the First Amendment must leave room for the government to intervene in the marketplace of ideas in such a way as to ensure that citizens have "a wide range of experiences—with people, topics and ideas—that would not have been selected in advance."—GRS

CASS R. SUNSTEIN

The Future of Free Speech

My purpose here is to cast some light on the relationship between democracy and new communications technologies. I do so by emphasizing the most striking power provided by those technologies: the growing power of consumers to "filter" what it is that they see. In the extreme case, people will be fully able to design their own communications universe. They will find it easy to exclude, in advance, topics and points of view that they wish to avoid. I will also provide some notes on the democratic nature of the guarantee of freedom of speech.

An understanding of the dangers of filtering permits us to obtain a better sense of what makes for a well-functioning system of free expression. Above all, I urge that in a heterogeneous society, such a system requires something other than free, or publicly unrestricted, individual choices. On the contrary, it imposes two distinctive requirements. First, people should be exposed to materials that they would not have chosen in advance. Unanticipated encounters, involving topics and points of view that people have not sought out and perhaps find quite irritating, are central to democracy and even to freedom itself. Second, many or most citizens should have a range of common experiences. Without shared experiences, a heterogeneous society will have a much more difficult time addressing social problems; people may even find it hard to understand one another.

A Thought Experiment: Unlimited Filtering
The central puzzle can be expressed as a thought experiment: an apparently utopian dream, that of complete individuation, in which consumers can entirely personalize (or "customize") their own communications universes.

Imagine, that is, a system of communications in which each person has unlimited power of individual design. If people want to watch news all the time, they would be entirely free to do exactly that. If they dislike news, and want to watch football in the morning and situation comedies at night, that

This essay borrows from CASS R. SUNSTEIN, REPUBLIC.COM (2001). The excerpts used here are reprinted by permission of Princeton University Press.

would be fine too. If people care only about America, and want to avoid international issues entirely, that would be very simple indeed; so too if they care only about New York, or Chicago, or California. If people want to restrict themselves to certain points of view, by limiting themselves to conservatives, moderates, liberals, vegetarians, or Nazis, that would be entirely feasible with a simple "point and click."

Our communications market is moving rapidly toward this apparently utopian vision. If you are interested in getting help with the design of an entirely individual paper, you can consult a number of sites, including individual.com and crayon.net. In reality, we are not so far from the thought experiment of complete personalization of the communications network. Thus MIT professor Nicholas Negroponte refers to the emergence of the "Daily Me"—a communications package that is personally designed, with components fully chosen in advance.

PRECURSORS AND INTERMEDIARIES

Of course this is not entirely different from what has come before. People have always had a great deal of power to filter out unwanted materials. People who read newspapers do not read the same newspaper; some people do not read any newspaper at all. People make choices among magazines based on their tastes and their points of view. But in the emerging situation, there is a difference of degree if not of kind. What is different is a dramatic increase in individual control over content, and a corresponding decrease in the power of general interest intermediaries. These include newspapers, magazines, and broadcasters.

People who rely on such intermediaries have a range of chance encounters, involving shared experience with diverse others, and also exposure to material that they did not exactly choose. You might, for example, read the city newspaper, and in the process come across a range of stories that you would not have selected if you had the power to do so. Your eyes may come across a story about Germany, or crime in Los Angeles, or innovative business practices in Tokyo, and you may read those stories although you would hardly have placed them in your "Daily Me." Reading *Time* magazine, you might come across a discussion of endangered species in Madagascar, and this discussion might interest you, even affect your behavior, although you would not have sought it out in the first instance. A system in which individuals lack control over the particular content that they see has a great deal in common with a public street, where you might encounter not only friends, but a heterogeneous variety of people engaged in a wide array of activities (including perhaps political protests and begging). I will return to this point later.

One question, which I mean to answer in the affirmative, is whether individual choices, perfectly reasonable in themselves, might produce a large set of social difficulties. Another question, which I also mean to answer in the affirmative, is whether it is important to maintain the equivalent of "street corners" or "commons," where people are exposed to things quite involuntarily. More particularly, I seek to defend a particular conception of democracy—a deliberative conception—and to evaluate, in its terms, the outcome of a system with perfect power of filtering. I also mean to defend a conception of freedom, associated with the deliberative conception of democracy, and oppose it to a conception that sees consumption choices by individuals as the very embodiment of freedom.

The Public Forum Analogy

The problems in individual filtering, and the value of shared experiences and unchosen exposures, are best approached through two different routes. The first involves an unusual constitutional doctrine, based on the idea of the "public forum." The second involves a general constitutional ideal, indeed the most general constitutional ideal of all: that of deliberative democracy. As we will see, a system of individualized filtering may violate that ideal. As a corrective, we might build on the understandings that lie behind the notion that a free society creates a set of public forums, providing speakers' access to a diverse people and ensuring in the process that each of us hears a wide range of speakers, spanning many topics and opinions.

In the popular understanding, the free-speech principle forbids government from "censoring" speech of which it disapproves. In the standard cases, the government attempts to impose penalties, whether civil or criminal, on political dissent, and on speech that it considers dangerous, libelous, or sexually explicit. The question is whether the government has a legitimate and sufficiently weighty basis for restricting the speech that it seeks to control.

But an important part of free-speech law takes a quite different form. The Supreme Court has also held that streets and parks must be kept open to the public for expressive activity.[1] Hence governments are obliged to allow speech to occur freely on public streets and in public parks—even if many citizens would prefer to have peace and quiet, and even if it seems irritating to come across protesters and dissidents whom one would like to avoid. To be sure, the government is allowed to impose restrictions on the "time, place, and manner" of speech in public places. No one has a right to use fireworks and loudspeakers on the public streets at midnight to complain about the size of the defense

---

1. Hague v. C.I.O., 307 U.S. 496 (1939).

budget. But time, place, and manner restrictions must be both reasonable and limited, and government is essentially obliged to allow speakers, whatever their views, to use public property to convey messages of their choosing.

A distinctive feature of this idea is that it creates a right of speakers' access, both to places and to people. Another distinctive feature is that the public forum doctrine creates a right, not to avoid governmentally imposed penalties on speech, but to ensure government subsidies of speech. There is no question that taxpayers have to support the expressive activity that, under the public forum doctrine, must be permitted on the streets and parks. Indeed, the costs that taxpayers devote to maintaining open streets and parks, including cleaning up each day, can be quite high. Thus the public forum represents one place in which the right to free speech creates a right of speaker access to certain areas and also demands public subsidy of speakers.

There is now good reason to expand the public forum well beyond streets and parks. In the modern era, other places occupy their traditional role. The mass media, including the Internet, have become far more important than streets and parks as arenas in which expressive activity occurs.

Nonetheless, the Supreme Court has been wary of expanding the public forum doctrine beyond streets and parks, perhaps on the theory that once the historical touchstone is abandoned, lines will be extremely hard to draw. Thus the Court rejected the seemingly convincing argument that many other places should be seen as public forums too. In particular, it has been urged that airports, more than streets and parks, are crucial to reaching a heterogeneous public; airports are places where diverse people congregate and where it is important to have access if you want to speak to large numbers of people. The Court rejected the argument, suggesting that the public forum idea should be understood by reference to historical practices, and airports certainly have not been treated as public forums from "ancient times."

At the same time, the Court has shown considerable uneasiness with a purely historical test. In the most vivid passage on the point, Justice Kennedy wrote: "Minds are not changed in streets and parks as they once were. To an increasing degree, the more significant interchanges of ideas and shaping of public consciousness occur in mass and electronic media. The extent of public entitlement to participate in those means of communication may be changed as technologies change."[2] What Justice Kennedy is recognizing here is the serious question of how to "translate" the public forum idea into the modern technological environment. And if the Supreme Court is unwilling

---

2. *See* Denver Area Educ. Telecommunications Consortium, Inc. v. FCC, 518 U.S. 727, 802–3 (1996) (Kennedy, J., dissenting).

to do any such translating, it remains entirely open for Congress and state governments to do exactly that.

WHY PUBLIC FORUMS?

The Supreme Court has given little sense of why, exactly, it is important to ensure that the streets and parks are open to speakers. This is a question that must be answered if we are to know whether, and how, to extend the public forum doctrine to contemporary problems.

We can make some progress here by noticing that the public forum doctrine promotes three important functions. First, it ensures that speakers can have access to a wide array of people. If you want to claim that taxes are too high, or that police brutality against African-Americans is common, you can press this argument on many people who might otherwise fail to hear the message. Those who use the streets and parks are likely to learn something about the substance of the argument urged by speakers; they might also learn the nature and intensity of views held by their fellow citizens. Perhaps their views will be changed; perhaps they will become curious, enough so to investigate the question on their own. It does not much matter if this happens a little or a lot. What is important is that for some people, some of the time, speakers are authorized to press concerns that would otherwise go ignored.

On the speakers' side, the public forum doctrine thus creates a right of general access to heterogeneous citizens. On the listeners' side, the public forum creates not exactly a right, but an opportunity, if perhaps an unwelcome one: shared exposure to diverse speakers with diverse views and complaints. It is important to emphasize that the exposure is shared, in the sense that many people will be simultaneously so exposed, and also that it involves seeing and hearing people whom one might well have refused to seek out in the first instance. Indeed, the exposure might well be, much of the time, irritating or worse.

Second, the public forum doctrine allows speakers not only to have general access to heterogeneous people, but also to specific people, and specific institutions, with whom they have a complaint. Suppose, for example, that you believe that the state legislature has behaved irresponsibly with respect to crime or health care for children. The public forum doctrine ensures that you can make your views heard by legislators, simply by protesting in front of the state legislature itself.

The point applies to private as well as public institutions. If a clothing store is believed to have cheated customers or to have acted in a racist manner, protestors are allowed a form of access to the store itself. This is not by virtue of a right to trespass on private property—there is no such right—but because a public street is highly likely to be close by, and a strategic protest will undoubtedly catch the attention of the store and its customers. Here speakers are permitted, by the public forum doctrine, to have access to particular audiences, and particular listeners have a duty, undoubtedly unwelcome in many cases, to hear complaints that are directed against them. In other words, listeners have a sharply limited power of self-insulation.

Third, the public forum doctrine increases the likelihood that people generally will be exposed to a wide variety of people and views. When you go to work or visit a park, it is possible that you will have a range of unexpected encounters, however fleeting or seemingly inconsequential. You cannot easily wall yourself off from contentions or conditions that you would not have sought out in advance, or that you would have chosen to avoid if you could. Here too the public forum doctrine tends to ensure a range of experiences that are widely shared—streets and parks are public property—and also a set of exposures to diverse circumstances. A central idea here must be that these exposures help promote understanding and perhaps in that sense freedom. And all of these points can be closely connected to democratic ideals, as we soon see.

GENERAL INTEREST INTERMEDIARIES

Of course there is a limit to how much can be done on streets and in parks. Even in the largest cities, streets and parks are insistently *local*. But many of the social functions of streets and parks, as public forums, are performed by other institutions too. In fact society's general interest intermediaries—newspapers, magazines, television broadcasters—can be understood as public forums of an especially important sort.

The reasons are straightforward. When you read a city newspaper or a national magazine, your eyes will come across a number of articles that you might not have selected in advance, and if you are like most people, you will read some of those articles. Perhaps you did not know that you might have an interest in minimum wage legislation, or Somalia, or the latest developments in the Middle East; but a story might catch your attention. What is true for topics is also true for points of view. You might think that you have nothing to learn from someone whose view you abhor; but once you come across the editorial pages, you might well read what they have to say, and you might well benefit from the experience. Perhaps you will be persuaded on one point or another. At the same time, the front-page headline, or the cover story in *Newsweek*, is likely to have a high degree of salience for a wide range of people.

Television broadcasters have similar functions, perhaps above all with respect to what has become an international institution: the evening news. If you tune into the evening news, you will learn about a number of topics that you would not have chosen in advance. Because of its speech and immediacy, television broadcasters perform this public forum–type function still more than general interest intermediaries in the print media. The "lead story" on the networks is likely to have a great deal of public saliency, helping to define central issues, and creating a kind of shared focus of attention, for many millions of people. And what happens after the lead story—dealing with a menu of topics both domestically and internationally—creates something like a speakers' corner beyond anything imagined in Hyde Park.

None of these claims depends on a judgment that general interest intermediaries always do an excellent job, or even a good job. What matters for present purposes is that they expose people to a wide range of topics and views at the same time that they provide shared experiences for a heterogeneous public. Indeed, general interest intermediaries of this sort have large advantages over streets and parks precisely because most of them tend to be so much less local and so much more national, even international. Typically they expose people to questions and problems in other areas, even other nations. They even provide a kind of backdoor cosmopolitanism, ensuring that many people will learn something about diverse areas of the world, regardless of whether they are much interested in doing so.

Of course general interest intermediaries are not public forums in the technical sense. Most important, members of the public do not have a legal right of access to them. These are emphatically not institutions with respect to which individual citizens are allowed to override the editorial and economic judgments and choices of private owners. A sharp constitutional debate on precisely this issue has resulted in a resounding defeat for those who claimed a constitutionally guaranteed access right. But the question of legal compulsion is really incidental. The general interest intermediaries, even without legal compulsion, promote many of the functions of public forums. They promote shared experiences; they expose people to information and views that would not have been selected in advance.

Deliberative Democracy

The public forum doctrine is an odd and unusual one, especially insofar as to create a kind of speakers' access right to people and places, subsidized by taxpayers. But the doctrine is closely associated with a long-standing constitutional ideal, one that is far from odd: that of republican self-government. From the beginning, the American constitutional order was designed to be a republic, as distinguished from a monarchy or a direct democracy. We cannot understand the system of freedom of expression, and the effects of new communications technologies and filtering, without reference to this ideal.

In a republic, government is not managed by any king or queen; there is no sovereign that operates independently of the people. The American constitution represents a firm rejection of the monarchical heritage, and the framers self-consciously transferred sovereignty from any monarchy (with an explicit constitutional ban on "titles of nobility") to "We the People." At the same time, the founders were extremely fearful of popular passions and prejudices, and they did not want government to translate popular desires directly into law. They sought to create institutions that would "filter" those desires so as to ensure policies that would promote the public good. At the same time, the founders placed a high premium on the idea of "civic virtue," which required participants in politics to act as citizens dedicated to something other than their self-interest, narrowly conceived.

The specifically American form of republicanism thus involved an effort to create a "deliberative democracy." In this system, representatives would be accountable to the public at large, but there was also supposed to be a large degree of reflection and debate, both within the citizenry and within government itself. The aspiration to deliberative democracy can be seen in many places in the constitutional design. The system of bicameralism, for example, was intended as a check on insufficiently deliberative action from one or another legislative chamber; the Senate in particular was supposed to have a "cooling" function on popular passions. The long length of service for senators was designed to make deliberation more likely; so too for large election districts. The Electoral College was originally a deliberative body, ensuring that the president would result from some combination of popular will and reflection and exchange on the part of representatives. Most generally, the system of checks and balances had, as its central purpose, a mechanism for promoting deliberation within the government as a whole.

From these points it should be clear that the Constitution was not rooted in the assumption that direct democracy was the ideal, to be replaced by republican institutions only because direct democracy was not practical in light of what were, by our standards, extremely primitive technologies for communication. Many recent observers have suggested that for the first time in the history of the world, something like direct democracy has become feasible. It is now possible for citizens to tell their government, every week if not every day, what they would like it to do. Indeed, websites have been designed to enable citizens to do precisely that, and we should expect more experiments in this direction. But from the standpoint of constitutional ideals, this is nothing to celebrate. Indeed it is a grotesque distortion of founding aspirations. The problem is that direct public communication, if accompanied by direct governmental response, would compromise the deliberative goals of the original design.

Counterspeech

We are now in a position to connect these points to a general theme in the theory and law of free speech. Frequently it is said, in response to the fear that certain speech is dangerous, that the proper remedy is not legal suppression but more speech—that a democracy responds to harmful speech with "counterspeech." This idea is generally quite sound. But its soundness depends on available channels for counterspeech. The faith in "more speech" is rooted in a belief that, in a democracy, people are generally going to hear, not echoes of their own voices, but a variety of diverse views, so that critics of a certain kind of speech are able to reach a large audience as well.

If the universe of free speech consists of countless versions of the "Daily Me," the premise behind our faith in counterspeech is greatly undermined. In such a universe, counterspeech will be ineffective, if for no other reason than that few people will hear it. We can now see that there are institutional prerequisites for faith in counterspeech; these include a robust set of public forums, or at least institutions, like general interest intermediaries, that can do the same work that they do.

Two Conceptions of Sovereignty

Now distinguish between two conceptions of sovereignty. The first involves consumer sovereignty; the second involves political sovereignty. The first ideal underlies enthusiasm for the "Daily Me." The second ideal underlies the democratic challenge to this vision, on the ground that it is likely to undermine both self-government and freedom, properly conceived.

Consumer sovereignty means that individual consumers are permitted to choose as they wish, subject to the constraints provided by the price system and also by their current holdings and requirements. This is the idea that lies behind free markets, and it plays a significant role in thinking about both politics and communications as well. When we talk as if politicians are "selling" a message, and even themselves, we are treating the political domain as a kind of market, subject to the forces of supply and demand. And when we act as if the purpose of a system of communications is to ensure that people can see exactly what they "want," the notion of consumer sovereignty is very much at work. Political sovereignty stands on different foundations. It does not take individual tastes as fixed or given. It prizes democratic self-government, understood as a requirement of "government by discussion," accompanied by reason-giving in the public domain. Political sovereignty comes with its own preconditions, and these are violated if government power is not backed by justifications, and represents instead the product of force or simple majority will.

Of course the two conceptions of sovereignty are in potential tension. A commitment to consumer sovereignty may well compromise political sovereignty if, for example, free consumer choices result in insufficient understanding of public problems, or if they make it difficult to have anything like a shared culture.

Fragmentation

I now turn to my central concern. In a system with public forums and general interest intermediaries, people will frequently come across materials that they would not have chosen in advance—and for diverse citizens, this provides something like a common framework for social experience. Let us suppose that the communications market became far more fragmented, in exactly the sense prophesied by those who subscribe to the "Daily Me." What problems would be created by this fragmentation?

It is obvious that if there is only one flavor of ice cream and only one kind of toaster, a wide range of people will make the same choice when they eat ice cream and purchase a toaster. It is also obvious that as choice is increased, different individuals, and different groups, will make increasingly different choices. This has been the growing pattern over time with the proliferation of communications options.

Consider some details. If you take the ten television programs most highly rated by whites and the ten most highly rated by African-Americans, you will find little overlap between them. Indeed, over half of the ten programs most highly rated by African-Americans rank among the ten *least* popular programs for whites. Similar divisions can be found on the Internet. Not surprisingly, people tend to choose like-minded sites and like-minded discussion groups. With respect to politics, for example, those with committed views on one or another topic—gun control, abortion, affirmative action—speak mostly with each other. It is exceedingly rare for a site with an identifiable point of view to provide links to sites with opposing views; but it is very common for such a site to provide links to like-minded sites.

Of course any system that allows for freedom of choice will create balkanization of this kind. Long before the advent of the Internet, and in an era of a handful of television stations, people made choices among newspapers and radio stations. Since the early nineteenth century, newspapers published by and for the African-American community have been widely read by African-

Americans, and these newspapers offer significantly different coverage of common issues and also make dramatically different choices among what issues are important.[3]

What is emerging is a change of degree, not one of kind, But it is no less significant for that. With an increase in options, and a greater power to customize, comes an increase in the range of actual choices, and those choices are likely, in many cases, to match demographic characteristics. Of course this is not entirely bad; among other things, it will greatly increase variety, the aggregate amount of information, and the entertainment value of actual choices. But there are problems: if diverse groups see and hear quite different points of view, or focus on quite different topics, mutual understanding might be difficult, and it might turn out to be hard for people to solve problems that all members of society face together.

Group Polarization in General

We can sharpen our understanding of the problem of fragmentation if we attend to the phenomenon of group polarization. This phenomenon raises serious questions about any system in which individuals and groups choose extremely diverse communications universes.

The term "group polarization" refers to something very simple: *after deliberating with one another, people are likely to move toward a more extreme point in the direction to which they were previously inclined, as indicated by the median of their predeliberation judgments.* With respect to the Internet, the implication is that groups of people, especially if they are like minded, will end up thinking the same thing that they thought before—but in more extreme form.

Consider some examples of the basic phenomenon, which has been found in over a dozen nations:[4] (a) A group of moderately profeminist women will become more strongly profeminist after discussion. (b) After discussion, citizens of France become more critical of the United States and its intentions with respect to economic aid. (c) After discussion, whites predisposed to racial prejudice offer more negative responses to the question whether white racism is responsible for conditions faced by African-Americans in U.S. cities. (d) After discussion, whites predisposed to racial prejudice offer more positive responses to the same question.

As statistical regularities, it should follow, for example, that those moderately critical of an ongoing war effort will, after discussion, sharply oppose the

---

3. For a fascinating discussion, *see* RONALD JACOBS, RACE, MEDIA, AND THE CRISIS OF CIVIL SOCIETY (2000).

4. For citations and general discussion, *see* Cass R. Sunstein, *Deliberative Trouble? Why Groups Go to Extremes,* 110 YALE L.J. 71 (2000).

war; that people tending to believe in the inferiority of a certain racial group will be entrenched in this belief as a result of discussion; that after discussion, people who tentatively think that the Second Amendment protects the right to own guns, and that government efforts at gun control are unconstitutional efforts to eliminate the public's power of self-defense, will end up thinking that these propositions are undoubtedly true, and call for an immediate public response.

The phenomenon of group polarization has conspicuous importance to the communications market, where groups with distinctive identities increasingly limit themselves to within-group discussion. If the public is balkanized, and if different groups design their own preferred communications packages, the consequence will be further balkanization, as group members move one another toward a more extreme position in line with their initial tendencies. At the same time, different deliberating groups, each consisting of like-minded people, will be driven increasingly far apart, simply because most of their discussions are with one another. Extremist groups will often become more extreme; as we will soon see, the largest group polarization typically occurs with individuals already inclined toward extremes.

TWO MECHANISMS

There have been two main explanations for group polarization, both of which have been extensively investigated. Massive support has been found on behalf of both explanations.[5]

Persuasive arguments. The first explanation emphasizes the role of persuasive arguments. It is based on the intuition that an individual's position on any issue is (fortunately!) a function, at least in part, of which arguments seem convincing. If your position is going to move as a result of group discussion, it is likely to move in the direction of the most persuasive position defended within the group, taken as a collectivity. Of course—and this is the key point—a group whose members are already inclined in a certain direction will offer a disproportionately large number of arguments supporting that same direction, and a disproportionately small number of arguments going the other way. The result of discussion will therefore be to move individuals further in the direction of their initial inclinations.

On this account, the central factor behind group polarization is the existence of a *limited argument pool,* one that is skewed (speaking purely descriptively) in a particular direction. If a group of moderately feminist women becomes more feminist, a group moderately opposed to affirmative action more

---

5. *See id.* for details.

extremely so, and so forth, one reason is that the argument pool of any such group will contain a preponderance of arguments in the direction suggested. It is easy to see how this might happen with discussion groups on the Internet, and indeed with individuals not engaged in discussion but consulting only ideas to which they are antecedently inclined. The tendency of such discussion groups, and such consultations, will be to entrench preexisting positions.

Social comparison. The second mechanism, involving social comparison, begins with the claim that people want to be perceived favorably by other group members, and also to perceive themselves favorably. Once they hear what others believe, they adjust their positions in the direction of the dominant position. People may wish, for example, not to seem too enthusiastic or too restrained in their enthusiasm for affirmative action, feminism, or an increase in national defense; hence their views may shift when they learn what other people and in particular what other group members think.

The dynamic behind the social comparison explanation is that most people (of course not all) want to take a position of a certain socially preferred sort. Within groups, no one can know what such a position would be until the positions of others are revealed. Thus individuals move their judgments in order to preserve their image to others and their image to themselves. A key claim here, supported by evidence, is that information alone about the actual positions of others—without discussion—will produce a shift. The point has implications for exposure to ideas and claims even in the absence of a chance for interaction. If group polarization will occur merely on the basis of exposure, it is likely to be a common phenomenon in a balkanized speech market.

Fragmentation, Polarization, Media

An understanding of group polarization casts light on the Internet, radio, and television more generally. On the Internet, like-minded people are frequently speaking only with one another, or consulting sites that appeal to their own preconceptions. Recall that mere exposure to the views of others creates group polarization; it follows that this effect will be at work for nondeliberating groups, in the form of collections of individuals whose communications choices go in a particular direction, and who do not expose themselves to alternative positions. Indeed the same process is likely to occur for newspaper choices.

Group polarization also raises more general issues about communications policy. Consider the "fairness doctrine," now largely abandoned but once requiring radio and television broadcasters (a) to devote time to public issues and (b) to allow an opportunity for opposing views to speak. Prong (b) of the doctrine was designed to ensure that listeners would not be exposed to any single view. When the Federal Communications Commission abandoned the fairness doctrine, it did so on the ground that this second prong led broadcasters, much of the time, to avoid controversial issues entirely and to present views in a way that suggested a bland uniformity.[6] Subsequent research has suggested that the elimination of the fairness doctrine has indeed produced a flowering of controversial substantive programming, frequently with an extreme view of one kind or another; consider talk radio.[7]

Typically this is regarded as a story of wonderfully successful deregulation, because the effects of eliminating the fairness doctrine were precisely what was sought and intended. But from the standpoint of group polarization, the picture is far more complicated. The growth of issues-oriented programming with strong, often extreme views creates group polarization. All too many people are now exposed to louder echoes of their own voices, resulting, on occasion, in social fragmentation, misunderstanding, and sometimes even enmity.

IS GROUP POLARIZATION BAD?

Of course we cannot say, from the mere fact of polarization, that there has been a movement in the wrong direction. Perhaps the more extreme tendency is better; indeed, group polarization is likely to have fueled many movements of great value, including, for example, the movement for civil rights, the antislavery movement, and the movement for sex equality. All of these were extreme in their time, and within-group discussion bred greater extremism; but "extremism" need not be a word of opprobrium. If greater communications choices produce greater extremism, society may, in many cases, be better off as a result. But when group discussion tends to lead people to more strongly held versions of the same view with which they began, and if social influences and limited argument pools are responsible, there is legitimate reason for concern. Consider discussions among hate groups on the Internet and elsewhere. If the underlying views are unreasonable, it makes sense to fear that these discussions may fuel increasing hatred and a socially corrosive form of extremism. This does not mean that the discussions can or should be regulated in a system dedicated to freedom of speech. But as we have seen, it does raise questions about the idea that "more speech" is necessarily an adequate remedy—especially if people are increasingly able to wall themselves off from competing views.

---

6. *Id.*

7. Thomas W. Hazlett & David W. Sosa, *Was the Fairness Doctrine a "Chilling Effect"? Evidence from the Postderegulation Radio Market*, 26 J. LEGAL STUD. 279 (1997) (offering an affirmative answer to the question in the title).

The basic issue here is whether something like a "public sphere," with a wide range of voices, might not have significant advantages over a system in which isolated consumer choices produce a highly fragmented speech market. The most reasonable conclusion is that it is extremely important to ensure that people are exposed to views other than those with which they currently agree, in order to protect against the harmful effects of group polarization on individual thinking and on social cohesion. This does not mean that the government should jail or fine people who refuse to listen to others. Nor is what I have said inconsistent with approval of deliberating "enclaves," on the Internet or elsewhere, designed to ensure that positions that would otherwise be silenced or squelched have a chance to develop. But the benefit of such enclaves is that positions may emerge that otherwise would not and that deserve to play a large role in the heterogeneous public. Properly understood, the case of "enclaves," or more simply discussion groups of like-minded people, is that they will improve social deliberation, democratic and otherwise. For these improvements to occur, members must not insulate themselves from competing positions, or at least any such attempts at insulation must not be a prolonged affair.

Of course education might be helpful here. Indeed, the need for general education, exposing people to diverse views and giving them an appreciation for the limitations of their own perspective, becomes all the more insistent in a world filled with numerous editions of the "Daily Me." My basic suggestion is that the adverse effects of group polarization thus show that with respect to communications, consumer sovereignty is likely to produce serious problems for individuals and society at large—and these problems will occur by a kind of iron logic of social interactions.

Social Cascades

The phenomenon of group polarization is closely related to the widespread phenomenon of "social cascades." No discussion of social fragmentation and emerging communications technologies would be complete without a discussion of that phenomenon.

It is obvious that many social groups, both large and small, seem to move rapidly and dramatically in the direction of one or another set of beliefs or actions.[8] These sorts of "cascades" often involve the spread of information; in fact, they are driven by information. A key point here is that if you lack a

---

8. *See, e.g.*, Sushil Bikhchandani et al., *Learning from the Behavior of Others: Conformity, Fads and Informational Cascades*, J. ECON. PERSP., Summer 1998, at 151.

great deal of private information, you may well rely on information provided by the statements or actions of others. A stylized example: if Joan is unaware whether abandoned toxic waste dumps are in fact hazardous, she may be moved in the direction of fear if Mary seems to think that fear is justified. If Joan and Mary both believe that fear is justified, Carl may end up thinking so too, at least if he lacks reliable independent information to the contrary. If Joan, Mary, and Carl believe that abandoned hazardous waste dumps are hazardous, Don will have to have a good deal of confidence to reject their shared conclusion.

The example shows how information travels, and often becomes quite entrenched, even if it is entirely wrong. The view, widespread in many black communities, that white doctors are responsible for the spread of AIDS among African-Americans is a recent illustration. Often cascades of this kind are quite local, and take different form in different communities. Hence one group may end up believing something while another believes the exact opposite, because of the rapid transmissions of information within the first group but not the second. In a balkanized speech market, this danger takes on a particular form: different groups may be lead to quite different perspectives, as local cascades lead people in dramatically different directions.

I hope that I have shown enough to demonstrate that for citizens of a heterogeneous democracy, a fragmented communications market creates considerable dangers. There are dangers for each of us as individuals; constant exposure to one set of views is likely to lead to errors and confusions. And to the extent that the process makes people less able to work cooperatively on shared problems, there are dangers for society as a whole.

Social Glue

In a heterogeneous society, it is extremely important for diverse people to have a set of common experiences. Most people understand this fact, and many of our practices reflect a judgment to this effect. National holidays, for example, help shape a nation by encouraging citizens to think, all at once, about events of shared importance. And they do much more than this. They enable people, in all their diversity, to have certain memories and attitudes. At least this is true in nations where national holidays have a vivid and concrete meaning. In the United States, however, many national holidays have come to mean merely a day off work, and the precipitating occasion—President's Day, Memorial Day, Labor Day—is all but forgotten or ignored. This is a serious loss. With the possible exception of Fourth of July, Martin Luther King Day is probably the holiday closest to having a genuinely substantive national character, largely because that celebration involves something that can be treated as concrete and meaningful. In other words, it is *about* something.

Communications and the media are of course exceptionally important here. Sometimes millions of people follow the presidential election, or the Super Bowl, or the coronation of a new monarch; and many of them do so because of the simultaneous actions of others. In this sense, some of the experiences made possible by modern technologies are *solidarity goods,* in the sense that their value goes up when and because many other people are enjoying or consuming them. The point very much bears on the historic role of both public forums and general interest intermediaries. Public parks are of course places where diverse people can congregate and see one another. General interest intermediaries, if they are operating properly, give a simultaneous sense of problems and tasks.

THE VALUE OF SHARED EXPERIENCES

Why might these shared experiences be so desirable? There are three principal reasons.

1. Simple enjoyment is probably the least of it, but it is far from irrelevant; and the reason people like many of the experiences they do is because they are shared. Consider a popular movie, the Superbowl, or a presidential debate. For many of us, these are goods that are worth less, and possibly worthless, if many others are not enjoying or purchasing them too. Hence a presidential debate may be worthy of individual attention, for many people, simply because so many other people consider it worthy of individual attention.

2. Sometimes shared experiences ease social interactions, permitting people to speak with one another and to congregate around a common issue, task, or concern, whether or not they have much in common with one another. In this sense they provide a form of social glue. They help make it possible for diverse people to believe that they live in the same culture. Indeed they help constitute that shared culture, simply by creating common memories and experiences, and a sense of common tasks.

3. A fortunate consequence of shared experiences—many of them produced by the media—is that people who would otherwise see one another as quite unfamiliar can come instead to regard one another as fellow citizens with shared hopes, goals, and concerns. This is a subjective good for those directly involved. But it can be an objective good as well, especially if it leads to cooperative projects of various kinds. When people learn about a disaster suffered by fellow citizens, for example, they may respond with financial and other help. The point applies internationally as well as domestically; massive

relief efforts are often made possible by virtue of the fact that millions of people learn, all at once, about the relevant need.

FEWER SHARED EXPERIENCES

Even in a nation of unlimited communications options, some events will inevitably attract widespread attention. But an obvious risk of an increasingly fragmented communications universe is that it will reduce the level of shared experiences, having salience to diverse people. This is a simple matter of numbers. When there were three television networks, much of what was broadcast had the quality of a genuinely common experience. The lead story on the evening news, for example, would provide a common reference point for many millions of people. To the extent that choices proliferate, it is inevitable that diverse individuals, and diverse groups, will have fewer shared experiences and fewer common reference points. It is possible, for example, that coverage of events that are highly salient to some people will hardly ever be seen by others. And it is possible that some views and perspectives that seem obvious for many people will, for others, seem barely intelligible.

This is hardly a suggestion that everyone should be required to watch the same thing. We are not speaking of requirements at all. In any case a degree of plurality, with respect to both topics and points of view, is also highly desirable. My only claim is that a common set of frameworks and experiences is valuable for a heterogeneous society, and that a system with limitless options, making for diverse choices, will compromise the underlying values.

Freedom of Speech

The points thus far raise questions about whether a democratic order is helped or hurt by a system of unlimited individual choice with respect to communications. It is possible to fear that such a system will produce excessive fragmentation, with group polarization as a frequent consequence. It is also possible to fear that such a system will produce too little in the way of solidarity goods, or shared experiences. But does the free-speech principle bar government from responding to the situation? If that principle is taken to forbid government from doing anything to improve the operation of the speech market, the answer must be a simple yes.

I believe, however, that this is a crude and unhelpful understanding of the free-speech principle, one that is especially ill suited to the theoretical and practical challenges of the next decades and beyond. If we see the First Amendment through a democratic lens, we will be able to make a great deal more progress.

On an emerging view, the First Amendment to the Constitution requires government to respect consumer sovereignty. Indeed, the Amendment is often treated as if it incorporates the economic ideal. Although it is foreign to the original conception of the First Amendment, this view can be found in many places in current law.

For one thing, it helps to explain the constitutional protection given to commercial advertising. This protection is exceedingly recent. Until 1976,[9] the consensus within the Supreme Court, and the legal culture in general, was that the First Amendment did not protect commercial speech at all. Since that time, commercial speech has come to be treated more and more like ordinary speech, to the point where Justice Thomas has even doubted whether the law should distinguish at all between commercial and political speech.[10] Justice Thomas has not prevailed on this count, but the Court's decisions are best seen as a way of connecting the idea of consumer sovereignty with the First Amendment itself.

Belonging in the same category is the continuing constitutional hostility to campaign finance regulation. The Supreme Court has held that financial expenditures on behalf of political candidates are protected by the free-speech principle—and also that it is illegitimate for government to attempt to promote political equality by imposing ceilings on permissible expenditures.[11] The inequality that comes from divergences in wealth is not, on the Court's view, a proper subject for political control. Here too an idea of consumer sovereignty seems to be at work. Indeed, the political process itself is treated as a kind of market, in which citizens are seen as consumers, expressing their will not only through votes and statements but also through expenditures.

Most relevant for present purposes is the widespread view, with some support in current constitutional law, that the free-speech principle forbids government from interfering with the communications market by, for example, attempting to draw people's attention to serious issues or regulating the content of what appears on broadcast networks. To be sure, everyone agrees that the government is permitted to control monopolistic behavior and thus to enforce antitrust law, designed to ensure genuinely free markets in communications. Structural regulation, not involving direct control of speech but intended to make sure that the market works well, is also unobjectionable. But if government attempts to require television broadcasters to cover public

---

9. Virginia State Bd. of Pharmacy v. Virginia Citizens Consumer Council, 425 U.S. 748 (1976).

10. 44 Liquormart, Inc. v. Rhode Island, 517 U.S. 484 (1996).

11. *See* Buckley v. Valeo, 424 U.S. 1 (1976).

issues, or to provide free air time for candidates, or to ensure a certain level of high-quality programming for children, many people will claim that the First Amendment is being violated. The same is true for government efforts to improve the operation of the Internet by, for example, enlisting the public forum doctrine so as to promote exposure to materials that people would not have chosen in advance (see below for proposals in this vein).

The First Amendment and Democratic Deliberation

There are profound differences between those who emphasize consumer sovereignty and those who stress the democratic roots of the free-speech principle. For the latter, government efforts to regulate commercial advertising need not be objectionable; certainly false and misleading commercial advertising is more readily subject to government control than false and misleading political speech. For those who believe that the free-speech principle has democratic foundations, and is not about consumer sovereignty, government regulation of television, radio, and the Internet need not be objectionable, at least so long as it is reasonably taken as an effort to promote democratic goals.

Suppose, for example, that government proposes to require television broadcasters (as indeed it now does) to provide three hours per week of educational programming for children. Or suppose that government decides to require television broadcasters to provide a certain amount of free air time for candidates for public office, or a certain amount of time on coverage of elections. For those who believe in consumer sovereignty, these requirements are quite troublesome, indeed they seem like a core violation of the free-speech guarantee. For those who associate the free-speech principle with democratic goals, these requirements are fully consistent with its highest aspirations.

There is nothing novel or iconoclastic in the democratic conception of free speech. On the contrary, this conception lay at the heart of the original understanding of freedom of speech in America. In attacking the Alien and Sedition Acts, for example, James Madison claimed that they were inconsistent with the free-speech principle, which he linked explicitly to the American transformation of the concept of political sovereignty. In England, Madison noted, sovereignty was vested in the king. But "in the United States, the case is altogether different. The People, not the Government, possess the absolute sovereignty." It was on this foundation that any "Sedition Act" must be judged illegitimate. "[T]he right of electing the members of the Government constitutes . . . the essence of a free and responsible government," and "the value and efficacy of this right depends on the knowledge of the comparative merits and demerits of the candidates for the public trust." It was for this reason that the power represented by a Sedition Act ought, "more than any other, to produce universal alarm; because it is levelled against that right of freely examining public characters and measures, and of free communication among the people thereon, which has ever been justly deemed the only effectual guardian of every other right."[12]

In this way Madison saw "free communication among the people" not as an exercise in consumer sovereignty, in which speech was treated as a kind of commodity, but instead as a central part of self-government, the "only effectual guardian of every other right." A central part of the American constitutional tradition, then, places a high premium on speech that is critical to democratic processes, and is hardly hostile to government efforts to promote such speech. If history is our guide, it follows that government efforts to promote a well-functioning system of free expression, as through extensions of the public forum idea, are entirely acceptable.

American history is not the only basis for seeing the First Amendment in light of the commitment to democratic deliberation. The argument can be justified by basic principle as well.

Consider the question whether the free-speech principle should be taken to forbid efforts to make communications markets work better from the democratic point of view. Some standard examples include educational programming for children, free air time for candidates for public office, closed-captioning for the hearing-impaired, and requirements that websites contain links to sites with different views. Perhaps some of these proposals would do little or no good, or even harm; but from what standpoint should they be judged inconsistent with the free-speech guarantee?

If we believed that the Constitution gives all owners of speech outlets an absolute right to decide what appears on "their" outlets, the answer would be clear: government could require none of these things. But why should we believe that? Broadcasters owe their licenses to a government grant, and owners of websites enjoy their rights of ownership in large part because of the law, which creates and enforces property rights. None of this means that government can regulate television and the Internet as it chooses. But if government is not favoring any point of view and if it is genuinely improving the operation of democratic processes, it is hard to find a legitimate basis for complaint. Indeed, the Supreme Court has expressly held that the owner of shopping centers—areas where a great deal of speech occurs—may be required to keep their property open for expressive activity.[13] Shopping centers are not

---

12. JAMES MADISON, *Report on the Virginia Resolution, Jan. 1800, in* 6 WRITINGS OF JAMES MADISON 385–401 (Calliallard Hunt ed., 1906).

13. Pruneyard Shopping Ctr. v. Robins, 447 U.S. 74 (1980).

websites; but if a democratic government is attempting to build on the idea of a public forum, so as to increase the likelihood of exposure to diverse views, is there really a reasonable objection from the standpoint of free speech itself?

In a similar vein, it makes sense to say that speech that is political in character, in the sense that it relates to democratic self-government, cannot be regulated without a special showing of government justification—and that speech that is not political in that sense can be regulated on the basis of a somewhat weaker government justification. I will not attempt to offer a full defense of this idea here, which of course raises some hard questions about where lines should be drawn. But in light of the importance of the question to imaginable government regulation of new technologies, there are three points that deserve brief mention.

First, an insistence that government's burden is greatest when it is regulating political speech emerges from a sensible understanding of government's own incentives. It is here that government is most likely to be acting on the basis of illegitimate considerations, such as self-protection, or protection of powerful private groups. Government is least trustworthy when it is attempting to control speech that might harm its own interests. When speech is political, its own interests are almost certainly at stake. This is not to deny that government is often untrustworthy when it is regulating commercial speech, art, or other speech that does not relate to democratic self-government. But we have the strongest reasons for distrust when political issues are involved.

Second, an emphasis on democratic deliberation protects speech not only when regulation is most likely to be biased, but also when regulation is most likely to be harmful. If government regulates sexually explicit speech on the Internet or requires educational programming for children on television, it remains possible to invoke the normal democratic channels to protest these forms of regulation as ineffectual, intrusive, or worse. But when government forbids criticism of an ongoing war effort, the normal channels are foreclosed, in an important sense, by the very regulation at issue. Controls on public debate are distinctly damaging, because they impair the process of deliberation that is a precondition for political legitimacy.

Third, an emphasis on democratic deliberation is likely to fit, far better than any alternative, with our most reasonable views about particular free-speech problems. However much people disagree about some speech problems, they are likely to believe that at a minimum the free-speech principle protects political expression unless government has exceedingly strong grounds for regulation. On the other hand, forms of speech such as perjury, attempted bribery, threats, unlicensed medical advice, and criminal solicitation are not likely to seem to be at the heart of free-speech protection.

An understanding of this kind does not answer all constitutional questions. It does not give a clear test for distinguishing between political and nonpolitical speech, a predictably vexing question. (To those who believe that the absence of a clear test is decisive against the distinction itself, the best response is that any alternative test will lead to line-drawing problems of its own.) It does not say whether and when government may regulate art or literature, sexually explicit speech, or libelous speech. In all cases, government is required to have a strong justification for regulating speech, political or not. What I have suggested here, without fully defending the point, is that a conception of the First Amendment that is rooted in democratic deliberation is an exceedingly good place to start.

Proposals

My goal here has been to understand what makes for a well-functioning system of free expression, and to show how consumer sovereignty, in a world of limitless options, is likely to undermine that system. I have also attempted to show that the First Amendment should not be taken to ban reasonable efforts on the part of government to improve the situation. I do not intend to offer a set of policy reforms or any kind of blueprint for the future. But it will be useful to offer a few ideas, if only by way of introduction to questions that are likely to engage public attention in the first decades of the twenty-first century.

In thinking about reforms, it is important to have some sense of the problems that we aim to address, and of some possible ways of addressing them. If the discussion thus far is correct, there are three fundamental concerns from the democratic point of view:

1. the need to promote exposure to materials, topics, and positions that people would not have chosen in advance, or at least enough exposure to produce a degree of understanding and curiosity;

2. the value of a range of common experiences; and

3. the need for exposure to substantive questions of policy and principle, combined with a range of positions on such questions.

Of course it would be ideal if citizens were demanding, and private information providers were creating, a range of initiatives designed to alleviate the underlying concerns. Perhaps they will; there is some evidence to this effect. In fact, new technology creates growing opportunities for exposure to diverse points of view, and indeed growing opportunities for shared experiences. It is certainly possible that private choices will lead to far more, not less, in the way of exposure to new topics and points of view, and also to more, not less, in the way of shared experiences. But to the extent that they fail to do so, it is worthwhile to consider government initiatives designed to pick up the slack.

There are many reform possibilities. Each of them would require a lengthy discussion. But if we draw on recent developments in regulation generally, we can see the potential appeal of five simple alternatives. Of course different proposals would work better for some communications outlets than others.

1. Producers of communications might be subject, not to regulation, but to disclosure requirements. In the environmental area, this strategy has produced excellent results. The mere fact that polluters have been asked to disclose toxic releases has produced voluntary, low-cost reductions. Apparently fearful of public opprobrium, companies have been spurred to reduce toxic emissions on their own. The same strategy has been used in the context of both movies and television, with ratings systems designed partly to increase parental control over what children see. On the Internet, many sites disclose that their site is inappropriate for children. The same idea could be used far more broadly. Television broadcasters might, for example, be asked to disclose their public interest activities. On a quarterly basis, they might be asked to say whether and to what extent they have provided educational programming for children, free air time for candidates, and closed captioning for the hearing impaired. They might also be asked whether they have covered issues of concern to the local community and allowed opposing views a chance to speak. The Federal Communications Commission has already taken steps in this direction; it could do in a lot more. Websites might be asked to say if they have allowed competing views a chance to speak. Of course disclosure is unlikely to be a full solution to the problems that I have discussed here. But modest steps in this direction are likely to do little harm and at least some good.

2. Producers of communications might be asked to engage in *voluntary self-regulation*. Some of the difficulties in the current speech market stem from relentless competition for viewers and listeners, competition that leads to a situation that many journalists abhor and from which society does not benefit. The competition might be reduced via a "code" of appropriate conduct, agreed upon by various companies, and encouraged but not imposed by government. In fact the National Association of Broadcasters maintained such a code for several decades, and there is growing interest in voluntary self-regulation for both television and the Internet. The case for this approach is that it avoids government regulation while at the same time reduces some of the harmful effects of market pressures. Any such code could, for example, call for an opportunity for opposing views to speak, or for avoiding unnecessary sensationalism, or for offering arguments rather than quick "sound-bites" whenever feasible.

3. The government might *subsidize speech,* as, for example, through publicly subsidized programming or publicly subsidized websites. This is of course the idea that underlies the Public Broadcasting System. But it is reasonable to ask whether the PBS model is not outmoded in the current communications environment. Other approaches, similarly designed to promote educational, cultural, and democratic goals, might well be ventured. Perhaps government could subsidize a "Public.Net" designed to promote debate on public issues among diverse citizens—and to create a right of access to speakers of various sorts.[14]

4. If the problem consists in the failure to attend to public issues, the government might impose "must carry" rules on the most popular websites, designed to ensure more exposure to substantive questions.[15] Under such a program, viewers of especially popular sites would see an icon for sites that deal with substantive issues in a serious way. They would not be required to click on them, but it is reasonable to expect that many viewers would do so, if only to satisfy their curiosity. The result would be to create a kind of Internet "sidewalk," promoting some of the purposes of the public forum doctrine. Ideally those who create websites might move in this direction on their own. If they do not, government should explore imposing requirements of this kind, making sure that any program does not draw invidious lines in selecting the sites whose icons will be favored. Perhaps a lottery system of some kind could be used to reduce this risk.

5. The government might impose "must carry" rules on highly partisan websites, designed to ensure that viewers learn about sites containing opposing view. This policy would be designed to make it less likely that people simply hear echoes of their own voices. Of course many people would not click on the icons of sites whose views seem objectionable; but some people would, and in that sense the system would not operate so differently from general interest intermediaries and public forums. Here too the ideal situation would be voluntary action. But if this proves impossible, it is worth considering regulatory alternatives.

These are brief thoughts on some complex subjects. My goal has not been to evaluate any proposal in detail, but to give a flavor of some of the possibilities for promoting constitutional goals in a dramatically changed environment.[16]

---

14. *See* ANDREW SHAPIRO, THE CONTROL REVOLUTION (1999).

15. *See* discussion in Andrew Chin, *Making the World Wide Web Safe for Democracy,* 19 HASTINGS COMM. & ENT. L.J. 309, 330–33 (1997).

16. *See* CASS R. SUNSTEIN, REPUBLIC.COM (2001), for more detail.

Beyond Censorship

My principal claim here has been that a well-functioning democracy depends on far more than restraints on official censorship of controversial ideas and opinions. It also depends on some kind of public domain, in which a wide range of speakers have access to a diverse public—and also to particular institutions, and practices, against which they seek to launch objections.

Emerging technologies are hardly an enemy here. They hold out at least as much promise as risk. But to the extent that they weaken the power of general interest intermediaries, and increase people's ability to wall themselves off from topics and opinions that they would prefer to avoid, they create serious dangers. And if we believe that a system of free expression calls for unrestricted choices by individual consumers, we will not even understand the dangers as such. Whether such dangers will materialize will ultimately depend on the aspirations, for freedom and democracy alike, by whose light we evaluate our practices. What I have sought to establish here is that in a free republic, citizens aspire to a system that provides a wide range of experiences—with people, topics, and ideas—that would not have been selected in advance.

EPILOGUE

STONE: As we bring this volume to a close, I suppose it's appropriate for us to speculate a bit about the future of the First Amendment. Before turning to the future, however, it may be useful to lay the foundation for that discussion with a few observations about the past.

If we divide the Supreme Court's experience with the First Amendment into two very loosely defined "eras," we can get some sense of how the nature of the problems confronting the Court have changed over time. In the first of these eras, which began with the Court's decision in *Schenck* in 1919 and ended with its decision in *Brandenburg* in 1969, the Court spent most of its energy attempting to work out the problems posed by dissident speech. Whether grappling with the rights of antiwar protestors during World War I, anarchists and syndicalists in the 1920s, Jevohah's Witnesses and neofascists in the 1940s, communists in the 1950s, or civil rights demonstrators in the 1960s, the Court's attention during these fifty years was largely absorbed by the need to reconcile the right of individuals to engage in speech highly critical of the established order with the preservation of order itself. These disputes raised a host of issues, including the meaning of "clear and present danger," the rights of public employees, the right of individuals to commandeer public streets and parks for speech purposes, the duty of the state to protect provocative speakers from hostile audiences, and the limits of licensing and prior restraints on marches, picketing, and demonstrations.

By 1969, which marks not only the decision in *Brandenburg,* but also the end of the Warren Court, the Court had established a more-or-less stable framework for evaluating these sorts of issues. As a consequence, since 1969 these types of questions have become much less prevalent within the Court. But in the more recent era, the Court has confronted a new set of issues. Among the most significant were the constitutionality of efforts to regulate the mass media and the financing of political campaigns, the special problems involved in government subsidized speech, the regulation of increasingly pervasive sexually explicit expression (most recently, on the Internet), and the level of First Amendment protection that should be accorded hate speech.

What can we learn from this? First, I would say that the Court's analysis of such issues as the regulation of sexually explicit speech and hate speech has largely followed the approach that evolved in the earlier era. That is, in each of these instances the Court has generally given very substantial protection to free expression and largely rejected efforts to regulate such speech on paternalistic grounds or on the claim that the speech is "dangerous." The hard-bought understanding of the need to adopt a highly skeptical view of government efforts to restrict the expression of particular ideas and to build a "fortress model" of the First Amendment has led the Court to grant very substantial protection not only to politically dissident expression, but also to sexually explicit (but nonobscene) speech and to hate speech.

Second, the nature of the issues confronting the Court has shifted over time from those involving primarily street-corner speakers to those focusing primarily on the mass media and the impact of money on the marketplace of ideas. From this perspective, too, the Court has tended toward a highly speech-protective view of the First Amendment. That is, it has strictly limited most forms of campaign finance regulation and most efforts to regulate the mass media. The Court seems generally to have concluded that the same basic presumptions about freedom of expression that developed in the earlier era for street-corner speakers should also prevail when the government attempts to regulate large political expenditures and complex enterprises engaged in the business of speech, such as television networks, newspapers, cable operators, and commercial advertisers.

A third observation I would make is that the issues that dominate the Court's attention at any particular time are likely—not surprisingly—to reflect developments in the larger society. The issues of hate speech and pornography arose out of the civil rights and feminist movements; the issue of sexually explicit expression arose out of changing social mores and the advent of new forms of technology; the issue of campaign regulation arose out of changes in the nature and cost of political campaigns, which were themselves trig- gered in part by the cost of mass media political campaigns; and the issue of government speech arose out of the increasing role government now plays in subsidizing various forms of expressive activities, such as through public universities, tax subsidies and exemptions, and the National Endowment for the Arts.

BOLLINGER: The question for the future, I think, is whether the scope of First Amendment rights articulated in the *Brandenburg* era reflects the distilled wisdom of historical experience, which makes it more likely to survive in future periods of social upheaval, or whether the *Brandenburg* era will turn out to be just one era among many, in which the freedom of speech varies widely and more or less according to the sense of security and tolerance prevailing in the nation at the time. The fact that the last thirty years since *Brandenburg* have been remarkably peaceful and prosperous means that the understandings we now have about the meaning of free speech have not really been tested. By the standards we now apply (that is, through the eyes of *Brandenburg*), just about every time the country has felt seriously threatened the First Amendment has retreated. There are thus two ways, at least, to view the twentieth-century experience.

I would add just a few thoughts on a couple of the specific areas you mention as likely to be developed in the future. The first is the problem of what limits the First Amendment places on the ability of the government in its funding decisions to attach conditions limiting speech. No solid framework has yet been laid down. On the one hand, one might think the state, like any private person, should be able to do pretty much as it likes with its own money, and if the recipients don't like the conditions attached they can look elsewhere for funding.

On the other hand, the massive presence of government in the society presents extraordinary opportunities for it to distort the marketplace of ideas. Virtually every university in the nation receives some form of federal funding (for financial aid, research, and so forth). Would it be constitutional for the government to demand that as a condition of receiving such funds a university must agree that no teacher, researcher, or student will criticize government policy, or advocate abortion? A majority of the Court has said no.

At the same time, however, reflecting the complexity of the problem, the Court has also upheld the power of the federal government to forbid recipients of federal funds for family planning programs (in that case, doctors of Planned Parenthood) from informing clients about the availability of abortion. If this seems surprising, what about a program that grants funds only to organizations that advocate nonsmoking? Must the government also give funds to groups that promote smoking? And what about museums, public broadcasting, and the National Endowments for the Arts and for the Humanities? The underlying problem is exceedingly difficult because the lines that must be drawn (namely, between government programs and between different types of restrictions within programs) are necessarily vague. Still, I see the Court over time developing a set of First Amendment protections for the autonomy of cultural institutions, such as universities and museums.

Another unresolved and critical area is that of the First Amendment and new technologies of communication. We have already talked about the "dual system" of freedom of the press: one set of First Amendment rules for print media and quite another for broadcast and cable media. Some have viewed the constitutional treatment of the electronic media as an unjustified aberration; others have seen it as a superior model that should apply to print media as well. I have argued for understanding the First Amendment benefits of a bifurcated approach. The Court will have to settle on a perspective for the future.

At the same time, however, we are witnessing the emergence of yet another new communications technology, the Internet. While experience teaches us that every new technology (from the printing press to the electronic media) stirs up fears of unwanted change and threats to the social order, that means only that we ought to be wary of claims for adjustments in the protections of the First Amendment, not necessarily unheeding of them. The fears increasingly voiced about the spread of hate groups over the Internet, for example, will surely eventually be presented to the Court. Unless the evidence of societal harms grows dramatically, however, I doubt that we will see a change in First Amendment direction.

There is a far larger question of scope that will confront the First Amendment as it develops. Every principle, one might say, contains within it the potential for virtually unlimited expansion. Freedom of speech is no exception in this regard. We might see three levels to its potential scope.

The first level involves securing, defining, and giving meaning to freedom of expression. This is mainly where our attentions have been focused over the last century. We pretty much take the world as it is and seek to establish within it a preserve—in a sense, a wilderness area—where state control is curtailed.

The second level involves efforts to correct or to counteract the perceived underlying deficiencies in the society that interfere with the fulfillment of the foundational purpose(s) of the First Amendment. At this level, we say that the function of freedom of speech and press is not only to stop censorship but also to reach truth, or good democratic decisions, or the proper balance of social tolerance. These basic functions naturally lead us to see how the structure of society—most notably, the economic system and its resultant unequal distribution of wealth—can distort the system of expression and its underlying goals. This produces in turn governmental intervention, and even First Amendment intervention, to limit some speech in order to enhance the quality overall. Hence, we see public access requirements or campaign finance reform. In our earlier dialogue and in several of the essays in this book, most of the significant, if tentative, moves the Court has permitted at this level have been discussed.

The third level continues with this logic but increases by an order of magnitude. This is where the Court has thus far not ventured. Take the educational system. Logically, the quality of the marketplace of ideas, the likelihood that truth will emerge from it, is significantly dependent on the quality of the basic system of education in the society. In theory, there would seem to be little stopping the Court from holding that the First Amendment imposes all kinds of obligations and responsibilities on the government with respect to the educational process. The methods of financing education would easily be an early candidate for judicial attention. And the purview of the First Amendment would continue on from there—from education to redistribution of wealth.

What we have seen over the past eight decades is extensive work at level one, considerable experiments at level two, and very little at all in the third level. Obviously, there is a hegemonic potential within the First Amendment that must be resisted. On the other hand, the willingness to expand and experiment further will also be tempting.

STONE: The risk of overreaching is an important one. Among the many constraints that operate on the constitutional process is the limited tolerance of the community for judicial action that limits the scope of democratic decision-making. There is a reason for judicial review, for granting the judiciary the authority to nullify majoritarian preferences through constitutional interpretation. An independent judiciary, which is largely (or at least somewhat) insulated from the passions, prejudices, fears, and anxieties of the larger society, can bring a measure of dispassion, objectivity, perspective, and balance to the protection of our most fundamental rights and liberties. On its best days, the Supreme Court can reign in the worst excesses and most intolerant tendencies of an overwrought majority, whether the triggering issue be war, sex, race, or speech itself. Moreover, some degree of boldness on the Court's part is often warranted. Among the Court's greatest triumphs, for example, are decisions that demonstrate judicial courage and independence, as exemplified by decisions like *Brown v. Board of Education* (racial segregation) and *Baker v. Carr* (legislative reapportionment).

But just as the Court must take care not to get swept up in the larger passions of the day, and thus lose its essential objectivity and its unique constitutional perspective, so too must it not get swept away by its own potential authority. It must exercise reasonable restraint. There is a limit to how much judicial direction—and how much free speech—society will stand. Should the Supreme Court order all states to provide equal educational funding per student as an application of the First Amendment? At the moment, that seems like a bit of a reach, though in principle it is far from outlandish. One of the constant challenges for the Court is to strike the right balance.

BOLLINGER: It would seem appropriate to close our discussion with one of the many profound observations of your professional namesake, Harry Kalven.

You and I conceived of this project because we have devoted a good portion of nearly three decades to thinking, writing, and teaching about the First Amendment and because, along with many others, we have been amazed by the ever-increasing hold the principle of freedom of speech and press has on the American imagination. Every one of the essays in this volume testifies to that fact.

In 1965, in the preface to his book, *The Negro and the First Amendment,* Kalven observed that the jurisprudence of the First Amendment is distinguished by an extraordinary "quest for [a] coherent general theory." Other areas of law seem comfortable with, or reconciled to, the inevitable inconsistencies and ambiguities that arise from case law over time, but that is not true of the First Amendment. This is so, Kalven argued, for one very simple reason: because "free speech is so close to the heart of a democratic organization that if we do not have an appropriate theory for our law here, we feel we really do not understand the society in which we live." That, at least, is the spirit animating this book.

CONTRIBUTORS

Lillian R. BeVier, Henry and Grace Charitable Foundation Professor and Class of 1948 Professor of Scholarly Research, University of Virginia

Vincent Blasi, Lamont Professor of Civil Liberties, Columbia Law School; Massee Professor of Law and Hunton and Williams Research Professor, University of Virginia

Lee C. Bollinger, president and professor of law, The University of Michigan

Stanley Fish, dean of the College of Liberal Arts and Sciences, University of Illinois, Chicago

Owen M. Fiss, Sterling Professor of Law, Yale University

Kent Greenawalt, University Professor, Columbia University

Richard A. Posner, judge, U.S. Court of Appeals for the Seventh Circuit; senior lecturer, The University of Chicago Law School

Robert Post, Alexander F. and May T. Morrison Professor of Law, University of California at Berkeley (Boalt Hall)

Frederick Schauer, academic dean and Frank Stanton Professor of the First Amendment, John F. Kennedy School of Government, Harvard University

Geoffrey R. Stone, provost and Harry Kalven Jr. Distinguished Service Professor of Law, The University of Chicago

David A. Strauss, Harry N. Wyatt Professor of Law, The University of Chicago

Cass R. Sunstein, Karl N. Llewellyn Distinguished Service Professor of Jurisprudence, The University of Chicago

INDEX

Abel, Richard, 216, 218, 220, 223, 226, 227, 228
    Speaking Respect, Respecting Speech, 209–14
Able v. United States, 187n. 50
Abrams v. United States, ix, 5, 24, 41, 48, 50,
        62n. 4, 73n. 63, 75n. 72, 128, 144
    and Espionage Act of 1918, 155–56
    Holmes's dissent in, 104, 105, 124, 129, 157–
        58, 167
ACLU. *See* American Civil Liberties Union
actual danger, vs. intended danger, 99, 104
Adair v. United States, 177n. 13
Adkins v. Children's Hosp., 177n. 12
advertising, 9, 21, 108, 132, 249–50
    and campaign financing, 146–47
    economic analysis applied to, 120
    gambling casino, 134
    and information packaging, 245
    and pharmaceutical prices, 179–80
    subsidy vs. suppression and, 137–38
    See also commercial speech
advocacy of ideas
    distinction between advocacy of action and,
        56
Aeschylus, 81
affirmative action, 145, 146
African Americans
    and Internet access, 259
    newspapers published by and for, 294–95
    spread of AIDs among, and social cascades,
        300
AIDS, 139, 300
airports, 149
A.L.A. Schechter Poultry Corp. v. United States,
        177n. 6
Alexander, Larry, 226, 227, 229
Allgeyer v. Louisiana, 177n. 7
American Booksellers Ass'n v. Hudnut, 135n. 25,
        176n. 1
American Civil Liberties Union, 193
American Motorcycle Ass'n v. Davids, 181n. 31
American Party of Texas v. White, 190n. 61
A & M Records, Inc. v. Napster, Inc., 191n. 65

anarchists, 311
antiabortion advertising, 137–38
anticigarette advertising, 137
antipornography
    advertisements, 137
    ordinance, 135
    and "silencing" argument, 187n. 52
antitrust regulation, and must-carry provisions,
        271–72
Areopagitica (Milton), 64, 66, 68, 70, 71
Aristotle, 81
*Arkansas Educational Television Commission v.
        Forbes*, 127, 130, 275
    Kennedy's opinion in, 275, 276, 277, 278
    Stevens's dissent in, 278–79, 280
assassinations, 21, 145
Associated Press v. United States, 273
Athenians (ancient), Brandeis's high regard for,
        80–82
Austin, J. L., *Speech Act Theory*, 216
autonomy, and free speech, 61

Bacchae, The (Euripides), 80
"bad tendency" test, 5
    Holmes's transformation of, 159
Baker v. Carr, 315
Barnes v. Glen Theatre, Inc., 22, 182n. 35
Beauharnais v. Illinois, 3, 7, 10
Bell Curve, The (Herrnstein and Murray), 140
Bethel School Dist. No. 403 v. Fraser, 169n. 76
BeVier, Lillian, ix–x, 232, 233
billboards, 258
Bill of Rights, 12, 39, 41, 43, 44
Black, Justice Hugo, 5, 35, 36, 55, 73
blackmail, 37
Blackmun, Justice Harry Andrew, 270
blacks. *See* African Americans
Blackstone, William, 42, 43, 48, 51, 58, 140
Blasi, Vincent, ix, 60, 120
blasphemy, 44
Board of Trade v. Dow Jones & Co., 252–53n. 59
Board of Trustees of the State Univ. v. Fox, 172n

319

Bollinger, Lee C., character and analysis of First
Amendment, 84n
Boos v. Barry, 169n. 73
*Bose Corp. v. Consumers Union of the United
States*, 234n. 5
Bowers v. Hardwick, 180n. 25, 181n. 30, 184n.
39
Brandeis, Justice Louis, 28, 51, 53, 83, 84, 211
ancient Greeks revered by, 79–81
"bad tendency" approach rejected by, 5
"clear and present danger" test refined by,
104–5
concurrence in *Whitney v. California*, 73–78,
82, 104, 105, 273, 283
and countervailing speech, 118
The Curse of Bigness, 83
and development of law of First Amendment, 47
dissenting opinion in *Abrams v. United
States*, 48, 49
dissenting opinion in *Gitlow v. New York*, 52
and free-speech tradition, 63
on inertia, 95
legacy of opinions on freedom of speech, 3,
5, 6
and sedition, 41
Brandenburg v. Ohio, 4, 5, 6, 17, 19, 37, 48,
62n. 5, 97n. 2, 103n. 10, 106–7, 113, 119,
129n. 18, 233n. 1, 311
and criminal counseling, 115–16
and McCarthy era, 54–57
Brennan, Justice William Joseph, Jr., 73
opinion in *New York Times v. Sullivan*, 239–
40n. 17
Breyer, Justice Steven, 256, 265, 275, 276, 277
concurrence in *Nixon v. Shrink Missouri
Government PAC*, 282–83
concurrence in *Turner II*, 273–75, 276, 277,
282, 283
opinion in *Denver Area* case, 262, 267, 268,
269
Bridges v. California, 53, 58
broadcast regulation, 1, 13, 152
Court's approval of, 168
and Meiklejohnian perspective, 170
Brown v. Board of Education, 315
Brown v. Hartlage, 111n. 37, 161n. 33
Buchanan, James, 177
Buckley v. Valeo, 146n, 168n. 64, 190n. 58, 283,
303n. 11
Bullock v. Carter, 190n. 61
Burke, Edmund, 52
on ideology of common law, 45–46
Burton v. Wilmington Parking Authority, 280
Butler, Judith, 226, 227, 228

*Excitable Speech: A Politics of the Performa-
tive*, 214–23
Butler v. Michigan, 264

Cable Act of 1992, 261, 264, 267, 270, 271
cable television, 256, 259–60
as decency police, 267–69
and *Denver Area* case, 262
economic power of, 274–75
and managerial censorship, 281–82
must-carry obligations of, 269–75
vertical integration in, 272
Cammermeyer v. Aspin, 184n. 37, 187n. 49
campaign financing, 14, 62, 188–90, 311
economic analysis applied to regulation of,
120
and "fair access," 146–49
and *Nixon v. Shrink Missouri Government
PAC*, 282–83
reform of, 29, 168, 174
regulation of, 144, 312
candidate debates, and television, 275–80
Cantwell v. Connecticut, 53, 54, 57, 73n. 64,
145n. 37, 169n. 71
Cardozo, Benjamin, 46, 56
Carson v. City of Beloit, 162n. 39
Case for Same-Sex Marriage, The (Eskridge), 140
censorship, 11, 14, 19, 25, 27, 31, 88, 89, 131,
143–44, 314
free speech, character, and, 86
and Internet, 150–51
"managerial," 256, 260, 265–67, 274, 275,
281–82
Milton's opposition to, 65, 66, 68, 70, 71–72
and Pentagon Papers, 17
placement of, inside First Amendment, 199–
200
Post's views on, 205–7
Schauer's views on, 228–29
state, 260–65, 266, 267, 278, 279, 281
Supreme Court's presumption against any
form of, 8
of television, 257–83
Censorship and Silencing (Post, ed.), 205
Chafee, Zechariah, Jr., 11, 40, 41, 44
Chaplinsky v. New Hampshire, 9, 53, 54, 57,
233n. 1
character
and censorship, 65–66
and free speech, 63–95
chat rooms, 150
checks and balances system
and deliberative democracy, 292
and free speech, 87
child pornography, and Internet, 149, 150

children, protection of, from sexually explicit
    material/programming, 264, 268
*Church of the Am. Knights of the Ku Klux Klan v.
    Safir,* 193n. 70
citizens and citizenship
    and evaluation of political information, 249–
        54
    and formal education system, 257
civic commitment, Brandeis's high regard for,
    79–80
civic participation, social psychology of, 90
civil liberties, 77
civil rights demonstrators, 57, 311
civil rights movement, 312
    and group polarization, 298
Clarke, Justice John, opinion in *Abrams,* 156
"clear and present danger" standard, 5, 16, 19,
        53, 128, 171, 311
    announcement of, by Supreme Court, 1, 2
    and *Brandenburg v. Ohio,* 56
    and criminal speech, 97–119
    Hand's concerns about, 6
    and McCarthy era, 55–57
    and *Pentagon Papers* decision, 58
    and political dissidents, 5
    and *Schenck v. United States,* 47–50, 97, 98–
        103, 123, 154, 155
    significance of "present" in, 101–2, 104
    subsequent decisions to *Schenck* and, 104–7
    during World War I, 7
Cohen v. California, 4, 73n. 67, 93, 169n. 70
Coke, Sir Edward, 34
collective action problems, 242–43
collective well-being
    character and, 87
    and free speech, 88, 91
*Colorado Republican Fed. Campaign Comm. v.
    Federal Election Comm'n,* 190n. 59
commercial advertising. *See* advertising
commercial speech, 37, 143, 152, 172, 182, 303,
        306
    and Court's treatment of false or misleading,
        240–41
    and First Amendment, 177–80
    and Meiklejohnian tradition, 170
    and regulation of "false ideas," 162
common law, First Amendment opportunism
        and nature of, 196–97
common-law approach
    central idea of, 45
    and "clear and present danger" principle, 56
    freedom of expression and, 44–47
    history behind, 34
    and *New York Times v. Sullivan,* 58
common-law Constitution, 32

and freedom of speech, 33–59
    and law of First Amendment, 59
Communist Party/Communist Party of the
    United States, 3, 4, 5, 7, 133, 311
    convictions of leaders of, 7
    and McCarthy era, 55
    and Smith Act, 105
computerized communication, 258, 259. *See also*
    Internet
Congress (U.S.), 33, 35, 39, 99, 261, 264
conscription, opposition to, during World War I,
    1, 5, 7, 96, 98, 122–23, 124–25, 154–55
consequentialists, and First Amendment, 200,
    201
conspiracy, criminal law of, 111
Constitution (U.S.), 97, 163
    Second Amendment to, 39
    Third Amendment to, 39
    Fourth Amendment to, 39, 193
    Fifth Amendment to, 39, 177, 185
    Sixth Amendment to, 39
    Seventh Amendment to, 39
    Eighth Amendment to, 39
    Ninth Amendment to, 39
    Thirteenth Amendment to, 98
    Fourteenth Amendment to, 39, 40, 131, 177
    See also First Amendment
consumer sovereignty, 293, 294, 304, 307
content-based regulations of speech, 15–16, 19,
    20–21, 22, 38
content-neutral regulations of speech, 15–16, 18,
    19, 20–21, 22
Contract Clause, 177
Contreras v. Crown Zellerbach Corp., 169n. 76
Coppage v. Kansas, 177n. 13
cost–benefit analysis
    of *Abrams* and *Schenck,* 124–25
    of free speech, 128–29
cost–benefit approach, to First Amendment, 120
costs, of free speech, 134
courage, Brandeis's high regard for, 74, 78, 79–
    80, 82
courts
    and antiwar advocacy, 98
    common-law approach in, 44
    and doctrines, 97
    See also Supreme Court (U.S.)
Cover, Robert, 78
Craig v. Boren, 185n. 42
criminal anarchy statute of New York, 159n. 27
criminal counseling
    and "clear and present danger" test, 119
criminal solicitation, 37, 111–19, 132
criminal speech, 96, 97–119
criminal threats, 132

Cromwell, Oliver, 72
cross-burnings, 23, 141
Curse of Bigness, The (Brandeis), 82
Curtis Publishing Co. v. Butts, 234n. 3
cyberspace, 1, 94, 151

"Daily Me" communications package, 286, 293, 294, 299
Debs, Eugene, 3, 155n. 12
Debs v. United States, 7, 8, 98n. 5
    and "bad tendency" approach, 5
    and "clear and present danger" standard, 1
    Holmes's opinion in, 155, 158
decency standards
    and Cable Act of 1992, 261
    and radio, 264
defamation, 4, 37, 57, 143, 233–34
defective products, and liability, 235, 236
deliberative democracy, 284, 287, 291–93
democracy, 23, 24
    deliberative, 284, 287, 291–93
    direct, 292–93
    First Amendment and rationale of, 152
    and formal education system, 257–58
    and new communications technologies, 285–86, 294–95, 297–300, 307–10
democratic self-government, and First Amendment, 165–68
democratic theory, ambiguities within, 165
demonstrations, 38
Dennis v. United States, 3, 5, 7, 8, 55, 56, 57, 105n. 25, 131, 133, 233n. 1
Denver Area Educ. Telecommunications Consortium, Inc. v. FCC, 173n, 256, 276, 276, 277
    Kennedy's opinion in, 270
    and managerial censorship concerns, 267
deregulation, and elimination of fairness doctrine, 298
designated public forums, 129
Dewey, John, 163, 167
Dickerson v. United States, 186n. 48
Doe v. Commonwealth's Attorney, 180n. 25
Doe v. University of Mich., 176n. 1
"Don't Ask, Don't Tell," 174, 183–87
Doran v. Salem Inn, Inc., 182n. 34
double-check provisions, of Cable Act of 1992, 267, 270, 271
Douglas, Justice William O., 5, 55
Downs, Anthony, 243n. 28
draft obstruction, during World War I, 5, 7, 16, 96, 98, 122–23, 125, 154–55
Due Process Clause, 177
"due process of law," 40
Dun & Bradstreet v. Greenmoss Builders, 234n. 3

Dunn v. Blumstein, 190n. 61
Dworkin, Andrea, 135, 137

easements
    commercial television, 280
    and public access channels, 267
    and risk of state censorship, 266
economic liberty, 180, 191
economic metaphors, for freedom of speech, 157, 158
education, 257–58, 315
Eighth Amendment, 39
elections, and campaign finance reform, 188–90
Ely, John Hart, 189, 190
Ely-Norris Safe Co. v. Mosler Safe Co., 234n. 6
Emerson, Ralph Waldo, 82
Equal Protection Clause, 177, 190
equal time provision, 13
Erznoznik v. City of Jacksonville, 183n
Espionage Act of 1917, 98, 106n. 28, 154, 155, 156
Espionage Act of 1918, 104, 155–56, 158
Euripides, 79
evil
    gravity of, and "clear and present danger" test, 105, 119
    Milton's views on "problem" of, 65
Excitable Speech: A Politics of the Performative (Butler), 214–23
extremist speech, 11, 25

"fair access," and campaign financing, 146–49
fairness doctrine, 13, 274
    and group polarization, 297–98
"false cry of fire in a crowded theater," 1, 2, 9, 123, 142
"false ideas," and *Gertz* case, 29–31
false statements, 37
    about public figures and public officials, liability for, 233–35
    restrictions of, 9
FCC. *See* Federal Communications Commission
FCC v. League of Women Voters, 266
FCC v. Pacifica Foundation, 264, 265
Federal Communications Commission, 13, 256, 260, 264, 297, 308
feminism, 135, 136, 312
Fifth Amendment, 33, 39, 185
    Takings Clause, 177
"fighting words," 4, 9, 25, 37, 54, 145
filtering
    via communications packaging, 285–86
    precursors and intermediaries to, 286–87
    and public forum analogy, 287
    unlimited, 285–86

First Amendment, ix, 32, 35, 103
  "affirmative" side of, 11
  architecture of, 21
  and campaign financing, 146
  celebrated status of, 33
  common-law Constitution and law of, 59
  cost–benefit approach to, 120
  development of law of, 46–47
  evolution of doctrine, 4–6, 14–15
  expansion of domain of, 233
  future of, 311–16
  and human nature, 31
  Madison's foundational essay on, 92
  and marketplace of ideas, 161–64
  modern history of, 3
  primacy of political dissent under, 56
  reasons for, 26
  reconciling theory and doctrine in, 168–72
  symbolic speech protected under, 22
  tradition of, against state censorship, 262,
    265
  underlying theory of, 23–29
First Amendment opportunism, 175–97
Fish, Stanley, ix, 140, 141, 198, 199
Fiske v. Kansas, 51n. 39
Fiss, Owen, x, 14, 256, 257
flag burning, 11, 22, 141, 203
Florida Bar v. Went For It, Inc., 169n. 76
"fora," jurisprudence of, 129–30, 149
Forsyth County v. Nationalist Movement, 145n.
    38
"fortress model" of free speech, 25
"Foucaultian perspective," Post's criticism of,
    207–9
Fourteenth Amendment, 39, 40, 131
  Due Process Clause, 177
  Equal Protection Clause, 177
Fourth Amendment, 39, 193
fragmentation, 284, 294–95
  polarization, media, and, 297–98
  See also group polarization
Frankfurter, Justice Felix, 47, 55
freedom of speech, 152, 302–3
  and accountability, 254–55
  benefits of, 236
  Brandeis's ideas and, 73–83
  central principles behind, 36–38
  and character molding, 84–86
  and common-law Constitution, 33–59
  cost–benefit analysis of, 124, 125–27
  development of American system of, 33
  and distinction between "high" and "low"
    value speech, 9
  economic analysis of, 120
  emergence of protection of, 50–54

  "fortress model" of, 25
  functions/purposes served by, 23, 27, 61–62
  future of, 285–310
  and good character, 61–95
  on Internet, 149–51
  and limits, 93–95
  Milton's ideas and, 63–72
  problem of measuring benefits of, 139–44
  and public streets and parks, 11, 12, 13
  reasons for, and varieties of communication,
    107–13
  subsidy vs. suppression of, 137–38
  See also First Amendment
freedom of the press, ix, 1, 152
  and accountability, 254–55
  "dual system" of, 13, 256, 313–14
  and market failure argument supporting
    freedom from liability, 239
Free Press Clause, 97, 98, 100
Freund, Paul, 79
Friedman, Milton, 177
Frohwerk v. United States, 98n. 5, 114n. 41
  and "bad tendency" approach, 5
  and "clear and present danger" standard, 1
  and rejection of free-speech claims, 3
"Funeral Oration" (Pericles), 79, 81

gambling, 134
Gannett Co. v. De Pasquale, 185n. 43
gays and lesbians, and "Don't Ask, Don't Tell"
    policy, 183–87
Gertz v. Robert Welch, Inc., 29, 234n. 3, 239–40n.
    18
Ginsburg, Justice Ruth Bader
  and Arkansas Educational Television Com-
    mission v. Forbes dissent, 278
  support for Breyer by, in Nixon v. Shrink
    Missouri Government PAC, 282, 283
Ginsberg v. New York, 264n. 16
Gitlow v. New York, 5, 52, 55, 103n. 10
good character, and free speech, 61–95
government, right to criticism of, 36–37, 40, 50,
    92
graffiti, 203
Greek Commonwealth, The (Zimmern), 79
Greeks (ancient), Brandeis's high regard for, 79–
    81
Greenawalt, Kent, ix, 96, 97, 120
"group libel," 3
group polarization, 284
  explanations for, 296–97
  fragmentation, media, and, 297–98
  in general, 295–96
  value of, 298–99
Guaranty Clause, 190

Gunther, Gerry, 5
Gusfield, Joseph, 210

Haas, Jacob de, 79
Habermas, Jürgen, 205, 214, 215, 223
Hague v. C.I.O., 12, 52n. 44, 287n. 1
Hahn v. Sterling Drug, Inc., 162n. 36
Hamilton, Alexander, 114
Hammer v. Dagenhart, 177n. 11
Hand, Judge Learned, 5, 6, 106n. 28, 113
Harlan, Justice John Marshall, 73, 93
Harper v. Virginia State Bd. of Elections, 190n. 61
hate speech, 3, 9–10, 23, 25, 108, 136, 137, 143, 149, 168
    within context of social developments, 312
    Court's analysis of regulation of, 311, 312
    economic analysis applied to, 120
    instrumental approach applied to, 132
    on Internet, 298, 314
    "problem" of, 229–30
    regulation of, 144–46
Hayek, Friedrich, 177
"heckler's veto," 145
Hess v. Indiana, 106–7, 115, 116
"high" value speech, 15, 16, 17, 20
    distinction between "low" value speech and, 9, 21, 37, 54, 56, 57
    and Meiklejohnian perspective, 167
Hobbes, Thomas, 35, 94
Holmes, Justice Oliver Wendell, Jr., ix, 8, 9, 24, 27, 31, 40, 47, 51, 53, 62, 75, 103, 142, 153, 154–61, 283
    "bad tendency" approach rejected by, 5
    and "clear and present danger" standard, 1, 2, 16, 19, 97, 103–5, 171
    on criminal counseling, 114, 115
    dissent in *Abrams v. United States*, 48, 49, 124, 129, 157–58, 167
    dissent in *Gitlow v. New York*, 52
    free speech defense and skepticism of, 142, 144
    Hand's correspondence with, 6
    influences on, 44
    legacy of opinions on freedom of speech, 3, 5, 6
    Lochner v. New York and Court's adoption of view by, 181
    and "marketplace of ideas" theory, 4, 157
    opinion in *Debs v. United States,* 155, 158
    opinion in *Schenck v. United States*, 48, 98, 99, 101, 120, 123, 131, 154–55, 158
Holmes v. California Army Nat'l Guard, 187n. 50
Holocaust, the, 107
Holt, Chief Justice, 42

homosexuals, and "Don't Ask, Don't Tell" policy, 183–87
Horton, Paul, 226, 227, 229
human nature, and First Amendment, 31
Hustler magazine, 141
Hustler Magazine v. Falwell, 141n. 33, 160n. 32, 161n. 34, 166n. 57, 169n. 69

immediacy, 123–24
    trade-off between gravity and, 124
indecent language
    in public places, 4
    restrictions on, 256
inertia, Brandeis on, 95
instrumental approach
    formalization and defense of, 125–31
    to freedom of speech, 121–22, 125
    implications of, for scholarship, 151
    operationalization of, 131–37
    origins of, 122–25
    for protection of free expression, 120
    values of, 129, 130
intended danger, relationship between actual danger and, 99, 104
interest groups, 146, 148
Internet, 258, 259, 264, 297, 299, 304, 305
    expansion of public forum and, 288
    and "free and independent media" model, 14
    free speech on, 131, 149–51
    and group polarization, 295
    hate groups on, 298, 314
    like-minded sites/discussion groups on, 294
    sexually explicit expression on, 311
intolerance, 11, 27, 28
invisible hand, 177
    of marketplace of ideas, 233–55
irrational speech, 169
issue-oriented programming, growth in, 298

Jackson, Justice Robert H., 73
Jackson, Thomas, 179–80
James, William, 158
James I (king of England), 34, 35
Jefferson, Thomas, 77
    influence of, on Brandeis, 80n. 82
Jeffries, John, 179–80
Jehovah's Witnesses, 193, 311
judicial review, reason for, 315

Kalven, Harry, 12, 52
    quotation by, on First Amendment, 315, 316
Kennedy, Justice Anthony M.

opinion in *Arkansas Educational Television Commission v. Forbes*, 275, 277–78

opinions in *Turner I* and *Turner II*, 270–71, 272

on public forum idea and modern technologies, 288

King, Dr. Martin Luther, Birmingham campaign of, 279

KKK. *See* Ku Klux Klan

Knights of the Ku Klux Klan v. Curators of the Univ. of Mo., 193n. 70

Konigsberg v. State Bar, 36n. 7

Ku Klux Klan, 4, 30, 106, 115, 193, 222

labor union protections, 53, 177

Lanham Trademark Act, 234

law
    authority of, 34
    defamation, 44, 57
    Milton's warning on excessive reliance on, 65n. 13

leased access television channels, 261

leased channels
    and must-carry obligations, 269, 271, 272
    segregate-and-block of indecent material on, 267

Levinson, Sanford, 230

liability
    press and lack of, 235–36
    three regimes of and rationales for, 237–41

libel, 9, 21, 25
    "group," 3
    seditious, 42, 43, 156, 157

libertarianism
    and First Amendment in service of commercial speech, 177–80
    sexual, 180–83

libraries, on World Wide Web, 258

licensing
    commercial television, 280
    and marches, picketing, and demonstrations, 311
    Milton on liberty of printing and, 66, 68–69, 71, 72

limited public forums, 129, 130

Lippmann, Walter, 75

Liquormart, Inc. v. Rhode Island, 36n. 6, 240n. 19, 303n. 10

local accountability, of public access channel managers, 268

Lochner v. New York, 178, 181

Locke, John, 94

Lovell v. City of Griffin, 52n. 44, 279

"low" value speech, 15, 19

distinction between "high" value speech and, 9, 21, 37, 54, 56, 57

and Meiklejohnian perspective, 167

obscenity as, 18

Lubin v. Panish, 190n. 61

Luther v. Borden, 190n. 63

Machiavelli, Niccolò, 63

MacKinnon, Catharine, 135, 137, 221, 222

Madison, James, 41, 44, 114, 157
    Alien and Sedition Acts attacked by, 304–5
    quoted, 92

"managerial censorship," 256, 260, 265–67, 281–82
    and *Arkansas Educational Television Commission v. Forbes*, 275–77
    danger posed by, to First Amendment interests, 267
    and fairness doctrine, 274

Marc Anthony problem, 6

marches, 22, 258

market failure, 124

marketplace of ideas, 4, 61, 144, 161–64, 168, 169, 172, 210, 313
    and campaign financing, 147
    "fair access" to, 148
    Holmes's theory of, 157
    invisible hand of, 233–55
    and "right of access," 17–18
    truth-seeking function in, 152

Martin Luther King Day, 300

Marx, Karl, 30

mass culture, and public opinion, 76

Masses, The (journal), 5, 6, 106n. 28

Masses Publishing Co. v. Patten, 6, 106n. 28, 113n. 40

maximum hours laws, 177, 178

McCarthy era, and *Brandenburg* synthesis, 54–57

McIntyre v. Ohio Elections Commission, 36n. 6, 160n. 32

media, 280
    and campaign financing, 147
    First Amendment and concentration of ownership of, 13–14
    fragmentation, polarization, and, 297–98
    regulation of, 256, 312
    and the state, 265–66
    See also newspapers; radio; television

Meiklejohn, Alexander, 20, 129, 165, 166, 169–72

Merchant of Venice, The (Shakespeare), 192

military personnel, and "Don't Ask, Don't Tell" policy, 183–87

Mill, John Stuart, ix, 24, 25, 26, 62, 128, 158, 164, 183, 219
  On Liberty, 132, 181, 220
  and "self"-regarding and "other"-regarding acts, 127, 135
Miller, Henry, 133
Miller v. California, 221, 263n. 14
Milton, John, ix, 77, 83, 84, 93, 95, 129
  Areopagitica, 64, 66, 68, 70, 71
  on connection between good character and free speech, 64, 65
  and free-speech tradition, 63
  Paradise Lost, 65, 70
  and political energy question, 63–65
  and process of renewal, 71
  The Ready and Easy Way To Establish a Free Commonwealth, 72
minimum wage laws, 177
Miranda v. Arizona, 186n. 48
Mississippi Univ. for Women v. Hogan, 185n. 42
Monaghan, Henry, 74
monarchical government, Milton's indictment of, 72
Moose Lodge No. 107 v. Irvis, 280n. 79
moral approach, 151
  to freedom of speech, 116–17, 121
moral pluralism, 84–85
Muller v. Oregon, 177n. 12
multiculturalism, 145
must-carry obligations/provisions, 256
  of cable operators, 269–75
  and Turner II, 281
  and websites, 309

National Association of Broadcasters, 193, 308
National Endowment for the Arts, 21, 264, 312, 313
National Endowment for the Arts v. Finley, 264n. 15
National Endowment for the Humanities, 313
national security, and injunction on Pentagon Papers, 261
National Socialist Party v. Village of Skokie, 28, 176n. 1
Nazis, 4, 28, 30, 107, 131, 139
Nazi speech, 131
Near v. Minnesota, 17, 51, 58
Negro and the First Amendment, The (Kalven), 316
Negroponte, Nicholas, 286
neofascists, 311
New Deal, 178
New England Naturist Ass'n v. Larsen, 182n. 32
New Orleans v. Dukes, 180n. 24

Newspaper Editors' "Statement of Principles," 247
newspapers, 13, 258
  and African American community, 294–95
  and Pentagon Papers, 17
  and "right-of-reply," 168
New York Times, 17, 261
  and Pentagon Papers, 58
New York Times Co. v. United States, 37, 73n. 66, 233n. 1, 261n. 7
New York Times v. Sullivan, 4, 36, 37, 50, 73n. 68, 92, 93, 233, 234, 239–40n. 17, 273
  and Pentagon Papers, 57, 58
  precursor to, 51
Ninth Amendment, 39
Nixon, Richard, 266, 278
  injunction on Pentagon Papers requested by, 261
Nixon v. Shrink Mo. Government PAC, 190n. 59, 282
nonconsequentialists, and First Amendment, 199, 200
nonpublic forums, 129
Noto v. United States, 56, 57
nudity
  First Amendment and nude dancing, 174, 180–83
  prohibitions on, 22–23

obscenity, 1, 4, 10, 21, 25, 37
  constitutional definition of, 263
  economic analysis applied to, 120
  restrictions of, 9
offensiveness, and free speech
  in cost–benefit analysis, 125, 126, 127
  and free speech, 131
  and pornography, 136
Ohralik v. Ohio State Bar Ass'n, 169n. 76, 172n
On Liberty (Mill), 132, 181, 220
orders
  boundaries of free speech and, 108–11
  requests and encouragements vs., 112
orthodoxy, and offensiveness, 131
"other-regarding" acts, 127, 135

parades, 22
Paradise Lost (Milton), 65, 70
Paris Adult Theatre I v. Slaton, 181n. 29
participatory theory, 152
  Meiklejohnian perspective contrasted with, 166–68, 170–71, 172
  and protection of irrational/abusive speech, 169
Patterson v. Colorado, 156–57n. 18
Payne v. Tennessee, 179n. 20

Peirce, Charles Sanders, 163

Pell v. Procunier, 185n. 43, 238n. 15

Pennsylvania Coal Co. v. Mahon, 177n. 9

Pentagon Papers, 8, 19, 37, 141
  injunction against publication of, 261, 262
  and *New York Times v. Sullivan,* 57–59

Pentagon Papers case, 16, 17, 19, 49, 265

People v. Poucher, 181n. 31

Pericles, "Funeral Oration," 79, 81

perjury, 37

Perry Educ. Ass'n v. Perry Local Educators' Ass'n, 129n. 19

pharmaceutical prices, prohibition on advertising of, 174, 179–80

Phelps Dodge Corp. v. NLRB, 177n. 13

Philadelphia Newspapers v. Hepps, 234n. 4

picketing, 141

Pittsburgh Press Co. v. Pittsburgh Comm'n on Human Relations, 179n. 20

Planned Parenthood, 313

Plato, 80, 143

Police Dep't v. Mosley, 233n. 1

political advocacy, 116–17

political campaigns, 258
  changes in nature and cost of, 312

political candidates
  equal time provision for, 13
  and fairness doctrine, 274

"political correctness," 136, 145, 150

political dissent, 86
  as central to First Amendment, 51
  opinions behind protection of, 50
  primacy of under First Amendment, 56
  and "seditious libel," 42–43

political dissidents, convictions of, upheld by Supreme Court, 5

political information
  market failure of, 242–44
  and quality, 246–54

political sovereignty, 293, 294

political speech, 21, 49, 124, 133, 147, 303
  and government regulation, 306
  political truth, Brandeis on, 75
  protections for, 37, 54

politics of rethinking, 219, 220

Popper, Karl, 189n. 57

pornography, 19, 108, 132, 139, 168
  child, 149, 150
  within context of social developments, 312
  and costs of enforcements against, 134–35
  and offensiveness, 136

Posadas de Puerto Rico Associates v. Tourism Co. of Puerto Rico, 134

Posner, Richard, ix, 120, 121

Post, Robert, ix, 152, 153, 214, 216, 218, 220, 223, 226, 227, 228
  Censorship and Silencing, 205–6
  "Recuperating First Amendment Doctrine," 201–204

presidential debates, 127

press freedom. *See* freedom of the press

printing, Milton's argument for liberty of, 65–66, 70

prior restraint, 3, 17, 48, 51
  and "clear and present danger" standard, 102–3
  and marches, picketing, and demonstrations, 311
  and Pentagon Papers, 58

private-school movement, 149

private speech, protections for, 117

privatization
  national trend toward, 149
  and strict enforcement of Free Speech Clause, 146

product warning labels, 164, 172

property rights, 242

"proximity and degree" tests, 155

Pruneyard Shopping Ctr. v. Robins, 305n. 13

public access channels, 267
  and must-carry obligations, 269, 270

public accountability, of public access channel managers, 268

Public Broadcasting System, 266, 309

public forum(s), 129
  doctrine, 3, 11, 12, 13
  functions promoted by doctrine of, 289–90
  and general interest intermediaries, 290–91

public officials, and liability for false statements of fact about, 233–34, 241

public opinion, and mass culture, 76

public policy, 146
  role of instrumental approach to, 151

public regulation model, and Supreme Court, 14

public streets and parks, freedom of speech exercised in, 11, 12, 13

public television, 266
  and candidate debates, 275–80

publishers, and liability issues, 233–34

R. v. Butler, 176n. 1

R. v. Keegstra, 176n. 1

racism, 86

racist speech, 3, 8, 11, 19

radio, 256, 258, 297, 304
  broadcasting regulations, 13
  and decency standards, 264

Railroad Retirement Bd. v. Alton R.R. Co., 177n. 6

Rand, Ayn, 177

"rational" person argument (Mill), 24–25, 26

R.A.V. v. City of St. Paul, 10, 176n. 1, 221

Rawls, John, 219

Ready and Easy Way To Establish a Free Commonwealth, The (Milton), 72

"Recuperating First Amendment Doctrine" (Post), 201–204

Red Lion Broadcasting Co. v. FCC, 160n. 32, 168n. 66

    revitalization of, 275

Redrup v. New York, 18

Red Scare, 6

Reformation, the, 71, 72

regulation of free speech

    alternatives to, 308–9

    in cost–benefit analysis, 126

    problems in measurement of, 139–44

religious responsibility, Milton on evasion of, 67

Reno v. ACLU, 169n. 72, 264

resilience, and free speech, 91

responsibility, and free speech, 90, 91

Rice v. Paladin Enters., 193n. 71

Richenberg v. Perry, 187n. 50

Richmond Newspapers v. Virginia, 18, 238n. 15

"right of access," and marketplace of ideas, 17–18

"right-of-reply" statutes, 168

Roberts, Justice Owen J., 73

Roe v. Wade, 191n. 66

Romer v. Evans, 184

Roosevelt administration, and New Deal legislation, 178

Rosenberger v. University of Va., 166n. 57

R.S. Royster Guano Co. v. Virginia, 177n. 8

Rubin v. Coors Brewing Co., 162n. 41

Rushdie, Salman, 211

San Antonio Indep. School Dist. v. Rodriguez, 190n. 58

Satanic Verses (Rushdie), 211

satellite transmission services, 260

Saxbe v. Washington Post, 185n. 43, 252n. 56

Schad v. Mt. Ephraim, 182n. 35

Schauer, Frederick, ix, 174, 175, 228–29

Schenck, Charles, 47–48, 50, 98, 101, 122

Schenck v. United States, 7, 8, 9, 16, 20, 96, 120, 128, 129, 131, 311

    and "bad tendency" approach, 5

    and "clear and present danger" standard, 1, 2, 47–50, 97, 98–103, 119

    Holmes's opinion in, 154–55, 158

    and instrumental approach, 122

    and rejection of free-speech claims, 3

    and relation of actual and intended danger, 102

    speech market and legacy of, 121–51

Schneider v. State, 20, 51–52, 55

Searle, John, 216

Second Amendment, 39

Sedition Act, 43, 44, 96

"seditious libel," 42, 156, 157

segregate-and-block provisions, 264

    of Cable Act of 1992, 262, 270, 271

Seinfeld, 259

Selective Service System, 186

self-expression, 108

self-government

    Brandeis's affirmation of, 73, 74

    controversy over constitutional meaning of, 165

    and free speech, 61

"self-regarding" acts, 127

"Self-Reliance" (Emerson), 82

Seventh Amendment, 39

sex discrimination, 185

sex equality movement, and group polarization, 298

sexist expressions, regulation of, 8

sexual liberty, 180, 191

sexually explicit speech

    children and protection from, 264

    Court's analysis of regulation of, 311, 312

    state censorship of, 261–65

sexual orientation, and First Amendment, 183–87

Shakespeare, William, 192n. 67

shared experiences, 286

    reduction in, 302

    value of, 285, 287, 301–2

Shelley v. Kraemer, 280n. 79

Shuttlesworth v. City of Birmingham, 279

"silencing" argument, and antipornography movement, 187n. 52

"situation-altering" communication, 108, 112

Sixth Amendment, 39

"slippery slope argument," 25

Smith, Adam, 177

Smith Act, 56

    and "clear and present danger" test, 105

Smith v. Goguen, 233n. 1

social cascades, 299–300

social comparison, group polarization and role of, 297

social conditions, freedom of speech relative to, 140–41

social glue, in heterogeneous society, 300–301

Socialist Party, 3, 122

social practices, and truth-seeking, 163, 164

Social Statics (Spencer), 181

Socrates, ix

"soft money" donations, 146, 147

Sophocles, 81

Souter, Justice David, opinion in *Arkansas Educational Television Commission v. Forbes*, 276, 278

sovereignty conceptions, 293–94

Speaking Respect, Respecting Speech (Abel), 209–14

special interest groups, 243

Speech Act Theory (Austin), 216

speech subsidies, 309

Spencer, Herbert, 177, 181

Spence v. Washington, 161n. 35, 162

Stanley v. Georgia, 171n. 88

state
  balance of power between federal government and, 41–42
  censorship, 260–65, 266, 267, 278, 279, 281
  commercial television and, 280
  and consensual activities, 181
  and the media, 265–66
  relationship between individual and, 74

"state action," 12

State v. Blyth, 111n. 37

Steffan v. Aspin, 184n. 37, 187n. 49

Stevens, Justice John Paul
  Forbes dissent by, 278–79, 280
  opinions in *Turner I* and *Turner II*, 270–71

Stewart, Justice Potter, 18

Strauss, David, ix, 32, 33, 96

Stromberg v. California, 50–51

Strum, Philippa, 78, 79

Stuart monarchy (England), 71, 72

substantive law of attempt, "proximity and degree" tests rooted in, 155

subversive advocacy, 8, 11, 96, 97, 106
  economic analysis applied to, 120
  evolution of law in, 5
  and permissibility of punishment, 119

Sunstein, Cass, x, 14, 284, 285

Supreme Court (U.S.), 8, 32, 38, 49, 52, 104, 114, 145, 146
  and *Arkansas Educational Television Commission v. Forbes*, 275
  "bad tendency" approach adopted by, 5
  Breyer's concurrence in *Turner II*, 273–75, 283
  and campaign finance reform, 168, 189
  "clear and present danger" standard announced by, 1, 2
  decision in *New York Times v. Sullivan*, 92
  and development of law of First Amendment, 47

and distinction between "high" and "low" value speech, 54, 56, 57
  and dual system of freedom of press, 13
  and early jurisprudence of free speech, ix
  and evolution of First Amendment doctrine, 4–6
  on "false ideas," 29–31
  First Amendment and "eras" of experience by, 311
  and hate speech regulation, 10
  jurisprudence of "fora" by, 129–30, 148–49
  libertarians and shape of, 177
  managerial censorship concerns and *Denver Area* case, 267
  narrow view of right to public forum by, 12
  and obscenity cases, 18
  obscenity definition and protection of children, 264
  and *Pentagon Papers* case, 58
  position on commercial speech, 172
  and post–New Deal legislation, 178
  and public forum doctrine, 288
  and *Red Lion Broadcasting Co. v. FCC*, 274
  on segregate-and-block provisions, 264
  and state censorship, 260
  and symbolic speech, 21–22
  television and decisions by, in *Denver Area*, *Turner*, and *Forbes*, 281

symbolic speech, 22

syndicalists, 4, 7, 311

Takings Clause, 177

talk radio, 298

Telecommunications Act (1996), 264

television, 13, 256, 297, 304, 305
  candidate debates and significance of, 280–81
  censorship of, 257–83
  crucial role of, in informal education system, 258–60
  racial divide over rating of, 294

television broadcasters, public forum–type functions performed by, 290–91

Terminiello v. Chicago, 169

Texas v. Johnson, 73n. 68, 161n. 35

Third Amendment, 39

Thirteenth Amendment, 98

Thomas, Justice Clarence, 303
  dissenting opinion in *Denver Area* case, 269

Thomasson v. Perry, 187n. 50

Thorne v. United States Dep't of Defense, 187n. 50

Thornhill v. Alabama, 53, 165

threats, 9, 37

Thucydides, 81

Time, Inc. v. Hill, 169n. 74
Tinker v. Des Moines Indep. Community School District, 163n. 44
Togstad v. Vesely, 162n. 39
tolerance, 11
tort law, 29, 57
torts opportunism, 196
trespass, 23
    Brandeis's discussion of, in *Whitney v. California,* 114
truth-seeking
    and freedom of speech, 23, 24, 61
    function of, and First Amendment, 161, 163
Turner Broadcasting Sys. v. FCC (U.S. 1993), 160n. 32
Turner Broadcasting Sys. v. FCC (U.S. 1994), 162n. 38. See also *Turner I*
Turner Broadcasting Sys. v. FCC (D.D.C. 1995), 272n. 42
Turner Broadcasting Sys. v. FCC (U.S. 1997), 269. See also *Turner II*
Turner I, 270, 282
    Kennedy's opinions in, 272
    and must-carry provisions, 270
    and *Red Lion,* 274
Turner II, 270, 273n. 47, 274n. 52
    Breyer's concurrence in, 273–75, 282, 283
    Kennedy's opinions in, 272
    must-carry provisions upheld in, 281
    and *Red Lion,* 274
    substantive differences between *Forbes* and, 276–77

United States v. Dennis, 123n. 8
United States v. O'Brien, 22
United States v. Schwimmer, 158n. 26
Universal Studios, Inc. v. Reimerdes, 191n. 65

Valentine v. Chrestensen, 179n. 20, 233n. 1
V-chip technology, 262
Vietnam War, 16, 17
    and Pentagon Papers, 58, 261, 263
Virginia Citizens Consumer Council v. Virginia Board of Pharmacy, 178, 179
Virginia State Bd. of Pharmacy v. Virginia Citizens Consumer Council, 233n. 1, 240n. 20, 303n. 9

voluntary self-regulation, by producers of communications, 308
"voter's paradox," 133
voting, 107, 245

Warren Court, 311
wartime
    and "clear and present danger" standard, 99, 101
    freedom of speech during, 123
    and free-speech protections, 3
Washington Post, 17
    and Pentagon Papers, 58
Wayte v. United States, 186
wealth redistribution, 315
websites, 150, 305
    and direct democracy, 292
    and filtering, 286
    and "must carry" rules, 309
welfare legislation, 29
West Coast Hotel Co. v. Parrish, 177n. 12
Weston, Peter, 227, 229
    "The Empty Idea of Equality" 224–26
West Virginia State Board of Education v. Barnette, 53, 73n. 65
Whitney v. California, 5, 14, 28, 41, 49n. 37, 62n. 5, 103n. 10, 104, 104n. 14, 105
    Brandeis's concurrence in, 73, 273, 283
    Brandeis's discussion of trespass in, 114
Widmar v. Vincent, 163n. 44
Williams, Judge Stephen, 272
Williamson v. Lee Optical, 179n. 23
Wisconsin v. Mitchell, 186
World War I, 7, 54
    antiwar speeches during, 4
    draft obstruction during, 5, 16, 98, 122–23, 125, 154–55
    freedom of expression system after, 44
    opposition to, 48, 96, 104, 122–23, 124, 311
    Supreme Court cases involving dissent against, 1
World Wide Web, 258, 259
Wycliffe, John, 71

Yates v. United States, 56, 57
Young v. American Mini Theatres, Inc., 182n. 33

Zimmern, Alfred, 79, 80
Zionism, 79